A New Orpheus

Kurt Weill, c. 1937 (photo by Blackstone Studios)

A New Orpheus

ESSAYS ON KURT WEILL

Edited by
Kim H. Kowalke

Yale University Press
New Haven and London

A New Orpheus was compiled and published with the assistance of the Kurt Weill Foundation for Music, Inc.

Designed by Nancy Ovedovitz and set in Baskerville type by Composing Room of Michigan. Printed in the United States of America by Edwards Brothers, Inc., Ann Arbor, Michigan.

Library of Congress Cataloging-in-Publication Data
Main entry under title:
A New Orpheus.
    "All but two of the essays included in this collection evolved from papers presented originally at the first international conference on Kurt Weill in New Haven, Connecticut, 2–5 November 1983"—Pref.
    "Chronology of Weill's life and works": p.
    Includes index.
    1. Weill, Kurt, 1900–1950—Criticism and interpretation—Addresses, essays, lectures.   I. Kowalke, Kim H., 1948–
ML410.W395N5   1986   782.81′092′4   85–29536
ISBN 0–300–03514–4 (cloth)
        0–300–04616–2 (pbk.)

The paper in this book meets the guidelines for permanence and durability of the Committee on Production Guidelines for Book Longevity of the Council on Library Resources.

10   9   8   7   6   5   4   3   2

In Memoriam
Lotte Lenya Weill
(1898–1981)

Contents

Editor's Preface

A collection of essays on Kurt Weill and his music would have been inconceivable ten years ago. At that time, the only published book focusing on the composer was Helmut Kotschenreuther's one-hundred-page *Kurt Weill* (Berlin, 1962), a superficial popular biography in German. The haphazard and error-laden entries on Weill in the fifth edition of *Grove's Dictionary of Music and Musicians* (1954) and *Musik in Geschichte und Gegenwart* (1968), then the two standard musicological reference works in English and German, merely reflected the scholarly neglect of Weill on both sides of the Atlantic. Not one of the basic musicological resources—catalogue of works, critical biography, collected writings and correspondence—was available in Weill's case. Furthermore, the primary sources in Europe were scattered throughout the Continent, with many documents in private hands. Access to Lenya's collection was restricted to her closest associates and David Drew, who had begun an "authorized" biography of Weill in 1956. Drew then facilitated, almost single-handedly, many performances and recordings, edited a number of scores, and published several essays on individual works. But the first book-length products of his two-decade devotion to Weill-research did not reach print until 1975, the seventy-fifth anniversary of Weill's birth, when Suhrkamp issued his anthologies, *Über Kurt Weill* and *Kurt Weill: Ausgewählte Schriften*.

At that time, I was just beginning work on my dissertation at Yale, published in 1979 as *Kurt Weill in Europe*. The last decade has also witnessed publication of four biographies aimed at a general readership (Ronald Sanders's and Douglas Jarman's in English, two by Jürgen Schebera in German), Gottfried Wagner's *Weill und Brecht: Das musikalische Zeittheater*, and numerous articles in periodicals, both populist and specialist. Performances, recordings, and first editions of a few of Weill's all-but-forgotten non-Brechtian European works added impetus to what was being called a Weill-renaissance. Drew's lengthy and exemplary entry on Weill in *The New Grove Dictionary of Music and Musicians* (1980) reflects not only the remarkable strides in Weill-research since the fifth edition had appeared in the 1950s but also the increasing acceptance within the scholarly community of Weill's importance. Although Drew's multi-volume biography is still keenly awaited, he graciously allowed authors of the essays herein access to a draft of his *Kurt Weill: A Handbook*, forthcoming from Faber & Faber.

Notwithstanding the widespread escalation of interest in the music of Kurt Weill, his principal publishers in both Europe and America have allowed a number of his compositions to go out of print. Until these original editions (despite their many inadequacies) are reissued and such major musico-dramatic works as *Der Kuhhandel, Der Weg der Verheissung, The Firebrand of Florence,* and *Love Life* are published for the first time, it would be merely wishful thinking to anticipate new critical editions of major works or to suggest the imperative need for a complete edition. Nevertheless, Weill scholarship has now progressed in terms of breadth, depth, quantity, and quality to the point where a collection of essays devoted to specialized historical and analytical topics is both feasible and necessary.

All but two of the essays included in this collection evolved from papers presented originally at the first international conference on Kurt Weill in New Haven, Connecticut, 2–5 November 1983. This conference, co-sponsored by the John Herrick Jackson Music Library at Yale University and the Kurt Weill Foundation for Music, brought together scholars, critics, performers, and associates of Weill and Lenya from three continents. The event had been envisioned in 1980, when I first introduced Lotte Lenya to Yale's music librarian Harold Samuel, with the hope of initiating discussions concerning a Weill/Lenya Archive at Yale. (My own association with Yale and the excellent productions of *Happy End, The Seven Deadly Sins, Mahagonny Songspiel,* and *Rise and Fall of the City of Mahagonny* by the Yale Repertory Theatre and School of Music had predisposed Lenya to that institution.) At the time, Lenya's large collection of autograph manuscripts and documents was stored in an out-of-the-way vault without even minimal climate control. By autumn of 1980, negotiations had advanced to the point where Lenya deposited at Yale, for an initial term of five years, all of the archival materials from the vault. I then laid plans for a Weill festival/conference to celebrate the opening of the collection.

Lenya did not live to see the event. Upon her death in 1981, the items on deposit at Yale were bequeathed to the University, and subsequently the Kurt Weill Foundation for Music added to the collection most of the documents still in Lenya's possession, including materials relevant to her own career. Prior to the conference, Yale had also obtained photocopies of some of the most important material in European archives. As a result, the conference was more than merely symbolic: it celebrated not only the official opening of the Weill/Lenya Archive at Yale and the Weill-Lenya Research Center in New York but also the beginning of a new era in Weill scholarship. Manuscripts and documents previously unavailable for study were now readily accessible, and their preservation was finally assured. On the last day of the conference, I also announced the discovery of fourteen autograph manuscripts containing eleven of Weill's early compositions (or portions thereof) that had been hitherto unknown or long presumed lost.

This volume is not the proceedings of the conference, however. Many of the papers included here have been revised and substantially expanded from the versions initially presented at Yale and benefit from access to material in the Weill/Lenya Archive. None of the contributions has been published previously in whole or in part. A number of preliminary studies also presented at the conference could not be included in this volume: Fritz Hennenberg's study in progress, "New Documents Concerning the Premiere of *Die Dreigroschenoper*," challenged the authenticity of the published text of Weill's score and suggested ramifications for performance practice; Susan Borwick's "Perspective on Lenya: Through the Looking-Glass" and Henry Marx's "The Americanization of Weill and Lenya" (a condensed version of which appeared in the *Kurt Weill Newsletter* 3 [Spring 1985]:5–7) addressed Lenya's career and her extraordinary role in the posthumous revival of Weill's music. Two of the conference papers have already been published elsewhere: Jürgen Schebera's comparative study of Weill's *Der Jasager* and Eisler's *Die Massnahme*, "Theater of the Future?" appeared in *Musik und Gesellschaft* 34 (March 1984): 138–45, and Horst Koegler's summary of Weill's influence on post–World War II dance theater in Europe was included in the *Kurt Weill Newsletter* 3 (Fall 1985):5–7. My own biographical and analytic study of the newly discovered correspondence and compositions, including a six-movement orchestral suite, a song cycle, and Weill's only surviving composition for solo piano, has been delayed by legal proceedings concerning access to and ownership of the documents.

Given the character and small number of previously published studies on Weill and the volume of documentary material now available for the first time, the revisionist tone of the seventeen essays included here is both unmistakable and inevitable. The startling historical revelations are matched by analytical and aesthetic insights which extend beyond Weill to wider issues of twentieth-century music, theater, dance, and cultural institutions. Because Weill's work was so often collaborative at every stage, from creation through production, it is not surprising that many of the essays also shed new light on figures such as Brecht, Kaiser, Reinhardt, Werfel, Ira Gershwin, Moss Hart, Klemperer, and Elisabeth Hauptmann. The authors' diverse backgrounds and approaches—musical, literary, dramatic, sociological, historical, critical—correspond to the various dimensions and concerns of Weill's own career and personality. As initial sorties into previously uncharted regions, many of the essays open up adjacent territories for further exploration. In this sense, the anthology is a reminder of how much remains to be done.

I have arranged the seventeen essays in an array roughly corresponding in chronology to Weill's career. My own introductory, historiographical piece provides a brief overview of Weill's career and invokes the Orpheus metaphor suggested by *Der neue Orpheus,* a stylistic turning point, to raise issues central to many of the essays that follow. The next four selections consider Weill's interaction with crucial contextual parameters of his European career. Christopher Hailey taps the single largest biographical source, correspondence between Weill and his publisher from 1924 to 1933, in tracing the development of the composer's stylistic path or *Linie* as he juggled commercial and artistic incentives with uncanny self-awareness. Hailey also evaluates Weill's attempts to balance his evolving forms directed toward a new mass audience with the grand traditions of European art music. (This resonates with Larry Stempel's and Matthew Scott's later discussions of Weill's analogous dilemma in the United States when confronted with the equally formidable tradition of the American musical.) Alexander Ringer identifies the effects on Weill's music of indigenous styles of proletarian music and draws parallels with the use of German folk poetry by Gustav Mahler, who was one of Weill's lifelong models. John Rockwell, in characterizing the nature and organization of state-subsidized opera houses in Germany and Weill's predominantly unhappy experiences within that system, demonstrates that Weill was already firmly committed to a commercial avenue when he first stepped onto Broadway. Rockwell claims that, in this sense at least, Weill's career in America was anything but a "sellout" to commercial instincts; on the contrary, it represented a direct continuation of his European efforts. Stephen Hinton examines the origin, meaning, and application of the terms *neue Sachlichkeit, surrealism,* and *Gebrauchsmusik* with respect to Weill's and his contemporaries' music and also discusses their usage in Adorno's and Bloch's critical writings.

The next four essays focus on Weill's major compositions from 1924 to 1932. Susan Cook discusses the genesis of Weill's successful one-act comic opera, *Der Zar lässt sich photographieren* (1927), and analyzes its synthesis of traditional operatic materials and techniques with elements derived from popular music and modern drama—before Weill's collaboration with Brecht. My summary of the historical points of contact between Schoenberg and Weill introduces Alan Chapman's seminal study of musical vocabulary common to both composers at stylistic junctions in their respective careers. Ian Kemp illuminates the musical structure and harmonic language of *Der Silbersee,* the last work Weill completed in Germany and his final collaboration with Georg Kaiser. Douglas Jarman speculates on the nature and effect of *Mahagonny*'s influence on the dramaturgy and music of Berg's *Lulu.*

Given the ill-informed and cursory treatment of Weill in much of the vast literature on Bertolt Brecht, the three essays by leading Brecht scholars are especially welcome. By sifting through dozens of contracts and hundreds of related documents, John Fuegi exposes the horrific business dealings of Brecht with Weill. His detective work accounts for Elisabeth Hauptmann's failure to complete the third act of *Happy End,* elucidates the personal reasons for Weill's rejection of Brecht's attempts to renew their collaboration in America, and unearths evidence that Brecht's financial treachery was not restricted to his dealings with Weill. Michael Morley tackles the elusive concept of *Gestus* in both theoretical and practical terms in his comparative study of Eisler's and Weill's settings of the same poems by Brecht. Dismissed by Brecht as "not very important," *Die sieben Todsünden* is nevertheless numbered among Weill's masterpieces. In the first published study of its origins, Ronald Shull demonstrates its uniqueness within the Brecht-Weill canon and traces the sources of its idiosyncratic content and structure.

David Drew contributes a revelatory study of *Der Kuhhandel* (1934– 35), Weill's satirical operetta about armament politics between the wars. The work has not been performed since 1935, when it was bastardized as *A Kingdom for a Cow,* and it has never been published. Concerned with an arms race in a not-so-mythical Caribbean setting, the work is stunningly topical today. Although it is a pivotal work within Weill's oeuvre, reflecting the international political realities of its time and foreshadowing traits of his Broadway scores to come, *Der Kuhhandel* was the last casualty of circumstances that plagued Weill's exile years in France and England. (Some of Weill's most distinctive "American tunes," including "September Song," were lifted from the dormant score of *Der Kuhhandel.*) Guy Stern provides much new information on Weill's other major work in European exile, *Der Weg der Verheissung,* which was severely compromised and compressed for its only production, as *The Eternal Road,* in 1937— much as *Der Kuhhandel* had been. The documents chronicling the troubled times of its creation suggest that in some respects *Der Weg der Verheissung* was Weill's and Werfel's "everyman" counterpart to Schoenberg's *Moses und Aron.*

In the past, few *musical* scholars have been attracted to either analytical or rigorous historical study of the repertoire of American musical theater. As a result, Weill's American works are allocated a smaller portion in this collection by default, not by design. Matthew Scott identifies a central problem for Weill's American works: composed specifically for production by the commercial theater in New York, representative of a genre that—almost by definition and with few exceptions—is especially dependent on ephemeral topicality, idiom, and stardom, and resistant to institutionalized revival as part of the "stock and amateur" repertory, Weill's "musicals" now must search anew for both a home and an audience. Basing his argument on Weill's correspondence with Ira Gershwin at the time, Scott suggests that Weill's American works cannot be revived without being subjected to a re-creative process. John Graziano asserts that although *Down in the Valley* is based on five American folk songs, its compositional techniques synthesize musical dialects from Weill's European and American domains into a convincing amalgam appropriate for the amateur and educational productions the opera was intended to encourage. Larry Stempel, on the other hand, argues that *Street Scene* falls short of Weill's goal for genuine American opera, because purely commercial considerations and collaborative compromises forced interpolations of "Broadway" numbers that defy either camouflage or incorporation within the structure and musical fabric of the opera that Weill had intended to compose. David Farneth's chronology of Weill's career reflects in its accuracy and comprehensiveness the wealth of new material now available to researchers.

It is my hope that the diversity inherent in this collection of essays will parallel Weill's own unique place in twentieth-century culture with an appeal that transcends arbitrary intellectual boundaries. Taken as a group, the essays bridge the geographic, political, and aesthetic disjunctures that have previously fragmented and compartmentalized our perception of his legacy. In light of the composer's international world view, his concern with major moral and social issues of his time, and his outreach beyond the "splendid isolation" of musical academia and contemporary art music to a larger audience, a collection of essays devoted to Weill can aspire to no less.

Los Angeles
February 1985

Acknowledgments

I am most indebted to the contributors themselves; their gracious cooperation has made my editorial task a rewarding one. I am also grateful to those other individuals and institutions who made the Kurt Weill Conference, and hence this book, possible, especially the staff of the Yale Music Library. My associates at the Kurt Weill Foundation for Music—David Farneth, Lys Symonette, and William Madison—have been involved in this project at every stage; their assistance in the production of this book has been indispensable. As always, David Drew was generous with his encouragement and valued counsel. Occidental College and my colleagues in the music department have been very supportive; I am especially thankful to Mrs. Lorraine Barnett, our administrative assistant.

The following publishers generously permitted use of musical examples: European American Music Corporation, B. Schott's Söhne, TRO/Hampshire House Publishing Co., T. B. Harms Co. (% The Welk Music Group), Belmont Music Publishers. The patience and expertise of the editorial staff of Yale University Press, especially Nancy Woodington, Elizabeth Casey, and Karla Knight, in guiding the multi-authored manuscript through the production process is gratefully acknowledged.

Finally, I appreciate the efforts of the Weill/Lenya Archive at Yale University and the Weill-Lenya Research Center in New York to open their collections to the contributors while still in the cataloging process. *The Weill/Lenya Archive of the Yale University Music Library* now contains the largest collection of original documents relevant to Weill and Lenya. Its holdings include musical manuscripts, correspondence, programs, clippings, photographs, interviews, writings, biographical material, and financial and legal items. With the assistance of a grant from the National Endowment for the Humanities, a formal register of the collection has been prepared by Adrienne Nesnow. Copies may be obtained from the Yale Music Library, P.O. Box 2104A Yale Station, New Haven, Connecticut, 06520.

The Weill-Lenya Research Center in New York was established by the Kurt Weill Foundation for Music. Its collection both complements and duplicates the archive at Yale in its goal of serving a wider public. In addition to its role as the primary repository for audio recordings, videotapes, published reference materials, dissertations, business records, and memorabilia, the Research Center is attempting to assemble a comprehensive collection of photocopies of material in other archives, as well as relevant documents concerning collaborators, and secondary sources dealing with the musical, theatrical, and social history of the time. The Foundation has deposited in the Weill/Lenya Archive at Yale original materials in need of increased security and sophisticated methods of preservation while ensuring scholars and especially performers the widest possible access to information and resources at the Research Center.

The Kurt Weill Foundation for Music, Inc. is a not-for-profit, private foundation established by Lenya in 1962 to preserve and perpetuate the legacy of Kurt Weill. After her death in 1981, the Foundation was bequeathed the royalties derived from Weill's works. In addition to the Weill-Lenya Research Center, the Foundation administers Weill's copyrights, provides information regarding availability of performance materials and clearance of performing rights, publishes a semi-annual newsletter, and awards grants to support excellence in research and performance. Its mailing address is 7 East 20th Street, Suite 3F, New York, New York, 10003.

A New Orpheus

1

Looking Back: Toward a New Orpheus
KIM H. KOWALKE

During the winter of 1925–26 Kurt Weill wrote an apologetic but revealing letter from Berlin to his parents in Leipzig:

> I sometimes wish that I could share in your lives more than I do. But now I have reached the point in the life of an artist when he is continually perched on a powderkeg. Unused energies must discharge themselves explosively, and this hyper-charged sensitivity produces a permanent state of excitement and stimulation. Only in this light can you understand some of the things about me that otherwise might seem incomprehensible. Now it has seized me again. I'm buried in this new opera, and I leave the house only to take care of the most important external matters. I must master a type of expression that is still new to me. To my satisfaction, I've confirmed what I already discovered in *Der neue Orpheus:* that gradually I'm forging ahead toward "myself," that my music is becoming much more confident, much freer, lighter—and simpler.
>
> This is also linked to the fact that I have become noticeably more independent, more confident, happier, and less tense. Of course, living with Lenja again accounts for much of this. That has helped me tremendously. It is the only way I could put up with living next to someone: co-existence of two differing artistic interests, without domestic ties, each one helping the other on his own course. How long will this last? I hope: a long time.[1]

---

1. The undated letter survived among documents in the possession of Rita Weill, wife of Kurt's older brother Hanns, at the time of her death in 1983. A portion of the letter was quoted by Franz Willnauer in "Vom Schiffbauerdamm zum Broadway—Weg und Werk Kurt Weills," *Opern Welt* (April 1970): 44–48. Willnauer apparently had access to photocopies of some of Mrs. Weill's documents that she had sent to the Akademie der Künste in Berlin with the hope of interesting that institution in purchasing her collection of manuscripts, correspondence, and photographs. When no sale transpired, the photocopies were included in the Akademie's "Theater in Exile" Collection, with the notation "Standort der Originale?" In January 1985 the Akademie provided the Weill-Lenya Research Center with duplicates of its photocopies, allowing scholars access to an important biographical source during the probate of Rita Weill's estate and ultimate disposition of her collection of documents. All letters of Weill and Lenya are quoted here by permission of the Kurt Weill Foundation for Music.

The letter is a remarkably accurate self-evaluation of a twenty-five-year-old man and artist in transition. At the time of this letter, he was finishing *Royal Palace*, a one-act ballet-opera with a libretto by Iwan Goll, which the composer eventually dedicated to Georg Kaiser, who had introduced Goll to Weill. But Weill suggests that evidence of his stylistic transformation could be discerned already in *Der neue Orpheus*, a cantata for soprano, solo violin, and orchestra, completed the previous September. It too had been based on a surrealist text by Goll—a poem written in French under the title "Le nouvel Orphée" during 1917. First published in 1918 and re-issued in a collection of Goll's poetry by Editions de la Sirène (Paris) in 1923, "The New Orpheus" had also been printed in the bilingual Goll's own German version by Schmiede-Verlag (Berlin) in 1924.[2] Claudio Arrau, who studied counterpoint, composition, and orchestration with Weill twice a week during 1925–26, recalled that at one of the parties held regularly in those days by a group of writers, architects, pianists, and composers who met to discuss problems of art and music, they "went over a sort of cantata Weill was composing at the time. One night, too, we went through Monteverdi's *Orfeo*, which at that time was a discovery, since it hadn't been performed for years."[3]

Goll's despairing vision of the modern world, in which even the forget-me-nots contemplate suicide and age-old forests suffocate, summons a "new Orpheus"—1.78 meters tall, weighing 68 kilograms, Catholic with brown eyes, and by profession a musician—to rescue from its wretched state a "new Eurydice"—now all of humanity, unredeemed, hopeless, and degraded. Imprisoned in a Hades of cement cities guarded by giant corporations, mankind can look only to itself for salvation. In the twentieth century, this new Orpheus must abandon Grecian heights for the boxing ring of daily struggles to soothe the pain of the hungry and

2. The information concerning the published versions of "Le nouvel Orphée" was supplied by Iwan Goll's wife, Claire, to whom the poem is dedicated, in a letter to George Davis of 13 November 1954. Davis's unpublished notes for his unfinished biography of Weill also include the following summary of Claire Goll's letter: "At the end of the year 1924, Iwan went to the premiere of his play *Methusalem*, directed by Wilhelm Dieterle in Berlin. He was for some time a guest in Georg Kaiser's house and there met Kurt Weill. They quickly became good friends, and Kurt set 'Der neue Orpheus' to music. He also asked Iwan to write him the libretto for an opera. In 1925 Iwan and Claire spent a few weeks in Varenna in the Lago di Como, and, inspired by the beautiful lake where their hotel was located, he wrote the libretto for *Royal Palace*."

3. Arrau's recollections are recorded in George Davis's notes, now in the Weill-Lenya Research Center, from an interview with Arrau conducted in the mid-fifties. Arrau recalled, according to Davis, that these "discussion-group parties" often included composers Vladimir Vogel and Erich Walter Sternberg, cellist Gregor Piatigorsky, the pianist Michael von Zadora, and Hans Mersmann, editor of *Melos*. Mersmann "suggested to Arrau that Weill would be a good teacher for what he was looking for."

thirsty with his balm of music. He is therefore everywhere: on Wednesdays at 2:30 at a little girl's piano lesson (also attended by her avaricious mother); in the evenings he precedes the contortionist in the cabaret; at midnight he's a clown banging the kettledrums in a circus: Sundays he conducts patriotic songs for veterans gathered in dance halls; in quiet vestries he plays the organ; in subscription concerts he drives unmercifully over hearts with Gustav Mahler; in suburban movie theaters he plays the Pilgrims' Chorus on the Torturepiano to lament the death of a virgin. Gramophones and pianolas spread his fame; on September 11 he'll present a wireless concert from atop the Eiffel Tower. Celebrated as a genius, the new Orpheus must rush from country to country. Finally he locates his beloved Eurydice in a railroad station. Still doomed, humanity slips away from his desperate attempt to reach her; alone in the waiting room, the new Orpheus shoots himself.

The unrhymed, free-verse poem depicts both a society and an art form in crisis, and it elicited from Weill a personal, perhaps even autobiographical response reifying his own aesthetic and technical turmoil. The "new type of expression" Weill discovered with *Der neue Orpheus* characterized the beginning of a shift away from the expressionist features prominent in the Violin Concerto (1924) and the Straussian, psychological aspects of *Der Protagonist* (1924–25) toward a sociologically motivated and morally committed art utilizing simpler idioms and incorporating "popular" materials. Although the brown-eyed Weill was only 1.61 meters tall and never a Catholic, it is tempting—for those so inclined—to draw parallels, some admittedly anachronistic, between his own career and the musical activities of the new Orpheus who inspired Weill to "find himself." As a teenager during the war, Weill composed patriotic war choruses.[4] During his years in Dessau, he too taught piano to young members of the ducal family. While studying with Busoni in Berlin, he supported himself by playing both piano in a Bierkeller (an incomplete draft of a slow foxtrot for voice and piano has survived from this period) and organ in a synagogue.[5] Although there is no record of an

4. In an interview with Hans Fischer in 1930, published as "Aktuelles Zwiegespräch über die Schuloper zwischen Kurt Weill und Dr. Hans Fischer" in *Die Musikpflege* 1 (April 1930): 48–52.

5. For an account of Weill's Bierkeller experiences, see Hans Heinsheimer, "Kurt Weill: From Berlin to Broadway," *International Musician* (March 1948): 17. In a postcard addressed to his father, Albert Weill, written from Berlin on 29 November 1920, Weill reported that a Mr. Guttmann had "talked with Dr. Karenski—one of the heads of the Jewish community (Dr. Mayer knows him)—about me and that by all means I should contact the congregation again about the organist job." The postcard is part of the Eve Hammerschmidt collection of correspondence preserved by Weill's younger sister, Ruth, now in the possession of the Weill-Lenya Research Center.

opportunity for Weill to "drive unmercifully over hearts with Gustav Mahler" during his season as conductor of the new opera company in Lüdenscheid (1919–20), he did write to his brother Hanns from Berlin in 1919:

> There is hardly an evening when I don't go to a concert. One hears much that is bad and much that is good, and one learns an extraordinary amount from both. A magnificent event was Mahler's Second Symphony, which utilizes a contralto solo on a genuine Mahlerian text from *Des Knaben Wunderhorn* in the fourth movement ("Urlicht") and in the fifth movement a marvelous chorus with alternating soprano and contralto solo. I think that here one finds the most promising form for future orchestral works, but it takes a genius to pour such comparatively simple musical thoughts into such a heavenly mold.[6]

As one of the first major composers to recognize the potential of film and radio as fertile fields for development of new genres of modern music, Weill eventually achieved both fame and fortune. After 1933, he rushed, like the new Orpheus, from country to country; despite his outreach to a mass audience on both sides of the Atlantic, Weill died in mid-mission, while still trying to communicate with his own Eurydice.

Versions of the Orpheus legend, of course, have inspired many composers, from Peri through Stravinsky, to create music of greatly contrasting character in diverse genres. But it is especially enticing to link Weill's attraction to Goll's surrealist treatment of the subject with such historical antecedents as the invention of *dramma per musica* by the Florentine Camerata in the late sixteenth century and the Gluckian reform of opera in the mid-eighteenth century. Since its birth, opera's original premises concerning the ideal relationship between the sister arts of music and drama have been continually reinterpreted in practice and periodically re-examined from a speculative viewpoint. These cycles of departure from original premises and subsequent reforms over a period of nearly four centuries have shared many issues, although the issues were sometimes disguised by changing terminology and cultural contexts. Within the German tradition, these central concerns have remained essentially unchanged since the seventeenth century. Such perennial topics as the differences between the demands of musical and non-musical theater, the appropriate subject matter for operatic treatment, the balance between textual and musical values, opera's capacity to influence the moral character of its audience, and the fundamental nature of dramatic music have characterized German operatic theory and debate.[7] Weill

6. Letter dated 17 March 1919; photocopy in the Weill-Lenya Research Center.

7. See Gloria Flaherty, *Opera in the Development of German Critical Thought* (Princeton, 1978).

spent virtually his entire career wrestling with these issues—speculatively
in his numerous essays on musical theater in its broadest sense and prag-
matically in his works for the stage. Fresh from his exhilarating, if informal, experiences with Berlin's equivalents to its Florentine counter-
parts—the November Group and Busoni's gatherings—Weill initiated
with *Der neue Orpheus*, described by Heinrich Strobel as a "scenic cantata,"[8] a path that later would lead to participation in other collectives,
also devoted in part to a reform of modern musical theater, as diverse as
Brecht's in Berlin and the Playwrights' Company in New York.

In essays published during the period immediately following the
composition of *Der neue Orpheus* and *Royal Palace* (in which the figure of
Orpheus also makes a brief appearance), Weill aligned himself with critics
of nineteenth-century developments which, he concluded, "had reached
their grandiose conclusion in Berg's *Wozzeck*." He called for a "renewal of
operatic form" that could serve as a "starting point for a new golden age
of opera."[9] This rebirth could be achieved only if modern opera abandoned its previous psychological premises in favor of a sociological, "com-
munity-engendering" [*gemeinschaftsbildenden*] approach, whereby crucial
moral and social issues of the era could be presented in universal and
enduring treatments. To do so, however, required collaboration with
modern playwrights of stature and talent equivalent to the composer's. By
thus breaking out of the traditional "opera business," Weill hoped that
modern musical theater would shatter the "splendid isolation" which was
again limiting opera's appeal to a small circle of aficionados. To attract a
broad public, the contemporary opera composer, taking his cue from
such predecessors as Peri and Gluck, would have to simplify his musical
language—but without dilution of substance or renunciation of the intellectual bearing of the "serious" composer. As a corollary, it eventually
became clear to Weill that the aristocratic, socially exclusive roots and
appeal of recent opera, at least in German-speaking countries, could be
supplanted only in the commerical arena, where a composer must continually submit his music to the ruthless judgment of a mass audience.

Although Weill had already articulated many of these ideas by the
time he wrote the prophetic letter to his parents, he summarized his new
direction most succinctly in a short essay entitled "Verschiebungen in der
musikalischen Produktion," dating from 1927:

> Today we're nearing completion of a clear separation between those com-
> posers who, filled with disdain for the public, continue to work toward
> solution of aesthetic problems as if behind closed doors, and those who

8. Heinrich Strobel, "Erinnerung an Kurt Weill," *Melos* 17 (May 1950): 134.

9. Kurt Weill, "Die neue Oper," *Der neue Weg* (16 January 1926): 25. Translated in Kim
H. Kowalke, *Kurt Weill in Europe* (Ann Arbor, 1979), pp. 464–67.

> associate themselves with any audience whatsoever . . . because they realize
> that there is a general human consciousness beyond the artistic one which
> springs from a social awareness of some kind and that this must determine
> the formation of an artwork. . . . In Germany it has been demonstrated very
> clearly that music must win a new justification for its existence. . . . The
> socially-exclusive (*gesellschaftslichen*) arts, originating in a different era and
> from a different artistic attitude, are losing more and more ground. Today
> new orchestral and chamber music, for which there used to be a regular
> public demand, is directed almost exclusively toward musical societies and
> organizations devoted to the cultivation of new music, whose circle of lis-
> teners comprises primarily other musicians. Therefore, music is seeking an
> approach to a broader audience, because only then can it maintain its
> viability. . . . Clarity of language, precision of expression, and simplicity of
> feeling, which new music has regained after a rectilinear development,
> form the reliable aesthetic bases for a broader impact of this art.[10]

During the next three years in his collaboration with Bertolt Brecht, these
precepts eventually coalesced, with respect to their theatrical implications
at least, as "epic opera," with *Aufstieg und Fall der Stadt Mahagonny* (1927–
29) documenting the various stages in Weill's continually evolving solutions to the formidable problems intrinsic to such an approach. In their
sweeping attempts to recapture in various forms of musical theater the
original function and cultural force of Greek lyric drama, Weill and
Brecht added their names to the list of influential operatic reformers
throughout history, many of whom had also returned to Orpheus as a
symbolic gesture of renewal.

In reasserting the power of music to alter the established order and
save modern society from its new Sirens, Weill himself might well be
compared, if only metaphorically, with the "old Orpheus" of Greek legend. According to Virgil and Ovid, Orpheus's head, severed from his
body by the Thracian women, continued to sing and prophesy after his
death:

> They slew the gentle musician, tearing him limb from limb, and flung the
> severed head into the swift river Hebrus. . . . His limbs they gathered and
> placed in a tomb at the foot of Mount Olympus, and there to this day the
> nightingales sing more sweetly than anywhere else.[11]

Weill, too, had been "torn apart" at the time of his death; the dire interwar
events in Central Europe had sliced his mature career into two segments,
geographically, aesthetically, and culturally so isolated from one another
that to speak of "two Weills" has become a seldom questioned critical

---

10. Kurt Weill, "Verschiebungen in der musikalischen Produktion," *Berliner Tageblatt,* 1
October 1927. Translated in Kowalke, *Kurt Weill in Europe,* pp. 478–81.
    11. Edith Hamilton, *Mythology* (New York, 1940), p. 105.

cliché. No passive victim of circumstances, however, Weill encouraged this posthumous split identity by suppressing in America, whether consciously or unconsciously, both the intellectual underpinnings and the musical products of his European career while enthusiastically assuming the role of populist composer for Broadway and assembling the image of a popular songwriter. He deflected virtually all of the admittedly few efforts by former collaborators and musical or theatrical cognoscenti to transplant his German-cultivated perennials onto American soil. During his fifteen-year tenure in the United States, not one of Weill's pre-1935 stage works was produced by a professional company. The appraisal of his estate for probate in 1950 testified to his success at carving out a radical new image in America: only "September Song" and *Down in the Valley* were assigned demonstrable monetary value—*Die Dreigroschenoper* did not appear on the list of assets. As David Drew has observed:

> While some notable artists have simply stopped creating at a certain stage in their careers and a few have put an end to their lives, Weill is perhaps the only one to have done away with his old creative self in order to make way for a new one. The pre-1934 composer had been acutely conscious of his roots and responsibilities as a German artist in post-war society; had felt himself to be a part of the modern movement and one of its leaders in the younger generation; and was accustomed to measure his talents and achievements against those of the most eminent of his German contemporaries, Paul Hindemith. The post-1940 composer was one who asserted that he had never thought of himself as a German composer, that his only roots were those he had now established in the USA, and that his responsibilities were to the American musical stage in its popular form. The composer whom he now saw as his chief rival was Richard Rodgers.[12]

The strident debates over the relative worth of the two Weills began long before his death and continue today as if a conclusive resolution of the partisan issues were actually possible by claiming victory for one Weill over the other. Ernst Bloch, T. W. Adorno, Otto Klemperer, Hanns Eisler, Brecht, and many other former admirers did not hide from the composer their contempt for the "new Weill." In both private and public, however, Weill argued that the "new" was nothing more than a logical extrapolation of the "old," which an audience within the vastly different cultural context of America could not yet be expected to understand or appreciate. If Weill exaggerated the connections linking his European and American works as a means of rationalizing artistic decisions that had immense financial ramifications, he nonetheless convinced Maurice Abravanel, who consistently served as his conductor on both sides of the

---

12. David Drew, "Weill, Kurt (Julian)," *The New Grove Dictionary of Music and Musicians* 20:307.

Atlantic. Meanwhile, a host of new admirers were blissfully unaware of esoteric criticism leveled against Weill as an "instant American" who had betrayed earlier promise by selling out to commercial enterprises.

In any case, Weill perceived early on that he had no options; he could neither join Schoenberg, Hindemith, Krenek, and Milhaud in their academic shelters nor accept for long the film industry's real intentions for and treatment of the musical craft of skilled émigré composers. Having already irrevocably terminated the collaboration with Brecht in Europe for artistic, ideological, and personal reasons, Weill knew both the playwright and the American theater well enough to recognize that Brecht's proposed projects would not find an audience in the United States during the forties. Nor could the Metropolitan Opera tempt Weill to seek what he called "the living theater" within its hopelessly retrospective repertory, especially since he had already despaired of more progressive operatic institutions in Germany. Once his tentative commitment to Broadway had been rewarded both financially and personally, regardless of any concomitant artistic frustrations, Weill could not turn back. If he was not to abandon his lifelong commitment to musical theater as his "special field of activity,"[13] clearly he would have to work from within the established system to effect changes in American musical theater—just as he had attempted (also with only limited success) within the state-subsidized operatic institutions in Germany. This decision, however, embodied risks greater than any he had encountered previously; his daring association with Brecht, for example, had alarmed only his publisher, and its consequences had alienated primarily the right wing of both New Music and society. But to embrace Broadway wholeheartedly presupposed severing his previous ties with "serious music" altogether. Addressing a new audience required Weill to disavow the old one, as Ernst Krenek noted with only partially camouflaged condescension in 1959:

> Composers whose American works point up new characteristics unknown in their earlier works should not for that reason be automatically accused of having struck an unethical compromise. That is, they should not be reproached for having taken great pains, against their better judgment, to cultivate modes of writing conditioned by their surroundings. If Kurt Weill in America seemed to exchange the aggressive, bald, and sarcastic style of his Brecht period for the sumptuousness, the mundane sentimentality, and the, if at all, circumspect irony of the Broadway manner, he was probably hardly aware of the fact that in so doing he descended in our eyes below the level of his tradition and his earlier works. Rather he did, as he himself told

---

13. Kurt Weill, Notes to the recording of *Street Scene*, Columbia 4139: "Ever since I made up my mind, at the age of 19, that my special field of activity would be the theater, I have tried continuously to solve, in my own way, the form-problems of the musical theater, and through the years I have approached these problems from all different angles."

me, what seemed necessary to comply with that natural, invincible urge of his to communicate via the musical theater: he adapted this communication to the only vehicle at his disposal, namely the Broadway stage.[14]

After his death, most American obituaries lauded Weill's contributions to the popular music and theater of his adopted country and cited the German titles of a few pre-1935 works as if hearsay had convinced the authors that at one time in the distant past of Weill's youth they had somehow been important. Only the most erudite of obituarists from academically oriented musical circles lamented an assumed capitulation to the ephemeral, if not innately inferior, genre of American musical theater, which automatically disqualified any of its successful practitioners as "serious" composers. Although *Lost in the Stars* was still running on Broadway in 1950, the remainder of his musicals were already yesterday's "used shows," no longer of interest to a commercial apparatus that had not yet instituted the notion of revival as standard practice nor yet inspired the maintenance of a standard repertory for stock and amateur outlets. "Mack the Knife" had not yet been introduced to either Bobby Darin or Louis Armstrong, much less the American public.

Conversely, of Weill's American works only *Down in the Valley* had been produced in Europe. Because the remaining "Sins of His Middle Age" were known there only by isolated reports and occasional recordings of individual popular songs, Weill's death gave occasion for critics on the Continent to lament his lapse into trivial pursuits in exile. Hitler's regime and World War II had left behind few survivors who remembered the extraordinary impact of the pre-1933 Weill, and the emerging generation of postwar European composers was almost single-mindedly devoted to sorting out the ramifications of Webern's legacy. On the basis of the few fragments of Weill's output still available for perusal in either cultural setting after his death, even those capable of surveying the entire range and nature of his oeuvre were unable to reconcile the dichotomies and paradoxes which characterize it on every level and at every stage. Weill remained, with qualitative judgment dependent almost entirely on the observer's point of view, at once European and American, "serious" and popular, German and Jewish, abstruse and accessible.

Had he survived into the next decade, Weill himself would have been forced to reconcile much more than the two pronunciations of his surname ("vile" in Germany, "wile" in the United States). Rediscovery in Europe of *Die Dreigroschenoper* would soon have prompted the curious to inventory the other contents of the abandoned European compartment of his career. At the very least, recognition in America of Brecht as one of

14. Ernst Krenek, "America's Influence on Its Emigré Composers," *Perspectives of New Music* 8 (Spring/Summer 1970): 115.

the century's great playwrights would have stimulated interest in the products of Weill's collaboration with him. Broadway now boasted of its "integrated" musical theater, and Weill's prophetic vision of American opera would have found less resistance there. Financially, technically, and culturally, Weill would have been in a position to reclaim whatever values had been compromised in earlier Broadway and Hollywood efforts by acknowledging the "old" Weill and synthesizing it with the "new." But while at work on *Huckleberry Finn*, a topic representative of classic Americana in the extreme and indicative of no incipient synthetic process, he evaded in death any resolution of the real or imagined paradox of the two Weills. It appeared as if his name would appear only as a small footnote in music history—a casualty of world events, a curious might-have-been.

Only a posthumous rediscovery could rescue Weill from the oblivion Goebbels had planned for him. But more than a few pieces of his shattered portrait were missing. Many of his scores had been left behind in Europe, entrusted to his publisher, Universal Edition in Vienna, or to family members and friends. Some had been consigned without his knowledge to hiding places during the war and had never been reclaimed. In 1947, Weill reported to Margarethe Kaiser:

> I'm very happy that Martin wants to produce *Der Silbersee* at the Hebbel Theater, and I also have nothing against the performance of *Der Protagonist* and *Der Zar lässt sich photographieren* by German opera houses. Unfortunately it is, however, very difficult for me to fathom clearly from here the entire publisher situation. I had a letter from Universal Edition with the laconic notification that all my full scores had been confiscated by the Gestapo. Of course, that is an unbelievable negligence of responsibility by a publisher with regard to its authors. I don't have a single partitur of my European works, and therefore at the moment I can't say if one can procure them anywhere.[15]

Even if Weill was actually willing to allow performances (in German opera houses only!) of his collaborations with Georg Kaiser, he was under the impression that all performing materials had been lost. In fact, when he died, *Aufstieg und Fall der Stadt Mahagonny* was still presumed lost; an intact full score and set of parts were not rediscovered until 1953, when it prompted the complete recording with Lenya singing a simplified version of Jenny's role. With the exception of *Die Dreigroschenoper*, which Brecht had now revised despite Weill's objections and which was still enmeshed in legal disputes when Weill died (where it remains today), the composer's other European works were presumably buried with him.

Lotte Lenya was devastated by Weill's death. Although their rela-

---

15. A copy of the letter, dated 1 May 1947, is in the Weill-Lenya Research Center. All translations are my own unless otherwise noted.

tionship had been a turbulent and "open" one, punctuated by periods of separation—including a divorce finalized in 1933, with remarriage in 1937—it is impossible to exaggerate the range and depth of emotional and artistic interdependence between Weill and Lenya that transcended their antipodean intellectual and psychological profiles. What Weill tried to explain in the letter to his parents quoted above about Lenya's effect on his life he had articulated more poetically in an earlier intimate letter addressed to her: "For the first time I begin to sense what I am as I see myself mirrored within you, as I am allowed to see myself like a reflection in clear water. . . . You must hover over everything I am trying to accomplish; but no one will ever recognize you—because you are far above anyone else."[16] These two artistic temperaments, so different in background and world view, somehow merged in Lenya's voice. During July 1926, almost six months after their marriage, Weill wrote from Berlin to Lenya, who was staying with the Kaisers in Grünheide:

> When I long for you, I think most of all about the sound of your voice, which I love like a very force of nature, like an element. You are entirely contained within this sound; everything else is only a part of you; and when I envelop myself in your voice, then you are with me in every way. I know every nuance, every vibration of your voice, and I can hear exactly what you would say if you were with me right now—and how you would say it. And then suddenly this sound is again alien and new to me, and then it is the greatest joy to realize what the fondling caresses of your voice hold for me. . . . And now, just as it was on that first day, I am no longer sad that your voice is sounding somewhere else—and I do not hear it.[17]

But contrary to popular myth that "Weill conceived all his works with Lenya's voice in mind," she created roles in only five of his stage works: Jessie in the *Mahagonny Songspiel* (1927), Jenny in *Die Dreigroschenoper* (1928), Anna I in *Die sieben Todsünden* (1933), Miriam and the Witch of Endor in *The Eternal Road* (1937), and the Duchess in *The Firebrand of Florence* (1945). The embarrassing reviews for her performance in *Firebrand* prompted her to retire from the stage, as the idiosyncratic accents of her talent seemed too foreign for the American audience of the forties. Despite her public pronouncements that she was perfectly content just to make a home for Weill at Brook House in Rockland County, Lenya was unhappy as a housewife.

---

16. The undated letter, probably written early in 1925, is in the Weill-Lenya Research Center. Lys Symonette and I are presently preparing an annotated edition of the Weill-Lenya correspondence, which includes more than four hundred items.

17. The letter, dated 23 July 1926, is addressed to "Frau Lotte Lenya-Weill, Notenquetschersagattin/bei Kaiser"; Weill and Lenya used humorous and endlessly inventive nicknames for each other throughout their correspondence. Translation by Lys Symonette.

After Weill's death, only a sense of responsibility (and even guilt, which she admitted to a very few friends in private) and the assistance and encouragement of her second husband, George Davis, prompted Lenya to a monogamous and unrelenting devotion to Weill's music for the next thirty years. She reluctantly returned to Berlin in search of lost scores; she collected Weill's published essays and assembled reviews from the original productions of his works. One by one she recorded Weill's works in renditions that have now become legendary: *Aufstieg und Fall der Stadt Mahagonny, Die sieben Todsünden, Happy End, Berlin Theater Songs, American Theater Songs*, and, of course, *Die Dreigroschenoper*. Marc Blitzstein's American adaptation of the latter ran for 2611 performances (more than the combined total of all Weill's musicals conceived for the American stage) at the Theater de Lys with Lenya in her original role of Jenny. Well, almost—the role now usurped Polly's "Seeräuber-Jenny," which Lenya had never sung on stage in the original production, and all of her songs were transposed down to accommodate the vastly different timbre and range of a woman in her mid-fifties. But the authority of her interpretations was indisputable; the extraordinary sense of style, the innate musicality, the detached irony, the dramatic instinct, the sparkling diction had grown only more evident. Hers had become the voice through which the world posthumously recognized Weill's. Unfortunately, imitators unable to match Lenya's interpretive gifts settled for duplication of the impinging vocal handicaps, as if these were somehow intrinsic to the style of the music. Even now it borders on the heretical in many circles to suggest that this aspect of Lenya's later renditions compromised certain values in Weill's music—an admission she herself often reiterated, particularly in reference to *Mahagonny*.

Largely because of Lenya's efforts both as a performer and as executor of Weill's estate to "put Weill back together," however, critics began to speak of a "Weill renaissance." But interest in his music tended to be restricted to his collaborations with Brecht. With no one to rebut Brecht's own claims—unpublished until after Weill's death—that he was responsible for the nature (if not even the melodies themselves) of Weill's songs, it was widely assumed, at least in the voluminous literature on Brecht, that the errant Weill-without-Brecht must be of marginal interest and inferior quality. Within a decade after his death, Weill was no longer recognized primarily as a Broadway tunesmith, but rather as a "threepenny" composer. One haphazard collection of myths was replaced by another, even more misleading and limiting.

In the context of our extended Orphic metaphor, this new mythology owed less to a reinterpretation of historical fact than to an altered political and cultural climate, in which Weill could be "rehabilitated" almost as a wayward prodigal son from Brecht's collective while still avoid-

ing issues fundamental to the phenomenon of Weill per se. If one accepted Brecht's assertion that he had rescued Weill from a prior "reactionary"
career in an atonal, psychologically-oriented idiom, it was also tempting to
join Adorno, Eisler, and the new Brecht exegetes in the corollary they
posited: Weill, as a *Mitarbeiter* carefully molded by Brecht in his own
image, was at his best only when he suppressed purely musical concerns in
favor of overriding dramatic or socio-political considerations. With the
model for distortion of musical values now discernible in Lenya's contemporaneous performances and implicit in Brecht's antedated and er-
roneous *Misuk*-notions, the Weill-Brecht works were popularized in mutilated versions in which musical demands were circumvented by omission,
re-scoring, transposition, and simplification. Few performers or producers resisted the temptation to convert all of the Weill-Brecht works
into "aggressive" pieces for singing actors along the lines of *Die Dreigroschenoper* and *Happy End,* in fact the only two among the nine major
products of their collaboration that utilized non-operatically trained
voices for most principal roles. As a result, Weill's scores written to
Brecht's texts have to this day only occasionally been performed in authentic versions by singers as skilled as those in the original casts. Certain
performers hailed widely today as Brecht/Weill specialists have built careers on their ability to capitalize on the supposed virtue of vocal and/or
musical disabilities when singing Weill. This misguided "performance
practice" has altered perception of the actual musical content of Weill's
works no less than equally well-intentioned editors and performers in the
nineteenth century distorted Renaissance and Baroque musical styles.

Another longstanding myth suggests that when Weill's music is deprived of its ironic banality or satiric subtext in the pre- and post-Brecht
periods it lapses into embarrassing sentimentality, caters to commer-
cialism, or suffers from obvious technical deficiencies. If Brecht is thus
used as a wedge to subdivide Weill's oeuvre into even more compart-
ments, the composer's wide stylistic range within several cultural settings
can be devalued to an uncanny ability, not much more sophisticated than
that of a keen-eared cocktail pianist, to mimic and assimilate diverse
idioms for purely financial incentives.[18] Armed with the formidable intellectual artillery supplied by Adorno directly and Schoenberg indirectly,
and fortified by the pronouncements of more "populist" (but far less
convincing) critics such as Peter Heyworth in England and Harold Schon-

18. See, for instance, Harold Clurman's *All People Are Famous* (New York, 1974), pp. 128–
29: "His powers of assimilation were extraordinary. He could write music in any country so
that it would seem as if he were a native. He did in fact write some good 'French' and
'English' music during his stays in Paris and London. If he had landed among the Hotten-
tots, he would have become the outstanding Hottentot composer of the Hottentot theater.
Weill was all theater and all 'mask.'"

berg in the United States, Weill's detractors could almost camouflage their substitution of a mythology, deceptively persuasive in its manipulation of certain elements of truth and half-truth, for a reasoned and even-handed consideration of the issues raised by acquaintance with his entire output.

The problems encountered in Weill scholarship may be symptomatic of those of twentieth-century music in general, as Christopher Hailey has suggested:

> In the best sense, Weill always sought an audience, and it is the mark of his success in that quest—in such disparate cultural environments as Weimar Germany and Depression and post-Depression America—that his musical profile and aesthetic integrity have been fragmented more by the impression of disparate audiences than by any inherent contradiction in the means he used to address them. It may be argued that the "problem" for Kurt Weill scholarship is in large part the sociology of twentieth-century musical life, for the exclusivity of our musical cultures has made a comprehensive approach to his music difficult.[19]

Such a comprehensive approach to Weill's music was probably not possible until a decade ago, when the process of reclamation—still far from complete—of the most deeply buried but still salvageable fragments of Weill's literary and musical legacy produced a series of major discoveries. But as late as 1979, in a biographical and critical survey in *The New Grove Dictionary of Music and Musicians* (highly recommended to readers unfamiliar with the basic outlines of Weill's career), David Drew lamented the missing pieces, particularly the earliest, that are essential if we are to see Weill whole:

> The loss of almost all the music Weill wrote between his 15th and 21st years is particularly regrettable in view of the striking talent revealed in the two works from those years which have chanced to survive, the B minor String Quartet and the Sonata for cello and piano. . . . Not even the weakest of his early works is without some decisive and intensely felt inspiration which justifies at least an occasional performance; and the best of them, above all the *Recordare*, deserve to be numbered among his major achievements.[20]

The earliest autobiographical sketch to survive and include a list of compositions dates from 1925, and it ends coincidentally with *Der neue Orpheus:*

> K. W. was born 2.3.1900 in Dessau, studied for a short time at the Berlin Hochschule (Humperdinck). Then 2 years as a theater Kapellmeister. 1921

---

19. Christopher Hailey, review of *Kurt Weill in Europe, Musical Quarterly* 66 (October 1980): 597.

20. Drew, "Weill, Kurt (Julian)," pp. 302, 308–09.

pupil of Busoni, lived in Berlin. Works: "Zaubernacht" (Pantomime, Berlin 1922); Divertimento op. 5 (Berlin 1922); Fantasia, Pass., Hymn. op. 6 (Berlin 1923); String Quartet op. 8 (Berlin 1923); Quodlibet for Orchestra op. 9 (Dessau 1923); Frauentanz op. 10 (Berlin and Salzburg 1924); Recordare (a cappella, op. 11); Orchesterlieder nach Rilke (Berlin 1925); Concerto for Violin and Winds op. 13 (Paris 1925); "Der Protagonist," opera by G. K.; "Der neue Orpheus," Cantata for Soprano and Orchestra, op. 15.[21]

Of the eleven works on Weill's list, all composed after he had joined Busoni's masterclass, only seven have survived intact.[22] Apparently Weill considered his earlier compositions to be *Jugendwerke*, since he even omitted from his list of works the *Berliner Sinfonie* (now known as Symphony no. 1), his first major composition to be completed after joining the master class. Composed from April to June 1921 without supervision from Busoni, the symphony, whose autograph score bore an epigraph from Johannes R. Becher's Festspiel, *Arbeiter, Bauern, Soldaten—Der Aufbruch eines Volkes zu Gott,* was a by-product of an anticipated commission, which never materialized, for a production of the play by Max Reinhardt. Weill had written to his brother Hanns on 17 November 1920:

> In February, Bing will probably bring out my Cello Sonata in Hannover. Moreover, I have in sight a commission for composition of a piece by Johannes Becher. It is an enormous thing ("Aufbruch eines Volkes zu Gott"), ecstatic tension, and the most eminent musicians tear themselves to pieces to get to it, since of the young poets Becher is considered to be the one with the greatest future. Therefore, one of them will surely beat me to it.[23]

Twelve days later Weill reported in a postcard to his parents that he had received the manuscript of Becher's drama; but when the commission was not forthcoming, Weill apparently converted his plans for a theatrical score into a symphonic poem, with rough programmatic outlines derived from Becher's play. Unperformed during Weill's lifetime, the score of the symphony was hidden in an Italian convent during the war among the personal papers of a Professor Fleischer, who responded to Lenya's advertisements in Berlin newspapers in 1955 and returned the autograph partitur.[24] Weill's failure to include the work in his list of compositions

21. The sketch is included among the Peter Bing Documents in the Weill-Lenya Research Center.

22. The orchestral score of *Zaubernacht* is missing entirely. Only two of the six movements of the Divertimento have survived in any form; the surviving sketch and draft of the *Sinfonia sacra* (Fantasia, Passacaglia, and Hymnus) are incomplete; only two of the orchestrated *Rilke-Lieder* are extant.

23. A photocopy of the letter is in the Weill-Lenya Research Center.

24. In 1929 the autograph orchestral score, along with a number of Weill's other early works, was entrusted by the composer to a Professor Fleischer, who was writing a biography of Weill. When the Nazi regime came to power in 1933, Professor Fleischer sent the manu-

may reflect its unfavorable reception when presented in a four-hand piano version at one of the sessions of Busoni's masterclass.

In addition to the symphony, the String Quartet in B minor (1918), and the Sonata for Cello and Piano (1920), the only pre-1921 compositions thought to have survived intact (until the most recent discoveries) were three lieder—"Reiterlied," "Im Volkston," and "Das schöne Kind;" a four-part male chorus entitled "Ich weiss wofür;" and two settings of the "Weberlied" from Act 2 of Gerhart Hauptmann's *Die Weber*. An unfinished "Volkslied" for voice and piano, and seven pages of sketches for *Sulamith*, a cantata for soprano, female chorus, and orchestra, completed the meager collection of pre-1921 compositions. Weill seldom mentioned any of his earliest works by name in any of his published essays or interviews. In 1930, when asked specifically about the compositions he had written during his Gymnasium years in Dessau, he stated that he "composed for the school orchestra and even wrote—amazingly enough, considering who I am today—war choruses." He described these student works as "still quite immature, without real stylistic impulse."[25] In various later interviews in America, Weill referred to three early attempts at operatic composition, all now lost and probably never completed. The earliest was an opera based on "an old German play about knights and their ladies" by Karl Theodor Körner (1791–1813), which in 1943 Weill remembered having started at age eleven. He also recalled deriving a libretto from Hermann Sudermann's novel, *Das hohe Lied* (1908), a psychological chronicle of a chaste prostitute who ends her career by marriage. There is no evidence to suggest that Weill completed the libretto, much less composition of the opera.[26] The third early stage work is mentioned only in a letter from Weill to his sister Ruth, dated 28 January 1920, wherein he expressed hopes of finishing a setting of a one-act play by Ernst Hardt, *Ninon von Lenclos* (1905), despite the overwhelming demands on him as Kapellmeister of a makeshift theater in Lüdenscheid during its over-ambitious and often disastrous first season:

---

scripts to Universal Edition in Berlin. Somehow the score of the symphony was included by mistake in a shipment of Fleischer's personal possessions that eventually weathered the war in an Italian convent where the caretakers removed the title page of the score to prevent confiscation. See *New York Herald-Tribune*, 22 May 1958; and *New York World Telegram and Sun*, 24 May 1958. Both reports refer to a "Walter Fleischer," but this is probably an error, since a Herbert Fleischer published an essay, "Kurt Weill: Versuch einer einheitlichen Stilbetrachtung," *Anbruch* 14 (September 1932): 135–37, whose content indicates that he had access to Weill's early compositions.

25. "Aktuelles Zwiegespräch über die Schuloper zwischen Kurt Weill und Dr. Hans Fischer," translated in *Kurt Weill in Europe*, p. 552.

26. David Drew has surmised that the Sudermann project was undertaken sometime between 1917 and 1921.

First to the matter of the young poet. I suppose it is all about a candidate for an opera libretto. I must tell you frankly that in this respect my demands have grown considerably. If theater life were to allow me more time and leisure for my own writing, I would complete the one-act piece by Ernst Hardt. In this work I would want to give—and would want to achieve—only one thing: beauty. In addition to all of the beauty Hardt has already poured into it—his beguiling language, the local color, etc.—it simply has to result in an exuberance of beauty when combined with the music I have in mind; if this succeeded, it could even become a model for an entirely new lyrical musico-dramatic creation. Now if, together with a poet, I were to create a new work of art, I would come up with totally new ideas for it; however they have as yet not ripened enough to be revealed to anyone.[27]

It is possible to piece together a slightly longer list of pre-1921 compositions from two biographical essays written in the 1920s by Rudolph Kastner and Heinrich Strobel. Kastner reported in 1926 that by the time Weill was ten years old he was already "filling notebooks with drafts of compositions without any formal training" other than his cantor father's limited guidance, and that his earliest compositions included some piano pieces and a song cycle entitled *Schilflieder*.[28] Strobel, who had access to some of Weill's early manuscripts, suggested that the "beginnings of Weill's musical development lay in the late romantic," and that by age twenty his musical sphere "extended up to Debussy and early Schoenberg." He described the "impressionistic sound and expressive melody of the choral fantasy *Sulamith*" and asserted that a symphonic poem based on Rilke's *Weise von Liebe und Tod* exhibited "the tensely melodic style" of Schoenberg's *Pelleas und Melisande*.[29] The final epitaph for Weill's earliest scores was a family rumor that a crate containing many of Weill's pre-

---

27. The letter to Ruth Weill is in the Weill-Lenya Research Center in New York. Translation by Lys Symonette.

28. Rudolph Kastner, "Kurt Weill: Eine Skizze," *Anbruch* 7 (October 1925): 454.

29. Heinrich Strobel, "Kurt Weill," *Melos* 6 (October 1927): 427–33. David Drew, relying on Strobel's account and a reference to a performance of an orchestral work by Weill at the Berlin Hochschule in February 1919, has speculated that the piece may have been the Rilke symphonic poem. Photocopies of the Rita Weill Collection of correspondence at the Akademie der Künste, however, allow us to date the beginning of composition for the Rilke piece as no earlier than March 1919. The same letter to Hanns (27 March 1919) mentions that "the orchestration of the Suite still is not ready." Drew has also claimed that Weill reported completion of a symphony ("No. 0") in a postcard to his parents of 10 December 1920, included among the Eve Hammerschmidt Collection at the Weill-Lenya Research Center. That assertion, however, was apparently based on a misreading of Weill's handwriting. The passage reads: "In dieser Woche hat sich einmal garnichts ereignet. Mein Vortrag ist fertig u., glaube ich, recht gut geworden. Er hat doch viel Arbeit gemacht. Es ist jetzt richtig kalt, doch hatte ich in den letzten Tagen viel in der Staatsbibliothek zu tun, so dass ich wenig gefroren habe." The "Vortrag" was probably the lecture on Beethoven Weill eventually delivered in Halberstadt at the Berend-Lehmann-Verein on 6 March 1921.

1925 manuscripts had been lost overboard and never recovered while being unloaded in Palestine when his parents emigrated there in 1935.

Speculation concerning Weill's musical roots, the determinant influences in his musical development, and their reflections in his mature compositions has therefore been based precariously on these few shreds of evidence. But in 1982 Weill's sister-in-law, Rita Weill, revealed that she possessed fourteen autograph musical manuscripts that preserve eleven pre-1921 compositions hitherto unknown to have existed or presumed lost and a large collection of correspondence between Weill and his family from the period. Although I was allowed to inventory some of the documents in September 1982, none was made available for study until after Rita Weill's death in 1983, when her daughter, Hanne Holesovsky, provided the Weill-Lenya Research Center with photocopies of ten musical manuscripts. The remainder of the material is still inaccessible because of probate proceedings. Although a detailed survey and evaluation of the documents has thereby been delayed, it is possible to present a rough chronology for the newly discovered compositions:

1. "Mi Addir: Jüdischer Trauungsgesang," undated setting for voice and piano of a traditional Hebrew wedding text.
2. "Es blühen zwei flammende Rosen," undated lied for voice and piano (poet unidentified).
3. "Ich weiss wofür," undated holograph draft of a four-part a cappella male chorus in B♭, differing from the version in A♭ previously preserved in a copyist's manuscript.
4. "Gebet," setting of text by Emanuel Geibel (1815–84) for four-part a cappella mixed chorus. Composed for Weill's sister's (Ruth) "confirmation."
5. "Sehnsucht: Eichendorff," lied for voice and piano without text underlay, dated 1916.
6. "Ofrah's Lieder," song cycle in five movements for voice and piano, with texts by Jehuda Halevi in German translation, dated September 1916.
7. "Abendlied," duet for two sopranos and piano with text by Otto Julius Bierbaum (1865–1910). Undated, but performed in concert by students of Emilie Feuge in Dessau on 6 February 1918.
8. "Maikaterlied," duet for two sopranos and piano with text by Otto Julius Bierbaum, performed with "Abendlied" on 6 February 1918, but completed prior to 15 November 1917, when Weill wrote to his brother Hanns that he "still [has] to copy over 'Maikaterlied' once more."
9. "Intermezzo," for solo piano, dated December 1917.

10. Orchestration of the Andante (movement 2) of Weber's Piano Sonata in A♭ major, dated March 1918.
11. String Quartet in B minor, holograph fair copy and corrected set of parts, dated 1918.
12. Orchestersuite in E major in six movements for double-wind orchestra, undated, but mentioned in a letter to Hanns of 27 March 1919: "The instrumentation of the Suite still isn't finished."
13. Sonata for Cello and Piano, undated and incomplete holograph draft.
14. "Die stille Stadt," lied for voice and piano with text by Richard Dehmel (1863–1920). Undated, but performed by Weill and Elisabeth Feuge in Halberstadt on 17 June 1920.

No less important for future biographical and stylistic studies is Rita Weill's parallel collection of correspondence, particularly letters from Kurt to Hanns, wherein he regularly reported in detail on his musical activities, composition projects, piano repertoire, score study, and reactions to concerts, conductors, and individual works. We learn, for example, of Weill's first encounter with *Rigoletto* and *Elektra*, his response to Nikisch's conducting of Beethoven's Fifth Symphony, the range of his piano repertoire, and his score study of *Fidelio, Die Walküre*, and *Palestrina*. Such documents are more than curiosities from a composer's youth; although "influence" and "development" can become areas of intellectual quicksand, so complex a figure as Weill and so difficult an interpretative challenge as his music presents demand profound understanding of the musical, theatrical, social, and political forces which originally informed (and continue to serve as subtext to) the compositions. The revisions in biography, chronology, and critical construct necessitated by the new material raises hopes for the eventual recovery of other missing links. *Na und?*, Weill's full-length comic opera on a libretto by Felix Joachimson (now Felix Jackson and living in Los Angeles), was lost after 1927 when it was rejected by both Universal Edition and Hans Curjel, the dramaturg of the Kroll Opera. Only thirty-four pages of a piano draft have survived. The orchestral material and full score of *Royal Palace* (1926) were not recovered after a production in Essen during 1929. The cantata *Fantômas*, based on a poem of twenty-five quatrains by Robert Desnos, commissioned by Radio Paris and broadcast on 3 November 1933, survives only in a corrupt arrangement of the "Ballad of Fantômas" recorded by Catherine Sauvage. Other missing works include incidental music for a radio production of *Herzog Theodor von Gothland* (1926), the Berlin production of *Mann ist Mann* (1931), and productions of *Two on an Island, It's Fun to Be Free, We Will Never Die*, and *A Flag Is Born* in the United States. Even scores which have survived intact have, for all practical purposes, been "lost." *Der Kuhhandel, Der Weg der Verheissung, The Firebrand of Florence,* and *Love Life,* major musical works all, have never been published or recorded for reasons that have little to do with their intrinsic merits.

Any current judgments, then, concerning Weill's ultimate stature as a composer or his impact on the musical course of the twentieth century must be viewed with some suspicion given the nascent state of research, publication, and performance. David Drew warned in 1975 that time alone will "not tell us anything other than the appalling lateness of the hour" in acknowledging the futility of positing "a precise evaluation of Weill's importance or lack of it."[30] Although that postponement is still necessarily in effect, the relevant issues are coming into better focus as Weill's image is gradually pieced back together and the cutting edges of musical theater on both "popular" and "serious" fronts demonstrate more and more affinities with Weill's vision. Although demythologized to some extent by recent studies, Weill remains a problematic figure of unique stylistic identity and paradoxical interpretative challenges. If the power of his art eventually proves to be that of a "new Orpheus" only in the sub-Olympian sense of a secondary master, his music will not easily be consigned to an obscure underworld.

> *So I sit in my half-dark room and feel such an intimate bond with all those others who have ever sought solitude in their little dens away from the rushing crowds in order to perceive more clearly the murmuring song of the stars. And with those who stretch out their hands to each other across the centuries. And all of them, all pray for reeling humanity.*
> —Kurt Weill, 1920.[31]

> *It's been five weeks now since Kurt died, and I haven't been able to take one step forward. The only thing that keeps me going at all is his music. . . . Only a few recognize its significance, especially here, where only a part of his work is known. And I believe I'll find my life's work in making this music known . . . . I hope that I'm choosing the right path by going on living—for him, so that he won't be forgotten too quickly in a time which has no time to remember what happened yesterday.*
> —Lotte Lenya, 1950.[32]

30. David Drew, "Introduction and Notes," Deutsche Grammophon recording 2563 584–586, p. 16.

31. The letter from Weill to his sister Ruth, written in 1920 from Lüdenscheid, is in the Weill-Lenya Research Center.

32. Letter dated 11 May 1950 to Manfred George.

2

Creating a Public, Addressing a Market: Kurt Weill and Universal Edition
CHRISTOPHER HAILEY

Kurt Weill belonged to the generation of German composers who came of age during the turbulent years of the Weimar Republic. It was a generation which had inherited its revolutions, a generation nurtured by the ideals of social and political revolt yet sobered by the realities of war and inflation, bred on a musical language in upheaval yet longing for a new classical balance, excited by the artistic possibilities of a technological age yet eager to explore the instrumental and vocal legacy of the past. Like no generation before, Weill and his contemporaries enjoyed generous sponsorship by state and municipal institutions, broad exposure in national and international music festivals, and the influential support of major publishing houses. Their works were more widely commissioned, published, and performed than those of any previous generation, yet the young composers of the twenties experienced unprecedented isolation from their audience and recognized a deep-seated crisis in their art.

The contradictions arising from these varied impulses and opportunities and the convulsive social, political, and economic background against which they were set are registered above all in the music of Kurt Weill. None of his contemporaries enjoyed such wide acclaim or captured such diverse audiences, and posterity has identified no other composer so closely with the spirit of that age. Yet at a time when Weill's music and career are in danger of becoming a cultural cliché, a convenient emblem for an eccentric era, it is well to look beneath the surface to explore the elements within his career which link him so inextricably with his contemporaries and the intellectual history of the century. Few documents afford us a better vantage point for that purpose than Weill's correspondence with his publisher, Universal Edition of Vienna. This correspondence, dating from Weill's first contact with the firm early in 1924 to the heyday of his European success in the late twenties and early thirties, is a dramatic chronicle of one of the most striking publishing successes of the Weimar period and a key document for Kurt Weill's musical and aesthetic development. Beyond that, however, these letters offer insight into the interplay between aesthetics and economics, between musical style and success, which has become such a hallmark of twentieth-century musical culture.[1]

Kurt Weill signed his first contract with Universal Edition (hereafter U.E.) in May 1924 after several months of negotiation and a recommendation from Busoni. His first works to be accepted into the U.E. catalogue were *Frauentanz, Quodlibet,* String Quartet (op. 8), and the Concerto for Violin and Winds, which had just been completed. Despite less than favorable terms, Weill could well be happy with his association with U.E., for his works—those which were accepted—would appear in print with what even then was considered the most prestigious publisher of twentieth-century music. U.E. had the influence to ensure some performances of his works and a well-oiled propaganda machine (including its house journal, *Die Musikblätter des Anbruch*) to promote any successes. By 1924 Germany's horrendous postwar inflation had been brought under control, and U.E. was undergoing a period of major expansion. New music was a profitable if circumscribed field of publishing activity, and to all appearances U.E. had nearly cornered the market by signing some of New Music's brightest lights. Among the firm's younger composers were Schreker's students, Ernst Krenek, Felix Petyrek, Wilhelm Grosz, Alois Hába, and Karol Rathaus, and Schoenberg's students, Anton Webern, Egon Wellesz, Alban Berg, and Hanns Eisler. Weill was the latest in a series of investments in the future, for U.E. hoped that in the long run this young member of the avant-garde would repay their initial printing costs with at least a modest return in royalties, sales, and rentals.

Weill's first years with U.E. were typical. He was but one of the many, and the correspondence reflects his frustration in trying to get his publisher's assistance in obtaining performances and providing what he considered timely publication or ample promotion of his scores. Nonetheless,

1. Weill's correspondence with Universal Edition is located in the U.E. Archive on loan to the music division of the City Library of Vienna (Wiener Stadt- und Landesbibliothek). The collection comprises roughly 1400 items, ranging from postcards and letters to slips and receipts, and covers a period from February 1924 to the end of 1933. Thereafter, Weill's correspondence with his publisher was increasingly sporadic, and only a few letters exist from the mid- and late thirties. While most of the correspondence appears to have been preserved intact, there are occasional gaps of several weeks, especially in the later years. Letters from the collection are identified by date in the text. The Weill-Lenya Research Center in New York holds the only copies of the correspondence in the United States. The correspondence is quoted here by permission of Universal Edition and the Kurt Weill Foundation for Music.

Weill could count on some small advances to supplement his meager income from private teaching and journalism. By the end of 1924, he was receiving one hundred marks a month, which was increased to two hundred marks by the end of 1925. With the premiere of his one-act opera, *Der Protagonist*, in March 1926, Weill entered the community of U.E.'s operatic composers, but the work's immense critical success did not bring commensurate box-office profits, something Weill blamed in part on U.E.'s lack of publicity, reluctance to produce a full score, and delay in printing the vocal score. At the beginning of 1927, Weill, who had long sought to improve the terms of his contract, vented his accumulated grievances in a letter to U.E.'s director, Emil Hertzka. Hertzka's reply of 29 January was frank and to the point:

> You know very well that not one of your works has covered its printing costs, let alone earned even a penny in profit. In April the contract will have been in effect for three years. We are in no way complaining about the fact that during these three years we have on the one hand helped you with advances and also invested very respectable sums in production and publicity, but we must find it regrettable that we never hear anything but expressions of your dissatisfaction. This might be understandable if we had enriched ourselves on your works and let you starve in the meantime. (29 January 1927)

Weill's precarious bargaining position with his publisher is best illustrated with a look at the circumstances surrounding the rejection of his first full-length opera, *Na und?*, in the spring of 1927. Weill first mentioned plans for *Na und?* in August 1925. He initially referred to it as an operetta, whose text was being prepared for him to his specifications by Felix Joachimson. By January 1926 he had begun work on the composition, which he completed at the beginning of the following year and offered to his publisher in April 1927. He then described the work to Hertzka in a letter dated 4 April as a "thoroughly unproblematic comic opera in an absolutely new style, which nonetheless seems suited to finding a larger audience." In the meantime Weill's topical second opera, *Royal Palace*, had been premiered in Berlin and had not even garnered the critical accolades of *Der Protagonist;* neither work seemed destined to balance Weill's ledger at U.E. Weill, though, was confident that *Na und?* would significantly improve his financial position. In a letter to Hans Heinsheimer, director of U.E.'s opera division, Weill called his new opera "the first attempt in opera to illuminate the essence of our era from within and not by means of obvious superficial props," and added, "it is the sort of comic opera which hasn't been developed since *Der Rosenkavalier* and is just what the theaters are looking for—not grotesque or burlesque, but jaunty and musical" (4 April 1927).

It is well known that neither Hertzka nor his assistant Heinsheimer shared Weill's enthusiasm for *Na und?*. However, the matter was not settled in their April meeting in Vienna, as discussions continued into the fall. At the beginning of August, following the success of the *Mahagonny Songspiel* at the Baden-Baden Music Festival, Weill wrote to pressure U.E. for a final decision on his opera, "since the Mahagonny success has opened entirely new perspectives for this piece" (4 August 1927). Weill insisted that the time was right for *Na und?* and what was more, that he had offers from other publishers and various performance opportunities. To forestall both eventualities, U.E. accepted *Na und?* in September and doubled Weill's monthly advance to four hundred marks; for his part, Weill agreed to proceed with other projects, including his next opera, *Der Zar lässt sich photographieren,* and to postpone a definitive decision on *Na und?* (7 September 1927).

U.E.'s initial rejection of *Na und?*, following as it did upon the poor returns from two operas, revealed the publisher's reluctance to embark on the expense of publishing a full-length opera by a not yet fully proven composer and its skepticism about the still cloudy future of *Zeitoper* in general. (Their objections, incidentally, concerned only the libretto; the music is never mentioned.)[2] It is apparent that, despite the success of the *Mahagonny Songspiel* and his continued confidence in his new opera, Weill was willing to sacrifice *Na und?* as a bargaining chip for the long-term benefits of better contractual conditions and a smooth working relationship with his publisher. Had this tactic failed, it is quite likely that he would have had the work performed and published elsewhere; undoubtedly the opera would then have survived in some form.

Weill's last-minute decision to write the *Mahagonny Songspiel* for the Baden-Baden Music Festival of 1927 was the turning point of his career, although the success of that work at the Festival did not make him immune from his publisher's criticism of his taste in librettos. When Weill informed his publisher that he was intent upon writing a full-length opera on the Mahagonny subject, Hertzka urged caution (15 August 1927). Hertzka's misgivings about Brecht's suitability as a librettist and Mahagonny as an operatic subject were based on his long experience with Germany's opera houses and their largely conservative audiences. Furthermore, he doubted if this material was really suited to operatic treatment. Weill, on the other hand, pointed to the demonstrated success of his Baden-Baden premiere. As he wrote to Hertzka on 25 August 1927:

> The reason I am drawn to Brecht is, first of all, the strong interplay of my music with his poetry, which surprised all those in Baden-Baden who were competent to judge. But further, I am convinced that the close collaboration of two equally productive individuals can lead today to something funda-

---

2. Weill described the musical form of *Na und?* as seventeen closed numbers with linking recitative or spoken dialogue to piano or chamber ensemble accompaniment (4 April 1927).

mentally new. There can certainly be no doubt that at present a completely new form of stage work is evolving, one that is directed to a different and much larger audience and whose appeal will be unusually broad. This movement, whose strongest force in the spoken drama is Brecht, hasn't had any effect upon opera to date (except in *Mahagonny*), although music is one of its most essential elements. In long discussions with Brecht I have become convinced that his views and mine regarding operatic texts are largely in agreement. The piece we are going to create won't exploit topical themes which will be dated in a year but rather will reflect the definitive shape of our time. For that reason it will have an impact far beyond its own age. The task is to create the new genre which treats the completely transformed manifestation of life in our time in an appropriate manner.

In addition to his lofty ambitions, Weill had a not-so-secret weapon in his musical arsenal which he promised would play a decisive role in his new work. As he wrote in December, "In the operatic style I am founding here, music has a much more fundamental role than in the purely action opera, since I am replacing the earlier bravura aria with a new kind of hit song [*Schlager*]" (27 December 1927).

Weill soon realized that his *Schlager* had a life and audience of their own, and he considered them a thing apart, not quite integrated with the main body of his works. After the premiere of *Die Dreigroschenoper* in August 1928, he wrote his publisher: "Every day I hear from all sides, from all circles of the public, that these pieces have a popular appeal unlike that of any music in years. Everyone bears me out that with the five or so pieces of this genre I have written to date, one could easily earn a small fortune" (25 October 1928). Weill urged his publisher to help him make the most of these popular songs in order to assure him financial independence. "I am convinced," he continued in his letter, "that my gift for writing a completely new kind of popular melody is absolutely unrivalled today. If this matter were organized in a thoroughly large-scale and novel way, there is no doubt that my hit compositions could take the place of the American jazz compositions that are already somewhat passé." After discussing various possibilities, Weill added a note of caution: "I don't know how many more pieces I'll be able to write as effective as the 'Alabama Song,' the 'Kanonensong,' the 'Tango Ballade,' the 'Ballade vom angenehmen Leben,' and the 'Moritat.'"

Weill's aspirations, his success, and the quandaries it posed for him and his publisher were symptomatic of German musical culture in the late twenties. In a 1929 article entitled "Der Musikverbraucher" (The Music Consumer), H. H. Stuckenschmidt noted that two recent premieres by Schreker and Strauss, composers who had dominated the operatic stage a decade earlier, had found little resonance:

They had to fail with the audience of 1928, with its interest so totally directed to the present and future. Today's music consumer will avoid reading through or even buying piano scores of *Helene* or *singende Teufel,* while on the other hand, he will play the songs and couplets of Weill and Spoliansky at home with pleasure.[3]

Linking Weill's name with that of the successful composer of revues and cabarets, Mischa Spoliansky (b. 1898), was indicative, for overnight a "serious" composer of the musical avant-garde had captivated public imagination as had nothing else in years. For young composers this breakthrough was cause for euphoria, and no doubt there was heady elation at the Karlsplatz offices of U.E., where no time was lost in exploiting these successes with all available "commercial" means. Individual "hit songs" from *Mahagonny* and *Die Dreigroschenoper* flooded the market, popular editions abounded,[4] recording contracts were signed, and arrangements were prepared for dance band, jazz ensemble, movie house orchestras, even military band, and, of course, U.E.'s publicity office was working at full capacity. Weill urged his publisher to keep the piano scores and arrangements of his works as simple as possible, for now the market was no longer the relatively sophisticated circle of new music enthusiasts, but the broader, relatively untrained music lovers of the mass audience.

The implications of these and other trends were not lost on contemporary observers. For Klaus Pringsheim, writing in 1930, it was nothing short of the most significant revolution in new music:

> The young people who were culpable of coercing this process of isolation for several years are beginning to understand better the signs of the times. . . . They are beginning to realize that the great musical revolution, whose driving power they feel themselves to be, is not taking place at the frontiers of the musician's preserve nor in the realm of new theories and systems of composition, but rather in the area of musical supply and demand—in the forms of dissemination, in the methods of marketing—not in a commercial sense, but rather in a much broader, more general sense. Music is divorced from life and separated from the people: that is what music has come to at the close of its bourgeois era.[5]

Weill recognized that he was a leader in this revolution. For over a decade he had been forming the aesthetic precepts which would lead him from what he called the "artfulness" [*Artistentum*] of his earliest works and the

---

3. *Die Musik* 21 (March 1929): 410–15. Stuckenschmidt refers to Schreker's *Der singende Teufel,* premiered in Berlin on 10 December 1928, and Strauss's *Die aegyptische Helene,* premiered in Dresden on 6 June 1928.

4. Among them was the 1929 *Musik für Alle* edition of hits from *Die Dreigroschenoper,* in which Paul Wiegler proudly noted in the preface that *Musik für Alle* was entering for the first time into the realm of atonal (!) music with this publication.

5. Klaus Pringsheim, "Die grosse Musikrevolution," *Die Weltbühne* 26 (1 July 1930): 22–24.

"snobbery" of the new music festivals to the full and unabashed embrace of the broader audience of the day.

A recurrent theme in Weill's writings and those of some contemporaries is the search for a so-called *gesellschaftsbildende* or socially formative role for new music. This type of sociological approach to art music had found adherents early in the century. One of its pioneering voices had been Paul Bekker, whose *Deutsches Musikleben* of 1916 broke new ground. Typical of Bekker's approach was his 1917 study of the symphony, in which he defined the achievement of the great symphonists from Haydn and Beethoven to Mahler in terms of the audience they had reached—the community their works attracted and the societal experience their compositions engendered.[6] A new work or body of works, Bekker argued, had progressive sociological value to the extent that it created or redefined a new and wider audience. This idea strongly appealed to the revolutionary impulses of young composers from Eduard Erdmann, Heinz Tiessen, and Ernst Krenek to the young Weill himself, whose early expressionistic symphony and other orchestral works seemed intent on achieving something of the same breakthrough to a new public, to a new humanity. Like much else in the immediate postwar years, these heady aspirations gave way to more sober realities. If the new humanity did not appear or failed to rally around the artists' work, then the artists had to go out in search of the audience—and it was an audience preoccupied with the social realities of the here and now, not the utopias of the future.

During these years there was palpable discontent among Weill's generation with many traditional forms of musical activity. An unprecedented array of new media from recording and radio to film, the democratization of political life, and the growth of a popular entertainment and sports industry seemed to support the thesis that modern civilization was outgrowing the elitist forms of the past and adapting itself to a new kind of mass culture. The music history of the late twenties is brimming with attempts of composers to meet this challenge in every genre, but perhaps nowhere so telling as in the theater. Ernst Krenek, whose *Jonny spielt auf* was hailed as the first jazz opera and the sensation of 1927, discussed the situation that same year:

> The theater has always had to treat themes which could find resonance in the widest circles. For what is a theater without an audience? . . . In earlier times, when there was still a homogeneous audience bound by great common ideas, the theatrical author had the inexhaustibly fertile soil of a living folk culture; on the other hand, he couldn't possibly go wrong, since he himself stood in the midst of this living culture. With today's inner disin-

---

6. Paul Bekker, "Die Sinfonie von Beethoven bis Mahler" (Berlin, 1917), later reprinted in the collection *Neue Musik* (Stuttgart and Berlin, 1923).

tegration of this folk culture, with the fragmentation of this homogeneity, with the planless dispersion of all instincts, it is enormously difficult to find any common denominator for these millions of disparate individuals. And on the other hand it is absolutely vital for the theater to bring things to the stage which interest the audience.[7]

Kurt Westphal put it still more directly when he wrote in 1930 that the question of new music had been turned upside down: "It is not the creator, but the listener who poses the question. It is for *him* to demand, for *him* to say what he wants. He holds the solution to the problem of a music rooted in our time and the spirit of our age."[8]

The audience of the 1920s was, in fact, a disparate and faceless entity, but its tastes were quantifiable through its profile as a market— through its purchase of recordings, radios, and sheet music, and through attendance at concerts, operas, films, theaters, cabarets, revues, and dance halls. In *Jonny spielt auf* Ernst Krenek had made an early attempt to reach broader elements of that audience by appealing to its topical interests; his work patched popular elements into the dramaturgy of an otherwise conventional operatic form and succeeded in conquering the opera houses of the world. Kurt Weill took that revolution a decisive step further; he virtually re-thought opera in light of popular forms and succeeded in bringing the world to the opera house.

But Weill's success by no means meant that he or his publisher could be wholly identified with the revolution Pringsheim had heralded. Universal, after all, was also the publisher of *Wozzeck*, an opera Pringsheim characterized as the "artistic will of a dying era . . . a reactionary front."[9] And Weill was also the composer of challenging concert works; he still maintained aspirations to "bourgeois art forms." The resultant schizophrenic split is clearly apparent in Weill's correspondence and strongly colors his post-*Mahagonny* production. During the late twenties and early thirties the letters of both composer and publisher vacillate between a determined sense of purpose and wariness, between defensiveness and mutual reassurances, reflecting their attempts to reconcile the demands of aesthetic principle and those of popular culture, between dreams of creating an audience and the business of exploiting a market. In the face of the almost irresistible lures of commercial success, both Weill and U.E. were interested in the development of the stylistic process Weill called his *Linie*, or path. But one is also aware of the efforts to maintain a foothold in

7. Krenek's remarks are quoted from a lecture given on 31 October 1927 in Kassel. A typescript is in the U.E. archive.
8. Kurt Westphal, "Neue Musik Berlin und die Musikpaedagogik," *Anbruch* 12 (September–October 1930): 245–46.
9. Pringsheim, p. 23.

two camps, to balance the evolving forms directed toward a new mass audience with the grand traditions of European art music.

There is a significant exchange of letters from the fall of 1929 which can serve as an example of the increasingly complex nature of Weill's relationship to his publisher and the web of interests in which both were caught. Early in October, while awaiting the March premiere of his *Mahagonny* opera, Weill was considering a lucrative offer to write four or five short songs for a *Volksstück* being produced by Stefan Grossmann in Berlin. He wrote his publisher:

> What attracts me to this project is the following: with a minimal loss of time (I can do these few songs in about a week) I can show a completely different side of myself for once; they won't be songs or "hits," no American milieu; it is quite outside the sphere of my most recent work for the theater. I think that would be of decisive importance, especially now **before** *Mahagonny*, because otherwise one might soon accuse me of one-sidedness. What is more, musically these short, folk-like songs are thoroughly in keeping with my latest compositions. Aside from such tactical and artistic considerations, I also think this piece has great chances for success throughout Germany, because there has never been a modern folk play of this kind. (8 October 1929)

In Hertzka's absence, Hans Heinsheimer replied, outlining his serious misgivings:

> The situation in which you currently find yourself is not simple. The style established in *Die Dreigroschenoper* and *Happy End* and continued in *Mahagonny*, whose most significant portions stem from the very period in which this style emerged, this style, and we are all in agreement about this, cannot be copied indefinitely. If I judge its place in your development correctly, it is, as it were, the breakthrough to a popular, simple musical style that radically liberated you from the style evident in, say, *Frauentanz*. But in the long run this song style can serve only as a springboard for your return to more profound and substantial musical creations. (10 October 1929)

Heinsheimer goes on to hail the recently composed alternative love scene in *Mahagonny*, the "Crane Duet," as the definitive break with the style of 1928 and the anticipation of the style of the coming years. He concludes his arguments with an extended appeal that Weill attend to long-range musical goals and turn away from the hothouse intellectualism of Berlin's literary circles:

> Perhaps it is more precisely because I don't live in Berlin and am therefore all the more conscious of the increasing isolation of Berlin's intellectualism that I can warn you with absolute conviction against expending your energies upon such things again. The strong opposition to Berlin's domination, which is currently apparent throughout Germany, doesn't surprise me in

the least. On the contrary, it is quite in keeping with an inevitable development. The German provinces are cultivating their own strong and admirable intellectual life. The vital forces which are at work throughout Germany, I am absolutely convinced, will determine the intellectual and artistic climate of the coming years. . . . You should and must free yourself once and for all from Berlin's commercialized artistic activity now that the success of your recent works has given you complete independence and freedom, not only financially, but also artistically; and now that precisely these popular works have completely freed you from the literary and artistic thicket, you must once again create works which can truly endure, works which aren't just created for the moment as accompaniment for plays, but which follow the great path of development I have always perceived in all your works.

Heinsheimer's letter no doubt reflected the publisher's disappointment with Weill's ill-fated *Happy End* and the fear that the composer might lose his compositional identity in a series of such works. Upon reflection, Weill agreed with Heinsheimer's arguments and put the Grossmann project aside. In his reply to Heinsheimer, however, he tried to place his own musical development in a more accurate context. He wrote:

Above all, I was pleased that you recognized the nature of the stylistic transformation I am undergoing. (There are not many who do notice it.) But one must date the beginning of this stylistic transformation much earlier than you do. By far the greater part of *Mahagonny* is already entirely free of the song style and reveals this new style which surpasses in seriousness, "stature," and expressive power everything I have written to date. Almost everything which was added to the Baden-Baden version is written in a completely pure, thoroughly responsible style, which I am convinced will endure longer than most of what is produced today. (14 October 1929)

Weill was at pains to establish his position against his publisher's misgivings. He defended the musical significance of *Happy End* and of his song style in general:

Just because some of my new works happen to be mounted badly in a bad play, we must not be misled into trivializing what was achieved through *Die Dreigroschenoper*, achieved not only for my music, but for musical life in general. From our standpoint the fact that my *Dreigroschenoper* music has been commercialized doesn't speak against it, but for it, and we would be falling back into our old mistakes if we were to deny some music its importance and artistic value simply because it found its way to the masses. You are right—I cannot copy this song style indefinitely, and with the works since *Mahagonny* I have demonstrated that I don't intend to copy it. But we cannot deny that this style has set a precedent and that today more than half of the young composers from the most diverse backgrounds make their living from it. That's why it's very easy for the general public to overlook the fact that I myself, who defined this style only a year ago, have in the meantime quietly continued on my own path. So you see that your arguments are essentially in complete agreement with my own views.

As for Berlin, Weill was adamant in its defense:

> On one point, however, I cannot concur with you: concerning what you say
> about Berlin and the German provinces. I know the German provinces. I
> grew up there, these days I often travel to provincial cities, and I read the
> papers. The "Spirit of the German Provinces" as portrayed in the papers is
> deeply reactionary, and it is absolutely inconceivable that a new, future-
> oriented artistic movement could emerge from one of these cities. In any
> case, opposition to Berlin's theatrical life can't be so strong when *Die Drei-
> groschenoper*, the most daring and revolutionary product of this much ma-
> ligned Berlin spirit, is enjoying full houses everywhere. No, dear friend
> Heinsheimer, the battle against Berlin being waged in certain well-known
> provincial circles is a part of that great offensive which reactionary forces
> have launched in recent years with the purpose of exerting influence over
> the artistic sphere as well. The provincial intellectual forces of which you
> speak have no more ardent desire than to come to Berlin. The develop-
> ments within the German theater over the last decade have come exclusively
> and entirely from Berlin, from Brahm, from Reinhardt, from Jessner and
> Piscator, and finally from the Theater am Schiffbauerdamm. Do you really
> believe that one can dismiss these achievements which make Berlin today's
> unrivalled theatrical capital of Europe with the expression "commercialized
> artistic activity"? And do you really believe that one can apply this descrip-
> tion to what I do? I am the only creative musician who for years has worked
> consistently and uncompromisingly in the face of opposition from the snobs
> and aesthetes toward the creation of fundamental forms of a new, simple,
> popular musical theater. Even my least significant music theater works dur-
> ing this time have been written with this sense of responsibility and have
> grown out of a constant effort to further a development which seems to me
> the only one possible. Is that commercialized artistic activity? Wouldn't it be
> much easier (and commercially more profitable) if, like most of the others, I
> were to carry on and vary the traditional operatic style a little further and
> adapt myself from the outset to the taste and mentality of the provincial
> opera-goer? No one knows the dangers of Berlin's literary scene as well as I
> do. But I have demonstrated that, as long as one doesn't fall victim to its
> pitfalls, the most substantial and the purest artistic achievements are possi-
> ble in precisely this atmosphere.

Shortly after these letters were written, the crash of the New York
stock market brought on a crisis which had devastating effects on Germany's economy. The brief span of stability and prosperity which had
begun around 1925 gave way to rising unemployment, increasing political polarization, and a series of governmental emergency decrees which,
among other things, had the effect of severely limiting state subvention
for the arts. For new music, and most particularly for contemporary
opera, it was an era of retrenchment. Germany's cultural and political
polarization now became a topic of major concern in Weill's correspondence with his publisher. But if Weill identified himself with the progressive forces, his criticism was just as often directed toward the left,

whose indecisiveness and often cowardly capitulation to the right was, he felt, responsible in large part for its threatened position.

For its part, U.E. was increasingly eager for Weill to diversify his production, to expand his performance opportunities in Germany and abroad, and to win back some of music publishing's more traditional concert constituency. U.E. welcomed the addition of *Der Lindberghflug* to Weill's concert works but also encouraged him to write so-called absolute music again. Erwin Stein, director of U.E.'s orchestral division, joined Heinsheimer's plea for a purely orchestral piece—something Stein found absolutely necessary from both an artistic and a practical point of view. Stein wrote:

> I understand very well why, for a man like you, to whom it is an artistic necessity to have a direct influence on the intellectual and social life of our time, it is not an easy decision to write "absolute" music today. But in order to expand your sphere of influence, to gain influence even where to date one has balked against you for topical reasons, I consider it essential that you make another appearance as an absolute musician. (16 May 1930)

Although Weill appears to have worked on at least one purely orchestral project during these years, it is indicative that he admitted the difficulty of finding the style (12 May 1932). Despite the obstacles, he remained committed to the theater, where he not only felt he could participate more directly in contemporary intellectual life, but where he found the stimuli best suited to his artistic temperament. Perhaps in response to the operatic crisis, Weill began exploring still other audiences. He felt a departure from the traditional operatic stage was crucial in developing his musical and dramatic language and a practical necessity in the face of such severe cutbacks. While searching for a subject for another major opera, Weill wrote the school-opera, *Der Jasager*, completed in April 1930. For Weill, the work represented "the decided departure from the song style" (14 April 1930) and an important step away from the *Dreigroschenoper* stereotype. What was more, it seemed to provide the stylistic basis for work on a new full-length opera.

From the end of 1929 Weill had been in search of material for another opera. After serious consideration of a number of subjects, including Hašek's *The Good Soldier Schwejk* and works by Jack London and Franz Kafka,[10] he informed his publisher of a new project in August 1930. When Weill began sketching the libretto of *Die Bürgschaft* with

10. Weill first mentions an interest in *Schwejk* in a letter dated 1 December 1929. In subsequent months he even secured the operatic rights to the novel from Hasek's family and continued to express interest in the project up to the time of his emigration. Weill mentions London and Kafka in a letter dated 6 August 1930. He gives no specifics, although he writes that Jack London's works have recently provided him with "all kinds of new ideas."

Caspar Neher, he felt he was about to take another major step in his development. "The opera I'm writing," he wrote on 19 January 1931, "isn't to be a seasonal hit, but a repertory piece." With *Die Bürgschaft* Weill confirmed that he had gone far beyond the style of his earlier successes and was eager to escape his reputation as a "song composer". He was apprehensive that the Berlin performance of *Mahagonny* in December 1931 might create the wrong atmosphere for the *Bürgschaft* premiere the following March and wrote his publisher in November 1931:

> It ought to be stressed in various places with absolute clarity that *Mahagonny* represents the end of a creative period which began with the Baden-Baden *Mahagonny*, and which I have already superseded, while *Die Bürgschaft* is the first major product of a new style, which began with *Der Lindberghflug* and above all *Der Jasager*. (19 November 1931)

Despite an exemplary production and critical and public acclaim, *Die Bürgschaft* could not establish itself in the tense atmosphere of 1932 and certainly did not show a profit for its publisher. The economic and political turmoil of the early thirties was having a debilitating effect on new music in Germany, and Weill found the artistic independence he had won just a few years before increasingly difficult to maintain. In considering his next projects, he wrote to U.E., "Naturally financial considerations also play a role. You know me well enough to know that I would be happy not only for myself, but also for the publisher if we landed a fat morsel. On the other hand, 1 don't want to depart from my firmly prescribed path" (15 June 1932). Weill turned once again to smaller works in what was becoming an established pattern of alternating the larger and often less profitable operas with smaller, more practical theater pieces which explored new audiences and stylistic regions. In his frustration over his experiences with *Die Bürgschaft,* Weill turned again to the development of a new operatic audience and conceived the idea of a so-called *Laienoper* or layman's opera, with which he hoped to circumvent both the timidity of theater directors and the conservatism of their audiences. In addition, he had plans for another school opera, "Naboths Weinberg," with a social theme in a biblical setting, as well as a proletarian Volksstück with a decidedly political message, though he was well aware that both ideas would be difficult to implement in the prevailing political atmosphere.

Over and against these plans, Weill was continually besieged by commercial theaters. "Here," he wrote in the same 15 June letter, "there still seems to be a real need for my music. The commercial composers have completely written themselves out, and it is obvious that there is no one but me who can write both artistically worthwhile and yet generally comprehensible music. At least that's what these people keep telling me."

Torn between two worlds, defined now less by aesthetic program and artistic principle than by the conflicting pull of political conviction and economic necessity, Weill entered into a series of negotiations for a commercial production with the German director and producer Erik Charell. Weill suggested four possibilities for collaboration: a folk opera, "Romeo and Julia," set in a working-class milieu with a happy end; a folk opera based on *Uncle Tom's Cabin;* a play with music about a comic incident at the 1920 Genoa Peace Conference; and an opera based on Georg Kaiser's play *Die jüdische Witwe* (The Jewish Widow). Informed of the plans, Heinsheimer welcomed the "new thrust into the broader public" and concluded, "the time for a re-orientation has come. You, dear friend, have already shown the way in two areas, in *Die Dreigroschenoper* and *Der Jasager*." Heinsheimer continued with the assurance: "I want to confront the suspicion head-on that, with an anxious look at your account, we want to force you into an attractive money-marriage with Charell. In the case of Kurt Weill you can be fully and absolutely assured of our generous and future-oriented publishing policies" (21 June 1932). Nevertheless, Heinsheimer, no doubt with Weill's dwindling account in mind, gave an enthusiastic endorsement to the *Romeo and Juliet* idea, which he found both commercially promising and well suited to Weill's intellectual and artistic temperament.

Charell, however, had different plans and eventually decided upon a musical setting of *Das Kabinett des Dr. Caligari*. Weill, who had his doubts about this project, insisted that Georg Kaiser be brought into the discussions to guarantee an intellectual foundation which Weill could reconcile with his previous works. Now as never before, Weill felt himself straddling the two worlds whose demands he had so far been able to balance. Although he assured his publisher that he was well aware of the artistic and financial advantages of the plan, he explained his dilemma: "For me, the line I don't want to cross under any circumstances lies at a point where, with an all-too-daring side leap, I rob myself of the possibility of afterwards continuing along my path, which I have so far followed with such good results and success" (29 June 1932).

Though nothing came of the plan with Charell, the renewed collaboration with Kaiser produced *Der Silbersee*. Weill wrote his publisher that he had long planned to wait with his next large opera until he had written "a few small, less demanding works for practical theater use." With *Der Silbersee*, he added, "I have the opportunity to carry out this plan on the highest level at no risk to my reputation. Also the transition to a project like the one with Charell would be easier after a piece like that rather than right after *Die Bürgschaft*" (2 August 1932). *Der Silbersee* was Weill's last work in Germany, and indeed, the last of his works to be published by U.E. One may well wonder about the opera Kurt Weill never had the chance to write because of all the intermittent smaller works intended "for practical theater use." Had he crossed that line of no return?

Weill's correspondence with Universal Edition offers a nearly continuous dramatic narrative of his European career and helps provide some answers to the stylistic and aesthetic riddles of the products of his American years. But Weill was not an isolated phenomenon. A look at other correspondences in the U.E. archives reveals similar questions, difficulties, and decisions and shows the extent to which the problems Weill confronted were symptomatic of his times, not unique to his person. It is clear from this that the publisher was not a passive factor, but exercised influence on the genesis, planning, and shaping of individual works, as well as on the overall trajectory of entire careers—most especially in the case of its more successful composers. Weill came to feel all the pressures of "style as commodity," of the market value of novelty, and of the twin perils of repetition and competition in the fast-turnover economics of new music. He experienced all the constraining limitations of success and the difficulties of defining his own artistic personality against a popularly held stereotype. On the other hand, Weill was challenging traditional concepts of both composer and publisher. His works, which hovered somewhere between the worlds of theater and opera, between bourgeois culture and revolutionary agitation, may well have been taking U.E. further than it was prepared to go with a "serious" composer.

These documents reveal the growing significance of the collaborative effort in Weill's career; during the years when the composer was seeking to redefine his role in a changing world and the publisher was exploring new markets, both were counting on their ability to identify and address, if not create, a new public. In what may be the ultimate collaborative effort, Weill's stylistic path is the sum of his artistic responses to the disparate audiences of his day—from the new music savants of Donaueschingen to the school children of Berlin, from the sophisticated literary circles of the Kurfürstendamm to the working proletariat of Kreuzberg. And with each new step he presented his publishers with new problems to solve and new markets to conquer. Ultimately, under the onslaught of economic chaos and political madness, those audiences— and those markets—fell into disarray. In the years that followed, Universal Edition "released" the composer from its roster and consigned the "unwanted products of a decadent era" to its warehouses, while Kurt Weill's style was being transformed by the challenge of a wholly new set of audiences.

3

Kleinkunst and Küchenlied in the Socio-Musical World of Kurt Weill
ALEXANDER L. RINGER

The unflagging love and admiration of Kurt Weill, the twentieth-century modernist, for Wolfgang Amadeus Mozart, the eighteenth-century idol of the romantic era, had many intricate roots. But whatever specifically musical affinities may have come into play, there was a deeply shared conviction that the artist endowed with special creative gifts was called upon to instruct as well as entertain his fellow man with effective images of the human condition in all its self-inflicted misery and to illuminate at the same time possible paths to self-redemption. Even so, neither the Jewish cantor's son, traumatized by the unprecedented horrors of World War I into ready acceptance of the messianic promises of socio-political revolution, nor the child prodigy, born to a Roman Catholic musician yet intoxicated by the pre-revolutionary air of the Enlightenment in Josephian Austria nearly a century and a half earlier, ever fell into the ready-made trap (which claimed so many victims during the intervening romantic age) of confusing the mission of the artist with that of the preacher. Quite to the contrary: like his favorite model, Weill never lost sight of the essentially symbolic nature of art which mandates often drastic sacrifices of specificity of the scientific sort at the behest of metaphorically generated intensifications of reality through which the genuinely creative individual speaks with a voice at once unique and universal.

By the same token, if somewhat paradoxically, the originality of any art so conceived is bound to be a reflection of its particular eclecticism. Thus, Mozart drew freely, as the occasion demanded, upon a large and variegated pool of contemporary musical idioms, from French and German popular tunes to specimens of the then prevailing Turkish rage, as well as solemn church chorales. Kurt Weill, for his part, every bit as enthusiastically explored and exploited the ever-expanding historical and sociological dimensions of the vast musical resources available to early twentieth-century composers willing and able to attune their hearts

37

and ears to the highly stratified society that nurtured and challenged them. In Ferruccio Busoni, young Weill found an inspired teacher who encouraged and equipped gifted pupils to assume cheerfully the awesome burdens of history handed down to them directly by great performer-composers like himself as well as indirectly through a veritable avalanche of musicological research and publication.

As for popular music, the urban environment that typified Central Europe in the wake of its all-embracing industrialization and concomitant proletarianization also ensured the propagation of a once primarily rural art by those whom economic forces beyond their control had displaced from their traditional habitat. Indeed, Béla Bartók by no means exaggerated in ascribing his early musical orientation as much to a kitchen maid's unselfconscious rendition of sentimental ballads from her native Hungarian village as to his mother's highly civilized piano playing in the family parlor. Surely, in Germany any musically sensitive youngster was apt to imbibe with his mother's milk at least some *Moritaten,* those unvariedly gruesome ballads with which the ubiquitous organ grinders entertained the wretched creatures from the countryside, who, having fled poverty and/or dishonor at home, earned their rarely generous room and board by cooking and cleaning for the urban bourgeoisie.

Much of this lower-class musical activity took place in the *Hinterhof* [courtyard] often formed by the two parallel wings of a U-shaped apartment building. Such buildings were inhabited in front by the well-to-do; in the rear servants and/or poor families were often crowded into shabby quarters that were accessible only through separate entrances and staircases. Social intercourse between the two classes of apartment dwellers was either non-existent or limited to absolute essentials. But sound travels easily across such artificial barriers erected by social convention and prejudice, especially where the architectural design ensures gratuitous additional amplification. In summertime, with all windows open, it would have been virtually impossible to avoid daily exposure to the sad balladry of the typical apartment building courtyard. Nor did single family houses fare much differently. Organ grinders unable to penetrate behind the garden gate simply did their act out front until a coin wrapped in a piece of paper and thrown at their feet encouraged them to move on. As for the kitchen maids, always easy prey for passing soldiers, they tended to feed their paramours quite openly within the confines of their particular realm of unencumbered responsibility, and many a *Küchenlied* enjoyed considerable popularity among the millions of lower-class Germans in uniform immediately preceding and during the First World War.

Thus, even if he had wanted to, Weill, the scion of a modestly middle-class family, could have avoided the Küchenlied no more than the quasi-operatic strains and pseudo-folk tunes heard at the time in many a

German synagogue like the one in Dessau where his father officiated. For all we know, though, the young Weill had no desire whatever to withdraw from what his unprejudiced musical mind must have perceived to be as genuine in its disarming simplicity and naive sentimentality as the poor souls who indulged in it. Unlike many a budding musician caught in the ideological web spun by anointed as well as self-appointed custodians of the Wagnerian inheritance, the cantor's son evidently listened attentively and with lasting consequences to the host of litanies bewailing the fate of the helpless victims of a system responsive only to power and status: those waylaid on their journey into town, those betrayed by their cynical city-lovers, those driven to despair, if not suicide, by unforgiving masters and mistresses, and always those ravaged by the unceasing wars that made up most of the history of Europe. To the post-romantic arbiters of public taste, such songs represented at best *abgesunkenes Kulturgut,* defective drippings of high-class cultural goods that had somehow caught the feeble imagination of the masses. And yet, as a musico-poetic mirror of the physical suffering and social malaise associated especially with the rapid process of urbanization which so radically transformed the socio-economic and political base of nineteenth-century Germany, the courtyard repertoire offered a proletarian alternative to the celebrated romantic collection of folk poetry that had struck such haunting chords in Kurt Weill's other lifelong model, Gustav Mahler. Though considerably less sophisticated in both form and content, the ubiquitous urban Küchenlied also rested on a principally oral tradition bewailing man's inhumanity to man in all its myriad guises and disguises: enforced poverty and un-deserved confinement; harsh, involuntary servitude, whether by deceitful conscription into some warlord's army or at the mercies of civilian taskmasters; ill-rewarded trust, relieved only by that pervasive, simple popular belief in the inevitability of eventual salvation.

That Mahler's idiosyncratic choices from *Des Knaben Wunderhorn,* especially the somber, grimly defiant marches so typical also of closely related symphonies like his Fifth, left their unmistakable imprints on many a Weill score goes without saying. The "Kanonensong" from *Die Dreigroschenoper,* the great *Mahagonny* finale, and, for that matter, "Der kleine Leutnant des lieben Gottes" in *Happy End* are ample proof to that effect. And the same holds for the Küchenlied, whether as a genre or in specifically motivic terms. The evocation of "The Maiden's Prayer" as the proletarian incarnation of "ewige Kunst" in the *Mahagonny* opera is but one obvious example of Weill's general indebtedness to Küche and Hinterhof in a context, moreover, that offers an extraordinary mix of fluffy parody and bitter satire.

A particularly compelling instance is the song of the liquor dealer in *Happy End,* perhaps because some Salvation Army tunes do bear striking resemblances to Küchenlieder for rather obvious socio-historical reasons. In this instance, a rueful liquor dealer, fat from profits made on the sufferings of others, is about to meet his Maker in an alcoholic dream. Anxious to ward off the expected bitter consequences of his unscrupulous life, he solemnly repents and promises all future "dirty money" to orphans, alcoholics, the aged, and others in dire need.[1] Similarly, "Die Räuberbraut," a well-known Küchenlied that became a favorite with German soldiers during the First World War, tells of the rural beauty abandoned by her lover, a robber and multiple murderer. Having resolved that their paths shall never cross again so that she may lead a normal, happy life, he leaves her his ring with the promise that upon his death she alone shall benefit from the fortune he has gathered by hook and crook as well as brute force. Even the most cursory comparison of some of the corresponding musical phrases is apt to demonstrate the miraculous artistic transformation which the unpretentious Küchenlied experienced in the crucible of Weill's creative mind and soul (ex. 1a, b).

Semi-oral tradition, though not exactly identical with that of the popular urban courtyard stage, accounted also for much of the very special flavor of *Kleinkunst,* the "minor art" practiced in often minuscule theaters, which, especially in Berlin, served the Republic's golden youth, its intelligentsia, and its political elite as watering and meeting places where the frustrations of the day found entertaining relief. Through sharp-witted comments and dramatic sketches, gifted lyricists, composers, and actor-singers subjected every possible manifestation of human weakness, whether private or public, endemic or passing, to their always humorous, at times devastating, analysis, frequently within hours of the event. Historically, Kleinkunst and Küchenlied, though one catered to the toiling masses, the other to the most sophisticated among their rulers and employers, shared close ties to the minstrels, those wayfaring singing newscasters traceable all the way back to antiquity. More directly, however, Kleinkunst was heir to the often highly cynical satire of nineteenth-century bourgeois values and customs by Heinrich Heine in literature and Jacques Offenbach on the musical stage. The latter in particu-

---

1. The text for this highly effective song derives from the considerably longer "Exemplary Conversion of a Liquor Dealer" in Bertolt Brecht's *Hauspostille* of 1927. Elisabeth Hauptmann combined the first four lines of the initial stanza with the last four lines of the second, then skipped to the two concluding stanzas (out of a total of eight). The refrain-like interjections "To the attack! Soul in trouble!" and the analogous "Soul is saved! Soul is Saved!" are apparently her own. That they inspired Arno Pardun's notorious "Volk ans Gewehr" [People to the Attack] refrain for the Nazi fighting song "Siehst Du im Osten das Morgenrot" [See How the Dawn Rises in the East] may seem paradoxical and/or ironic yet typifies a situation where the radical left and right shared not only street battle tactics but also many elements of their respective battle songs.

lar, a Jewish cantor's son, too, and an equally fervent Mozartian, had managed to turn musical irreverence into a lucrative business. By doing so, he had mortally offended the priestly souls dedicated to the preservation of aesthetic purity who saw in him, not without some justification, the very incarnation of the Jewish spirit, that is, the devil in musico-theatrical guise. The same was soon to be said of Gustav Mahler and, before long, of Kurt Weill.

By Weill's time, the romantic yearning for purity had become an irreversible German obsession leading straight to the racial policies of the Third Reich. Indeed, 130 years after A. F. J. Thibaut published his treatise *Über Reinheit der Tonkunst,* Karlheinz Stockhausen still reiterated the conviction that all great art was predicated on stylistic purity.[2] Irony, parody, and outright satire, on the other hand, thriving on "impurity" almost by definition, pervade the work of Jewish intellectuals and artists from Heine to Karl Kraus and from Offenbach to Rudolf Nelson, the uncrowned king of Berlin Kleinkunst. There is little in principle, therefore, that distinguishes Meilhac-Offenbach's city fathers under the scrutiny of public opinion at the opening of *Orphée aux enfers* from Brecht-Weill's view of the forces of law and order in *Die Dreigroschenoper.* Both pairs of authors certainly considered comedy more effective than tragedy as a means of raising man's sensitivity to his own failings, perhaps because in comedy, when all is said and done, the dramatis personae "embrace each other in life, not in death."[3] Mozart, for one, had subscribed to that basic notion. If he had Pergolesian opera buffa to build on, Offenbach could turn to Mozart and French opéra comique, not to speak of Parisian vaudeville with its established pattern of poking fun at serious opera, at times so rapidly that the first-night footlights had hardly been extinguished before the parody got under way on a small stage nearby. Kurt Weill in the 1920s looked to Kleinkunst as a precedent where no public figure could claim immunity, no historical event was off limits, where, in fact, any and all social, political, or economic taboos were smartly brushed aside. On the Kurfürstendamm—*Kudamm* in popular parlance—the center of all this iconoclastic activity, even matters of life and death surfaced in the guise of off-hand conversational remarks.

2. Robert Schumann's teacher, A. J. F. Thibaut, published his essay *Über Reinheit der Tonkunst* as early as 1824 (1825, according to the official imprint). Stockhausen paid his homage to *Stilreinheit* in 1955 with reference to the oeuvre of Anton von Webern. Webern, for his part, though devoted to Mahler and Schoenberg, expressed outright contempt for Weill who, in his judgment, operated outside "the great Middle-European tradition," as he explained to his visitor Luigi Dallapiccola in 1942. See Hans and Rosaleen Moldenhauer, *Anton von Webern* (New York, 1968), p. 537.

3. The formulation is that of Dieter Roth in his Nestroy review "Carrozza kaputta," *Rhein-Neckar Zeitung* 39 (24 May 1983): 2.

Clever conversation was a hallmark of the cabaret as envisaged by Rudolf Nelson, who greatly expanded the role of the informal narrator, the *Conférencier*. Previously, whether in Paris, its nineteenth-century birthplace, or in Vienna, where its German-speaking literary counterpart was spawned, the Conférencier's role was either non-existent or limited to introductions of songs and an occasional sketch. But in Nelson's cabaret, and ultimately in Robitschek's *Kabarett der Komiker,* the Conférencier, with his sophisticated banter full of in-jokes and risqué anecdotes, his little poems ridiculing the continuous states of crisis that beset the ill-fated Republic, became a focal and much-debated figure.[4] Even the news of the day, however, was invoked by the Conférencier primarily for its broader ramifications in a rapidly changing world about to lose its bearings altogether. The spectacular feat of the Swiss scientist Piccard, who explored the stratosphere in a specially constructed balloon capsule, is a case in point: it stimulated not only brilliant verbal commentary of a mostly half-serious nature but also one of Rudolf Nelson's funniest patter songs, which pointed to the essential futility of such acts of human folly. As for Charles Lindbergh's sensational crossing of the Atlantic, Berlin Kleinkunst mulled over its personal, social, and economic implications well before Weill and Hindemith wrote their radio cantata on the subject.

During its brief but intense time of glory, the musico-theatrical counterculture of the German cabaret circuit attracted some of the finest German literary talent, from Wedekind and Ringelnatz to Zuckmayer and Brecht, satirists all, some sweet, some bitter, most bittersweet. Hence, despite the improvisational aspects of Kleinkunst (conditioned in part by the very nature of its concern with daily happenings), and despite its eventual degradation by political fiat and the subsequent systematic murder of most of its outstanding practitioners, literary specimens have been preserved in sufficient quantity to reveal a remarkable diversity of traditions fused into a uniquely modern genre. This genre offered novel creative opportunities to both the professional Jewish merrymakers of the *Badkhen* variety and the Gentile descendants of a long line of popular *Bänkelsänger,* who gladly exchanged the small bench on which their fore-fathers had stood in rural market squares for slightly larger indoor stages. Composer, poet, and performer were one and the same in a number of notable instances, a modern continuation of a longstanding unity. Before long, however, even Bertolt Brecht, who liked to write his own simple tunes, concluded that the roaring twenties required a great deal more musical know-how than he and others sharing his basic attitude could muster. He therefore turned to Weill, and it was Weill who imbued Kleinkunst with the lasting spirit of true musical art.

4. See Alexander L. Ringer, "Dance on a Volcano: Notes on Musical Satire and Parody in Weimar Germany," *Comparative Literature Studies* 12: 3 (1975), p. 251.

The Brecht-Weill collaboration acquired its almost immediate momentum at a most propitious moment. The socio-political situation in Weimar Germany had reached the point where Brecht's hard-hitting lines and Weill's unforgiving music were bound to find sympathetic ears, especially among the relatively affluent, ever ready to spend considerable sums of money on entertaining recitals of their own sins. As if by design, the first fruit of Weill's association with the radical bard of the left, the *Mahagonny Songspiel,* saw completion in May 1927, the very month the Berlin stock exchange experienced its first "black Friday" and the month Berlin's police commissioner felt constrained to ban the Nazi Party in the public interest. Nor was it sheer accident that Kleinkunst had just recently been transformed into big-time entertainment, thanks primarily to a savvy producer-director named Erik Charell (of later *Im Weissen Rössl* [White Horse Inn] fame), who saw a chance for larger theaters to cash in on the tuneful, pithy creations of cabaret veterans like Rudolf Nelson, Mischa Spoliansky, and Friedrich Holländer, or newcomers like Willy Rosen. Charell's Berlin Revue, as it came to be known, combined elements of the traditionally intimate cabaret with leggy costume displays *à la* Folies Bergères and Broadway in a most successful attempt to capture a broader public. In the words of one qualified contemporary, the Revue had "no particular public in mind. Like nature, the street song, the tavern, and the detective story, it appeals to all."[5]

H. H. Stuckenschmidt, who wrote these words in 1926 "in praise of the Revue," might have used them as well with reference to *Die Dreigroschenoper,* which embarked on its worldwide triumph two years later. How deliberately Weill and Brecht set out to appeal "to all" follows from Stuckenschmidt's own experience when he visited Weill in 1928. Pointing to the *Dreigroschenoper* score-in-progress, the young composer said: "I am working on something there that could be successful."[6] And when its triumph was no longer in question, was in fact already legendary, he observed with pride that, in his eyes, it was its "successful penetration of a consumer industry which until now had been the exclusive preserve of an entirely different sort of musician and author" that represented the work's most important historical achievement.[7] Paradoxically and ironically, if its social message was to come across where it really counted, the commercial arena seemed indeed the indicated venue, as long as the immediacy and spontaneity of Kleinkunst could be somehow sustained,

5. H. H. Stuckenschmidt, "Lob der Revue," *Anbruch* 8 (March 1926): 155. In 1932 Charell and Weill entered into negotiations for a production of a new musical theater work Weill was to compose, but nothing materialized.
6. H. H. Stuckenschmidt, preface to Philharmonia score no. 400 of *Die Dreigroschenoper,* (U.E. #14901), p. v.
7. Kurt Weill, "Korrespondenz über *Dreigroschenoper,*" *Anbruch* 11 (January 1929): 24.

radically changed physical conditions notwithstanding. Thus, if Rudolf Nelson was still in a position to lead his small group of instrumentalists from the keyboard, much as Joseph Haydn had at eighteenth-century Esterházy, Weill at least preserved the small quasi-popular instrumental ensemble with its preponderant wind and percussion sonorities, the singing actors, and a modicum of planned informality. An example is the "Wedding Song" (no. 5) of *Die Dreigroschenoper,* which is to be sung "at first *a cappella,* embarrassed and boringly" and "later possibly" as printed in the full score. That contemporary dance rhythms contributed decisively to the lean, dramatic expressiveness of this at once timely and timeless play, in which social degradation and human folly combine to make the perfect human comedy, goes without saying. On the other hand, that echoes of the Küchenlied would also reverberate in the world of "Seeräuber Jenny" should come as no surprise to anyone familiar with the composer's socio-musical background and orientation.[8] Jenny's "Salomonsong" certainly fulfills every expectation along these lines, with its monotonous Alberti bass in the harmonium accompaniment marked "in der Art eines Leierkastens" [in the manner of a hurdy-gurdy]. As regards Brecht's and Weill's consistent preference for the English word *song,* beginning with the five *Hauspostille* poems on which the *Mahagonny Songspiel* is based, again Kleinkunst had pointed the way when, in a deliberate act of alienation, it rejected the customary German term *Lied* as a symbol of precisely that *petit bourgeois* spirit which was the principal target of its musico-literary poisoned arrows. At times, Kleinkunst artists actually used English lyrics, as Hauptmann-Brecht did in two of the "Mahagonny-Gesänge"; some, like Nelson, born Rudolph Lewinsohn, went so far as to anglicize their family names.

Perhaps inevitably, *Die Dreigroschenoper* remained a work sui generis, acclaimed not merely by sophisticated theater-goers everywhere but also, in Weill's own words, by those who either "did not know us at all, or denied us the ability to generate interest among members of an audience well beyond the limits of the musical and operatic public."[9] Neither *Mahagonny,* too intimate as a song-play and somehow too furiously overwhelming as a full-fledged Kleinkunst opera (where, by the way, the narrator-Conférencier has been given a new dramatically integrated role), nor *Happy End,* which as a kind of sequel to *Die Dreigroschenoper* has all the earmarks of Kleinkunst with a somewhat artificial ideological twist, has held anything like the well-nigh universal appeal of *Die Dreigro-*

---

8. Bertolt Brecht, for his part, saw in "so-called 'cheap' music, particularly that of the cabaret and operetta," the original "gestic" music. See John Willett, *The Theatre of Bertolt Brecht,* 3d ed. (New York, 1968), p. 130.

9. Weill, p. 24.

schenoper, that bitingly disarming remake of a pre-industrial morality play in the image of the industrial age. But in its own disjointed way, the *Mahagonny* opera is nevertheless a thoroughly moving masterpiece in the direct succession of Alban Berg's *Wozzeck*, more so possibly than Berg's own *Lulu*.[10] And *Happy End*, its unquestioned dramatic limitations and contingent production problems notwithstanding, offers some unadulterated Weill in the best tradition of the late twenties. In so doing, however, it also serves to demonstrate the composer's tenuous relationship to big-time Kleinkunst in the post-*Dreigroschenoper* phase. As originally conceived, the satirical parable of charity embodied in the tale of good men and women of the Salvation Army getting the better of evil was set in a German *Gasthof,* which offered a respectable facade for the criminal gang's activities centered on its courtyard, the Hinterhof.[11] Only after Brecht sent what was no more than an outline to his collaborator Elisabeth Hauptmann who, under the pseudonym Dorothy Lane, assumed ultimate responsibility for the book, was the decision made to reframe the story in the form of fifteen boxing rounds fought in the city of Chicago. This may have satisfied Brecht's personal passion for prize fights and fighters, but not only did it violate the Kleinkunst credo of dramatic straightforwardness, easy accessibility, and ready producibility, it also deprived a play permeated by Küchenlied-sentimentality of a most logical scenic symbol.

Philosophically, *Happy End* takes the co-existence of good *and* evil more or less for granted, whereas *Die Dreigroschenoper* still posed questions of good *or* evil. Similarly, the self-destructive tendencies of that modern Valhalla, the big city, hovering over *Mahagonny* as an ever-present threat, have been mitigated to the point where, as the title suggests, even the city's endemic contradictions, so intractable in *Mahagonny,* vanish before the irresistible truth that in the end all humankind winds up the same way.[12] That latter thought, by happenstance, runs like the proverbial red thread through an extremely successful Nelson Revue, pointedly entitled *Der rote Faden* and premiered at just about the same time with several actors, including Kurt Gerron, who had been in the original cast of *Die Dreigroschenoper.* Among Nelson's many hit songs, one in particular lends

10. See Alexander L. Ringer, "Schoenberg, Weill and Epic Theater," *Journal of the Arnold Schoenberg Institute* 4 (June 1980): 98. See also Douglas Jarman's essay in this volume for a different viewpoint.

11. Jan Knopf, "Happy End und kein Ende," in *Happy End,* program booklet of the Schauspiel Frankfurt 1982/3, p. 84.

12. Brecht's original outline for Elisabeth Hauptmann reads as follows: "Milieu: Salvation Army and criminal hangout. Content: struggle of good and evil. Resolution: victory of good." See "Dorothy Lane an der Strippe," in *Happy End,* Schauspiel Frankfurt 1982/3, p. 82.

itself to comparison with a number in *Happy End,* thanks to textual con-
cordances as well as crucial differences that make for a rather intriguing
case. Nelson clearly took his motivic cues from Johann Strauss's "Bitte
schön" polka, except that in Nelson's song the persistent "please" and
"thank you" motive stands for the vain appeals of masses of powerless
pedestrians whose freedom of movement has been severely curtailed by
the relentless flood of automobiles pouring into the city streets (ex. 2).
Tired of merely protesting their technologically enforced state of servitude, the poor pedestrians, representing the vast majority, threaten
open rebellion against the privileged few who terrorize them with their
soulless machines:

> May we boss, may we, please, get across, or are
>   we, in the end no more on your list?
> May we boss, thank you, boss, could we try
>   without loss, or are we no more being
>   missed?
> We are sick of all that "may we boss, thank you
>   boss," once we're dead we'll have our
>   rendez-vous, thank you, too,
> And then, to your disgrace, you will face on
>   your knee, the rebellious city infantry.[13]

In the hereafter, there is no gasoline, the symbol of oppression, and
therefore no class struggle (ex. 3).

Nelson's lightfooted little march with its insistent logogenic drum
motive leaves the serious ramifications of a very real socio-economic problem ostensibly untouched. Kleinkunst never teaches; at best, it enlightens.
By contrast, Weill broaches the same underlying issue (in Brecht's admittedly quite different formulation) with a characteristic thrust straight to
the heart of the matter. Eschewing Nelson's popular verse and chorus
structure, he opens with a strident instrumental call to arms. The song
proper evolves hesitantly, at first almost disorientedly, in recitative-like
fashion into an ominous march proceeding as inexorably as the vision of a
better future that informs it. "Careful, be careful," the "little lieutenant of
the Dear Lord" warns,

> Here a man is drowning.
> There, they are crying for help.
> And there a woman waves.
> Bring those cars to a halt. Stop all traffic.
> All around us men are sinking, and nobody even looks.

The city dwellers' obliviousness to the plight of their unfortunate fel-
lowmen and women evokes no tuneful appeal to reason nor, for that

---

13. All English translations included in this essay are those of the author.

matter, manifestations of enlightened self-interest. The little lieutenant's repeated "Obacht" is uttered not merely for the protection of the hapless beings whom a hedonistic society has cast aside but also as an implied threat to the culprits rushing by in their comfortable mini-palaces on wheels.[14] Nor does she plead with them; instead, she orders them to stop. Hers is a different kind of *Grossstadtinfantrie*, advancing irresistibly to somber march strains recalling a peculiarly heartrending passage in Gustav Mahler's Wunderhorn-Lied, "Der Tambourgesell." Finally, snatches of the "Internationale" and the communist fighting song "Brüder, zur Sonne, zur Freiheit," merge into a solemn hymn, an "Onward, Christian Soldiers" of messianic socialism, as it were (ex. 4). And such is its melodic-rhythmic drive that few in any audience, of whatever status or class, are likely to remain unseared by the moral flame that lit this revolutionary summons to social action.

In early 1925, months before he completed his own first foray into moralistic opera, a young Weill, reflecting on the rather conventional story line underlying Mozart's *Entführung*, exclaimed in undisguised awe: "But what a distance between that simple account of such an innocent sequence of events and its ethical transformation in the crucible of Mozart's genius."[15] Later that year, *Der neue Orpheus* evoked for the first time those unmistakable musical associations with the cabaret, the neighborhood movie house, the dance hall, the circus, the political demonstration, and popular religion that were to become the hallmark of Weill's mature stage works created during the closing years of the ill-fated Weimar Republic in the spirit of Mozart, the old Orpheus, though in the idiosyncratic guise of the new. By then, however, it was *Die Zauberflöte* which had Weill's undivided attention, if only because it, too, had been commissioned by a "commercial" theatrical entrepreneur and had become, with his active collaboration, "the best example of the ideal combination of popular music and the highest degree of artistic intensity."[16] Characteristically, the composer added, its artistic qualities had often been underestimated, "because they are popular, generally accessible, and have immediate effect upon the public."

One of its greatest admirers once characterized Mozart's ultimate bequest to German opera, written within a year after the death of the enlightened Emperor Joseph II, as a work which "under the cloak of

14. Toward the end of the short-lived economic boom which preceded "Black Friday" also in Germany, the automobile figured prominently in the work of many a socially conscious author. Illya Ehrenburg's 1929 novel, *Ten PS*, typically depicts this favorite symbol of brute industrial power as bent on "the extermination of man."

15. Reprinted in Kurt Weill, *Ausgewählte Schriften*, ed. David Drew (Frankfurt, 1975), p. 141.

16. Ibid., p. 81.

symbolism" treats of "rebellion, consolation, and hope."[17] Better words could hardly be found to describe what the new Orpheus and his Sarastro wrought in their determined effort to entreat the twentieth-century forces of night about to engulf humankind. In the service of that desperate cause, modern Kleinkunst and the Küchenlied effectively replaced the eighteenth-century vaudeville and street song with the understanding that they, too, underwent that "ethical transformation" which has distinguished moral art at all times from merely moralizing propaganda. At least in this respect, surely the new Orpheus proved himself worthy of the old.

Examples

Example 1. a. "Das Lied vom Branntweinhändler" from *Happy End*, mm. 4–19.
b. "Die Räuberbraut," after Hartmann Goertz, *Lieder aus der Küche* (Munich, 1974), p. 8.

Example 2. "Bitte schön" (chorus) by Rudolf Nelson; transcribed from a recording by the author.

17. Alfred Einstein, *Mozart: His Character, His Work* (New York, 1945), p. 465.

Example 3. "Tausend Autos rasen" (verse) by Rudolf Nelson; transcribed from a recording by the author.

Example 4. a. "Brüder, zur Sonne, zur Freiheit." Lyrics by Leonid P. Radin; German translation by Hermann Scherchen. After Inge Lammel, *Das Arbeiterlied* (Frankfurt, 1973), p. 118.
b. "Die Internationale," conclusion. Lyrics by Eugène Pottier; German translation by Emil Luckhardt; Music by Pierre Degeyter. After Lammel, p. 102.

Example 4 continued
c. "Der kleine Leutnant des lieben Gottes" from *Happy End,* mm. 48–56.

4

Kurt Weill's Operatic Reform and Its Context
JOHN ROCKWELL

From the early 1920s until his death in 1950, Kurt Weill did not just compose a dizzying range of works for the musical theater. He also wrote a series of journalistic essays in which he expounded his shifting theories of operatic reform. It is not my purpose here to recapitulate those ideas or to offer new insights into their internal evolution. But for anyone who has encountered Weill's casual use of such terms as *epische Oper, Schuloper, Zeitoper, Laienoper,* and *gesellschaftsbildende Oper,* it might be helpful to recall the world in which such terms were common parlance.

That world is German opera, considered not so much aesthetically as institutionally, sociologically, economically, and even politically. A sketch of the operatic world of the Weimar Republic and of the efforts at Socialist operatic reform during that troubled, wildly optimistic time may help to explain not just Weill's operatic ideals before his emigration, but also his seemingly paradoxical willingness in America to embrace the commercial theater, a theatrical environment against which his early intellectual upbringing might otherwise have prejudiced him irrevocably. For all the confusion, almost schizophrenia, in Weill's own utterances about his roles as a serious composer and a vernacular populist, there does seem to be a long-range evolution in his development, from a conventional young classical composer to an unashamed, if still idealistic, composer for the commercial stage. It is my contention here that the aspirations and failures of Berlin's leftist operatic reformers during the Weimar Republic played a crucial contextual role in that evolution.

The struggle of composers to find solutions to the problems posed by post-Wagnerian operatic (and musical) development lies at the heart of the modernist movement in music—and of the post-modernist reaction of which Weill was such a significant forerunner. Weill himself wrote often and eloquently about this topic—about how young German composers, in the wake of Wagnerianism, turned first to abstract music, then

51

to the musical stage again, but with a freshly-felt need to work out a new relationship between word and text and between composer and public. This strictly aesthetic context of Weill's ideas for reform has been discussed extensively elsewhere.[1] What interests me instead is the place of opera in German society and how that changed during the Weimar Republic, the debates about how opera should relate to the public, and the specific methods used in attempting to overcome what many leftist intellectuals perceived as a crisis. I am concerned with how German opera had evolved in the late nineteenth century, how it changed with the "revolution" of 1918, and how the frustration of Socialist reform efforts encouraged Weill to conceive of the commercial theater as the most promising avenue for a socially minded operatic populism.

Partly because Weill's career was centered in Berlin, it is on Berlin that I wish to concentrate—specifically on the efforts of key Independent Socialist *Referenten* in the Prussian Ministry of Culture to bring the policies and performances of the Berlin State Opera into line with the larger aims of the Republic. This is only one of many efforts toward operatic reform in Germany at the time; it doesn't even account for all of Berlin's operatic life, with its Municipal Opera, its private operas, and such fringe experiments as the commercial productions of *Die Dreigroschenoper* and *Aufstieg und Fall der Stadt Mahagonny.* But the specific tale of the Prussian governmental reformers is not only a revealing paradigm for the troubles the Republic faced in its efforts to cast off the weight of German tradition; it also has many fascinating points of direct contact with Weill's own career.

Before the revolution, opera in Germany had been patronized in three different ways. The predominant method was royal: opera as a gracious dispensation of the ruler, it being remembered that before the unification of Germany in 1870, there were hundreds of rulers, their fiefdoms ranging in size from mighty Prussia to the most minute principality. This particularism was maintained operatically after 1870 in the continued existence of such royal operas as those in Munich and Berlin. There were also municipal operas, the best-known and longest-lasting of which was Hamburg's, and purely private ventures. Some of these modes of patronage overlapped: for example, a royal opera could provide an impresario with a fixed subsidy, after which he was liable for subsequent losses but entitled to any profits. Angelo Neumann in Leipzig was such a royally subsidized, private impresario.

The notion of opera as a gift from ruler to ruled was linked conceptually with the larger tradition of German philosophical idealism and the

---

1. See especially David Drew, "Kurt Weill and His Critics," *Times Literary Supplement* 3838 (3 October 1975): 1142–44, and 3839 (10 October 1975): 1198–1200; and Kim H. Kowalke, *Kurt Weill in Europe* (Ann Arbor,1979), pp. 98–150.

various conservative theories of politics and society associated with that school of thought. The monarch was believed to incorporate the diverse aspects of the state into his royal person and therefore to transcend grubby partisan politics. Politically this expressed itself in the tradition of non-political service to the state, not just by the monarch, but also by his large, efficient, ever-proliferating bureaucracy. Of course, such "non-political" service actually served the narrow dynastic interests of the monarch, but the bureaucrats saw themselves as grander and more dispassionate than that, and such political naiveté or even hypocrisy carried over into the supposedly democratic, overtly political Weimar Republic in a way that made the Prussian bureaucracy either ineffective in fighting political battles that needed to be fought or unwilling to soil itself with such battles in the first place.

The monarchs took it upon themselves to espouse a rather windy, self-aggrandizing form of idealism, a post-Bismarckian, blood-and-iron degeneration of nobler, purer, early nineteenth-century idealism. For example, a speech given in 1901 by Kaiser Wilhelm II included such phrases as "an Art which transgresses the barriers and limits established by Me ceases to be an Art," "the often-used word 'liberty' leads to license," and "Art must help educate the people."[2] In other words, royalists saw art as a didactic tool wielded by the monarch for the moral benefit of the populace.

It may seem like a mighty leap from Wilhelm II to the Social Democratic Party, but unfortunately it was not. The SPD was the principal Marxist party after its unification with the LaSalle faction in 1875 and might have been expected to be a cauldron of provocative leftist alternatives to royalist aesthetics. (In a sense it was: the party had an active cultural program and several further-left offshoots that served to invigorate the prevailing Marxist orthodoxy. The SPD had been deeply involved for decades before the Weimar Republic with worker education and cultural presentations. Their policy was codified in 1906 with the establishment of the SPD Bildungsausschüsse, which coordinated the party's multifarious cultural activities.) Unfortunately, the SPD never developed a coherent, articulate vision of what art within a materialist philosophy actually was, or what role it should play in a post-revolutionary society. Most of the party's intellectuals came from the bourgeoisie and represented in their aesthetic views an unthinking prolongation of German idealism. They perceived art as abstractly beneficent, floating above the class struggle they assumed shaped other aspects of life. Art was merely a benefit that a post-revolutionary state would provide its citizens in greater measure than the monarchs had provided it, but in a similar

2. Quoted by Gerhard Masur in *Imperial Berlin* (New York, 1970), p. 211.

manner—from on high. Apart from naturalism, which was really welcomed only by the left wing of the party, no avant-garde devoted to a radical art reflecting new visions of mankind and predicated on new social relations was fostered by the SPD.

The principal Socialist cultural organization, although it was not a part of the SPD *Bildungsausschuss* apparatus or even formally linked with the party, was the Volksbühne. This organization, which had branches in every large city, sometimes presented its own theatrical productions but served mostly to provide workers and other low-income members with blocks of inexpensive seats at theaters and opera houses. For the most part, before and during the Republic, this was fundamentally a conservative organization, aesthetically speaking. However, there was a spin-off from the Volksbühne called the Freie Volksbühne, which was allied with naturalism. Eventually, the two reunited, but the split prefaced the large division in 1917 between the SPD and the more radical USPD, or Independent Socialists.

In general terms, what happened to opera in the wake of the 1918 revolution was a transferral of the former royal operas to the new democratic states, or *Länder* (not the national government); thus, the Royal Opera in Munich became the Bavarian State Opera; the Royal Opera in Berlin became the Berlin State Opera, under the aegis of the Prussian state government. The shift in funding did not in itself invariably affect the policies of these companies, which, especially in the large cities, remained museums of the operatic past. But in the provinces, by the early to mid-1920s, both state and municipal operas often became lively centers for experimentation. New operas were commissioned and performed, but the real friskiness was seen in production styles, wherein visual artists of the day were imported to decorate the operas of the past (e.g., Cubist productions of Handel operas). In Berlin, the peak of experimentation came only in the late twenties. Still, Berlin is important not just because Weill and Brecht were living there: Prussia dominated Germany numerically, geographically, and economically, and Berlin dominated Prussia. Thus, reform efforts in Berlin had a national resonance that no other city could match.

When the revolution came about in 1918, the Socialists assumed power almost accidentally. They solidified their parliamentary grasp by making a deal with the Independent Socialists whereby ministries, from the top down, would be shared by representatives of both parties. In Prussia prior to the revolution, the Ministry of Culture had had nothing to do with opera and theater; its domain had been education and religion, and the royal theaters had been funded and administered directly by the Hohenzollerns. But with the collapse of the monarchy, the Ministry of Culture wound up almost by default with the Prussian theaters. The

Independent Socialist co-minister at the outset of the Republic was Adolf Hoffmann, portrayed by his detractors as a buffoon but by his champions as a populist hero. Hoffmann took personal responsibility for the theaters and brought in two USPD allies to be Referenten, or specialist advisers, for music and theater. These men, Leo Kestenberg for music and Ludwig Seelig for theater, shared opera, but Kestenberg was more directly concerned with it. He became the dominant figure in Berlin's operatic reform until nearly the end of the Weimar Republic—and the prime villain, the chief Jewish musical Bolshevist of Weimar, in the eyes of the increasingly vocal right wing in the Prussian Landtag. Despite all the shifts of power within the Prussian cabinet, and the different Ministers of Culture, Kestenberg and Seelig remained in their posts from 1919 to 1932, years after Hoffmann and the USPD had faded from the scene.

Kestenberg had many personal and ideological connections with Weill. Kestenberg was a pianist of some distinction and a student of Busoni; he even served as that composer's private secretary for many years. In 1919, in one of his first acts at the ministry, Kestenberg summoned Busoni to Berlin and installed him in a special niche as a professor of composition. Kestenberg's socialist beliefs, it should be added, horrified Busoni.

Kestenberg had come to his ministerial position with strongly formulated opinions as to what was wrong with German operatic life and what should be done to try to put it right. He had been actively involved with Socialist cultural activities before the war, when he had already experimented with foisting musical modernism onto working-class audiences. Such music had been ignored or despised by the workers, but Kestenberg had perhaps learned the wrong lesson from those disappointments. His conclusion was not that workers would resist defiant atonalism and always prefer Johann Strauss, but that more and better concerts of modern music would ultimately elicit a more favorable response.

Like Kaiser Wilhelm, however, both Kestenberg and Seelig were unquestioning believers in the government's role in dispensing culture to the masses; it was just that the two bureaucrats disagreed with the emperor as to what that culture should be. Seelig was a violent opponent of commercial theater, which he considered to be an insidious corruption of German idealism and the inherent good taste of the working classes. In the heady, optimistic early days of the Weimar Republic, Kestenberg and Seelig dreamed not only that they could reform opera from above, but that they could also thereby elevate popular taste and play a role in the creation of an earthly socialist paradise. The eventual irony for Weill was that his bitter experience with the finest fruit of these reform efforts, the Kroll Opera, helped to convince him that his own best hope for operatic reform lay in just the commercial theater—am Schiffbauerdamm, am

Kurfürstendamm, and eventually on Broadway—that for Kestenberg and Seelig represented the ultimate evil.

The ministry's attempts to reform Berlin's opera in the early twenties were almost constantly frustrated, for a variety of reasons. One was that, in the first years of the republic, the ministry was swamped with seemingly more pressing problems—education and a policy for religion in a supposedly atheist state—and tended to let the theaters go their own ways. Furthermore, the very democratic machinery established by the Socialists reinforced conservatism. Throughout Germany in the revolution's early days, democratically elected "workers' councils" were intended to spearhead society's socialization. The Socialists respected majority opinion within these councils, and at the Ministry of Culture this respect was combined with a naive residue of a philosophy of "art above politics." Since there was a considerable hold-over of personnel from the old Royal Opera in Berlin to the new State Opera, the "workers"—meaning the stars and administrators as well as the stagehands—voted to preserve the status quo, and there wasn't much Kestenberg could do about it. The newly elected Intendant was the conservative composer Max von Schillings, who had no use whatsoever for socialism or the Republic, let alone worker-oriented modernism.

In addition, the ministry found itself in possession of a large opera house called the Kroll, which it didn't know quite what to do with. The Unter den Linden home of the State Opera had to be rebuilt, so in the short term the Kroll served as a home for the main opera during its reconstruction. With the completion of work on the Staatsoper Unter den Linden, the Kroll was transformed into a subsidiary of the main company with spin-off productions by artists from the State Opera. One reason for this decision was the Ministry's ideological and financial commitment to the Berlin Volksbühne. Kestenberg had long been associated with the Volksbühne and saw in it the best way to provide workers with culture. He now managed to forge with the Berlin branch of the organization a contractual relationship by which a certain number of operatic performances were guaranteed each year. Since the Unter den Linden house was small and required for Berlin's traditional opera audience, as well as for the attraction of much-needed foreign currency from tourists during a time of rampant inflation, it was decided that the State Opera needed a subsidiary, in large part to fulfill the contractual obligation to provide the requisite number of performances for the Volksbühne's working-class membership.

The subsidiary was also designed in part to forestall a company entitled the Grosse Volksoper, which had right-wing leanings and which, as a private venture, was anathema to Seelig especially. Despite its capitalist basis, the Volksoper got under way in the early twenties with considerable venturesomeness of repertory and production styles. But it soon degenerated into star turns by famous singers and eventually petered out during the peak inflationary year 1924.

In 1925, Kestenberg finally forced the issue and managed to fire von Schillings—who, among other failings, had never been much interested in Kroll performances—as the Intendant of the State Opera. His successor was the young Erich Kleiber, who proved somewhat more progressive. By this time, however, Kestenberg had resigned himself to leaving the Staatsoper Unter den Linden more or less alone as an inherently conservative house and had turned his attentions to creating an artistically independent, progressive company at the Kroll Theater, administratively still linked to the State Opera but artistically separate, with its own company and its own policy of worker-oriented avant-gardism.

Unfortunately, the new Kroll was cursed by a crucial aftershock of the firing of von Schillings. Almost accidentally, the funding for the State Opera after the revolution had remained with the former Hohenzollern estates, which had not been legally dissolved. The annual subsidies were thus protected from the direct political review that normal parliamentary appropriations underwent annually. In 1925, with the resolution of the legal uncertainties surrounding the Hohenzollern estates, subsidies for state theaters began to appear in the regular budget of the Ministry of Culture. But this was just the time when von Schillings was fired and thus transformed into an instant martyr and political cause célèbre—a conservative (eventually Nazi-sympathizing) German composer subverted by vicious Jewish, Bolshevist intrigues—or so the right wing howled in the Landtag. With his thick glasses and lips and round cheeks, Kestenberg was as much a subject for anti-Semitic cartoons as Weill. Kestenberg became the focus for repeated attacks and debates in the Landtag from the mid-twenties to the early thirties, and the supposedly non-political operatic policies of the ministry were fatally politicized.

Still, the Kroll Opera, from its eventual establishment in 1927 until its demise in 1931, was the high point of Weimar operatic progressivism—the darling of the left-wing intelligentsia, the principal forum in the capital for the earlier provincial operatic experimentation and, not least, the springboard for Otto Klemperer's erratic but important international career as a conductor.[3] The Kroll ceased to exist in 1931 because the

3. Today Klemperer, the artistic director of the Kroll, is remembered primarily as a magisterial exponent of the Germanic classics. In his younger years, however, he was a leftist, avant-garde firebrand, at least in comparison with other major conductors of his generation. But it is not the artistic successes and failures of the Kroll that are my concern here; the reader is referred to Peter Heyworth's superb *Otto Klemperer: His Life and Times*, vol. 1: 1885–1933 (Cambridge, 1983), which includes an extensive account of the Kroll. For a more complete discussion of the operatic reform attempted by the Prussian Ministry of Culture, see my "Prussian Ministry of Culture and the Berlin State Opera, 1918–1931" (Ph.D diss., University of California, Berkeley, 1972).

Prussian Landtag decided that in a time of depression there was not enough money to support three public opera companies in Berlin and that the Kroll had less justification for survival than either the Staatsoper Unter den Linden or Bruno Walter's Städtische Oper. But the actual basis for that decision was Kestenberg's ineffectiveness. Crippled by his position as public scapegoat and ineffective as a parliamentary infighter because of his anachronistic, neo-idealistic ideas about art's inviolability, Kestenberg failed to defend the company adequately. His opponents were the right, gleefully appalled by the Kroll's left-wing avant-gardism. But his potential allies, the center and especially the SPD itself, had been shaken in their support because the ideological foundation of the company had crumbled. That foundation had been the forced marriage of the avant-garde with the working classes, as represented by the Volksbühne. From the outset the Volksbühne held the largest single block of seats at the Kroll, but its membership and administration proved profoundly indifferent, not to say hostile, to the prestigious premieres and outrageous productions that set the intelligentsia atwitter. With the onset of the Depression, the Volksbühne's membership declined sharply, compromising its ability to honor its commitments to the Kroll, even if its members had supported the company's policies wholeheartedly. Instead, they wanted *La Bohème* with stars, and the starry prestige of the Staatsoper Unter den Linden made them feel as if they were being fobbed off with inferior operatic goods at the Kroll.

All these tensions had their principal impact on Weill during the controversy over whether *Aufstieg und Fall der Stadt Mahagonny* was to be performed at the Kroll. Brecht and Weill had assumed during the composition of this full-scale opera that it would be done there. But after characteristic indecisive agony, Klemperer rejected the score in 1929—in the face of fervent enthusiasm for it by his chief administrators at the Kroll. Although this seems to have been exclusively the conductor's personal, aesthetically and morally based decision, the rejection was interpreted by Weill as a sad timidity by both Klemperer and Kestenberg in the face of Volksbühne conservatism and growing right-wing opposition to the ministry's reform policies and the theater's artistic and social mandate. Weill's champions within the Kroll—principally the dramaturg, Hans Curjel, who subsequently made himself the theater's most comprehensive documentarian—regarded the rejection of *Mahagonny* as a turning point in the history of the company.[4]

Curjel even wrote Weill a letter in July 1929 suggesting that perhaps the time had come, for the purposes of advancing the cause of progressive opera, to consider the establishment of a private company: "I do con-

---

4. See Hans Curjel, *Experiment Krolloper 1927–1931* (Munich, 1975).

stantly ponder whether the moment has not come to set up an uncompromising musical theater on a private basis."[5] Socialist operatic reformism had come full circle, and this when the Weimar Republic was still ostensibly at its peak. What had begun as an idealistic hope that the state could reform the depravities of royal and private opera had turned into a bitter despair that nothing could be expected from the ministry and that composers like Weill had to enter the capitalist arena to reach the people and reform a dangerously moribund art form. Weill wrote a newspaper article at the time of the rejection of *Mahagonny* in which he made reference to "a broadly progressive movement [that] gradually becomes a reactionary danger (in the process of coalition politics that levels everything)."[6]

Despite his personal disappointment about the failure of a Kroll production of *Mahagonny,* Weill shared with other republican intellectuals a bitter sense of defeat when the Kroll finally collapsed in 1931. His newspaper articles of 1931 and 1932 returned time and time again to the need for a broadly accessible opera that would reach out and solve not just the crisis of opera, but that of operatic subsidy, about which he had grown disillusioned after the Kroll's demise.[7] Composers must, he now felt, strive to write operas that, without descending to the level of the cheap popular operetta or revue, would still command a wider audience. He wrote these articles at a time when his own sense of confusion about his dual roles as a "serious" composer and a purveyor of socially-committed music theater in a vernacular idiom seemed particularly acute.

In this light, the subsequent condemnation by the European left of Weill's Broadway musicals as a cynical sell-out of his former ideals must be qualified by an understanding of the context from which Weill emerged. His commercially produced musicals, both in Europe and in the United States, were a logical response to his experiences in Berlin, the appropriate avenue for his continued efforts to reach a broader public and to make an economically viable, self-sufficient form of musical theater. The commercial musicals Weill composed in New York were a direct consequence of the failure of state-mandated operatic reform in Berlin.

5. Quoted in Heyworth, p. 296. Weill himself discussed such a possibility in "Musikfest oder Musikstudio?" *Melos* 9 (May–June 1930): 230–32. Translated in Kowalke, pp. 527–29.
6. Kurt Weill, "Aktuelles Theater," *Melos* 8 (December 1929): 524. Translated in Kowalke, p. 510.
7. See, for example, "Situation der Oper," "Das Formproblem der modernen Oper," and "Wirklich eine Opernkrise?" in David Drew, ed., *Ausgewählte Schriften* (Frankfurt, 1975); translated in Kowalke, pp. 541–44. Weill wrote two essays that dealt specifically with the Krolloper: "Gesellschaftsbildende Oper," *Berliner Börsen-Courier,* 19 February 1929; and "Rettet die Kroll-Oper," *Das Tagebuch* 11 (15 November 1930): 1854.

5

Weill:
Neue Sachlichkeit,
Surrealism, and
Gebrauchsmusik
STEPHEN HINTON

"The credit for coining the phrase *Neue Sachlichkeit*," as the art historian Wieland Schmied remarked, "must go to G. F. Hartlaub."[1] As director of the Mannheim Art Gallery, Gustav Friedrich Hartlaub planned an exhibition of paintings under this title in May 1923, although it did not open until 14 June 1925. In his initial invitation, dated 18 May 1923, he wrote:

> In the autumn I would like to mount a medium-sized exhibition of paintings and graphic art which might perhaps have the title "Die neue Sachlichkeit." I am interested in bringing together representative works by those artists who over the last ten years have been neither impressionistically vague nor expressionistically abstract, neither sensuously superficial nor constructivistically introverted. I want to show those artists who have remained—or who have once more become—avowedly faithful to positive, tangible reality.[2]

Although it literally put an end to the string of "isms," from romanticism and naturalism through impressionism and expressionism to cubism and

---

This essay originally comprised a chapter, here abridged slightly, of the author's doctoral dissertation, "The Idea of *Gebrauchsmusik:* A Study of Musical Aesthetics in the Weimar Republic (1919 to 1933) with Particular Reference to the Works of Paul Hindemith," University of Birmingham (England), 1984.

1. Wieland Schmied, "Neue Sachlichkeit and the German Realism of the Twenties," *Neue Sachlichkeit and German Realism of the Twenties* [Arts Council Catalogue] (London, 1978), p. 9. "To render 'Die neue Sachlichkeit' . . . by 'the new objectivity,' as is commonly done in English-speaking countries, is only partially right, and we have to be careful not to let the looseness of the term lead us to use it in contexts where the Germans would not have used it themselves." The title of John Willett's book, *The New Sobriety* (London, 1978), from which this warning comes, is an obvious allusion to *Neue Sachlichkeit,* if not an actual attempt at translation. Because of the difficulty of translating the word "Sachlichkeit," implying as it does not only objectivity, impartiality, detachment, and matter-of-factness but also utility, practicality, and appositeness, the following discussion will retain the German.
2. Quoted by Fritz Schmalenbach in "Der Name 'Neue Sachlichkeit,'" *Kunsthistorische Studien* (Basel, 1941), p. 22.

surrealism, the term *Neue Sachlichkeit* was, of course, required to fulfill a function similar to that of its predecessors as a label identifying a movement, trend, or style in the arts.

In Germany, as the subtitle of Hartlaub's exhibition ("Deutsche Malerei seit dem Expressionismus") and the title of Franz Roh's celebrated book *Nach-Expressionismus* (1925) suggest, the new era was defined negatively as post-expressionism. Similarly, Emil Utitz called his 1927 book surveying the cultural scene *Die Überwindung des Expressionismus*— the overcoming or surmounting of expressionism. Two years later, Utitz summarized his ideas in a pamphlet entitled *Über die geistigen Grundlagen der jüngsten Kunstbewegung* (1929). Like Hartlaub, he saw the essence of the new art expressed in a changed relationship to tangible reality: "Expressionism sought the wonderful beyond the world, as it were; now the call is: to acknowledge the existing world in its totality, in its complete reality, and thus to discover the wonderful in it. That is why there is talk of a *Neue Sachlichkeit*."[3]

In painting, the art form for which the term was originally coined, Neue Sachlichkeit is frequently described in terms of both a new style and a new way of seeing: "it reflects a radical commitment to the modern environment and everyday life."[4] It is reduced to stylistic characteristics such as "a new and intentional fidelity to the outlines of objects . . . concentration on everyday things . . . isolation of the object from any contextual relationship . . . static pictorial structure . . . manifest construction of a picture out of heterogeneous details . . . eradication of the traces of the process of painting;" or more generally as "visual sobriety and acuity, an unsentimental, largely emotionless way of seeing . . . a new mental relationship with the world of objects."[5]

Utitz, however, does not limit his discussion just to painting or the visual arts. He finds evidence for expressionism having been overcome, and a Neue Sachlichkeit consequently established, in several cultural spheres. Indeed, the term *Neue Sachlichkeit* quickly caught on in other art forms, thus suggesting an aesthetic and cultural correlation, and Hartlaub's original restriction to painting was soon forgotten. As Henrich Besseler wrote in his 1927 essay "Grundfragen der Musikästhetik," "although the concepts of expressionism and Neue Sachlichkeit were first of all coined in painting, nothing stands in the way of their being carried over into the musical sphere."[6] One of the first to follow in Besseler's

3. Emil Utitz, *Über die geistigen Grundlagen der jüngsten Kunstbewegung* (Langensalza, 1929), p. 13.

4. Schmied, p. 13.

5. Ibid.

6. Heinrich Besseler, "Grundfragen der Musikästhetik," *Jahrbuch der Musikbibliothek Peters für 1926* (Leipzig, 1927), p. 65.

footsteps was the critic Hans Heinz Stuckenschmidt. In 1927 he wrote an article entitled "Neue Sachlichkeit in der Musik," in which he commented on parallels between music and painting. "Just as, for example, in a portrait, the emphasis is on material similarity—the spiritual utterance favored by the expressionists thereby being brought into line with this similarity—so the most modern music concerns itself with strict depiction [*Zeichnung*] and a clear definition of line." Stuckenschmidt described this change as being "closely related to the new classicism."[7]

Although Stuckenschmidt considered Neue Sachlichkeit in music to be symptomatic of the "start of a new musical culture resulting from sociological shifts," his discussion largely dealt with questions of style, just as Schmied's study of painting did. In March 1929, Hanns Eisler introduced a very different definition of Neue Sachlichkeit whose influence has been far-reaching, still making itself felt in recent commentaries. In the context of a newspaper article entitled "Zeitungskritik," Eisler wrote of an "Entindividualisierungsprozess der Wirtschaft" (depersonalization process in the economy) "that is reflected in all cultural and intellectual spheres; the modern style in music, 'die neue Sachlichkeit,' is such a 'reflection.'" Eisler's analysis was, of course, directly influenced by the Marxist model of base and superstructure and the theory of reflection whereby, in the classic (some would say "vulgar") version at least, the phenomena of the cultural superstructure can be related directly to the economic base. "We therefore see," Eisler continued, "that music also follows the tendencies of economic development. It does not develop according to immanent laws but reproduces on a different level the development of the economy."[8]

Nearly a year before, Eisler had illustrated what music he had in mind when he wrote a review of Paul Hindemith's *Cardillac*, giving it the title "Relative Stabilisierung der Musik" (the relative stabilization of music), obviously referring to the post-inflation buoyancy of the Weimar economy, the Stresemann era. Jost Hermand's recent study of Neue Sachlichkeit quotes from Eisler's review, describing the following passage as a "collective judgment of the movement which is still valued as a model for Marxist criticism today":

> Here a small group of artists apparently wishes to opt out of the present in
> much the same way as one opts out of school. Their helplessness in the face
> of the situation of their class has a simply tragic effect. But: the modern
> musician affirms all the technical achievements of the present. He uses
> them. He loves the city, its noise, and is in love with the precise rhythm of

7. *Vossische Zeitung*, 7 May 1927.
8. Hanns Eisler, "Zeitungskritik," reprinted in *Musik und Politik: Schriften 1924–48*, ed. Günter Mayer (Leipzig, 1973), p. 95.

machines. Yet the people who operate the machines are of no interest to him. And in his art he strives towards the highest degree of expressionlessness, of objectivization. Behind all these vague phraseologies, behind this apparently radical progressiveness, behind this rejection of the sentimental experience of nature and love, there is nothing but the *petit-bourgeois* wanting to trick his way into escaping the fate of his class. The bourgeois musician, in search of a content for his art and finding nothing, propagates contentlessness as the purpose and meaning of his art. Incapable of understanding the social situation, he writes music which is elevated above everything human.[9]

In Eisler's review, Hindemith is called a great talent, one of the leading figures of modern, objectivized music. Yet the significance of this particular short piece of criticism lies not so much in Eisler's insights into Hindemith's music, which are minimal, as in the influence of his approach.

One of the first to take up Eisler's interpretation of Neue Sachlichkeit was Ernst Bloch, who, in the course of his essays published in Zurich in 1935 under the title *Erbschaft dieser Zeit,* incorporated the gist of Eisler's ideas into an expanded theoretical tract on the Weimar Republic. Writing as a communist during the years of the Republic and those immediately succeeding the seizure of political power by the National Socialists, Bloch devoted substantial passages of the book to an attempted analysis of the forces that led to that seizure. What results is a complex set of interrelated ideas concerning contemporary German culture and history:

> Here a broad view it taken. The times are at once decaying and giving birth. The condition is miserable and despicable, the way out twisted. But there is no doubt that its end won't be bourgeois. . . . Does the declining bourgeoisie in its decline contribute elements toward the construction of a new world and, if so, what are these elements?[10]

Bloch's aphoristic, elliptical style betrays him as the philosopher of expressionism that he once was when he wrote *Geist der Utopie* (1918, revised 1923), and, indeed, the significance of *Erbschaft* rests largely in the contribution it made to what has become known as the "Expressionism Debate." Expressionism, the art of "the declining bourgeoisie," could, he thought, contribute "elements toward the construction of a new world." (Bloch intentionally stressed the activity of inheritance [*Erbschaft*] rather than the passive acceptance of heritage [*Erbe*].) Others, notably Georg Lukács, thought differently. It is against the background of the ensuing debate— initiated in the late 1930s and taken up again in the newly founded

---

9. Translation revised from Jost Hermand, "Unity within Diversity? The History of the Concept 'Neue Sachlichkeit,'" *Culture and Society in the Weimar Republic,* ed. Keith Bullivant (Manchester, 1977), p. 177.

10. Ernst Bloch, *Erbschaft dieser Zeit* (Frankfurt, 1962), p. 15.

German Democratic Republic in the 1950s—that Jost Hermand's later comments can be understood, his view being that the "proper," "progressive" kind of Neue Sachlichkeit should really be seen as a continuation of the expressionist tradition.

For Bloch, Neue Sachlichkeit was equatable with the "Golden Twenties," in which "the Nazi horrors germinated." Bloch's ideological interpretation of Neue Sachlichkeit is part of what has become known as a "fascism theory," a theory of what made National Socialism possible. His short, essentially Marxist answer to this question is: capitalism. His explanation of what makes up capitalist reality is long and involved, shunning simpler notions of reflection and introducing instead the complex theoretical concepts of "simultaneity" (*Gleichzeitigkeit*) and "dissimultaneity" (*Ungleichzeitigkeit*). Although economics, politics, and culture are all of a piece for Bloch, simultaneity is first and foremost an economic category. It is an expression of the "unequivocally dominating influence of the logic of capital"; "completely simultaneous" can be translated as "oriented precisely toward the most advanced form of economy." Dissimultaneity, on the other hand, represents a "contradiction to capital," however "padded or upholstered"; "impulses and reserves are at work from pre-capitalist days and superstructures too, ensuring the continued existence of a sinking class's consciousness." Bloch speaks in quasi-Freudian terms of the "unresolved past" that has not yet been "subsumed" (*aufgehoben*) capitalistically. Something that is not socially integrated can, in Bloch's eyes, be positively subversive; for example, expressionism. Not so Neue Sachlichkeit. Here cultural and economic mechanisms go hand in hand in perfect simultaneity:

> The de-spiritualization of life, men and things becoming commodities—all this becomes polished as if it were in order, even order itself. Here the *Neue Sachlichkeit* is the overriding, most distinguished form of diversion. . . . Its light, gaiety, and clarity present a mere part as the whole thing itself, the shop window as the whole enterprise. . . . In the place of the expressionist dreams, "explosive concentrations" [*Ballungen*], even storms, an incomparable "realism" set in, namely that of a restabilized world, of a truce with bourgeois existence. Naturally, this type of *Sachlichkeit*, in business as in architecture and ideology, at best becomes a facade; behind the installed rationalities remains the utter anarchy of economic profiteering.[11]

Seen in the context of this analysis of Neue Sachlichkeit as simultaneity, Bloch's seemingly harmless remark about Hindemith's being a "born, instinctive social democrat" takes on not just a negatively critical but also a polemical, even malicious character. The charge is backed up by calling him *musikantisch*, something which is "falsely immediate"—though

11. Ibid., pp. 22, 112–14, 117, 216.

Bloch might have said "simultaneous," for, according to him, Weimar simultaneity is a phenomenon óf social democracy. This rather condescending polemic against Hindemith forms part of Bloch's strategy of presenting an apology for Kurt Weill's *Dreigroschenoper*. He wishes to free Weill of the charge of Neue Sachlichkeit by contrasting him with Eisler, whom Bloch classified as "radically monotonous and exact," leaving it open whether he intends this to be pejorative or not. He prefers to compare Weill with the Stravinsky of *L'Histoire du soldat*. Both of these composers, Bloch maintained, can be linked with surrealism. Reality is reflected, yes; but it is the surrealist vision of the "torn, shabby environment phosphorescing at the edges," not the shop-window effect. "Weill's music," Bloch argued, "is the only music today possessing any socially polemical impact."[12]

Bloch's distinction between *Neue Sachlichkeit* and surrealism bears a striking resemblance to T. W. Adorno's contemporaneous system of values. Bloch even mentions Adorno in his review, thus acknowledging the obvious mutual influence of the two philosophers. For Adorno, the conversion to Weill initially entailed an element of concession. His argumentation in response to the Frankfurt production of *Die Dreigroschenoper* in 1928 runs as follows:

> How distant I at first feel from music that does not draw any consequences from the current state of musical material, but rather seeks its effect by transforming old, atrophied material: Weill achieves this effect with such force and originality that, faced with the fact, the objection pales. In Weill there is a regression, one which exposes the demonic traits of dead music and uses them. . . . With courage and confidence Weill has entered a realm which Stravinsky discovered and promptly recoiled from: a realm which, by being music from the neighborhood of madness, gains explosive, illuminating power.[13]

Despite his reservations about musical material—and partly because of them—Adorno finds that Weill has written "*Gebrauchsmusik* that can really be used"—music which serves a critical function by distorting the Gebrauchsmusik of the past and present, dance music and jazz, and which thus necessarily ignores what Adorno sees as the demands made by "the current state of musical material." He is at one with Bloch both in finding a predecessor in the Stravinsky of *L'Histoire du soldat* and, as a later and much longer review from 1929 remarks, in suggesting that Weill's music is "*Gebrauchsmusik* . . . that cannot be used to cover up what it is."[14] Ador-

---

12. Ibid., pp. 230, 256, 232.

13. Adorno's review originally appeared in *Die Musik* 21 (December 1928): 221–22. It is reprinted in David Drew, ed., *Über Kurt Weill* (Frankfurt, 1975), pp. 37–38.

14. *Die Musik* 22 (March 1929): 424–28; reprinted in Drew, pp. 39–44.

no similarly entertains the notion of musical surrealism. In 1930 he described Weill's *Mahagonny* as "the first surrealist opera." "Its surrealism," he wrote, "is radically different from all *Neue Sachlichkeit* and classicity." He defines that difference as being an intention "supported by the music, which, from the first to the last note, is itself directed at the shock produced by a head-on confrontation with the dilapidated world of the bourgeoisie."[15]

Adorno systematized these ideas on Weill's music and incorporated them into his study "Zur gesellschaftlichen Lage der Musik" (1932). He differentiated four types of contemporary music, illustrating each by naming its leading exponents. The first type, "modern music," is the sole preserve of Schoenberg and his school; the second, "objectivism," is represented by Stravinsky; the third is the "surrealism" of Weill in his collaborations with Brecht; and the fourth type he calls "community music," which he sees as related to neo-classicism and therefore objectivism, but which forsakes its "immanent form" in the cause of fulfilling particular functions, and whose chief exponents are Hindemith and also Eisler in his "proletarian choral works."[16] The second type, objectivism, is in effect synonymous with Neue Sachlichkeit, which Adorno described, significantly with the same terminology as Bloch, as "false facade," as "diversion away from social conditions." And in his description of Weill's music he uses almost exactly the same formulation as Bloch: "Unquestionably, Weill's is the only music today of genuine socially polemical impact."[17]

Bloch and Adorno were not alone in distinguishing between Neue Sachlichkeit and surrealism. Acknowledging Adorno's influence, Krenek presented a similar typology of contemporary music in *Über neue Musik* (1937). What Adorno termed "modern music" is, according to Krenek, "New Music" emanating from Vienna and "continuing the tradition of expressionism." His second and third types are neo-classicism and surrealism; what Adorno preferred to call *Gemeinschaftsmusik* Krenek calls Neue Sachlichkeit; or, at least, the latter is seen as the starting point of, as Krenek remarks cynically, the *Blockflötenkultur* (recorder culture). And it is implicit throughout his text that when he speaks of Neue Sachlichkeit he really also includes neo-classicism, all of which lives "under the fictitious belief that somehow in society an indefinable change had taken place, making possible a new immediacy." Not so New Music. Here Krenek joined Adorno in saying that New Music, "having drawn the most extreme constructive consequences by virtue of its radical expressionism

---

15. *Die Musik* 23 (December 1930): 198–200; reprinted in Drew pp. 73–75.
16. T. W. Adorno, "Zur gesellschaftlichen Lage der Musik," *Zeitschrift für Sozialforschung* 1 (1932): 108.
17. Ibid., p. 120.

and thus having transcended old forms, articulates with total truth the condition of society." Surrealism, he wrote, also contains "an eminently polemical trait . . . from the outset the intention of unmasking the illusion." But he has reservations. Like Adorno, he sees the surrealist technique as "refunctioning" old music so that it can become critically new. However,

> this process of "refunctioning," whose essential means is a montage technique and consists of splitting up the usual unity of text and music and imposing on each half a new meaning opposed to the earlier one—this process is unfortunately reversible, and it can occur only too quickly that surrealist music, freed from the compromising text, returns to its original home: one only has to rectify a couple of wrong bass notes and within the chamber of horrors it becomes rather cozy.[18]

This is doubtless true, in which case the distinction between Neue Sachlichkeit and surrealism—as one between harmless illusion or facade and critical exposure—disappears; and Krenek's types of music become reducible to two.

Bloch and Adorno were also aware of the danger that surrealism could lose its critical barbs and thereby its justification for being distinguished from Neue Sachlichkeit. Bloch laid the blame squarely at the feet of the public. *Die Dreigroschenoper* was a resounding success with the bourgeois public, as is well known. In *Erbschaft*, Bloch remarked that Weill's surrealism was comfortably misunderstood. Adorno, in his 1932 essay, is more circumspect:

> The misunderstanding on the part of the public, whereby the songs of *Die Dreigroschenoper*, which after all are their own and their public's enemy, are peacefully consumed as hit tunes—this misunderstanding may be legitimate as a means of dialectical communication. The further course of things, however, reveals ambiguity to be a danger: the unmasked appearance turns into false positiveness, destruction into the community art of the status quo.[19]

Nevertheless, despite the public's apparent incomprehension of the music's surrealistic force, Adorno still thought that Weill "would not succumb to the danger of the harmless." When he again turned his attention to Weill, in his *Einleitung in die Musiksoziologie* in 1962, he had revised his views considerably. As a composer of Gebrauchsmusik, Weill was now, according to Adorno, a prototype of the musician who "largely directs his production towards the desiderata of reproduction and consumption" and was symptomatic of a "false rationalization."[20] The positive aspects of

---

18. Ernst Krenek, "Über neue Musik (Vienna, 1937), pp. 13, 97, 92, 10, 11.
19. Adorno, "Zur gesellschaftlichen Lage," p. 122.
20. T. W. Adorno, *Einleitung in die Musiksoziologie*, 3d ed. (Frankfurt, 1975), pp. 228–29.

his interpretation of Weill's music as surrealism have disappeared altogether. This is not to say that Adorno ceased to talk of surrealism. In his
Aesthetische Theorie (1974), for example, he employed the term profusely.
And his definition in *Minima Moralia,* first published in 1951, is a concise,
aphoristic version of what he meant during the Weimar years: "Surrealism breaks the *promesse du bonheur.* It sacrifices the appearance of
happiness conveyed by every integral form in favor of the idea of
truth."[21] He had not changed his interpretation of surrealism. This indeed comes very close to his definition of what he saw as the task of art: "to
bring chaos into order."[22] But his interpretation and assessment of
Weill had changed.

Although it might usefully serve to describe an aspect of Weill's
compositional technique—namely, the incorporation of dance music and
jazz by way of a montage effect—the main function of the term surrealism
for the authors who use it in a musical context is undoubtedly a political,
ideological one. Yet it would appear that the ideological basis of such an
interpretation is wholly untenable: what today is surrealism can tomorrow become Neue Sachlichkeit. Rather than describing an artistic procedure, surrealism was used to articulate an ideological interpretation,
which, in the first place, was most probably not shared by the public at
large and ultimately was called into question, if not actually rejected, by
two of the three authors who had proposed this usage of the term. By the
same token, if critical exposure can so easily turn into a harmless facade,
who can deny that the opposite may not be true? Such a definition of Neue
Sachlichkeit primarily implies the interpretation of social forces that in
turn are dependent on the complex process of a work of art's reception. Is
it therefore not too prone to individual likes and dislikes, to individual
whim, to be of any lasting significance? Admittedly, this ideological usage
of the term Neue Sachlichkeit has gained great currency and has found
favor with many distinguished critics writing at a time when *Ideologiekritik*
was in many circles the lingua franca of intellectual practice. Against the
intellectual traditions of the Frankfurt School of Critical Theory and
other Marxist theories, Neue Sachlichkeit serves as a central concept
within a strategy of criticizing ideologies, a shorthand term for what are
seen as cultural forces of reaction during the Weimar Republic. As such,
the term has had an important and distinguished career.

In Eisler scholarship, for example, it has become common practice
to accept the composer's definition of Neue Sachlichkeit and see it, to
quote a recent contribution, as covering "essentially phenomena of the
super-structure in the phase of capitalism's relative stabilization in Cen-

21. T. W. Adorno, *Minima Moralia* (Frankfurt, 1979), p. 300.
22. Ibid., p. 298.

tral Europe during the years 1924 to 1929."[23] Sharing these sentiments, Albrecht Betz has written that "Eisler kept his distance from the fashionable *Neue Sachlichkeit,* which reacted in a stringently formal and emotionally atrophied way to the changes wrought by the rapid onslaught of technology."[24] Betz, in turn, acknowledges the central study representing this direction of thought, Helmut Lethen's book, *Neue Sachlichkeit, 1924–32* (1970), whose telling subtitle translates as "Studies on the Literature of 'White Socialism.'" That Lethen is dealing specifically with literature is immaterial. As the phrase "White Socialism" suggests, his concerns are ideological and political, and his definition of Neue Sachlichkeit is based on a clear if misguided methodological premise. His introduction makes this quite plain. No punches are pulled:

> The illusion of the state having a "golden mean" aligns itself with the real process of power resulting in fascism. A critique of *Neue Sachlichkeit* that ignores the relations of production, the symptom of which was this cultural phenomenon, turns into apology. The representative literary documents of this period cannot be dealt with outside the context of the capitalist culture industry.[25]

Lethen's notion of Neue Sachlichkeit unequivocally takes up Eisler's Marxist model of reflection—cultural phenomena as symptomatic of the relations of production—and adds a further political dimension by including an interpretation of "the real process of power" in the Weimar period. By linking the art of the period so closely to the economic forces, Lethen smuggles into his interpretation the idea of tacit complicity. Neue Sachlichkeit, a reflection of what Lethen sees as the powers that led to National Socialism, is seen as symptomatic of, and is thus held indirectly responsible for, Weimar's political decline. In political terms, Lethen defines Neue Sachlichkeit as "White Socialism," which from his further left, "red" perspective means "social democratic" and therefore regressive. Neue Sachlichkeit tacitly complies with the forces of reaction. According to Lethen, it is primarily an ideological category; only secondarily does it have any aesthetic significance, although he would argue that aesthetics and politics are inseparable.

To concentrate on ideology, however attractive and necessary the practice may have seemed in the past, entails two essential problems. The first is that the ideological content of art, particularly music, presents insuperable difficulties of interpretation, not only of the artist's inten-

23. Hartmut Fladt, "Eisler und die neue Sachlichkeit," *Hanns Eisler* (Berlin, 1975), p. 86.
24. Albrecht Betz, *Hanns Eisler: Political Musician,* trans. Bill Hopkins (Cambridge, 1982), p. 69.
25. Helmut Lethen, *Neue Sachlichkeit, 1924–32: Studien zur Literatur des "Weissen Sozialismus"* (Stuttgart, 1970), p. 2.

tions, but, above all, of their realization and reception. Symptomatic here is the apparent misunderstanding on the part of the public of Weill and Brecht's *Dreigroschenoper* as well as Adorno's later rejection of his former position vis-à-vis the progressive content of that work. The second problem is that the ideological interpretations of Weimar art nowadays inevitably become part of more general theories of fascism; they describe less what artists were doing than what were the supposed political consequences of their actions. It cannot be a historian's task to describe past events using terms defined according to connotations subsequently acquired, that is, to take as a point of reference the consequences that are visible now. Rather, the task should be to restore to past events the open-endedness in which they occurred; otherwise the essence of the historical act (as opposed to the scientific fact), freedom, is extinguished. Thus, an aesthetic concept that is historically valid has more to do with aspects of artistic production at the time than with what came afterwards. Since the figure of contention in the musical discussions was more frequently than not Weill, we might usefully turn our attention away from his critics and admirers and instead look to what he himself thought.

Like Adorno, Weill categorized much of his music of the later Weimar years as Gebrauchsmusik. He did not, however, speak of surrealism or attempt to distinguish his music from any other with recourse to ideological matters. His intentions when theorizing were artistic, which included seeing himself within a broader artistic movement rather than singling himself out. But, as he wrote in 1927 in an article entitled "Verschiebungen in der musikalischen Produktion" (Shifts in Musical Production), published in the daily newspaper *Berliner Tageblatt*, "If from the position of a creative musician I am to answer questions concerning the current musical situation, then I must limit myself to viewing this situation from the point of view of my own production and development." This he did both in that and an equally little-known article carried by the same newspaper two years later and entitled "Die Oper—Wohin?" (Opera—Whither?).[26]

Divided into two sections—"Gebrauchsmusik and its limits" and "Trends in the development of opera"—the 1929 article is essentially programmatic; it deals chiefly with Weill's own compositions, offering a condensed and cogent summary of his musical aesthetic. Although it does not appear in David Drew's edition of Weill's selected writings, this article is one of the group of writings that, as Drew stated in his preface, "are

26. "Verschiebungen" appeared in the *Berliner Tageblatt* on 1 October 1927; "Die Oper—Wohin?" on 31 October 1929. Both are translated by Kim H. Kowalke in *Kurt Weill in Europe* (Ann Arbor, 1979), although translations of passages cited in this essay are my own.

intended to underpin theoretically his own creative output."[27] Weill begins the article with his own concise definition of Gebrauchsmusik:

> The idea of *Gebrauchsmusik* has manifested itself in all those camps of modern music that are within its reach. We have lowered our aesthetic sights. We have realized that our artistic production must again be given its natural breeding ground; that music in its significance as the simplest human need can also be presented with heightened means of expression; that the boundaries between "art music" and "use music" [*Verbrauchsmusik*] must be brought closer together and gradually erased and transcended.

The editors of the paper reminded the reader that Weill was writing at a time when he had recently achieved fame as the composer of *Die Dreigroschenoper* and was looking forward to the forthcoming premieres of the cantata *Der Lindberghflug* and the full-scale opera *Mahagonny*. The composer himself remarked that, as a "representative of serious music," he was supporting views that a few years before would have been unthinkable. According to Weill, composers should start by asking themselves the fundamental question: "Is what we do useful to the general population? It is only second that we ask whether what we produce is art; for that is only decided by the quality of our work." He wished "to let the people of our time speak," and, in pursuing artistic goals as a secondary consideration, he therefore sought to mediate between what he called *Kunstmusik* and *Verbrauchsmusik*. The result of that mediation he called Gebrauchsmusik.[28] Although it was not usual to make such a distinction, Weill's argument rests on distinguishing between Verbrauchsmusik and Gebrauchsmusik. Several of his contemporaries thought the *Ver-* and *Ge-* to be interchangeable. For Weill, the distinction was essential:

> In no way is it the aim of these efforts to compete with composers of hit-tunes [*Schlagerkomponisten*], but rather merely to bring our music to the masses. This can only be achieved if our music is capable of expressing simple human emotions and actions, if it reproduces natural human attitudes.

No one can deny that Weill had succeeded in bringing his music to the masses, certainly as far as *Die Dreigroschenoper* was concerned. The masses represented for him the "natural breeding ground" for his music—music that he said should be capable of expressing "natural human attitudes." Critical minds are wary of the use of the epithet "natural."

27. Kurt Weill, *Ausgewählte Schriften*, ed. David Drew (Frankfurt, 1975), p. 11. Both essays, however, are included in English translation in Kowalke.

28. In view of the ideas contained in Weill's article, Kowalke's statement that Weill "shunned association with such catchwords as *Gebrauchsmusik* and *Zeitoper*" (Kowalke, p. 110) needs revising: he shunned the concept of *Zeitoper*, yes; *Gebrauchsmusik*, however, was a central concept within his musical philosophy around 1929.

Here its use is for Weill the most forceful way of conveying his normative, even ontological intention. Weill himself is far from uncritical. Verbrauchsmusik also reaches the masses. Yet he distances himself from this genre because of its lack of aesthetic value, an aspect of his music that he is under no circumstances prepared to forsake. "In our attempt to develop this genre [Gebrauchsmusik]," he wrote, "we naturally perceive the dangers of this whole movement."

> Not for a moment should the impression be given that we want to sacrifice the intellectual bearing of the serious musician in order to compete fully on the market with the producers of lighter wares. . . . We may only change our music to the extent that we can carry out our intellectual tasks—the tasks of the artist in his time—in a language that is acceptable and understandable to all.

Weill prefers to see the effect of his music as "provocative" rather than as "enticing," a quality of light music. He concedes that a superficial, even hostile observer to a certain extent hits upon salient qualities of his music, that "the musical means of expression have been simplified to a considerable degree, that the question of 'tonal or atonal' is here no longer a subject for discussion, the question of originality no longer primary." He states that "the fear of banality has finally been overcome (something demanded by Busoni ten years ago)" and that "with the use of the elements of jazz, easily graspable melodies that superficially bear a strong resemblance to light music are produced."

All this Weill conceded, insisting at the same time that "the public expects something else from the development of this type of music than it does from the older forms of Verbrauchsmusik." The difference is "the intellectual bearing" which is "thoroughly serious, bitter, accusing, and, even in the most pleasant context, ironic." Gottfried Wagner has defined Weill's Gebrauchsmusik as the technical aspect of "negating and transcending" sociologically determined musical clichés by integrating elements of light music from the 1920s and thereby touches upon the relationship of Weill's music to Verbrauchsmusik.[29] For Weill, though, the concept of Gebrauchsmusik subsumes still more than that.

Weill's own notion of Gebrauchsmusik is very broad, as can be seen from his definition at the outset of his 1929 article. He saw it in terms of an ideal embracing a musical movement that "seems especially suited to influence the development of opera," where his own inclinations lay. The movement did not itself constitute a movement of operatic composers; rather, he saw himself as an operatic composer sharing aims similar to those of various composers in various genres. He made this point es-

---

29. Gottfried Wagner, *Brecht und Weill: Das musikalische Zeittheater* (Munich, 1977), p. 94.

pecially clear in response to questions from the editors of the music journal *Anbruch* concerning the "sensational success of *Die Dreigroschenoper.*" That work, he wrote,

> aligns itself with a movement that has taken over almost all young composers. The forsaking of the *l'art pour l'art* standpoint, the turning away from an individualistic principle of art, the ideas on film music, the joining up with the youth music movement, the simplification of the musical means of expression connected with all these things—these are all steps along the same path.[30]

One of those young composers was Paul Hindemith, as Weill had specifically mentioned in his essay two years earlier. There he had acknowledged Hindemith's joining up with the youth music movement—a step that he himself had not taken but which he felt belonged with his composing *Die Dreigroschenoper* and was part of common artistic pursuits, especially of reaching out to a new, wider audience. Weill's search for that audience led him to go beyond the bounds of "the clearly defined, typical opera public," which is "numerically not very large and expects in the opera house certain impressions that are not allowed to go beyond the traditional definition of opera."

In redefining the concept of opera, in consciously bringing about new developments, Weill felt he could best reach his new audience by drawing opera closer to the "theater of the times." He viewed the ensuing enrichment as reciprocal in "Die Oper—Wohin?":

> Modern theater strongly complies with these endeavors, for its most important representatives have realized that certain stylistic elements of contemporary theater can only be accomplished musically. Since this new theater endeavors to represent man, what he says and does, it fits in with our endeavors, because we are also looking for new expressive possibilities for simple human actions and relationships.

Weill is proposing here nothing less than a simultaneous reform of opera and theater, to be achieved by inaugurating a rapprochement of the two. And this is not only the wish of the opera composer. The readiness for reform is also apparent on the part of playwrights and other "leading men of the spoken theater." Without offering details, Weill views his ideal as having already been put into practice. "It is today already possible in a private Berlin theater to produce an opera with a libretto of literary worth and with forces that are not too large." Just as he confirms the application of his claims with a reference in a footnote to his *Happy End* and *Die Dreigroschenoper*, so he uses the latter work as an illustration of the type of

---

30. Kurt Weill, "Korrespondenz über *Dreigroschenoper*," *Anbruch* 11 (January 1929): 24. Reprinted in *Ausgewählte Schriften*, pp. 53–56.

song composition developed along the lines of his new ideas. The private Berlin theater to which he is referring is the Theater am Schiffbauer-damm, and the work *Die Dreigroschenoper,* premiered there on 31 August 1928. Similarly, when mentioning "leading men of the spoken theater," he chiefly has in mind the author of that "libretto of literary worth," Bertolt Brecht.

The nature of Weill's article is clearly programmatic, and his statements are apologetic. The mention of Brecht, however, raises problems as to the details of this apology. True, the music Weill composed for his collaborations with Brecht is central to the development of what he described as his Gebrauchsmusik. Yet circumspection is called for, particularly if Weill's status is not to be devalued to that of one-half of purported collective intentions or, worse still, to that of musical executor of Brecht's ideas and inspiration, something to which Brecht exegetes are all too prone, as their reams of literature testify.[31] The implied unity of the formula "Brecht-Weill" really conceals as many differences and reflects as many misunderstandings as it expresses similarity and agreement. The dangers of the formula can be seen as both ideological and musical: ideological, in that many Brecht scholars tend to view the Brecht-Weill episode as an essentially immature period, the prehistory to Brecht's Marxism after 1930; musical, in that concentrating on the collaboration with Brecht conceals the significance of the composer's achievement, not only within the collaboration but also on either side of it. To focus exclusively on the years 1927–30 (leaving aside 1933, the year of *Die sieben Todsünden*) precludes taking a broader view—a view that reveals the individuality and continuity of Weill's own development while illuminating for what it is the substance of his contribution within the collaboration with Brecht.

The song style of the *Mahagonny Songspiel* and *Die Dreigroschenoper* did not develop spontaneously as a result of Weill's collaboration with Brecht. In fact, if we consider the technical aspects of the style, which above were called surrealistic, then we can certainly find its genesis in *Der*

---

31. Concerning the premiere of *Mahagonny* in its opera version, Ernst Schürer, for example, wrote that "the audience undoubtedly felt that something new was being offered; but, since it was not acquainted with the theoretical foundations or did not understand them, the premiere in Leipzig on 9 March 1931 [recte 1930] was a failure" (*Georg Kaiser und Bertolt Brecht* [Frankfurt, 1971], p. 65). Since Brecht did not formulate the theory until after the premiere, it can hardly be expected that the audience should have been acquainted with it. What most probably prompted Brecht to these theoretical utterances was the differences of opinion between himself and Weill over the "essence and function of the opera" (Weill, *Ausgewählte Schriften,* p. 212), differences that had become apparent on account of, among other things, Weill's own notes written jointly with Caspar Neher. Brecht may have felt that the opera had not turned out the way he would have liked; but the audience could not have known that either.

neue Orpheus (1925), the cantata for soprano, solo violin, and orchestra to a text by the surrealist poet Iwan Goll, in the operas *Royal Palace* (1926), also a collaboration with Goll, and *Der Zar lässt sich photographieren* (1927), to a libretto by Georg Kaiser.[32] In these works, the contrast of musical clichés, such as dance idioms, and art music is indeed much greater and the surrealist effect therefore more marked than in the later works. If anything, then, Weill's development in the Weimar years can be seen as a gradual integration of popular elements into his musical language to a point, say in *Der Silbersee* or *Die sieben Todsünden*, where he achieved a homogeneity of style, a truly personal idiom, in which the surrealist effects have all but disappeared.[33] What in the earlier works was intrinsically aesthetic opposition to art-for-art's sake, a clash of styles, becomes in the later works a more constructive attempt to fashion a popular, unified musical language.

The early works nevertheless constitute an important basis and precondition for that style. Yet related styles do not necessarily constitute part of the same musical aesthetic. Indeed, Weill himself saw the later works, the collaborations with Brecht, as products of a new attitude and philosophy of music. In other words, the earlier works do not come under the category of Gebrauchsmusik as Weill defined it. Can they, however, be seen as constituting a Neue Sachlichkeit and, if so, in what way does Weill's philosophy of Gebrauchsmusik differ from the idea of Neue Sachlichkeit? Gebrauchsmusik is not, it would appear, the same thing as musical Neue Sachlichkeit, although the one is obviously related to the other—or, at least, the former is an aspect of the latter. In order to examine this relationship more closely, it is necessary to return to the question of defining more precisely what is meant by Neue Sachlichkeit.

Seeing Neue Sachlichkeit in ideological terms, as has been shown, has led historians and aestheticians into all sorts of methodological traps and impasses. To define it in terms of style is almost as problematic, though this approach does, of course, have the advantage of pinpointing manifest changes and developments in artistic technique. This is, after all, one way that Hartlaub's definition can be and has been understood. Difficulties nevertheless arise when it comes to using the term in an interdisciplinary context, as rapidly became the case after Hartlaub's exhibi-

32. The "Alla marcia" after figure 21 in Weill's String Quartet No. 1, op. 8 (1923), reveals an even earlier example of this type of surrealism and an obvious connection with comparable techniques in the music of Gustav Mahler. While looking back to Mahler's fondness for writing pseudo-military music, for putting his music in quotation marks, this work also looks forward, with its closing chorale, to the final scene of *Die Dreigroschenoper*.

33. If the final major chord of *Die sieben Todsünden*, for example, is intended to be ironic, then it is a very subtle brand of irony, without exclamation marks, as it were.

tion. Since direct analogies between the techniques employed in various artistic media can seem either forced or merely whimsical, it would be wise to look elsewhere for links between those media. If we still take Hartlaub's definition seriously, then the question to resolve is how we interpret the positive part of it. Negatively defined, Neue Sachlichkeit constitutes for him a rejection of impressionism and expressionism. Positively defined, this rejection represents a move towards becoming "avowedly faithful to positive, tangible reality." In painting, the consequences of this change are obvious. We need only think of the paintings on display at the 1925 exhibition—by artists such as Beckmann, Dix, and Grosz—and we are aware of what Hartlaub had in mind. These paintings now form for many the very image of the Weimar Republic. What about the other arts?

Emil Utitz's field of investigation covered mainly the visual arts, yet in speaking of Neue Sachlichkeit as a call "to acknowledge the existing world in its totality, in its complete reality" he was aiming, as the title of his pamphlet announces, at the "spiritual and intellectual foundations" of the arts in all their manifestations. His reflections are therefore general and philosophical; and, although he does not actually mention Heidegger by name, it is his school of philosophy to which Utitz is directly indebted. In his 1927 book he made this evident with a bow of respect to Husserl, the founding father of phenomenology. In the 1929 pamphlet he expressed it thus:

> This contemplation of reality pervades recent philosophy as a kind of leit-motiv. Since the science of being is called ontology, we might say that this latest philosophy conducts its struggle on the basis of ontology. That would mean, applied to man: the establishment of man's full being through insight into his essence. He becomes neither idolized as a god nor brutalized as an animal.[34]

Against this philosophical background, Utitz analyzes changes and developments not only in the visual but in all the arts.[35] His reflections on Neue Sachlichkeit range from considering man's portrayal of himself in paintings to a more general discussion of contemporary aesthetics. To the extent that modern phenomenology informs his argumentation he can be said to share a common frame of reference with the Freiburg school of musicology, in particular with Heinrich Besseler. Just as Besseler sought to relativize the importance of aesthetics as such, or rather the notion of aesthetic autonomy, by adapting Heideggerian categories and confronting the concept of *Darbietungsmusik* with its more primordial form of

34. Utitz, *Über die geistigen Grundlagen*, pp. 13, 20.
35. Utitz (1883–1956), a cultural philosopher and a professor at the University of Halle, studied philosophy with Franz Brentano, Husserl's teacher.

Gebrauchsmusik, so Utitz warned against "a flight, however aristocratic, into the aesthetic realm": "The origin, the fundament, cannot and should not be an aesthetic one. That would still mean—albeit perhaps in the most noble form—bypassing the reality of being. The beauty of being is not being as such."[36] In more general terms, then, Utitz saw Neue Sachlichkeit as a reaction against art-for-art's-sake, hence his polemic against such figures as Stefan George and, of course, against the later expressionist generation.

> Neither the spiritual nor the purely instinctive possesses full autonomy; it is ultimately [moral] values that are decisive for both and repeatedly spur them on to common deeds. Therefore, it is neither aesthetics nor the beautiful that bring about and inaugurate a relationship here but rather the objective being of intrinsic values.

The "fullness of life," Utitz argued, "can only be understood from the 'Sachlichkeit des Wertseins,'" and the same is true of artistic activity; it is this renewed attempt to consider art as an integral part or function of human existence or being that lies behind Utitz's explication of Neue Sachlichkeit.

> The aesthetic dimension cannot be the central value . . . because its essence is a value of expression and because it is aimed at the "appearance," not at full, whole being. . . . In the end, what matters is not how we "express" ourselves but how we "are."[37]

Neue Sachlichkeit is much more, then, than a new realism and "sobriety" in painting. Developments in this medium registered at the 1925 exhibition in Mannheim were really only a symptomatic aspect of a broader movement. As an overall shift in the philosophy of art, which, as Utitz's writings testify, had a theoretical foundation in contemporary phenomenology, Neue Sachlichkeit's central premise rests on an opposition to artistic autonomy. Expressed paradoxically, it is an anti-aesthetic aesthetic. Painting, although it prompted the coining of the term, thus really represents a rather marginal aspect of the movement, because the medium of painting is an essentially autonomous one. If painting were to question autonomy, logically it would end up confronting and negating the justification for its own existence, or at least painting for art galleries would.

Hartlaub was only too aware of this central aspect of Neue Sachlich-

---

36. Emil Utitz, *Die Überwindung des Expressionismus* (Stuttgart, 1927), p. 85. For a discussion of Besseler, Heidegger, and the Freiburg School in relation to the concept of Gebrauchsmusik, see the author's above-mentioned dissertation, *The Idea of Gebrauchsmusik*, esp. pp. 6–23.

37. Ibid., pp. 96, 115.

keit. Applied solely to painting, the term is essentially synonymous with a new kind of *Verismo*, as Hartlaub's preface to the exhibition catalog pointed out. However, between the planning and the mounting of the exhibition, Hartlaub published an important and telling article in which he gave vent to some reservations concerning the tendencies of some of the younger generation. In mentioning "one of the strongest and most original of our 'Veristen'" who had appeared in court on the charge of "supposed indecency," Hartlaub doubtless had Grosz in mind, one of the artists exhibited most prominently at Mannheim. Naturally, as director of a major gallery, Hartlaub felt obliged to include the work of a leading artist. But, with the questioning title of his article, "Zynismus als Kunstrichtung?" (first published in the *Frankfurter Zeitung* in 1924), he was articulating his fear that such artists as Grosz may have been threatening the very existence of art, in which he passionately and devotedly believed. For him, it was not so much that the new art was immoral or indecent, but "what it offers extends to utility [*Gebrauchszweck*], to tendentiousness." Some artists, he felt, "do not believe whole-heartedly any more in *art*." Significantly, on the occasion of this article's being reprinted, he remarked that "the mounting of an exhibition that became famous and also the coining of a title that had far-reaching consequences . . . does not by any means preclude an inner distance felt by the organizer, even at the time."[38] This inner distance also explains his apologetic tone in the 1925 catalogue ("what we want to show is merely that art is still with us"), as well as the fact that for the exhibition mounted in Mannheim in 1932 and given the title *"Beschauliche Sachlichkeit"* (which, as the preface to the catalog suggests, Hartlaub would probably have found most adequately translated as "contemplative representationalism") he had to venture to the provinces and turn to *Heimatkunst* (regional art) to find evidence of the assertion that "it is not true that art is dying."[39]

A natural consequence of the developments from which Hartlaub distanced himself can be seen particularly clearly in John Heartfield's turn towards photo-montage, whereby the artist put his talents at the service of a functionalized art form. By the same token, the main achievements of Neue Sachlichkeit are found less in the work of the artists exhibited at the Mannheim exhibitions than in that carried out by the Bauhaus artists. "The Bauhaus had in mind," Hans Wingler writes, "that the artist should consciously experience his social responsibility towards the community and that, on the other hand, he should be supported and sus-

38. G. F. Hartlaub, "Zynismus als Kunstrichtung," *Fragen an die Kunst* (Stuttgart, n.d.), pp. 42–43, 39.
39. Reprinted in Joachim Heusinger von Waldegg, *Neue Sachlichkeit* (Munich, 1982), p. 18.

tained by that community. . . . The integration of art into life was the aim."[40] Painting in its own right was not in a position to realize the idea of "transcending the division and differentiation between 'free' and 'applied' art."

Alban Berg transposed the gist of this dichotomy into musical categories when objecting in 1928 to the fact that Schubert was generally held to be closer to Johann Strauss than to Beethoven: "Perhaps such a lack of detachment in judging art can hardly be surprising at a time when even the likes of us cannot make up their minds in favor of a 'Drei-Groschen-Oper' or a 'Zehntausend-Dollar-Symphonie.'"[41] In an imaginary hierarchy of the arts, a panel picture hung in an art gallery might well rank with what in music Berg calls a "ten-thousand-dollar symphony." By obviously conceding that Weill is to be included among the "likes of us," he clearly registers that Weill, for his part, by deciding in favor of the "threepenny opera," has contributed to a "lack of detachment in judging art," toward upsetting the hierarchy. Indeed, it is precisely the lack of detachment that has become a positive virtue in the minds of serious artists. Writing in the same connection as Berg, namely, on the occasion of Schubert's centenary, Weill commented on the fact that Schubert's "popular melodies have found their way into the hearts of the people," adding that this is "perhaps the highest thing that an artist can achieve."[42] Weill propagated that lack of detachment precisely in terms of forsaking art-for-art's-sake and lowering his aesthetic sights. For him, these steps were a necessary part of an attempt to re-establish what, as mentioned already, he called "a natural breeding ground" for his music. Art should arise, as he put it in 1927, "from some sense of communal belonging [*Gemeinschaftsgefühl*]."

The concept of the community also plays an important part in Utitz's theories. He too writes of Gemeinschaftsgefühl and *Gemeinschaftsgedanke* (the idea of the community). In rejecting the expressionist approach to music which, quoting Kurt Zeidler's *Die Wiederentdeckung der Grenze* (1926), he described as "making music into a hotbed of the individual's needs to exclaim and confess," Utitz singled out the name of Fritz Jöde as someone who personified the new direction taken by the *Jugendbewegung*, a direction that embraced the community idea and that Hindemith also began to take at the time Utitz was writing, 1926–27. As an overcoming of expressionism, Neue Sachlichkeit in music is, therefore, not only a more sober, matter-of-fact approach to musical style and

40. Hans Wingler, *Kleine Bauhaus-Fibel* (Berlin, 1974), p. 5.
41. Alban Berg, "Zu Franz Schuberts 100. Todestag," in *Schriften zur Musik*, ed. Frank Schneider (Leipzig, 1981), p. 308.
42. Reprinted in *Ausgewählte Schriften*, p. 126.

expression, but also implies a conscious attempt on the part of the composer to integrate his art into the community. In that respect, these two aspects of style and use are interdependent.[43]

It might appear that musical Neue Sachlichkeit and Gebrauchsmusik are to be understood as essentially one and the same. This would assume that composers who turned away from expressionism and musical autonomy instantly found "a natural breeding ground" for their music, which was obviously not the case. Many went through a transitional period of doubt and questioning following their rejection of a romantic musical aesthetic and preceding their attempts to write Gebrauchsmusik proper. In several senses, then, these transitional works can also be subsumed under the label Neue Sachlichkeit. In Hindemith's output there exists a large corpus of works composed before 1926 that come under this category.

Before Hanns Eisler began to write with particular uses and functions in mind around 1928, there was a period of a few years when he was breaking free from the aesthetic of his teacher Schoenberg and composing music that is both within and against the tradition of autonomy. The best known and most representative of these compositions is the collection of songs with piano accompaniment *Zeitungsausschnitte,* op. 11 (1925– 27). They are certainly not in any sense Gebrauchsmusik. The musical language still belongs too much to the esoteric world of the Schoenberg School; the general idiom is still too much a part of the late-Romantic lied tradition. And yet, by employing banal, everyday texts expressing aggression and caricature (doubtless prompted by Karl Kraus) and by including passages of tonal writing which offset the atonal sections and thereby create an eclectic effect, Eisler is participating in a kind of artistic protest that relates to Neue Sachlichkeit. True, such contact with "reality" (for example, the setting of "lonely hearts" notices) and such musical eclecticism can best be defined in negative terms as "épatez les bourgeois." Its parody proclaims an antithesis to the old, rather than a new synthesis.

---

43. The fact that in his biography of Otto Klemperer (*Otto Klemperer: His Life and Times,* vol. 1: 1885–1933 [Cambridge, Eng., 1983]) Peter Heyworth writes of his protagonist as being "attacked and praised as an arch-exponent of *die Neue Sachlichkeit*" (p. ix) is indicative of the way that he restricts his definition of the concept purely to matters of style, either to trends in contemporary composition, as witnessed in Klemperer's championing of Hindemith's music written for concert purposes, or to the conductor's manner of interpretation, such as his "approach to Bach" (p. 302). It is this restricted understanding of Neue Sachlichkeit that doubtless leads Heyworth to talk of a "flaw in Weill's character," of a "desire to have his cake and eat it" which "was to prove fatal during his later years on Broadway." He mentions Weill's being "eager that his new opera [*Mahagonny*] should be seen by the audiences that had flocked to *Die Dreigroschenoper*" (p. 294). Seen in the context of the Weimar years, that desire—positively to seek popular recognition—was not so much a flaw as quintessentially "neu-sachlich."

That it also takes a step in a new direction which must lead elsewhere is nevertheless undeniable.

The same might be said of certain works written by Weill around the same time, in particular of such a work as *Der neue Orpheus*. This cantata, composed in 1925, is one of the most curious and elusive works in Weill's output. It seems to fall between all the slats—chronologically and in terms of genre between the Violin Concerto and the theatrical works (if one ignores *Der Protagonist*, written just before), stylistically between highly charged expressionism and bitter parody, aesthetically between concert and cabaret. Who, then, is the new Orpheus? He is certainly a figure of crisis. He is also someone who is sensitive and circumspect. He is like everyone else ("jeder ist Orpheus"); yet he is a genius who travels from country to country and whose signature alone costs a thousand marks. He is, of course, a musician, but one who is at home in all genres: tearing at people's hearts along with Mahler in subscription concerts; the skinny organist in church; the player of the tortuous piano in the local cinema. By trade a *Musikant,* he is in favor of democracy, looking for his Eurydice: unredeemed humanity. But Eurydice wears too much lipstick. Orpheus loses her to the underworld, to everyday life, to suffering. Alone in the station waiting room, he kills himself.

In terms of Weill's biography, it is not difficult to see what it was about Goll's surrealist poem that attracted the twenty-five-year-old composer to set it to music: he too was a kind of new Orpheus, as his eclectic setting proves. He too was looking around him, finding his feet. And here he was given the perfect opportunity to employ stylistic quotation, to stand back from the integrity of "serious," autonomous music, and to experiment with a new kind of urbanity. In that, *Der neue Orpheus* marks a significant stepping-stone to *Die Dreigroschenoper,* to what Weill saw as his real Gebrauchsmusik. For Neue Sachlichkeit in music encompasses the whole dynamic of art's movement away from the tradition of autonomy, whereas Gebrauchsmusik, a consequence of that movement, signifies attempts to find new, positive uses for composers' skills. *Der neue Orpheus,* for all its affinities with the tradition of *espressivo,* signals Weill's own allegiance to that movement, to a Neue Sachlichkeit.

6

Der Zar lässt sich photographieren: Weill and Comic Opera
SUSAN C. COOK

The years 1926–29 were especially productive ones for Kurt Weill: he completed seven large-scale works for the stage and more than a dozen incidental scores and concert pieces.[1] Among these works, *Der Zar lässt sich photographieren* stands out as his only surviving comic opera. In it, he simultaneously affirmed his link with the traditions of pre-Wagnerian comic opera and introduced musico-dramatic means characteristic of contemporary drama. As such, it manifests a compositional and aesthetic transition incorporating ideals of both the "new classicism" and *Zeittheater*.

In *Na und?* (an unpublished and unperformed full-length comic opera now surviving only in thirty-four pages of sketches) and the *Mahagonny Songspiel*, Weill had turned away from the expressionism of *Der Protagonist* and the surrealism of *Royal Palace*. Despite their pervasive comic elements, *Die Dreigroschenoper* and *Happy End* rely on singing actors and spoken dialogue to such an extent that they remove themselves from the realm of Weill's other operas. But in *Der Zar,* within the formal outlines of traditional comic opera, Weill fused technical mastery of the New

---

1. See Kim H. Kowalke, *Kurt Weill in Europe* (Ann Arbor, 1979), pp. 395, 398, 400, 403, 410, 428. *Royal Palace,* his surrealist one-act opera with a libretto by Iwan Goll, received a prestigious premiere at the Berlin Staatsoper under Erich Kleiber on 2 March 1927. A comic opera, *Na und?,* composed during 1926 but unpublished and unperformed, has subsequently been lost. The *Mahagonny Songspiel* showcased the new *Song* style in July 1927 at the Baden-Baden Music Festival. Weill immediately began work with Brecht on the libretto of the full-scale opera *Aufstieg und Fall der Stadt Mahagonny.* A second comic opera, *Der Zar lässt sich photographieren,* was composed from March to August of 1927 and premiered on 18 February 1928. By the summer Weill was composing *Die Dreigroschenoper,* whose unexpectedly successful premiere occurred on 31 August. A year later, Weill, Hauptmann, and Brecht failed to duplicate that popular success with *Happy End.* During the period 1926–29, Weill also managed to compose the score for a radio production of Grabbe's *Herzog Theodor von Gothland; Vom Tod im Wald;* incidental music for Strindberg's *Gustav III,* Leo Lania's *Konjunktur,* Arnolt Bronnen's *Katalaunische Schlacht,* and Feuchtwanger's *Petroleuminseln; Das Berliner Requiem; Kleine Dreigroschenmusik; Der Lindberghflug;* and several songs and workers' choruses.

Music with popular idioms, integrated now to such an extent that thereafter the comic elements of satire and burlesque continually question the meaning of both medium and message in his works. Weill also incorporated nascent features of what was to become epic opera, initiated here without the assistance of Bertolt Brecht. Finally, in his attempts to stage *Der Zar* as the complement to *Der Protagonist*, Weill confronted the obstacles of a state-subsidized repertory system without the options that commercial theaters would offer to *Die Dreigroschenoper* and *Happy End*. Within two years, these two works emancipated themselves from dependence upon the German opera houses' monopoly of legitimate voices and large orchestras that had barred *Der Zar*'s escape.

That Weill identified *Der Zar* as an opera buffa, a term no longer in common usage, underscores both its comic nature and its historical precedents. Few composers still labeled their operas as either comic or tragic. Ernst Krenek, for example, called *Jonny spielt auf* merely "an opera in three parts." Weill's use of an antiquated descriptive subtitle suggests an intimate acquaintance with such pre-Wagnerian models as opera buffa, opéra bouffe, and *komische Oper*. Indeed, in his reviews for *Der deutsche Rundfunk* from this period, Weill specifically discussed works by Mozart, Offenbach, and Lortzing that typified the various national traditions of comic opera.[2] Above all, Weill shared Busoni's great love for Mozart, the acknowledged master of the opera buffa, and aligned himself with the sceptics of post-Wagnerian music drama.[3]

From the outset, Weill conceived *Der Zar* as a contrasting yet complementary companion piece to his earlier one-act tragic opera, *Der Protagonist*, which had attained a respectable place in the repertory of a number of German opera houses. (*Royal Palace* had forfeited its claim to that role after its ill-received premiere in Berlin.) As such, *Der Zar* would do double duty both as showcase for Weill's new sociologically grounded approach to opera and as counterbalance within a Kaiser-Weill double bill. As Weill summarized in an interview from the eve of *Der Zar*'s premiere in Leipzig:

> Here it was a matter of creating a complementary work for *Der Protagonist* . . . a contrasting work of another genre yet not inferior in intensity or effectiveness. My ideal subject would lack that psychological quality of earlier operas and instead turn towards the larger issues of our time which are subjects worthy of theatrical treatment.[4]

2. See Kurt Weill, *Ausgewählte Schriften*, ed. David Drew (Frankfurt, 1975), pp. 141–57, and Kowalke, pp. 545–49.

3. See Kurt Weill, "Die neue Oper," *Der neue Weg* 55 (16 January 1926): 24–25. Translated in Kowalke, pp. 464–67.

4. "Kurt Weill über seine Oper," *Leipziger neueste Nachrichten*, 18 February 1928.

As a complementary work then, *Der Zar* was to be as comic as *Der Protagonist* had been tragic, but the new work would manifest contemporary themes centering on the role of the individual within society, whereas both *Der Protagonist* and *Royal Palace* had dwelt on the psychological or private (erotic) aspects of their main characters.

After the resounding rejection accorded both *Der neue Orpheus* and *Royal Palace*, it is hardly surprising that Weill turned away from the radical approach of Iwan Goll to the tested but now almost outmoded one of Georg Kaiser. Although still recognized as the preeminent expressionist playwright, Kaiser was no longer on the cutting edge of modern drama, and his credentials made him an unlikely candidate for comic librettist in any case. Although his early play *Die jüdische Witwe* (1911) is a satirical comedy, his later, internationally acclaimed works, *Von Morgens bis Mitternachts* (1916) and the *Gas* trilogy (1917–20), are anything but lighthearted. Perhaps Weill recognized that the creation of a genuinely complementary work required both consistency and contrast, and so he wisely persuaded Kaiser to undertake the project.

Weill initially referred to the opera in letters to his publisher as *Photographie und Liebe*,[5] and the work was first announced in *Die Musik* (July 1927) under that modish title. On 4 August, Weill wrote to Universal Edition that he now wanted to call the work *Der Zar lässt sich photographieren*. But only two days later, he wrote again; after visiting Kaiser, he wished to abridge the title to "Der Zar lässt sich . . . .". Weill specified that this new title should not end with a mere ellipsis but with nine widely spaced dots. He and Kaiser felt that the new title would suggest more effectively the special quasi-realistic, ambiguous atmosphere of the piece. In German, the many possible implications for completion of the title include a wide range of activities that the Czar might be "having done for himself," from having his palace cleaned to overtly obscene actions. (Many expressionist authors, including Kaiser, had utilized unusual titles that embodied multiple, suggestive meanings.) But before the premiere, Weill wrote once more, to ask if there was still time to change the title back to *Der Zar lässt sich photographieren*.[6] He explained that he and Kaiser had been persuaded that the abbreviated title might be a little offensive.

Throughout the relevant correspondence with his publisher, Weill stressed the importance of having *Der Zar* and *Der Protagonist* performed together. He spent considerable time and energy trying to convince opera houses to mount the works as a double bill, and he persistently urged his

5. Weill to Universal Edition, 14 May 1927. Photocopies of the complete Weill-Universal Edition correspondence are available at the Weill-Lenya Research Center. All of Weill's correspondence is cited by permission of the Kurt Weill Foundation for Music.
6. Postcard from Weill to Universal Edition, 2 December 1927.

publisher to present the works as two halves of a whole when acting as his agent. Initially Weill envisioned a premiere at the Krolloper, which had opened in the fall of 1927 under Otto Klemperer. Peter Heyworth claims that Hans Heinsheimer of Universal Edition offered Klemperer the premiere of *Der Zar* instead of the projected triple bill of one-act operas by Ernst Krenek that Klemperer had specifically requested following the sensation of *Jonny spielt auf*.[7] Although Klemperer held out for his bid on the Krenek trio, he belatedly showed interest in producing *Der Zar*—but only after the success of the *Mahagonny Songspiel* in Baden-Baden. Although Karlheinz Martin hoped to produce both works at Berlin's Städtische Oper, its Intendant, Heinz Tietjen, was not enamored of *Der Protagonist*.[8] Many directors now shared Tietjen's distaste for Weill's older one-act opera, perhaps as much for its formidable casting demands as for its outmoded expressionist libretto. After the phenomenal success of Krenek's Zeitoper, many managers hoped to capitalize on the box-office draw of popular, topical comedies. Thus, most of Weill's attempts to have *Der Protagonist* and *Der Zar* presented together were stymied.

The influential theatrical company directed by Erwin Piscator also expressed interest in staging the first production in Berlin of *Der Zar*. Weill recognized that such a bold move outside the traditional home of contemporary opera would offer distinct monetary and artistic advantages, even in the face of musical obstacles that were sure to arise in a nonoperatic theater.[9] Piscator's reputation could all but guarantee an audience, and such a theatrical production would allow Weill to "break out of the old opera business." Preferring to have the work produced by one of the three opera houses in Berlin, Universal Edition was less positive about the idea. Bruno Walter had expressed an interest, and Hans Curjel at the Krolloper indicated that if Klemperer wouldn't conduct it, he might pass it on to Klemperer's assistant, Alexander Zemlinsky.[10] Weill suggested that Universal Edition could play off the various parties against each other and extract a guarantee that *Der Protagonist* would be performed with *Der Zar*.[11]

After Weill abandoned his hopes for the premiere in Berlin, he entered into negotiations with the opera house in Leipzig. He had become acquainted with its principal stage director, Walther Brügmann, when

7. Peter Heyworth, *Otto Klemperer: His Life and Times*, vol. 1:1885–1933 (Cambridge, 1983), p. 246.

8. Weill to Universal Edition, 20 September 1927.

9. Weill to Universal Edition, 8 March 1928.

10. Weill to Universal Edition, 16 March 1928, and Universal Edition to Weill, 3 April 1928.

11. Ibid.

Brügmann directed, with Brecht, the *Mahagonny Songspiel* at the Baden-Baden Festival. Weill believed that the work might be more favorably received in Leipzig,[12] but the production encountered more than the expected set of problems for a new opera. Conductor Gustav Brecher claimed that his schedule at the Gewandhaus precluded sufficient rehearsal to premiere *Der Zar* on the same bill with *Der Protagonist,* but he promised performances of *Der Protagonist* for the following fall.[13] *Der Zar* was then oddly coupled with Nicola Spinelli's *A Basso Porto.* Weill complained to his publisher that Brecher was "pedantic," that he overexaggerated the difficulties of the score, had old-fashioned musical tastes and sensibilities, and forced an inappropriate style of declamation on *Der Zar.*[14] Weill subsequently felt it necessary to make changes in the score to allay Brecher's fears, changes which did not ultimately appear in the published score.[15] The date of the premiere, 18 February 1928, conflicted with the opening of a Gluck revival in Berlin, so many critics from influential newspapers did not attend. Nevertheless, the Leipzig premiere was a critical success. Weill rejoiced that, of the twenty reviews which he collected after the premiere, only five were negative.[16] *Anbruch, Melos,* and other important music journals featured prominent reviews of the opera.[17]

Nine other houses presented a total of thirty-nine performances during the opera's first season, but it was not coupled with *Der Protagonist* until 22 April 1928 in Gera, the fifth house to stage the work, with Maurice Abravanel conducting.[18] Ultimately *Der Zar* did not make it to Berlin until 14 October 1928—at the Städtische Oper under Robert Denzler, in tandem with *Der Protagonist.* Weill then expressed intentions to his publisher of arranging *Der Zar* for chamber orchestra with a view toward performance in America, as Kaiser had achieved some notoriety in theatrical circles there. He also hoped to get performances in Russia, although he conceded that a Russian production would necessitate making the Czar an even more outlandish character.[19] Neither the adaptation nor any performances in commercial theaters seem to have materialized.

12. Weill to Universal Edition, 20 September 1927.
13. Weill to Universal Edition, 23 October 1927.
14. Weill to Universal Edition, 23 October, 2 November, and 10 November 1927. Weill must have changed his opinion of Brecher's abilities; he dedicated the score of *Der Jasager* to Brecher and entrusted the premiere of *Aufstieg und Fall der Stadt Mahagonny* to him, again after Klemperer had refused the project for the Kroll.
15. Weill to Universal Edition, 12 February 1928.
16. Weill to Universal Edition, 23 February 1928.
17. *Anbruch* 10 (April–May 1928): 119–22, and *Melos* 7 (December 1928): 557.
18. Wilhelm Altmann, "Opernstatistik 1927/28," *Anbruch* 10 (December 1928): 434.
19. Weill to Universal Edition, 23 February 1928.

In the interview published in the *Leipziger neueste Nachrichten*, Weill credited Kaiser with the original idea for the plot, which centers on the seemingly routine attempt by an enlightened Czar visiting Paris to get his photograph taken. But anti-czarist conspirators commandeer the studio of the famous Angèle and replace the lovely photographer and her assistants with impostors. The false Angèle attempts to "shoot" the Czar with a gun concealed in her camera. The Czar foils the plot unwittingly by falling in love with his phony photographer. When he insists upon taking her picture first, he delays the terrorists' "shot" until the police arrive, but the assassin and her fellow conspirators escape over the rooftops of Paris.

As complements, the title characters in both *Der Zar* and *Der Protagonist* experience a tension between their public roles and their private identities and are unable to distinguish reality from illusion. The Protagonist immerses himself so completely in his acting that he confuses his own identity with the characters he portrays. This psychological confusion leads him to murder onstage his beloved sister, whom he mistakes for the unfaithful wife in the play. The tragedy of *Der Protagonist* is a personal one, caused by the artist's inability to differentiate his art from life.

The Czar is equally imprisoned by his public role. His official responsibilities and royal facade limit his personal freedom as an ordinary "modern" man and prevent him from public identification with the democratic ideals he professes to Angèle. Ensnared in the assassination plot and surrounded by impostors, he too is unable to distinguish between what is real and what is acted. When the real Angèle returns after the conspirators' departure, the Czar is surprised by the change in her appearance. Angèle explains that there has been no change: the darkened studio can be blamed for his befuddlement. Once light is literally shed on the subject and order is restored, the Czar again presents his public facade to the real Angèle's camera. Topsy-turvy events have arisen from the Czar's desire to indulge his private, erotic self, but in this comic counterpart to *Der Protagonist*, the "hero" escapes only to suppress his private self in favor of the public—the "psychological" must yield to the "social."

Whereas *Der Protagonist* resides in the Shakespearean past, *Der Zar* captures the vitality of the twenties. The political references central to the plot—a dictatorial aristocrat and proletarian assassins—were certainly topical in 1927. The assassination of Archduke Franz Ferdinand in 1914, precipitating World War I, and the murder of Czar Nicholas II and his family in 1918 would have been all too familiar reference points for the audience. And in the fledgling Weimar Republic, political assassinations continued to be grim and not infrequent occurrences, although the victims were more often revolutionaries than rulers. The murders of Karl Liebknecht and Rosa Luxemburg were still debated. *Der Zar*'s setting also underscored its modernity, as photographic portraiture was evolving into a popular new art form in the 1920s.[20] Lotte Jacobi and Elli Marcus were both already well-known in Berlin for their stunning portraits of leading citizens. (Jacobi photographed both Weill and Lenya [c. 1929], and Marcus, who specialized in portraits of Berlin's stage personalities, photographed Brecht's wife, the actress Helene Weigel, in 1930.) Finally, with an attitude characteristic of postwar Germany, the opera does not shy away from sexual candor.

Despite *Der Zar*'s topicality, Kaiser's libretto fulfills Busoni's injunction to create an operatic world of pretense, of life reflected and distorted in a comic mirror,[21] and incorporates many traditional elements of farce, satire, and burlesque. Both the amorous Czar and the vigilant assassins are presented as the exaggerated caricatures populating political satire as far back as the commedia dell'arte troupes, the model for the acting company in *Der Protagonist*. By parodying literary and musical conventions and juxtaposing serious and comic elements, *Der Zar* sometimes borders on burlesque. With its caricature of a member of the upper class and his social predicament, *Der Zar* is a modern comedy of manners—a twentieth-century equivalent of a typical eighteenth-century comic libretto relying on class distinctions, buffoonish aristocrats, deception, impostors, and unwitting actions on the part of main characters. If the Czar invites comparison with Mozart's Count Almaviva in *Le Nozze di Figaro*, the false Angèle, like Susanna, pretends to succumb to the aristocrat's sexual advances. Angèle, too, manages to extricate herself at the last minute; the embarrassed ruler is left to face public scrutiny.

Kaiser's plot also echoes nineteenth-century comic opera traditions. The choice of a czar as central character suggests, at least superficially, a connection with *Zar und Zimmermann* by Gustav Albert Lortzing (1801–51). This komische Oper was regularly performed in the 1920s, and Weill reviewed a performance in 1925.[22] Lortzing based his topical work on Peter the Great's exploits while traveling incognito as a shipbuilder. In both *Der Zar* and *Zar und Zimmermann*, the czars shed their public roles in an attempt to become ordinary citizens, but neither is successful. When Peter the Great's identity is revealed, he resumes his royal duties and sails back to Russia, just as Weill's Czar finally poses for his official portrait. Offenbach's *La Grande Duchesse de Gérolstein* also presents a ruler, in this case female, who tries to evade her official duties. While disguised as a mere lady of the court, the young duchess attempts to seduce Fritz, a

20. Peter Salz, "The Artist as Social Critic," in Louise Lincoln, ed., *German Realism of the Twenties* (Minneapolis, 1980), p. 33.

21. Ferruccio Busoni, "Entwurf einer neuen Aesthetik der Tonkunst," trans. Rosamund Ley, *The Essence of Music and Other Papers* (New York, 1965), p. 40.

22. See Weill, *Ausgewählte Schriften*, pp. 146–47. The same review, published on 26 April 1925 in *Der deutsche Rundfunk*, discussed Offenbach's *Orpheus in der Unterwelt*.

member of the lower class who has already offended a number of nobles. Fritz's rebuff prompts the duchess to join with these other aristocrats in a plot on Fritz's life. As in *Der Zar,* the farcical assassination attempt is aborted when the young Duchess finally resumes her duties and settles down with an appropriately aristocratic mate.

Weill claimed that Kaiser's Czar was modeled on the screen persona of Paramount Pictures' film star Adolphe Menjou. Chaplin's *A Woman of Paris* in 1923 and *Ace of Cads* from 1926, for example, presented Menjou in his perennial role of the seductive ladies' man with debonair manner, smoothed-back hair, and thin triangular moustache. As Weill's suave Czar turns the tables on his murderous photographer, "a modern woman with political tendencies,"[23] the action becomes almost slapstick, with the Czar and the false Angèle each trying to force the other in front of the deadly camera. Kaiser's dialogue for the Czar and Angèle depends on dramatic irony, as the audience recognizes what the Czar fails to understand—the real meaning of the false Angèle's banter:

> *Zar:* Genügt das Licht?
>   Es ist ja Dämmerung.
>   Wie lang muss ich sitzen stocksteifstill?
> *falsche Angèle:* Ich habe Blitzlicht in der Kamera.
> *Zar:* Werd' ich erschrecken?
> *f. Angèle:* Das wird sich finden!
> *Zar:* Sie glauben fest, ich werde gut getroffen?
> *f. Angèle:* Ich treffe wie der Schütze seine Scheibe.[24]
>
> *Czar:* Enough light?
>   It's almost dark.
>   How long must I sit here so stiff and still?
> *False Angèle:* I have a flash in the camera.
> *Czar:* Will it frighten me?
> *False Angèle:* We'll see.
> *Czar:* Do you really believe it will hit me right?
> *False Angèle:* Like a sharpshooter, I hit my target.

The comedy results from an in-joke between the false Angèle and the audience: they know something that the Czar doesn't. As the scene proceeds, suspense builds, and humor increases in direct proportion.

Weill's musical treatment of Kaiser's libretto emphasizes its breakneck pace and farcical qualities. The composer's primary comic device was a male chorus seated in the orchestra pit. Weill summarized its function:

> A male chorus, added later by myself, has the primary function of juggling the Czar around and at times even commenting in a somewhat unseemly

23. "Kurt Weill über seine Oper."
24. Piano-vocal score of *Der Zar lässt sich photographieren* (Vienna, 1928), pp. 61–62.

manner on the stage action without gaining influence over this action, and it underscores the *opera buffa* character of the work.[25]

Isolated from the stage and commenting upon rather than participating in the action, the chorus spoofed the Greek revivalism reflected in French and German art of the time. Composers such as Egon Wellesz and Darius Milhaud, whose *opéra minute, L'enlèvement d'Europe,* had shared the Baden-Baden stage with the *Mahagonny Songspiel,* favored a return to the old-fashioned operatic chorus. Wellesz, composer of the Greek-inspired *Alcestis* (1924), was also influenced by new productions of Handel's operas. Initiated in 1920 with the Göttingen production of *Rodelinda,* the so-called Handel revival relied on large, static choruses.[26] Weill himself had a passing flirtation with Greek drama: in a 1927 letter to Universal Edition, in which he first mentioned work on *Der Zar* and before he conceived the *Mahagonny Songspiel,* he voiced his intent to compose a "klassische Tragödie" on *Antigone* or a similar subject to fulfill his commission for the Baden-Baden Festival.[27]

Weill's use of a male chorus may also reflect acquaintance with Pro-kofiev's *Love for Three Oranges* (1919), a popular comic work which features several male choruses. Though this work received its Berlin premiere on 9 October 1926—well before Weill's composition of *Der Zar*—any similarity between the works is only superficial, as the choruses differ markedly in their functions. Prokofiev's choruses are given collective personalities, dividing into warring factions of *Les Tragiques* and *Les Comiques,* and the two groups are situated on the stage, where they occasionally take part in and influence the course of the action. Weill's chorus is nameless and merely comments upon the action with no attempt to intervene.

A more probable inspiration for Weill's chorus is Stravinsky's *Oedipus Rex,* which received a concert performance in Paris during May 1927 while *Der Zar* was being sketched. One of the notable features of *Oedipus Rex* was its Greek chorus, situated to the side of the stage and commenting on the action throughout the opera. Stravinsky opened and closed the work with the chorus, as Weill did in *Der Zar.* Although the gala production of *Oedipus Rex* under Otto Klemperer at the Krolloper (which Weill reviewed for *Der deutsche Rundfunk*)[28] followed the premiere of *Der Zar,* it is possible that Weill had learned of the work already in 1927. Young German composers, especially Weill, were cognizant of Stravinsky's importance and probably would have been aware of this neo-classic composition, since the Paris premiere of *Oedipus Rex* had been widely reviewed in French- and English-language journals. Although

---

25. "Kurt Weill über seine Oper."
26. Walter Panofsky, *Protest in der Oper* (Munich, 1964), p. 74.
27. Weill to Universal Edition, 23 March 1927.
28. *Der deutsche Rundfunk* 10 (16 November 1928): 3180.

Weill may not have known the musical score of *Oedipus Rex* before the Krolloper production, he certainly could have read descriptions of Stravinsky's use of chorus. In an article published in October 1927, Weill even discussed the new French preference for ancient subject matter and singled out *Oedipus Rex* as an example.[29]

The similarity between *Oedipus Rex* and *Der Zar* did not escape producers or critics of the time.[30] *Oedipus Rex*, rather than *Der Protagonist*, even doubled the bill with *Der Zar* on a number of occasions, apparently with Weill's approval.[31] Not only did the two works share the "Greek" chorus, but *Oedipus Rex* is similar to *Der Protagonist* in its tragic but detached presentation of an individual forced to take responsibility for his rash actions. Thus, a double bill of *Oedipus Rex* and *Der Zar* maintained the intended tragic-comic balance. Given the comic nature of *Der Zar lässt sich photographieren*, the chorus utilizes Stravinsky's ancient convention with tongue in cheek, and presentation together enhances the burlesque of incongruous juxtapositions.

Although neither partitur nor libretto gives any indication of the chorus's appearance or demeanor, photographs from the Leipzig premiere show a group of old men with exaggerated moustaches and long white beards and dressed in dark coats and top hats (fig. 1).[32] A publicity photograph from the production at the Städtische Oper in Berlin features a similarly attired group, with each chorus member carrying a briefcase (fig. 2).[33] Apparently the chorus's distinctive but homogeneous dress manifests the dramatic convention of *typification*, a technique employed by many expressionist playwrights. Characters were typified by costuming that indicated their social function or communal identity, eliminating the need for personal names or individual traits. Many expressionist plays dating from the early 1920s and critical of modern society clothed capitalist figures such as businessmen, industrialists, or bankers in full evening dress, dark coats, and top hats regardless of situation, season, or time of day. Kaiser's own early play, *Von Morgens bis Mitternachts* (1916), generally considered to be his first expressionist work, includes several male

29. Kurt Weill, "Verschiebungen in der musikalischen Produktion," *Berliner Tageblatt*, 1 October 1927. Translated in Kowalke, pp. 478–79.

30. See Paul Stefan, "Antinomie der neuen Oper: Kurt Weill und Strawinsky," *Anbruch* 10 (March–April 1928): 119–22; T. W. Adorno's review in *Die Musik* 20 (September 1928): 923–24.

31. Weill to Universal Edition, 18 November 1927.

32. This publicity photograph, the original now in the Leipzig Museum für Stadtgeschichte, was published in *Anbruch* (April–May 1928): 121. The costumes were designed by Anna Ulrich and Leopold Schneider.

33. A publicity photograph from the Städtische Oper production appears in H. H. Stuckenschmidt, *Oper in dieser Zeit* (Hannover, 1964), p. 128. Reviews from the Frankfurt production also mention the distinctive dress of the chorus.

Figure 1. The premiere of *Der Zar lässt sich photographieren* in Leipzig. (The original photograph is now in the Museum für Stadtgeschichte in Leipzig.)

characters, dressed in smoking jackets and silk hats, who act as umpires at a bicycle race. The play's main character, known only as a bank cashier, arrives at the bicycle race dressed in evening clothes (with top hat), ready to partake in the new delights of capitalism. At the end of the play, the bank cashier is robbed by four other well-dressed men.[34] Ernst Toller's *Massemensch* (1920) contains a dream scene in which the heroine pleads with four bankers for financial aid: "The sound of coins clinking: the bankers in top hats dance a foxtrot around the stock exchange table."[35] A character in one of Toller's later plays, *Hinkemann* (1922), is a *Budenbesitzer* or showman, and he comes to represent the evils of capitalist society as he forces the hapless Hinkemann to perform in a freak show. Near the end of the play, when the Budenbesitzer refuses to release Hinkemann from his contract, this corrupt capitalist is costumed in a dress coat and top hat.[36] Even Dr. Caligari, the title character in one of the most famous contributions to expressionist cinema, *Das Kabinett des Dr. Caligari,* sports a top hat. Whoever originally conceived its costuming, the chorus func-

---

34. Georg Kaiser, *Werke,* ed. Walther Huder (Frankfurt, 1972), 1:490, 492, 505.
35. Ernst Toller, *Prosa, Briefe, Dramen, Gedichte* (Reinbek bei Hamburg, 1961), p. 303.
36. Ibid., p. 421.

Figure 2. The male chorus of *Der Zar lässt sich photographieren* in the Berlin Städtische Oper's production from 1928.

tioned again as a synthesis of elements drawn from contemporary drama and from the neo-classic equivalent of a traditional comic opera chorus comprising undifferentiated groups of villagers, hunters, or peasants.

The chorus sings on ten occasions in *Der Zar.* Some entries are brief, only a measure or two of music, but several passages are lengthy and represent self-contained choral units in keeping with the formal organization of earlier comic operas. The chorus performs variously in unison, in two-, three-, or four-part harmony, both accompanied and a cappella, with and without text. As Weill indicated, the chorus does not participate in the action per se. But in an often mock-serious manner with distinctive music, the chorus serves to remind the audience that regardless of what transpires on stage, the opera remains a comedy. Although Weill claimed to have added the chorus independently,[37] it is unclear whether he supplied the new texts or whether Kaiser wrote them later at his request. Weill did caution his publisher to use the piano-vocal score to derive the authentic libretto, because the typescript of the text in Universal Edition's possession, he warned, had undergone significant changes and revisions.[38]

The chorus opens the opera by proclaiming the title of the work, like a cabaret *conférencier* or variety-show emcee who announces the evening's

37. No chorus appears in the first scenario Weill sent his publisher (4 April 1927). Weill does not refer to the chorus until a letter of 6 August 1927, by which time the music was largely composed.
38. Weill to Universal Edition, 4 January 1928.

entertainment. The attendant music (ex. 1), with its cymbal downbeat, melodic fifths, and triplet rhythms, is reminiscent of a fanfare in tribute to the Czar's elevated station. The full orchestra then proceeds with a short overture. The chorus sings again before the curtain rises to restate the title, this time in three-part harmony and with an orchestral accompaniment echoing the opening triplet rhythm. Humming in slower four-part harmony as the curtain rises on Angèle's studio, the chorus brings the overture to a close.

As in many earlier comic operas, the chorus concludes the finale as well. As the real Angèle prepares to photograph the Czar, an onstage entourage breaks into a march that gives way to a return of the opening choral and orchestral fanfare. The work ends with the chorus reiterating the title, as in the opening measure, but transposed up a semitone and now followed by a final cymbal tag. This repetition of the opening choral gesture stresses the opera's paradox of role-playing and reality, for once the assassination plot and the Czar's attempted seduction have both failed, all that has transpired is indeed that the Czar has had his picture taken. The implicit circularity of the returning chorus shows that the plot has come full circle, and with the true Angèle behind the camera, order has been restored to maintain the status quo.

Two other times the chorus breaks in to repeat the opera's title and clarify its central action. When the real Angèle learns of the Czar's impending visit, she states the title to the same triplet rhythm as in the opening gesture, but with a different melody. The chorus follows Angèle's restatement of the title with eight measures of humming in four-part harmony. The chorus's slower-moving a cappella part is in marked contrast to the preceding music, distinguished by its rapid sixteenth-note scalar passages, and it musically italicizes Angèle's proud announcement. When the false Angèle makes her first attempt to "shoot" the Czar, the chorus again declaims the title to the triplet, fanfare-like rhythm and in three-part harmony. This repetition ironically reminds the audience that the Czar is supposedly *only* being photographed.

The remaining choral entrances spoof the stage action and add moments of false suspense to the drama. When the terrorists first enter Angèle's studio, the leader reveals the assassination plot: "It's time for our Czar to pay with blood." The five other assassins emphatically reiterate, "With a Czar's blood."[39] The chorus repeats this phrase in a pianissimo that heightens the dramatic impact. Later the entire group of terrorists swears allegiance to its political beliefs and affirms its mission. This murder will be a signal for the oppressed who hunger for liberation; it will

---

39. "Anführer: 'Sie wird mit eines Zaren Blut bezählt.' Männerchor: 'Mit eines Zaren Blut!'" See piano-vocal score, pp. 20–21.

open the door to freedom and justice and break the chains of imprisoned brothers. The chorus asserts that the assassination will, shall, and must succeed, after which the terrorists exit with their hostages, leaving the false Angèle to await the Czar. The chorus then sings a separate choral number. The text reminds the audience that the revolver is in the camera and summarizes the assassins' philosophy. The number closes with a final reminder to the audience of the loaded camera, as members of the Czar's retinue search the studio. Weill sets this passage (ex. 2) in mock-military style, with three-part harmony making prominent use of open fourths and fifths and the accompaniment reduced to a single snare drum. The tongue-in-cheek military manner and the mysterioso melodramatic quality invoked by the rapid crescendos and decrescendos prevent the terrorists' philosophy from receiving the credence it otherwise might. The number also serves as a suspenseful interlude before the Czar's arrival; an ironic, shortened version of this choral reminder appears later as the Czar first takes a seat in front of the loaded camera.

The chorus also interacts with the Czar, or "juggles" him, as Weill said. After receiving news of a possible attempt on his life, which he considers boring, the Czar launches into a soliloquy, lamenting his special predicament: "A Czar can rule everything except his own life. I'm just a concept."[40] Weill sets the Czar's solo in the style of recitative, marked as such parenthetically in the score and reminiscent of the traditional parody awarded blustering aristocrats in the various national forms of earlier comic opera. The chorus, intoning a grating major second, serves as the Czar's only accompaniment. After a more lyrical outburst from the Czar accompanied by full orchestra, the humming chorus returns as the Czar, reflective again, compares himself to Napoleon entombed in the nearby Invalides. Weill's musical treatment effectively derails any tendency of the audience to sympathize with the Czar's predicament.

Weill employed distinctive music to clarify the action and amplify the notion of private versus public. Most notable are the passages that invoke the dance idioms of jazz.[41] Next to the chorus, Weill's use of jazz, particularly the "Tango-Angèle," was the feature most often cited by contemporary critics. By 1927, jazz had already stormed Germany, with such composers as Wilhelm Grosz and Erwin Schulhoff routinely employing aspects of dance rhythms and jazz instrumentation in their classical compositions. Other composers, such as Ernst Krenek and Paul Hindemith, had explored the new sound too. Avant-garde musical journals including *Anbruch* and *Auftakt* published special jazz issues in an

40. "Über alles soll ein Zar gebieten nur nicht über sein Leben. Denn ich bin ein Prinzip." See piano-vocal score, p. 100.

41. Kowalke, pp. 120–22, provides an extensive list of the occurrences of various modern dance idioms in Weill's works from this period.

attempt to report on the popular phenomenon.[42] In an opera that dealt, as Weill claimed, with modern issues, jazz was almost to be expected, but in *Der Zar* it is used as ironic commentary.

The Czar makes his first stage entrance to the unlikely strains of a foxtrot (ex. 3). A solo trumpet and clarinet carry the melody and the dotted-rhythm countermelody respectively, while piano and lower strings accompany with harmonies few authentic jazz bands had ever played. The jaunty rhythms underscore the first encounter between the Czar and the false Angèle, and the melody returns after the Czar states his wish to be photographed not as a ruler, but as "a man who walks the street with other men who are all equals."[43] A shorter version of the foxtrot recurs as the Czar poses for Angèle, after he has been assured that he will be repaid for this royal favor. Weill's use of this modern dance is pure burlesque—a foxtrot is hardly music suitable for a ruler, even an "enlightened" one caught up in the invigorating Parisian atmosphere. But use of the foxtrot also heightens the public-versus-private issue, in that this popular music clarifies the personality of the Czar, who secretly longs to be an ordinary man.

The "Tango Angèle," so designated in the score and announced by the false Angèle herself, appears at the climax of the opera. It elicited the most comment from critics—not for its well-worn dance rhythms but for its innovative accompaniment by an onstage gramophone (ex. 4). Again in his Leipzig interview, Weill described the dramatic reasons for creating this tango:

> I attempted to achieve the [climactic] effect through a completely new sound form, and for me this was the gramophone. I orchestrated a tango expressly for the gramophone, which enters for the first time as a soloist while the orchestra is silent, and whose melody is countered by the singers. . . . The opposition of an action rising to its greatest tension [the arrival of the police] and a simple dance-like recording seemed to me to be precisely the way to achieve the climactic effect.[44]

The published full score of the opera does not indicate the instrumentation for the tango, which was later released as a single by Parlophon-Beka.[45] The tango was widely recognized as a couple dance with particu-

42. *Anbruch* 7 (April 1925) and *Auftakt* 6 (no. 10, 1926).

43. "Als Mensch, der auf den Strassen geht mit andern Menschen, die alle seinesgleichen sind." See piano-vocal score, p. 43.

44. "Kurt Weill über seine Oper."

45. The recording of the Tango-Angèle was made in Berlin on 11 January 1928 in Weill's presence and perhaps under his direction (David Drew, *Kurt Weill: A Handbook*). The recording, which was leased with the orchestral parts to opera houses, is still available for rental from Universal Edition, but the score and parts for the tango have been lost. [A year later, Weill again utilized the gramophone in the theater when he composed incidental music for Arnolt Bronnen's *Katalaunische Schlacht*. In order to preserve the versatility of a pit band and

larly seductive and erotic undertones. As Angèle pretended to submit to the Czar's advances, its extramusical connotations would have been appreciated by all but the most out-of-touch viewer. The entrance of the tango, immediately following the Czar's soliloquy in recitative, creates another comic juxtaposition—the unlikely contrast of an old-fashioned operatic convention and a twentieth-century popular one.

In contrast, the "Gemessener Marsch" and "Alla marcia" sections ironically depict the Czar's unwanted social station. The "Gemessener Marsch," scored for brass and piano, appears immediately after the second, shorter use of the foxtrot as the Czar first sits for his photograph. The Czar has just stated his wish to leave his public duties behind, and he complains to Angèle that the formal pose is uncomfortable. The false Angèle, at last behind the deadly camera, sees the Czar only as a political symbol, not as a flesh-and-blood man trapped by his role. Therefore, the march characterizes the Czar's political and public nature as misunderstood by the false Angèle. The "Alla marcia" section, featuring a prominent trumpet solo, is longer and forms part of the finale discussed earlier. At this point, the assassination plot has been uncovered, and the true Angèle reappears to take the Czar's picture. The Czar is so confused by the turn of events that he wonders if he is still Czar. His followers march onstage with sabers swinging and sing of their loyalty to him. This march answers the Czar's question: after all that has transpired, he is indeed still Czar. As the chorus closes the work, the Czar is photographed, not as the ordinary man of the foxtrot, but as the Czar of the military march. All of these musical techniques demonstrate Weill's dramatic invention while at the same time showing his reliance on models from a past tradition of comic opera.

In his review "Der neue Kurt Weill," Alfred Baresel stated that, after the impudence of the *Mahagonny Songspiel*, *Der Zar* represented a clarification of Weill's style within the structure of a high-quality comic work.[46] Baresel could not have foreseen that Weill would develop further the "impudent" style of the *Mahagonny Songspiel* in *Die Dreigroschenoper* and *Happy End*. But as a transitional work, *Der Zar* did act as a clarification of Weill's dramatic and aesthetic sensibilities. Kim Kowalke has noted the transitional aspects of *Der Zar* in the "rudimentary gestic function" of the "Tango-Angèle," and the sectional organization of the opera based on ostinatos and motor rhythms which adumbrated Weill's closed song forms.[47] In aiming to make the opera a true complement to his earlier

yet operate within the production's meager budget for musicians, the entire score was recorded on disk and then played at each performance on an offstage gramophone. K. K.]

46. Alfred Baresel, "Der neue Kurt Weill," *Neue Musik Zeitung* 48 (1928): 384.

47. Kowalke, pp. 106, 285.

tragic work, Weill relied heavily on satire and parody brought to life solely through the music as commentary on, not accompaniment to, the events on stage; these techniques remain a central component of his later collaborations with Brecht. Weill's integration in *Der Zar* of conventions from earlier traditions of comic opera and modern subject matter and treatment, leavened with irreverent social commentary, prepared the way for his "neo-Baroque" formulation of the "prototype" for modern opera in *Die Dreigroschenoper.*

Two other aspects of *Der Zar* suggest nascent features of the epic opera. Weill's Greek chorus acts as a distancing agent, as described later by Brecht. The chorus continually reminds the audience that the work is a comedy in which the world portrayed on stage should not be viewed as real. The chorus functions irrationally and non-naturalistically in this Zeitoper; its secondary function as narrator (a dramatic technique more fully developed in *Aufstieg und Fall der Stadt Mahagonny*), is reinforced by the inherent typification of its dress. This technique would become a crucial aspect of Weill's theatrical vocabulary as he and his collaborators focused on character "types" and "typical" behavior,[48] again in opposition to naturalistic theater.

The frustration Weill encountered in his attempts to have *Der Protagonist* and *Der Zar* performed together as a dramatic unit greater than the sum of its two parts undoubtedly contributed to his growing distrust of the state-subsidized operatic system in Germany. Fighting to preserve his artistic integrity in the face of formidable odds, Weill had hoped to escape "the old opera business" by mounting *Der Zar* in Piscator's independent theater. *Die Dreigroschenoper*'s restriction of musical means can then be seen as the logical and practical compromise necessary to achieve the goal that had eluded *Der Zar.*

Despite its relative obscurity today, *Der Zar lässt sich photographieren* is a consummately skillful work that attests to Weill's dramatic and musical maturity before his collaboration with Brecht. It is a work both tied to the past and carrying within it seeds for the future. Although Weill continued to employ aspects of *Der Zar*'s compositional procedures in later works, its non-parodistic operatic elements were temporarily all but suppressed within Brecht's epic model. It remained—until *Der Kuhhandel* (1934) and *Knickerbocker Holiday* (1938)—an isolated but worthy testament to Weill's neo-classic, but highly original, vision of comic opera.

---

48. See Kurt Weill, "Das Formproblem der modernen Oper," *Der Scheinwerfer* 5 (February 1932): 3–6. Translated in Kowalke, pp. 541–42: "Today we are on the way to a theatrical form that projects great, enduring contemporary ideas in simple, typical events and which thereby leads back again to the original purpose of theater: representation of types of human behavior."

Examples

Example 1. *Der Zar lässt sich photographieren*, opening.

Example 2. *Der Zar lässt sich photographieren*.

Example 3. *Der Zar lässt sich photographieren*.

Example 4. "Tango Angèle" from *Der Zar lässt sich photographieren,* mm. 1–8, 19–22.

7

Crossing the Cusp: The Schoenberg Connection
ALAN CHAPMAN

Editor's Preface

In an oft-quoted and frequently misinterpreted interview published in the *New York Sun* on 3 February 1940, Kurt Weill summarized his own approach to composition by contrasting it with Arnold Schoenberg's:

> I'm convinced that many modern composers have a feeling of superiority toward their audiences. Schoenberg, for example has said he is writing for a time fifty years after his death. But the great "classic" composers wrote for their contemporary audiences. They wanted those who heard their music to understand it, and they did. As for myself, I write for today. I don't give a damn about writing for posterity.[1]

Weill's deliberately provocative statement denying the primacy of purely aesthetic considerations in his own works undoubtedly made usable journalistic copy in promoting the next day's broadcast of *The Ballad of Magna Carta*, but it also testified to his final and irrevocable severance of any vestigial links with the technical/aesthetic concerns of European musical modernism. Already at work on *Lady in the Dark*, Weill had long before rejected the nineteenth-century, art-for-art's-sake aesthetic whereby art and artist had become increasingly isolated from society as a whole—sometimes through the conscious calculation of the composer. Weill's selection of Schoenberg as the foremost representative of the continuation of this path into the twentieth century was not arbitrary. In 1924 Schoenberg himself had issued an equally shocking statement in which he lamented the "fairest, alas bygone, days of art when a prince stood as a protector before an artist, showing the rabble that art, a matter for princes, is beyond the judgment of common people."[2]

In 1924 Weill already would have disagreed with Schoenberg's elitist viewpoint. Having recently completed his studies with Busoni, Weill embraced the neo-classic ideal of functional art characteristic of eighteenth-century masters, even though his "populist" tendencies were not yet linked to specific sociological

---

1. William G. King, "Music and Musicians," *New York Sun*, 3 February 1940.
2. Quoted by Geoffrey Skelton, *Paul Hindemith* (New York, 1978), p. 71.

concerns. Less than two years later, however, with the hope of shattering the "splendid isolation" of contemporary music, Weill would add elements of popular music, aspects of the new theater, and topical subject matter from the socio-political arena to his Busoni-inspired arsenal of simplicity, concision, and emotional detachment. In seeking a larger audience for modern music at precisely the time Schoenberg was solving the technical impasse of non-tonal music with the abstractions of a twelve-tone method, Weill was initiating a course that would eventually lead him closer to Gershwin than to Schoenberg. Yet even as Weill was taking his first tentative step with *Der neue Orpheus*, he championed Schoenberg's music at every opportunity as music critic for *Der deutsche Rundfunk*. In 1925, Weill wrote that Schoenberg "has had to struggle against universal misunderstanding and animosity," because he

> renounced tonality, common chords, symmetrical melody, rhythmic and formal constraints and substituted a wonderful interweaving of long melodies, a free polyphony that is sustained with prodigious skill, rich in inspiration, and unquestionable honesty.[3]

In a later essay Weill perceptively characterized Schoenberg's work as "an entirely organic outgrowth of the nineteenth century" and asserted that "even his opponents must recognize in him the purest, most noble artistic personality and the most powerful intellectual force in today's musical life."[4] Four months later, Weill again cited him as "the pathbreaker of new music, whose full significance for the musical public will probably be first recognized only after several decades."[5]

Weill's public statements about Schoenberg—boldly prophetic and courageous in 1925—were not merely the impassioned exclamations of a Young Turk as he jumped on the modernist bandwagon. In an anguished letter to his family written from Berlin during 1919, while he was studying at the Hochschule für Musik, Weill lamented his inability to work productively:

> I want to accomplish this much—and only through Schoenberg can I do it—that I write only when I have to, when it comes honestly from the depths of my heart. Otherwise, it will turn out to be merely music of the intellect, and I hate that. The "Weise" does come from the heart; I live in this music. But even that embarrasses me.[6]

3. *Der deutsche Rundfunk* 3 (1925), translated by David Drew in his insert notes to the Angel recording of Symphony No. 1 (S–36506).
4. *Der deutsche Rundfunk* 4 (28 February 1926): 582; quoted and translated in Kim H. Kowalke, *Kurt Weill in Europe* (Ann Arbor, 1979), pp. 156–57.
5. *Der deutsche Rundfunk* 4 (27 June 1926): 1796; trans. in Kowalke, p. 157.
6. Undated letter with opening page(s) missing. The original was in the collection of Weill's sister-in-law, Rita, when I inventoried her holdings on 8 September 1982. Photocopies of the fragment are held by the Academy of Arts in Berlin and the Weill-Lenya Research Center. In a letter to his brother Hanns dated 27 March 1919, Weill outlined his plans for the symphonic poem; on 3 July 1919, Weill wrote again to Hanns and reported: "The 'Weise' is finished up to the closing chords of the middle section. Next week I'll go on to the orchestration." Photocopies of both letters are in the Weill-Lenya Research Center.

The "Weise" was a symphonic poem based on Rilke's *Die Weise von Liebe und Tod des Cornets Christoph Rilke;* it has disappeared without a trace. However, in a survey of Weill's compositions published in 1927, Heinrich Strobel mentioned the orchestral work, claimed that it had been influenced by Schoenberg's *Pelleas und Melisande,* and perceived in it a "cautious departure from the superficial pathos of late romantic decadence in art."[7] Weill's admiration for Schoenberg is also reflected in the First Symphony (1921), which owes much in both materials and conception to Schoenberg's First Chamber Symphony. Maurice Abravanel recalls that Weill insisted that all his students purchase Schoenberg's *Harmonielehre,* although Abravanel cannot remember that Weill made any reference to it in the actual harmony and composition lessons.

Schoenberg's influence survived Weill's period of study with Busoni. In a letter to Lenya postmarked 28 October 1925, written while he was in Dessau for the German premiere of his Violin Concerto, Weill wrote that "before one can understand this music, one must have already digested with good intentions a portion of Schoenberg."[8] Weill also sometimes rationalized negative reviews for his works if the offending critic had also disapproved of Schoenberg. In another letter to Lenya, postmarked 19 July 1926, he rationalized such an attack by Adolf Weissmann: "After his devastating judgment about Schoenberg, his remarks about me are just malicious enough not to endanger my musical reputation."[9] Even after Schoenberg's rejection of the post-*Dreigroschenoper* Weill, they shared many contacts within the Viennese circle: Alexander von Zemlinsky (Schoenberg's brother-in-law), who conducted the Berlin premiere of *Mahagonny;* Karl Rankl (one of Schoenberg's students), who premiered two workers' choruses by Weill; Hermann Scherchen; and Karl Kraus. In what may be the most curious biographical sketch of Weill published during his lifetime, Gdal Saleski described Kurt Weil [sic] in *Famous Musicians of a Wandering Race* as "one of the prominent ultra-modern composers" and a follower of "Schoenberg and the whole school of our ultra-modernists."[10]

Schoenberg, in turn, evidently found much to admire in some of Weill's pre-1927 compositions; early in 1928 he nominated Weill for membership in the Prussian Academy of Arts. But Schoenberg's only recorded public pronouncements on Weill postdate the incredible success of *Die Dreigroschenoper.* Having been inordinately rewarded for what Schoenberg could only view as squandering his talent, Weill now "constituted a betrayal of the cause of modern music which the once-gifted Weill had fought for. Schoenberg dissected one or two of the songs for the benefit of his Berlin masterclass and maintained that they were

7. Heinrich Strobel, "Kurt Weill," *Melos* 6 (October 1927): 427–28.

8. The letter is held by the Weill-Lenya Research Center in New York and is quoted by permission of the Kurt Weill Foundation for Music.

9. The letter is in the Weill-Lenya Research Center.

10. New York: Bloch Publishing Co., 1927; pp. 92–93. Although the entry lists "Photography and Love," the abandoned title of *Der Zar lässt sich photographieren,* among Weill's works, there is no mention of Brecht, the *Mahagonny Songspiel,* or the use of elements derived from popular music.

technically inferior to Lehár.[11] Weill's lighthearted but inflammatory response to the *Berliner Tageblatt*'s 1928 Christmas invitation to address an essay to a class of students on the subject of his life and works so exasperated Schoenberg that he scribbled extensive and scathing comments in the margin of the newspaper clipping.[12] In his marginalia, Schoenberg prophesied that "in the end, all those communally oriented artists will have addressed their idiocies only to each other."[13]

Weill and Schoenberg had been on a collision course. In 1927, while Weill was criticizing composers who "continue to work toward the solution of aesthetic problems as if behind closed doors" and asserting that a social consciousness of some kind must determine the characteristics of an artwork in order to reach a broader audience,[14] Schoenberg wrote that it was "self-evident that art which treats deeper ideas cannot address itself to the many." If Schoenberg was not willing to modify his dictum that "in the end, art and success have to part company"[15] to accommodate *Die Dreigroschenoper*, he could react in only one way to the crisis which that work must have represented for him. Since the success of *Die Dreigroschenoper* was indisputable, it simply could not be art; as a corollary, Weill no longer could be considered an artist. Schoenberg's own "artistic" response, *Von heute auf morgen*, was subliminally intended to demonstrate that *Die Dreigroschenoper* led only from a "shaky hand to a greedy mouth." The common fate of exile only exaggerated the distance that separated their diverging aesthetic, technical, and economic paths. But their erstwhile mutual admiration for each other's music suggests that, for a time at least, their musical idioms were not antithetical.[16]

*   *   *

11. David Drew, "Kurt Weill and His Critics," *Times Literary Supplement* 3838 (3 October 1975): 1143. See also Drew's comments in the same essay regarding other parallels in the careers of the two composers.

12. See Alexander Ringer, "Schoenberg, Weill and Epic Theater," *Journal of the Arnold Schoenberg Institute* 4 (June 1980): 77–98.

13. Arnold Schoenberg, notes to "Der Musiker Weill," trans. in Ringer, p. 87.

14. Kurt Weill, "Verschiebungen in der musikalischen Produktion," *Berliner Tageblatt*, 1 October 1927; translated in Kowalke, pp. 478–80. In "Der Musiker Weill," Weill stated his position even more clearly: "If music cannot be placed in the service of society as a whole, it forfeits its right to exist in the world today. . . . Music is no longer a matter of the few" (Ringer, p. 86).

15. Arnold Schoenberg, "The Future of Opera" (1927), in *Style and Idea*, ed. Leonard Stein (New York, 1975), p. 336.

16. Ringer points out a number of parallels in their careers to show that "Weill and Schoenberg did not really stand as far apart as might appear at first blush" (p. 79). There is no evidence of any direct contact between Weill and Schoenberg in exile. However, on 19 June 1934, an employee of Universal Edition wrote to Weill in Louveciennes, France: "I have just now heard through Rudolf Kolisch (Kolisch-Quartet) that Georg Schoenberg, Arnold Schoenberg's son, who, as you may know, earlier lived in Germany, is now in Paris, Grand Hotel de Lorraine, 6 Passage de Clichy. He is in very bad financial straits and lives with his wife and children in the bitterest poverty. Apparently he earns almost nothing and receives from Schoenberg in America only a small monthly sum. Schoenberg also apparently doesn't earn very much in America for the time being and probably can't send a larger amount." The representative of Universal Edition then recommends the young Schoenberg to Weill as a copyist and asks him to help in any way possible. (Weill himself had been

At a critical stage in each composer's career—a period of transition from one organizing principle or compositional procedure or style to another, which I refer to as a *cusp*—Weill and Schoenberg shared a number of elements of musical vocabulary. For Schoenberg, this cusp dates from 1907 to 1909, when he made the transition from tonal composition to his earliest atonal pieces.[17] The corresponding cusp in Weill's career occurs from 1925 to 1927, when he moved from the "modern" compositional idiom of the Violin Concerto and *Der Protagonist* to a more "traditional" tonal idiom in *Royal Palace* and the *Mahagonny Songspiel* (even though their structure and dramaturgy are altogether radical in other ways). In relation to Schoenberg, Weill crossed his cusp eighteen years later and *stylistically* in reverse! Of particular interest here is that in both cases certain musical elements exist on each side of the cusp yet function differently in the varying contexts. With Weill and Schoenberg themselves pointing to a connection that can be documented historically, we begin our investigation of musical elements common to the compositions from the cusp periods of both composers.

Example 1 presents two musical excerpts for comparison. In example 1a (from the accompaniment to the sixth song of Schoenberg's "Fünfzehn Gedichte aus *Das Buch der hängenden Gärten* von Stefan George" [*George-Lieder*], opus 15, composed in 1908–09) two three-note groups have been identified as A and B. A might be described as a tritone joined with a perfect fourth. In such terms, B could be described as two perfect fourths joined together. These two three-note groups combine with the coincident notes of the bass line to produce four-note groups. In example 1b, from Weill's one-act opera *Der Zar lässt sich photographieren* (1927), the upper three voices are exclusively devoted to the presentation of either A or B. Here a number of occurrences of B appear in the more compact voicing exemplified by the first appearance at the beginning of the excerpt. As in example 1a, these forms of A and B combine with the simultaneous bass notes to produce four-note groups.

Another comparison is offered in example 2. In example 2a, the opening passage from the ninth of the *George-Lieder*, A is combined with two other notes, D and E, to form a five-note sonority. In the second

---

"released" by Universal Edition the previous October, with U. E. claiming a percentage of royalties Weill earned from works placed with other publishers in the future!) Weill replied to the request for help for Georg Schoenberg on 9 September: "Forgive me for not answering your last letter. I have in due course attempted to undertake something for the son of Schoenberg, but you can imagine that it's not easy. I will in any case keep it in mind if I hear of something." Copies of the correspondence are in the Weill-Lenya Research Center.

17. See Allen Forte, "Schoenberg's Creative Evolution: The Path to Atonality," *Musical Quarterly* 64 (April 1978): 133–76, for a detailed discussion of Schoenberg's transition to atonal composition and "set consciousness."

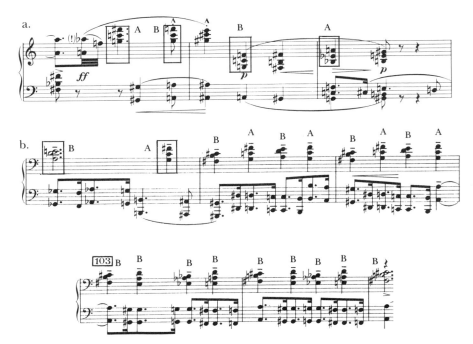

Example 1. A comparison
a. Schoenberg, "Fünfzehn Gedichte aus *Das Buch der hängenden Gärten* von Stefan George," (*George-Lieder*), op. 15, no. 6, mm. 10–12.
b. Weill, *Der Zar lässt sich photographieren.*

Example 2. Another comparison
a. Schoenberg, *George-Lieder,* op. 15, no. 9, mm. 1–2.
b. Weill, Konzert für Violine und Blasorchester, op. 12 (Violin Concerto), mm. 45–46.

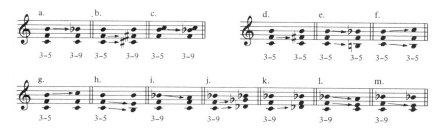

Example 3. Set names for three-note sonorities

measure, another form of *A* is combined with the bass notes, D and E. In example 2b (from Weill's Violin Concerto of 1924) *A* is combined with two other notes, C and D♯ to form a five-note sonority.

In example 3, the widely used names for these three-note groups are introduced. The names 3–5 and 3–9 for *A* and *B* respectively are pitch-class set names, as codified by Allen Forte in *The Structure of Atonal Music* (1973). The first number in each name indicates the cardinality of (number of pitches in) the set: three. The second number indicates the position of each set, among sets of the same cardinality, on Forte's comprehensive list. There are twelve distinct "trichords" (three-note unordered sets) in all. The usefulness of such pitch-class set names, as evidenced by their widespread employment, at least for purposes of identification of non-triadically based pitch collections, is seldom challenged. This approach recognizes the equivalence of forms of the set related by transposition and inversion. In addition, a name like 3–5 is a more manageable identifier than "the collection of three pitches which, in one of its possible voicings, is a perfect fourth joined with a tritone." The latter label is not only unwieldy, but it implies tonally-derived intervallic interpretations that may not be appropriate to the musical context.

Example 3 also illustrates a number of possible voice-leading relationships that exist among 3–5, 3–9, and some other three-note pitch combinations. Examples 3a, 3b, and 3c illustrate semitone melodic motions which may connect 3–5 and 3–9. Examples 3d, 3e, and 3f demonstrate the capacity of 3–5 to change from one form to another by semitone motion in one or more voices. (In ex. 3f, the pitch content remains constant through a voice exchange effected by contrary motion in the outer voices.) Examples 3g through 3m explore semitonal voice-leading connections between 3–5 or 3–9 and a number of sets with traditional tonal associations. Especially interesting are the relationships between 3–9 and major and minor triads (exx. 3i through 3l) and between 3–9 and a dominant seventh with fifth omitted (ex. 3m). These relationships are particularly significant, since our discussion will include the generation and employment of these trichords within tonal frameworks.

Although 3–5 and 3–9 are the focus of the present investigation, this comparative approach could easily (and must eventually) be extended to include a larger collection of pitch combinations, particularly those containing four or more pitches. These two trichords, then, are intended as models by which certain analytic procedures can be clearly demonstrated. The emphasis on 3–5 and 3–9 is also consistent with the importance placed by Ian Kemp and Kim Kowalke on Weill's use of semitonal voice-leading and chords constructed from fourths.[18]

Example 4 illustrates a harmonic facet of Schoenberg's compositional evolution between 1907 and 1909. The opening and closing passages of the first song of opus 14 ("Ich darf nicht dankend" in ex. 4a), composed in December 1907, feature 3–5 and 3–9 prominently within a tonal context. The two trichords, connected by two semitone motions, begin the accompaniment. At the song's end, 3–5 (duplicating the pitch content of its initial appearance) serves as a cadential embellishment of the tonic triad, B minor. The introduction to the other song of opus 14, "In diesen Wintertagen," composed in February 1908, also features these trichords within a tonal context. In Example 4b, 3–5 arises twice in a linear fashion, as part of a suspension of one of the notes in a minor seventh chord. In the first measure, the suspended B resolves to A over a change in harmony. In the sequentially related second measure, D resolves to C. The move toward dominant harmony in the third measure creates 3–9 through B's displacement by C.

Many music theorists hold certain truths to be self-evident: any sonority can be generated in a linear context, and any sonority thus generated has the inalienable right to life, liberty, and the pursuit of independent meaning. Examples 4c through 4f demonstrate this pursuit of independent meaning by 3–5 and 3–9 in Schoenberg's *George-Lieder*. 3–5 is prominent as a harmonic building block in the opening measures of several of these songs. (See also the opening of op. 15/9, ex. 2a.) In the first measure of op. 15/12 (ex. 4f), two successive forms of 3–5 appear. In the third measure of the same song, 3–9 (B-E-A) and 3–5 (F-B-E) interlock to form a four-note chord.

The importance of the chronological position of the opus 15 songs is underscored by a survey of some atonal works by Schoenberg: Three Piano Pieces, op. 11 (1909), *Erwartung*, op. 17 (1909), Six Little Piano Pieces, op. 19 (1911), *Herzgewächse*, op. 20 (1911), and *Pierrot Lunaire*, op. 21 (1912). Detailed analyses of these works reveal a collection of characteristic atonal sets, that is, a recurrent harmonic vocabulary which includes 3–5 and 3–9 among its members, although this vocabulary is

18. Ian Kemp, "Harmony in Weill: Some Observations," *Tempo* 104 (1973): 11–15; and Kowalke, pp. 183–307.

Example 4. Schoenberg crosses the cusp
a. "Ich darf nicht dankend," op. 14, no. 1, opening and closing.
b. "In diesen Wintertagen," op. 14, no. 2, opening.
c. *George-Lieder,* op. 15, no. 5, opening.
d. *George-Lieder,* op. 15, no. 6, opening.

Example 4 continued
e. *George-Lieder,* op. 15, no. 10, opening.
f. *George-Lieder,* op. 15, no. 12, opening.

especially rich in four-note sets. Weill certainly took notice of this harmonic development. Writing in 1926, he asserted that "with the opus 11
piano pieces, Schoenberg quite consciously takes the step into unknown
territory."[19]

As the above comparisons may have already suggested, Weill also
carried the trichords 3–5 and 3–9 across his cusp. They appear in works
from the early twenties as well as in compositions written after 1927. The
present examination of examples drawn from two representative works
by Weill uses three criteria to evaluate the significance of pitch combinations:

1. The pitch combination occurs frequently in a composition. It may
   recur with the same or varied (through transposition or inversion)
   pitch content.
2. The pitch combination serves as a building block for larger sonorities.
   We might expect that in certain cases it might be highlighted (through
   register or orchestration, for example) as a subset of those larger
   sonorities.
3. The pitch combination is employed melodically as well as harmonically.

Examples 5a through 5d (drawn from the piano reduction) are a
clear indication of the recurrence of 3–5 and 3–9 in the non-tonal con-

19. *Der deutsche Rundfunk* 4 (27 June 1926): 1796.

Example 5. Weill crosses the cusp
a. Violin Concerto, mvt. 3, mm. 15–17.
b. Violin Concerto, mvt. 1, mm. 86–92.

c.

d.

Example 5 continued
c. Violin Concerto, mvt. 3.
d. Violin Concerto, mvt. 2b (Cadenza), opening.

text of Weill's Concerto for Violin and Wind Instruments. In examples 5a and 5b, their role as accompanimental trichords can be seen. In example 5c, the trichords are featured in metrically prominent positions; in the second system of the excerpt, 3–5 (G♯-D♯-A) is embellished by the neighbor harmony F♯-E-F. Example 5d reveals 3–5 as the opening sonority of a movement; in addition, 3–9 appears in a linear context similar to those seen in example 3. In sequential passages a recurrent sonority is truly emancipated from its linear origins, since its capacity to follow itself denies its dependence on another chord. (A notable precedent is Hugo Wolf's use of augmented triads in parallel.) Here, in exam-

Example 5 continued
e. *Der Zar lässt sich photographieren.*
f. *Der Zar lässt sich photographieren.*

ples 5e and 5f, such sequential usage in *Der Zar lässt sich photographieren* is evident. In example 5e, most of the harmonic material consists of the trichords 3–5 and 3–9. In example 5f, 3–9 appears as the exclusive accompanimental trichord, harmonizing a bass line which ascends a minor tenth from G to B♭ (and repeating its final steps in the last two measures of the excerpt).

Examples 6a through 6h explore 3–5's role as the clearly delineated subset of larger sonorities in the Violin Concerto. In the opening of the work (ex. 6a), 3–5 (F-B♭-E) is presented by the brass (E by the trumpet, B♭

Example 6. Larger sonorities in Weill's Violin Concerto
a. Mvt. 1, opening.
b. Mvt. 1, mm. 45–46 and mm. 136–37.
c. Mvt. 1, mm. 53–54 (also in m. 49).
d. Mvt. 1, mm. 15–16.
e. Mvt. 1, mm. 65–67.

Example 6 continued
f. Mvt. 1, mm. 6–8.
g. Mvt. 3, m. 51.
h. Mvt. 3, mm. 41–43.

and F by the horns); the coupling of this trichord with brass color is consistent in six of these eight excerpts, the exceptions being 6g and 6h. In example 6a, 3–5 is rhythmically combined with the bassoons' C and D♯ to form a five-note sonority. The disposition of this five-note sonority (brass plus bassoons) is the same in examples 6b through 6e. Other instruments, however, make differing pitch contributions to give rise to a variety of even larger sonorities. (In ex. 6c, the piano reduction does not indicate the contrabasses' A below the bassoons.) In example 6f, the brass trichord remains the same, but the bassoons offer C and D♭, rather than C and D♯; this five-note set combines with the upper voices (clarinets) to generate a melodically embellished seven-note sonority.

In examples 6g and 6h, the pitch content of 3–5 remains the same, but the orchestration changes to create two interesting situations. In example 6g, as in the preceding examples, E is taken by the trumpet, while B♭ is allotted to one of the horns. Here, however, the F, which had been the property of the other horn, is shared by the bassoon and contrabass. The second horn is now given a D♯, and, by virtue of this choice, the brass are able to present a different form of 3–5 (B♭-D♯-E). In example 6h, 3–5 is coupled with woodwind color: B♭ in the clarinet, lower F in the oboe, and octave Es in the bassoons; the piano reduction omits the doubling of F

Example 6 continued
i. Mvt. 1, mm. 187–93.
j. Author's reduction.

and B♭ in the upper octave by the other clarinet and the two flutes. Even in the simplified picture presented by the piano reduction in Example 6i, the importance of 3–5 and 3–9 is readily apparent. My reduction of measure 190 (the two top staves of ex. 6j), which includes all notes except the melodic top voice, reveals the true multiplicity of forms within the texture. These forms are displayed on the bottom staff of ex. 6j. Example 7 contains several instances of 3–5 and 3–9 as harmonic building blocks in *Der Zar.* In the third measure of example 7a, two forms of 3–9 combine to form a six-note chord built from perfect fourths. The excerpt also features 3–9 and 3–5 as subsets of five-note sonorities within a large-scale linear connection (semitone motion) which spans the last five measures of the example. It is particularly significant that the five-note set which contains 3–5 (measure 52) is precisely the same as that which we have already observed in the Violin Concerto (Examples 6a through 6e); here, however, the low D♯ appears as the enharmonically equivalent E♭.

In example 7b, a four-note chord is created by the conjunction of a melodic line and an accompanimental trichord (3–9). In example 7c, a four-note accompanimental chord containing 3–9 as a conspicuous subset is created at a point of melodic repose, sustained for two measures, and repeated after two measures. The well-emphasized harmonic goal in example 7d is again a four-note chord formed by A♭ and the trichord 3–5 (C-D♭-G), with the trichord initially distinct rhythmically from the "added note." (I would not necessarily advocate classifying all of these larger sonorities as significant harmonic structures; to describe Weill's harmony solely in terms of vertical pitch combinations is to ignore the generative role of melody. On the other hand, to describe Weill's harmony exclusively in terms of melodic connections is to ignore the fundamental role of certain harmonic combinations.)

Example 8 deals with one such harmonic combination, the tetrachord (four-note set) 4–23. (Remember that the "4" indicates that there are four pitches; "23" refers to its position on Forte's list. There are twenty-nine distinct four-note sets.) In example 8a, the addition of a note either a fourth below or a fourth above 3–9 will yield 4–23. (The two forms are, of course, inversionally related.) In example 8b, the beginning of a section from *Der Zar*, 3–9 combines with the pitch C to form 4–23. Example 8c contains many occurrences of 3–9; it also features what could be called a harmonic rhyme. At the end of the first system, the accompanimental 3–9 (A♭-B♭-E♭) combines with the voice's quarter-note D-flats (the fourth above) to form 4–23. At the end of the second system, the same trichord combines with the voice's quarter-note Fs (the fourth below) to create another form of 4–23.

The third indicator of a pitch combination's significance is its tendency to be used linearly (melodically) as well as vertically (harmonically). Example 9 explores such melodic usage of the trichords under consideration in the Violin Concerto. In example 9a, 3–5 is prominent both melodically and harmonically. The bass line contains three melodic statements of 3–5. The third (F-E-A♯) is the retrograde of the second (B♭-E-F); A♯ is actually spelled B♭ in the full score. This is precisely the pitch content seen in the harmonic combinations of example 6. Of the five harmonic appearances of 3–5 indicated, the last deserves special mention for its role in sectionalization: it is reached as a harmonic goal immediately preceding the re-entry of the violin. In examples 9b and 9c, 3–5 is also melodically prominent in the bass line; in 9b two forms (G♯-A-

Example 7. Larger sonorities in *Der Zar lässt sich photographieren*
a. 8 measures before 53.
b. 6 measures after 19.

D and G♯-D-C♯) overlap. In example 9d, such overlapping occurs in the
top voice and extends to four forms of 3–5. Conspicuous again is the
pitch combination F-E-B♭. In example 9e, the horn's melodic line contains this combination as well, with one enharmonic respelling: B♭-F-F♭.
The elaboration of the stepwise motion from F to F♭ (by the eighth notes
A and B♭) creates a second form of 3–5 "in the foreground," and a third
form (B♭-F♭-E♭) follows.

Example 10 shows that such melodic usage can be found in *Der Zar*
as well. Examples 10a and 10b contain overlapping melodic forms of 3–5.
Early in example 10c, the "melodic" voice within the accompaniment

c.

d.

Example 7. continued
c. 5 measures before 97.
d. 2 measures before 99.

Example 8. A consistently important tetrachord
a. Derivation of 4–23 from 3–9.
b. *Der Zar lässt sich photographieren.*
c. *Der Zar lässt sich photographieren.*

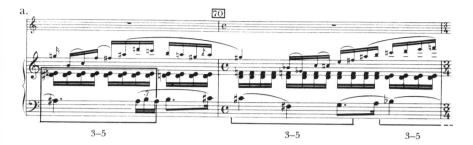

Example 9. Melodic usage of 3–5 in Weill's Violin Concerto
a. Mvt. 1, mm. 69–76.
b. Mvt. 1, m. 24.

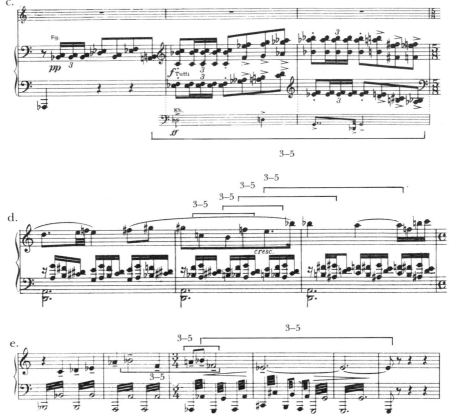

Example 9 continued
c. Mvt. 2c (Serenata), mm. 25–27.
d. Mvt. 1, mm. 31–33.
e. Mvt. 1, mm. 129–34.

features five overlapping occurrences of 3–5, coupled with a distinctive rhythm. The Czar then sings 3–5 ("Madame ich sitze"); I have enclosed the C, not part of the trichord, in parentheses to reflect its role as an "embellishing tone" to the G. Although the false Angèle is an impostor in the opera, perhaps we can accept her reductive analysis here. She sings 3–5 ("Endlich sitzen sie"), a transposition of the Czar's statement, but without embellishment. The excerpt concludes with another melodic statement by the Czar, with the intervals reordered.

Several instances of the continuing employment of these trichords in the post-cusp *Mahagonny Songspiel* are presented in example 11. Kim

Example 10. Melodic usage of 3–5 in *Der Zar lässt sich photographieren*
a. 2 measures after 99 .
b. 4 measures after 100 .
c. 97 .

Example 10c continued

Kowalke has written of this work that "the harmonic language remains remarkably similar to that of *Der Zar* and *Royal Palace,* but the clarity of texture, vitality of rhythms, and unobscured tonal implications of the bass-line make the overall idiom seem simpler."[20] In example 11a, 3–5 and 3–9 seem to be "connective tissue" within a tonal framework. In Example 11b, where 3–5 is a cadential prefix to a C-minor triad, the situation is not unlike that at the close of Schoenberg's song, op. 14/1 (ex. 4). The presence of 3–5 and 3–9 within larger sonorities is apparent in examples 11d through 11f.

By way of conclusion, example 12 offers a summary of three ways in

20. Kowalke, p. 286.

Example 11. Weill, *Mahagonny Songspiel*

a. 2 measures before 32 .

b. 15 measures after 32 .

c. 8 measures after 60 .

d. 43 .

e. 4 measures after 44 .

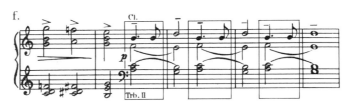

Example 11 continued
f. 2 measures after 45.

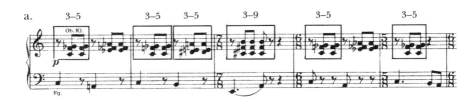

Example 12. The *Threepenny* connection
a. Violin Concerto, mvt. 3, mm. 243–47.
b. *Die Dreigroschenoper*, Polly's Lied, opening.
c. *Mahagonny Songspiel*, 6 measures after 39.

which our two trichords may be used. Example 12a shows these trichords as independent entities within the Violin Concerto. Example 12b, from *Die Dreigroschenoper*, shows these combinations as "substitutions" within a tonal context. Finally, in example 12c, 3–5 (Ab-Db-G) and 3–9 (Ab-Db-Gb) serve as linear embellishments within a tonal framework and, as such, point directly back, across another composer's cusp, to opus 14 of Schoenberg.

This limited discussion of only two three-note building blocks demonstrates that the historical evidence linking the music of Weill and Schoenberg at diverse points in their respective careers is reflected by some similarities within their compositional idioms before their paths diverged so radically. Before more far-reaching conclusions about a Weill-Schoenberg connection can be drawn, however, the harmonic language of Weill and his contemporaries must be subjected to the same comprehensive scrutiny Schoenberg's has received. Then it might be possible to demonstrate analytically, with confidence that similarities were not merely elements shared by a whole generation of composers, Alexander Ringer's claim that "Kurt Weill and Arnold Schoenberg did not really stand as far apart as might appear at first blush."

8

Music as Metaphor: Aspects of *Der Silbersee*
IAN KEMP

Der Silbersee is a play with music. What is a play with music? Kaiser's and Weill's interpretation may be a familiar one, but it is no less deliberate for that: the genre should involve the extraordinary or the supernatural. It will have no justification unless music is *necessary*—in other words, unless it is pitched at a level where words and music are interdependent or where rational, explicative words embody tensions that can find release only in irrational, revelatory music. This is the conceptual basis of *Der Silbersee,* and the work's subtitle, "fairy-tale," is thus of crucial significance. Why did Kaiser and Weill write a fairy-tale? They certainly wanted to write something which would become popular; but their deeper reason, one may suppose, was that they wanted to recreate a myth.

A fairy-tale has its forest and castle, its banquet and ball, its miracle, its happy ending. *Der Silbersee* has all these in one way or another. Kaiser described it as a *"Wintermärchen,"* a winter fairy-tale, and considering that the work was written in 1932, it could hardly not have been affected by that bleak time. Its hero, exploited like Cinderella, is unemployed and starving. His image of transcendent beauty is not a princess but a pineapple. He steals a pineapple. His wound is not a prick from a spindle but a bullet in the leg. After a crisis of conscience, the policeman who shot him becomes the good fairy (his ministrations made possible by the appearance of miraculous riches at the hands of a lottery agent), and the hero recuperates in a castle—not, however, in the stillness of sleep, but in a turmoil of vengeance against his (as yet incognito) assailant. Eventually he masters his emotions and is reconciled with his benefactor, but not before he has let in the wicked witch, a loathsome fascist, who swindles the policeman of his castle and riches and leaves them both to a hopeless fate. So it is an upside-down fairy-tale, but all is put right at the end with that extraordinary twist where the hero and the policeman are redeemed by the kiss of the princess or, here, by the voice of the anima.

The important question emerging from this is not so much *how* Weill interpreted the genre as *why* a composer who had been almost contemptuously opposed to the idea of fantasy in the theater should now commit himself to a work depending on just that. Against all the odds, *Der Silbersee* ends with a transformation scene, in which the tone is switched from stark reality to magic—a revelation of the power of the human spirit to transcend its earthly miseries and strive after paradise. Furthermore, the agent of this catharsis is Goethe's *Ewigweibliche* (in *Der Silbersee,* the voice of the young girl Fennimore). Of course, 1932 was a Goethe centenary year; but this can hardly have meant much to artists driven by a moral imperative to speak to their own time rather than pay homage to the great departed. Of course, Kaiser was an expressionist, and the power of the human spirit (*Geist*) was precisely what his earlier plays had been attempting to uphold; but this hardly explains why in *Der Silbersee* he suppresses the idea throughout, only to release it abruptly at the end. The obvious answer to the question remains the best one. The situation in Germany in 1932 had become so ominous that it was already too late to use the theater to condemn the society which had brought this about or to alert audiences to imminent danger. All that could be done was to make a direct and dramatic appeal to the deepest layers of humanity, offering a psychological truth more enduring than anything Hitler could serve up: offering it, moreover, in his terms. Hitler traded in vengeance and retribution. In Kaiser's and Weill's "winter's tale" these emotions are mastered by friendship and trust, and the result is not disaster, but wonder. This is the modern myth of *Der Silbersee.*

As far as Weill was concerned, his artistic standpoint had now shifted toward the romantic aesthetic that art embodies the universal and that messages about the universal can be transmitted subliminally and symbolically. His profound message of hope was not to be impeded by too sharp a focus on the particulars of contemporary politics. So his music no longer protests or provokes: it engages the audience's sympathies. Instead of reporting, it interprets. It no longer interrupts the narrative: it carries the narrative. When Weill does make a sharp political point in his earlier manner, as in the "Ballade von Cäsars Tod," which is placed at the focal point of the whole work, the effect is stunning because it is so unexpected.

Weill's withdrawal from epic theater into the so-called theater of illusion coincided with a comparable process in Kaiser, but from the opposite direction. For Kaiser, *Der Silbersee* represented a repudiation of what might be termed Social Expressionism in favor of Social Realism. "Kaiser, who had tried to avoid in his plays direct references to contemporary historical and political events, could no longer close his eyes to the existing conditions."[1] Thus, while *Der Silbersee* remains, in essence, a variant of Kaiser's central theme of the regeneration of the individual

1. Ernst Schürer, *Georg Kaiser* (New York, 1971), p. 136.

thwarted by society, that society is portrayed more incisively. In addition to the warning to Hitler in the "Ballad of Caesar's Death," there are exposés of an amoral police force, of commercial malpractices, of a corrupt and decadent aristocracy, which nevertheless will outlive the political upheavals that inconvenience it from time to time. Kaiser's and Weill's paths met in *Der Silbersee*, which accounts for the peculiar electricity of this, their last collaboration.

The collaboration came about because, after the disappointing response to *Die Bürgschaft*, Weill probably wanted both to write a more popular piece and to work with a better librettist than Caspar Neher. One of the ideas he considered was an operatic version of Kaiser's *Die jüdische Witwe*, a somewhat scandalous updating of the apocryphal story of Judith. This was not so surprising as it might seem; after all, by slaughtering Holofernes (read Hitler), Judith saves the Jewish nation. Although this idea was dropped, as was the really surprising idea of a musical version of *Das Kabinett des Dr. Caligari* with a libretto by Kaiser, the important considerations here were that Weill had reacted against his previous theatrical works (overreacted, as it turned out, since the eventual *Der Silbersee* is closer in spirit to *Die Bürgschaft* than to *Die jüdische Witwe*) and that he was thinking of reviving his collaboration with Kaiser. He approached Kaiser in July 1932. Kaiser quickly developed a plan for an entirely new work. This would be not an opera, but something in-between, which, as Weill preferred, would involve fairly large musical resources and be of a difficulty comparable to Offenbach's operettas. Operettas were, of course, good business in the financially strapped German theater of the early 1930s, but Weill was more concerned with a clear-cut departure from the *Dreigroschenoper* genre, with its simpler songs sung by singing-actors. By the beginning of August, they had prepared a draft of "a kind of modern fairy-tale," rather like a *Singspiel*. By the middle of the month, an exact design had been worked out with the musical numbers set in place. By November the whole work was complete.[2]

2. This paragraph is drawn from letters Weill wrote to Universal Edition, Vienna. The following excerpts are reprinted by kind permission of the Kurt Weill Foundation for Music. Letter of 29 July 1932: "Kaiser will mir ein musikalisches Volksstück schreiben. . . . Es soll keinesfalls eine Oper werden, sondern ein Zwischengattungsstück. Es bleibt mir vorbehalten, ob ich daraus ein 'Stück mit Musik,' also mit ganz einfachen Liedern mache, die von reinen Schauspielern gesungen werden können, oder ob ich doch mit etwas grösseren musikalischen Ansprüchen herangehe und eine Musik im Umfang und im Schwierigkeitsgrad etwa einer Offenbach-Musiquette schreibe. Das letztere würde mich mehr reizen, weil ich hier über den in der *Dreigroschenoper* geschaffenen Typus hinausgehen könnte." Letter of 2 August 1932: "Wir haben den Entwurf eines sehr schönen Stückes fertig, eine Art von modernem Märchen. . . . Es handelt sich keineswegs um eine Oper, sondern um ein Stück mit gut eingebauten Musiknummern, etwa in der Art eines Singspiels." Letter of 15 August 1932: "Wir . . . haben jetzt schon die ganze Handlung bis in die

The authors' intentions are already apparent from the title, *Der Silbersee: Ein Wintermärchen,* which subtly combines the idea of popular appeal with that of social criticism. "Der Silbersee" sounds beguiling on its own account; but, in addition, it is an allusion to *Der Schatz im Silbersee* (The Treasure in the Silver Lake), a story by the most popular of all popular writers in Germany, Karl May (1842–1912). May specialized in Westerns—in which respect Kaiser was exploiting the vogue for all things American in the Weimar Republic—and provided German expansionist instincts with much to feed on: romanticized descriptions of the Wild West, continuous action (especially the gratuitously violent), struggles for power and wealth in which the only "good guys" among white men are Germans, who alone can draw out the nobility of the Indians. Hitler regarded May very highly. The treasure of *Der Schatz im Silbersee* is both mythical, a kind of Holy Grail (here, riches hidden by the Indians in a submerged city), and real, namely a silver mine. The heroes find the latter but not the former. Whether or not Kaiser is inferring that they should have kept to the former can only be guessed at. His allusions to *Deutschland: Ein Wintermärchen,* Heine's bitterest commentary on Germany, and to Shakespeare's *Winter's Tale,* which, like *Der Silbersee,* sets gross inhumanity against miraculous fantasy, must be intentional, however.

As is well known, the premiere of *Der Silbersee* on 18 February 1933 in Leipzig (with simultaneous premieres in Erfurt and Magdeburg) was an outstanding success, despite Nazi barracking. Hitler had been chancellor for only a fortnight; but on 28 February, the day after the Reichstag fire, he promulgated a decree suspending all civil liberties. A Leipzig performance on 4 March was canceled, and all future performances of the works of both Kaiser and Weill were banned. *Der Silbersee* has not been performed intact since.[3]

Einzelheiten wie auch die geistige Grundlage des Ganzen volkommen festgelegt. . . . Ich habe bereits die Stellen, an denen die Musiknummern stehen sollen, und den Charakter dieser Musiknummern genau festgelegt."

3. A mutilated version was staged in Berlin in 1955, and there were concert versions at the Holland Festival in 1971 and the Berlin Festival in 1975. None of these represented the real *Der Silbersee.* In 1980 the New York City Opera mounted an adaptation entitled *Silverlake,* which had even less to do with the original. In 1982 the departments of music and drama of the University of Manchester, England, mounted *The Silver Lake,* in an English translation by Raymond Furness, with student actors and musicians. This was an attempt to be faithful to the original, although the actors' singing parts were assigned to a group of four soloists positioned within the orchestra and independent of the stage action. In this respect the production was not the real *Der Silbersee* either. But it convinced the present writer, who initiated and conducted the performances, that such a production is feasible. This was also the view of Stephen Walsh of the *London Observer,* who wrote (20 June 1982) that the work "can very well stand up in its own clothes, patches and all." The production of *Der Silbersee* in Zurich during 1983 utilized a greatly condensed script and a compromised musical text. [During 1985 *Der Silbersee* was produced as a play with music (with some cuts in dialogue) in Gera and Karl-Marx-Stadt in East Germany and in Recklinghausen in West Germany.]

Why this is so may be ascribed in part to its casting demands. There are roles for four principal actors, of whom two must be able to sing very well and two moderately well, and five supporting actors, four of whom must also sing moderately well. In addition, there are parts for seven other actors, two of whom must sing tolerably well, and there are walk-on parts, an orchestra of at least thirty, and a chorus to match. No opera company has been able to cast the work. It was written for theater companies with access to the resources of affiliated opera houses in German cities. Even so, more theater companies might have mounted the work, one suspects, had Kaiser's reputation not been in decline since the late twenties.

Given its hybrid characteristics, any reassessment of *Der Silbersee* must begin with its text. Every one of *Der Silbersee*'s political points has remained topical, so the oft-cited objection that the work is a period piece can be dismissed, as can the irrelevant objection that Kaiser does not write like Brecht.[4] A criticism that *does* merit consideration is that the work is simply too long. There may be a need to make small cuts in order to prevent it from extending beyond four hours' playing time. But this criticism is really a veiled objection to either Kaiser's dramatic pacing or the quality of his material. It should be remembered here that any such contemporary criticism is of necessity based only on readings of his text and is therefore one-dimensional. Kaiser was nothing if not a man of the theater (*Der Silbersee* was his fortieth stage work). His understanding of such matters as scenic effect, lighting, dramatic pacing, and the tone of a scene was as highly developed as he was experienced. If the quality of his dramatic pacing must remain an open question until the work has been given a professional production in its original form, it should all the same be noted that *Der Silbersee* is inherently episodic, a method of construction which opposes continuous flow and which is entirely appropriate to a fairy-tale, where the important thing is what happens or, more exactly, what happens next. Characters come and go with the logic of a dream. The story twists and turns, and then straightens out.

Der Silbersee is a play with music: not only does the music itself bind this episodic material together, but the relationship between words and music is carefully controlled so that neither dominates; there emerges a structural cohesion with a strength of its own. This is illustrated in example 1. Some scenes have no music, some have occasional music, others are framed by music (notably the first, where the tone of the work has to be established from the start), and others have more or less or actually continuous music. Kaiser was obviously well aware of how the presence of music would influence the design, as well as the substance, of his text. A hierarchy of values can be perceived, where music is present in propor-

4. See, however, Ernst Schürer, *Georg Kaiser und Bertolt Brecht* (Frankfurt, 1971).

ACT I
Scene   Overture
1 Forest
2 Shop
3 Ditch
4 Police Station
5 Hospital

ACT II   Prelude 7a
1 Castle Gates
2 Inside Castle
3 Banqueting Hall
4 Luber's Bedroom
5 Fennimore's Bedroom
6 Hall

ACT III   Introduction 13
1 Attic
2 Cellar
3 Banqueting Hall
4 Ditch
5 Forest

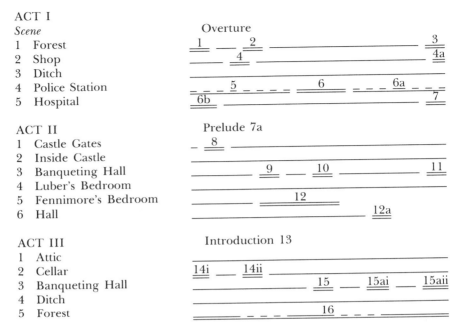

Example 1. The structure of *Der Silbersee* (Single lines indicate dialogue; double lines music; dotted and continuous lines, melodrama. Numbers refer to the musical numbers in Weill's score.)

tion to the degree of human feeling. In act 1, scene 3, the police are revealed as amoral puppets, capable of panicking and committing murder. What has music to do with that? In the next scene Olim, the policeman who has shot Severin, gains a conscience—the stuff of music—and music predominates.

Singing is apportioned in a similar hierarchy. The most sympathetic and human characters are Severin, Fennimore (the young niece of the villainous Frau von Luber), and Olim.[5] Severin, the central figure representing the underprivileged and dispossessed, has the most (and the most varied) music to sing. Fennimore hardly speaks at all: she expresses her-

---

5. Kaiser chose his names with care. Unlike the heroes of Karl May, Kaiser's present an international front. Fennimore seems American, recalling James Fenimore Cooper, the author of the original Westerns. (She is not however a Cooper heroine, being neither pale and virginal nor dark and sensual. She is a tougher version of both types, a modern woman whose very name confounds sexual stereotyping). Olim is Latin for "once upon a time." Severin sounds French, perhaps a reference to a character in one of the novels of the French imitator of Cooper, Gustave Aimard (1818–83). Only Kaiser's villains are given German names.

self almost entirely through music.[6] Olim sings only once, but his developing humanity is expressed through melodrama. As for the other characters, some are magnified, others are caricatured, others are affectionate vignettes. The two shopgirls, who are obliged to subscribe to a commercial practice they despise, have one song, as do the two lads, who at the beginning of the work dig a grave for an effigy of hunger. By this line of reasoning, the unsavory characters should not have been given any music at all. The Fat Policeman indeed has none. The tango for the Lottery Agent (who embodies a familiar dramatic device in Kaiser's works) could be justified on the grounds that an important turning point in the story must be emphasized by music. But there is no reason why Frau von Luber and her paramour Baron Laur should finally get a unison duet. It seems that Kaiser and Weill were not entirely consistent. *Der Silbersee* contains relics of Weill's earlier manner, in which respect it is a transitional work and an especially poignant reminder of what might have been.

Kaiser's ability to integrate and capitalize on the dramatic potential of music—to use it as dramatic catalyst—can best be demonstrated by narrowing the focus to a single scene, where his economy of writing, his skillful interweaving of various threads, symbolic and concrete, and his taut structure can be analyzed in some detail. It may be tendentious to draw attention to scene 3 of act 2, for certainly there are others with less theatrical impact. But Kaiser's and Weill's genius here in using music to control dramatic tension is undeniable and may be taken as representative of its presence elsewhere.

Recovering from his wound, Severin is consumed with thoughts of vengeance upon the policeman who shot him, not knowing that Olim, whom he treats with sullen indifference, is that same policeman. Olim seeks gratitude for his philanthropy and will do anything to gain it. He provides a castle for his charge's recovery and an expensive doctor, who has prescribed a distraction, namely music, to help Severin overcome his black moods. Frau von Luber, hired as housekeeper, has told Olim that she can provide what is required in the form of Fennimore, who plays the harp, an instrument traditionally associated with both chaste sweetness and healing. Thus the stage is set for a banquet at which Severin will be soothed by Fennimore's playing. Fennimore duly completes the picture by appearing dressed in pink, with almond blossoms in her hair. She is asked what she is going to play. The answer is "Caesar's Death!" Accompanying herself on the harp, she sings her song: strident, knowing, menacing. Her strokes on the harp sound like the sharpening of a knife.

---

6. In *Im Banne des Expressionismus* (Leipzig, 1926), p. 667, Albert Soergel wrote of Kaiser's early plays, and of *Die jüdische Witwe* in particular, that "those who live, don't speak, and those who speak, don't live" [reden die nicht, die leben, leben nur die, die nicht reden.]

This coup de theatre astonishes both the audience and the characters on stage. Fennimore's song infuriates Frau von Luber, who had planned that her niece would seduce Olim and thus extract the secret of his strange behavior from him. It embarrasses Olim, whose hopes for Severin's gratitude are confounded. And it fuels Severin's lust for vengeance. Fennimore is told to make amends for her tasteless performance. She offers a dance executed by bread rolls. She says that the rolls on the table are too round for her purposes and that she needs long, pointed ones. She asks for bananas instead. Servants bring a fruit bowl, crowned with a pineapple. Fennimore takes two bananas, sticks a fork in each, and, sitting at the table with her back to the audience, she wiggles the bananas and makes them dance. Their movements can be imagined from the movements of her shoulders. Weill's music is, appropriately, a shimmy, a 1920s foxtrot featuring shaking of the shoulders. All this is an allusion to a famous scene in Chaplin's *Gold Rush* (1924), in which he takes two forks, sticks them into a pair of bread rolls, and, with neat movements of his wrists, performs a dance with forks for legs and bread rolls for boots.[7]

Olim and Frau von Luber find Fennimore's dance extremely amusing; so does Fennimore herself. But the allusion also serves to identify her with Chaplin, the spokesman of the underprivileged, and thus with Severin. By using bananas, she shows, as had Severin with his yearning for a pineapple, that she too can make the imaginative leap from a lifestyle associated with bread rolls to a better one. As for Severin, his eyes are on both bananas-cum-boots, which stir up his resentment that his own feet cannot function normally, and on the pineapple in the fruit bowl, which represents everything he has been denied. His expression grows ever more alarming until he grabs a knife and stabs the pineapple repeatedly. Luber and Fennimore hurriedly depart, while Severin reveals to Olim that he is determined to wreak vengeance on the criminal who destroyed his paradise. This is the first time he has explained his behavior to anyone, and his pent-up fury now floods into his vengeance aria, which ends the scene. Severin's fury is not impotent, for the scene has introduced him to an ally, and it is through Fennimore that he will discover the identity of his assailant and the basis for reconciliation.

Given a dramatist of the caliber demonstrated here, it is not surprising that Weill should have been stimulated to write some of his finest and

---

7. In *Gold Rush* Chaplin has invited his girlfriend and her three companions to a New Year's Eve dinner party in his little shack in snow-swept Alaska. They have not turned up, but in a dream sequence Chaplin imagines that they have. By way of after-dinner entertainment, he performs the dance described in the text above. *Gold Rush* could conceivably have given Kaiser and Weill the idea for the whole of *Der Silbersee* and not merely this one episode.

most expressive music in *Der Silbersee*. (It is not surprising either that he should have reworked some of it in his next two scores, *Die sieben Tod-sünden* and Symphony no. 2). The most significant consequence of Kaiser's ability to grade between dialogue and musical number, as in the scene just described, was the melodrama, where the two are combined. Melodrama is a dramatic technique particularly associated with operas of the late eighteenth and early nineteenth centuries, and here again we find Weill, like all his major contemporaries in the 1930s, coming to terms with his nineteenth-century inheritance. His melodramas may resist the purely illustrative and may still be composed in the self-contained forms of absolute music, but they now admit the imaginative. It is impossible to account for the psychology that lies behind Weill's peculiar compound of ruthless willpower and anxiety to please: maybe it was because he was prepared to accept banality as a norm for modern life, while at the same time having the vision to charge it, via its metaphor in popular song, with precision and passion. The compound itself does, however, begin to explain why his characteristic forms are short and schematic. The essence of large forms is the resolution of conflict; if conflict is intrinsic, nothing much can be done with it beyond presentation.

In this connection *Der Silbersee* is of special interest because, in its melodramas, Weill began to disentangle the components of his inner conflict, the ruthlessness and the charm, and in the process to announce the gradual retreat of the former and the growing strength of the latter. But *Der Silbersee* remains very much a work of Weill's European years, and his subsequent career cannot be extrapolated from the evidence of this score. What its melodramas show in their masterly and economic manipulation of short forms of greatly varied expressive content is the possibility of a more dialectical mode of musical thinking, to be fulfilled in his Symphony no. 2. In the meantime, Weill demonstrated how, with the help of a dramatic scenario, he could make his music breathe. His melodramas sound more extended than they actually are precisely because of their varied expressive content. There are three of them (nos. 5, 6a, and 16). An examination of the last, *Der Silbersee*'s finale, will illustrate some of these points.

The scene is designed in two parts of about equal length, rather like a scena and aria. The first accompanies what Severin and Olim imagine to be their last journey together, to the waters of the silver lake where they will sink into oblivion. The music starts with a chorale accompanied by shivering tremolando lines. A chorale, however bleak, is an expression of faith, and after the perplexed dialogue of Severin and Olim (Why should it be snowing when it has just been raining?), the outcome of the chorale is a kind of benediction from an offstage chorus, which sings a melody of the utmost tenderness, just on the right side of sentimentality. While Severin and Olim seem not to understand what the voices are saying, they now go to their deaths content.

Weill lays out this part in a kind of mirror form, as if to close off that period in their lives. In the central melodrama proper, the instrumental passages diminish in length, gradually capitulating to the influence of the chorus, whose melody is related rhythmically to the chorale and is thus a metaphor for the hope that can spring from darkness. The table below indicates the musical contents of this part. (The middle line indicates musical material; bottom line, number of bars.)

A		B					A	
chorale		melodrama 1					chorale	
orch. (varied repeat)		tr.	chor.	fl.	chor.	cl.	chor.	orch.
a + b a + c		d	e(a$_1$)	d$_1$	e$_1$	d$_2$	b	a
8 + 8 8 + 8(+1)		11	12	7	12	6	7½	8(−1)

Linking the two parts is an eight-bar tutti passage, fortissimo and in the threatening rhythm of no. 5, where it was associated with the transformation of Olim's character. Onstage a sudden, violent storm sweeps away the snow and reveals spring foliage; the lake is frozen and sparkling in the sunshine.

The second part, the transformation scene, is, by contrast with the closed form of the first, an open-ended ABC form, a metaphor this time for burgeoning hope. The introductory melodrama 2 is a transformation of the melodic kernel of melodrama 1; the chorus provides a variant of its earlier melody, while the voice of Fennimore introduces the only real novelty, as it must, for what she sings is the revelation. Weill here has written music which is both the authentic voice of genius and the vernacular of the comrade—a duality entirely characteristic of him. We may also note the skill with which he has ensured that his revelation will be fresh but not arbitrary, for melodrama 2 has been foreshadowed in act 2, scene 5, where Fennimore had shown Severin something of the spirit which drives her on.

A	B				C
melodrama 2	song with choral refrain				coda
trumpet	soprano	chorus	soprano	chorus	tutti
oboe/clarinet	(v. 1)		(v. 2)		
flutes					
g (d)	h	i (e)	h$_1$	h$_2$	h$_3$
2 + 32 + 2	32	24	16	16 + 4	6 + 4 + 16

The structural skill exhibited in this scene is typical of that exhibited on a smaller scale in individual numbers, which similarly are self-contained organisms—sometimes in closed tonal schemes, sometimes in open, according to the dramatic situation. When words and music are so interdependent, it is indeed vital that the music should be coherently organized; otherwise its status, and hence the rationale behind the genre, will be undermined. Weill does not impose an independent, abstract tonal design on his work because perhaps that would be inaudible to most listeners. Instead he uses tonal symbolism to set up a network of relationships determined by common tonalities, themselves determined by expressive considerations. Behind this lies a tradition stretching back to Mozart and Beethoven (and beyond to the baroque). There are four principal tonalities, D, G, E, and E♭, their major and minor modes representing opposites of each other. The central D minor is the tragic tonality, associated with cold and burial: D major is regenerative and spring-like. G minor is associated with anxiety and suppressed anger; G major with calm and peace. E major is the tonality of fantasy or wishful thinking; E minor of stern reality. E♭ major is the tonality of defiant stoicism (an ironic comment on the tonality of *Die Zauberflöte*, the Eroica Symphony, or *Ein Heldenleben*). Other tonalities, notably D♭ major, which represents promise and delight, play their part. These verbal analogues are, to be sure, crude, but they are unlikely to be contentious. Example 2 illustrates the complete network of tonal relationships.

If Weill's tonal organism is conditioned by the need for expression, it follows that the generator of that organism, namely his harmonic language, will be conditioned by the same thing. The agent of expression in *Der Silbersee* remains Weill's harmony. The questions how harmony fulfills this role and what sort of expression emerges from it are best approached through his harmonic progressions. A theoretical basis for an under-

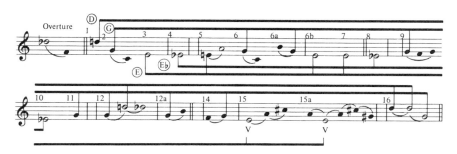

Example 2. Network of tonal relationships in *Der Silbersee* (Numerals indicate musical numbers; see Example 1. Single barlines indicate scenes; double barlines, acts. White notes indicate major tonalities; black notes, minor.)

Example 3. Der Silbersee, no. 4: Duet for two shopgirls

standing of them would begin by taking note of their inclination to drop to the flat side of a tonic. This is a consequence of Weill's fondness for root progressions which move from the tonic to the subdominant, to the subdominant of the subdominant, and so on, in bass patterns of downward-moving perfect fifths. Example 3 provides a simple eight-bar illustration. The force of such progressions is so strong that the bass sounds like a root, even if technically it is not: the fourth harmony in example 3 is actually a first inversion of an E minor chord, although it sounds like G because of the bass progression. Other instances of this phenomenon (see ex. 4) underline a characteristic ambivalence in Weill, where implication is stronger than fact.

The influence of the subdominant naturally affects Weill's harmonic vocabulary as well, and it gives rise to a particular chord which bears his

Example 4. Der Silbersee
a. No. 2: March for the effigy of hunger.
b. No. 12: Severin-Fennimore duet.

a-1.

a-2.

a-3.

b.

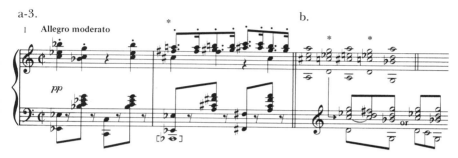

Example 5. Der Silbersee
a-1. No. 12, from the introduction.
a-2. No. 7a (Introduction to Act 2).
a-3. No. 10, Fennimore's Dance.
b. Chord progression of the introduction to no. 12.

imprint almost as strongly as any other. This is a subdominant with a leaning towards its own subdominant, as in the putative completion of the implied progression (see ex. 5b). The chord in question is marked with an asterisk in the passages given in example 5a.

The consequences of subdominant attraction may be pursued by constructing a model of the possible relationships. Example 6 treats C as tonic and illustrates (1) subdominant, (2) subtonic—subdominant of subdominant, (3) flat mediant, and (4) flat submediant relationships. The remaining relationships are considered later.

Example 6. Possible subdominant relationships

Weill is especially fond of chord pairs combining 1 and 2 (see ex. 5), and, in the process, of more extended progressions from tonic to sub-

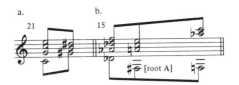

Example 7. Der Silbersee
a. No. 2.
b. No. 16 (Melodrama 2).

dominant and, most characteristically, from tonic to subtonic. This last is perhaps the most individual of all his progressions, appearing many times in all his post-1927 European works. Example 5a-1 presents a simple example from *Der Silbersee*. Others include the introduction to the "Ballad of Caesar's Death" and the junction between the melodrama of no. 5 and the tango for the Lottery Agent, no. 6. It is not surprising to find that Weill pursues the implications of subtonic emphasis by favoring progressions to the subtonic of the subtonic (flat submediant) relationships. Instances of this can be found, for example, within the introduction to Severin's "Ulysses" song, or, more dramatically, in the coda to his vengeance aria, a progression from B minor to G minor. Flat submediant relationships are also common in chord pairs, where they function as expressive color (see ex. 7).

There remains the flat mediant relationship, 3 in example 6. This is not so common, but it is present. Example 8a provides a more complex example than before, an interweaving of A minor and C minor. Example 8b illustrates flat relationships in combination.

Example 8b introduces another progression, E to E♭, a descending semitone. Example 6 shows that this is the last in the cycle of downward fifths, or, to put it another way, the fifth in a cycle of upward fifths. The

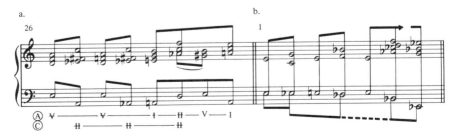

Example 8. Der Silbersee
a. No. 9 (The Ballad of Caesar's Death).
b. No. 5 (Olim's melodrama).

Example 9. Der Silbersee
a. No. 9 (The Ballad of Caesar's Death).
b. No. 5.
c. No. 16 (Melodrama 2).

last three steps in both cycles yield exactly the same notes, though in reverse order. Therefore, when any one of these progressions is used, it is not clear from which direction it has been approached, and accordingly the effect of such relationships is ambiguous, disorienting, or even fantastic. Example 9 indicates (a) Caesar's amazement that he is being murdered, (b) Olim's disturbing conscience, and (c) Severin's and Olim's wonder at the miracle of the frozen lake.

I have already begun to suggest how Weill's harmony achieves its expressive effects. To draw a bolder conclusion, it may be said that it does so by perfectly traditional means, capitalizing on the inherited expressive associations of upward or downward cycles of fifths. (Upward cycles do exist in Weill's music, but they are not characteristic.) Tonal direction towards the flat side of a tonic has always been associated with introversion, darkening, pessimism, tragedy—away from a positive, dynamic way of seeing things. Weill's European music may be characterized as fundamentally tragic. But, and this is the important point, he also and persistently injects his music with colorings from the sharp side, as most of my examples illustrate. He accepts the tragic and will not accept it. He accepts the banality of life and resists it. In these contradictions lie the peculiar tensions of his musical language and the poignancy of *Der Silbersee*.[8]

8. The author thanks Christopher Hailey, J. M. Ritchie, and Rhys Williams for help in preparing this paper.

9

Weill and Berg:
Lulu as
Epic Opera
DOUGLAS JARMAN

In his essay "Tradition and Reform in Opera," Carl Dahlhaus contrasts
the work of Weill and Brecht, which he cites as typifying the way in which
progressive artists of the 1920s and 1930s reacted against the Wagnerian
ideal, with Alban Berg's *Wozzeck*, which "must be understood in relation
to the tradition of Wagner's music dramas," since Berg "took over almost
unchanged the idea of music dramas, the principle that music is a means
of serving the drama."[1] Dahlhaus is here expressing the generally accepted view of the operatic situation in Germany during the period between
the wars: a view, on the one hand, of Weill—representing the new socially
conscious opera, an opera with a new simplicity of content and means of
expression, an opera that would reach a wide audience—and, on the
other hand, of Berg—representing a continuation of the traditional Wagnerian music drama, opera which maintains the traditional relationship
between music and text and which uses a complicated and advanced
musical language to arouse the traditional (what Weill and Brecht sometimes called "narcotic") emotional response, appealing only to an elite.

It is a view that was generally held by Berg's and Weill's own contemporaries. When Erich Kleiber mounted a new production of *Wozzeck* at
the Berlin Staatsoper in November 1932, Max Marschalk, the critic of the
Vossische Zeitung, wrote:

> From this distance we can see that the new opera has two main paths. One
> path goes from Wagner through Strauss to Berg, where it seems to have
> ended for the moment. The other, going from Musorgsky and Debussy to
> Janácek and Stravinsky and then on to Milhaud and Kurt Weill, is the really
> modern and new path. The essential difference becomes clear at two points.
> Berg holds himself aloof from the modern epic theater—although Büch-
> ner's *Wozzeck*, with its loosely ordered succession of short scenes and the
> cold, objective attitude of the poet toward his characters, stands close to the
> repressed emotions of epic theater.

1. Carl Dahlhaus, "Tradition and Reform in Opera," *Esthetics of Music*, trans. William
Austin (Cambridge, Eng., 1982), p. 69.

Through his music, however, Berg turns the whole of the drama into something emotional . . . just as earlier operas did. Stravinsky and Weill write music against the words; Berg composes wholly from within the words, drawing from their emotional content a psychological, poeticizing music.[2]

Weill had seen *Wozzeck* in a similar light. Reviewing the Berlin premiere of the opera in 1925, Weill called *Wozzeck* "a masterpiece of tremendous power" and described the performance as "the greatest event in Berlin's musical life for many years."[3] He regarded the work, however, as "the grandiose conclusion" to the Wagnerian tradition.[4] Unlike Busoni's *Doktor Faust*, which he believed could become the starting point for a new golden age of opera, Weill saw *Wozzeck* as a work that had little relevance to what he himself hoped to achieve in the "new opera."

The view that places Weill and Berg at opposite poles of German opera at that time is, of course, supported by what we know of the very different aesthetic positions adopted by Weill and the Second Viennese School. In his "Notiz zum Berliner Requiem" which Weill published in May 1929, he remarked that "content and form [of radio compositions] must be capable of interesting a large number of people of all classes, and the means of musical expression also must not cause any difficulty for the untrained listener."[5]

Six months earlier, Arnold Schoenberg, infuriated by an earlier article that Weill had published, had jotted down a remark to the effect that "it is evident that art which treats deeper ideas cannot address itself to the many. Anyone regarding [art for everyone] as possible is unaware how 'everyone' is constituted and how art is constituted."[6] There could, we may feel, be no more succinct summary of the differences between Weill and Schoenberg (and by implication, between Weill and the whole of the Second Viennese School). Admittedly, in his notes on the *Berlin Requiem*, Weill was not talking in general terms, but only about the peculiar problems facing the composer writing a work for radio performance. Yet the difference between the aesthetic, philosophical, and social stances revealed by these two statements is so great that the gap between their authors seems unbridgeable.[7]

2. Max Marschalk, *Vossische Zeitung*, 23 December 1932. Reprinted in K. Vogelsang, *Dokumentation zur Oper "Wozzeck" von Alban Berg* (Regensburg, 1977), p. 113.

3. Kurt Weill, "Alban Berg: *Wozzeck*," *Der deutsche Rundfunk* 3 (27 December 1925): 3422; reprinted in *Ausgewählte Schriften*, ed. David Drew (Frankfurt, 1975), p. 152.

4. Kurt Weill, "Die neue Oper," *Der neue Weg* 55 (16 January 1926): 24–25; trans. by Kim H. Kowalke in *Kurt Weill in Europe* (Ann Arbor, 1979), p. 465.

5. *Der deutsche Rundfunk* 7 (17 May 1929): 613; trans. in Kowalke, p. 504.

6. Arnold Schoenberg, "The Future of Opera" in *Style and Idea*, ed. Leonard Stein (London, 1975), p. 336.

7. For discussion of the Schoenberg-Weill relationship, see Alexander Ringer, "Schoen-

Weill and Marschalk were, I think, correct in their assessment of the historical position of *Wozzeck*. Despite its innovative features, the aesthetics of *Wozzeck* are those of nineteenth-century opera and Wagnerian music drama. Certainly Berg's own remarks about *Wozzeck* in his 1928 article on "The 'Problem of Opera' " reveal in unmistakable terms his allegiance to the Wagnerian aesthetic.[8] The very fact that, as Dahlhaus has noted,[9] Berg places the phrase "Problem of Opera" in quotation marks in the title of his essay suggests that he did not even accept the notion that such a problem existed.

In 1928, the same year that Berg wrote "The 'Problem of Opera,' " *Die Dreigroschenoper* received its first performance, and Berg himself began work on a new opera, *Lulu*. Until very recently we have known Berg's second opera only as a two-act fragment, and our approach to the incomplete *Lulu* has inevitably been affected by our knowledge and our fuller understanding of the complete *Wozzeck*. With the crucial third act of *Lulu* in its place, we can now see that the later opera functions dramatically in a way that is very different from *Wozzeck* and that even our previous understanding of acts 1 and 2 was falsified by the absence of Act 3. The performance and publication of the complete *Lulu* force us to reassess Berg's operatic achievement and to re-examine our assumptions about Berg's position in relation to that of Weill and the "new opera."

Unlike Schoenberg and Webern, Berg seems to have made no disparaging public observations about Weill's music. For Schoenberg, Weill's music was the "only music in the world" in which he could "find no quality."[10] This opinion, voiced shortly after Weill's phenomenal popular success with *Die Dreigroschenoper,* conflicts greatly with his earlier attitude toward Weill. As for Webern, we know from Dallapiccola that the mere mention of Weill's name was enough to make him explode with anger: "What," he is reported as having said, "do you find of our great Middle-European tradition in such a composer?"[11] Amid all Berg's letters and writings, amid all the reminiscences published by those acquainted with Berg, there are, as far as I know, only two passing references to Weill's works. The two references are almost identical, and both appear in letters

berg, Weill and Epic Theatre," *Journal of the Arnold Schoenberg Institute* 4 (June 1980): 77–98; and Kim H. Kowalke, "Weill, Dallapiccola, and 'Committed' Music," insert notes to the recording of Weill's *Recordare* (Nonesuch 79050).

   8. Alban Berg, "The 'Problem of Opera,' " reprinted in Willi Reich, *Alban Berg* (London, 1965), pp. 63–66.

   9. Dahlhaus, p. 64.

   10. Quoted by Kowalke in *Kurt Weill in Europe*, p. 3.

   11. Luigi Dallapiccola, "Incontri con Anton Webern (1945)," quoted and translated in Hans Moldenhauer, *Anton von Webern: A Chronicle of His Life and Works* (London, 1978), p. 537.

from Berg (respectively to Schoenberg and Universal Edition) written in December 1929 when, worried about the forthcoming production in Essen of *Wozzeck,* Berg half jokingly protested that Caspar Neher's sets for the opera threatened to turn the piece into a "Two-Penny Opera by Neher, after Büchner by Berg."[12]

The lack of any more forthright comment by Berg on Weill is significant. Berg may (if we believe Adorno's account of his reaction to the successful premiere of *Wozzeck*)[13] have shared Schoenberg's distrust of popular acclaim, but it would be wrong to assume that he shared Schoenberg's views on everything else. We know that Berg did not subscribe to Schoenberg's views on the nature of opera (Schoenberg was originally opposed to Berg setting Büchner's *Woyzeck* because he thought that the subject of the play was not fitting for an opera), and there is no reason to believe that Berg endorsed Schoenberg's views on Weill's music or on epic theater. As the most eclectic of the Second Viennese School and the one most aware of and open to outside influences, Berg was prepared to take on board any idea that might be useful for his own work. As a man of the theater, Berg could not afford to ignore and could not fail to be interested in what was happening in the "new opera."

It is possible that Berg, like Schoenberg, knew some of Brecht's and Weill's writings on epic theater in general and perhaps specifically on *Mahagonny.* Berg certainly knew *Mahagonny* itself and attended rehearsals of a greatly abridged studio production when it was being performed in Vienna in 1932; it was conducted by Berg's pupil Gottfried Kassowitz and directed by Hans Heinsheimer of Universal Edition's opera department. If Berg made no public statement on Weill's music or on the "new opera," it was, I suggest, not because of ignorance or because of lack of interest on Berg's part, but because of an unwillingness to dissociate himself publicly from the views of his teacher.

Berg's acquaintance with Weill's work and with the precepts of epic theater may have influenced Berg's own conceptions of *Lulu.* In his article "Schoenberg, Weill and Epic Theatre," Alexander Ringer has suggested that, had it not been for an unfortunate journalistic jeu d'esprit which Weill published in December 1928 (and which provoked Schoenberg to make the remarks quoted earlier), "Berg might have managed to bridge the rapidly widening gap between Weill and Schoenberg."[14] In creative,

12. See E. Hilmar, *"Wozzeck" von Alban Berg* (Vienna, 1975), p. 60. [See, however, Stephen Hinton's citation of a published and not unfavorable reference by Berg to *Die Dreigroschenoper* on p. 80 of this volume.]

13. T. W. Adorno, *Alban Berg: Der Meister des kleinsten Übergangs* (Vienna, 1968), p. 18.

14. Ringer, p. 87. [Ringer based his article on Schoenberg's annotated clipping of Weill's essay in the Arnold Schoenberg Institute in Los Angeles. Ringer surmised: "Conceivably, therefore, Berg might have managed to bridge the rapidly widening gap between Weill and

if not in personal terms, Berg did bridge that gap in his second opera, and it is only an accident of history that has prevented us from seeing *Lulu* as the one work to come from the Second Viennese School in which the ideas of epic opera were fruitfully absorbed into a style and an aesthetic which, at first glance, seems so far removed from them.

In asserting this, I am referring to the basic conception of *Lulu* and to the way in which it works in the theater. I am not referring to the more obvious ways in which Weill's work might have influenced certain aspects of Berg's opera—for example, the similarity (which David Drew has already pointed out) between Berg's use of a silent film to chart the progress of his heroine at the central point of act 2 and Weill's prior use of a film for the same purpose in *Royal Palace,* or Berg's use of jazz, or the fact that the pantomime in act 3, scene 1 of *Lulu* finds its precedents in the two pantomimes of Weill's *Der Protagonist.*[15] Nor, obviously, am I referring to any similarity between the musical language of Berg and Weill. Indeed, the

---

Schoenberg, who was to remember *Wozzeck* so audibly in *Moses und Aron,* had not Weill, buoyed by the frenetic career of *Die Dreigroschenoper,* chosen at the crucial moment to regale his Berlin fans with a journalistic prank, published shortly before the 1928 Christmas holiday under the title 'The Musician Weill,' that made light of everything Schoenberg held dear. Although it was by no means aimed at him, Schoenberg was shocked by this somewhat sophomoric buffoonery of a young colleague brazen enough to deal with serious aesthetic views in the comic manner of a typical German high school lesson parodied down to the last detail, including the typical conditioning ritual of 'Get up . . . sit down . . . get up,' etc., preceding the lesson proper." It is doubtful that Schoenberg would have reacted to the article so vituperatively (or that Ringer would have interpreted it quite as he did) if either had known the complete source of the clipping. It was published in the *Berliner Tageblatt* on Christmas Day, 1928, under the heading, "Gastspiel vor der Quarta." The editor had asked a number of well-known artists how they would address an audience of school-children (age twelve or thereabouts) on the subject of their own life and works. Among the ten contributors were Heinrich Mann, Otto Klemperer, the critic Alfred Kerr, the Swiss author Jakob Schaffner, biographer Annette Kolb, the expressionist author Arnold Ulitz, and the "musician Weill." Far from a "journalistic prank," Weill's contribution was an intentionally simplistic, if miscalculated, response to the editor's invitation. What Ringer described as "sophomoric buffoonery" in "dealing with serious aesthetic issues in the comic manner of a typical German high school lesson" was in fact only an exaggerated reply in kind to the request. Unfortunately, *Das Orchester* reprinted only some sections of the essay on 15 January 1929; when *The Musical Times* (70 [1 March 1929]: 224) further condensed and translated sections of the "lesson," the article's original light-hearted context and intent had been lost. The fragments of the essay were then taken at face value and are still widely quoted as an accurate exposition of Weill's aesthetic viewpoint. K. K.]

15. See David Drew, "Musical Theatre in the Weimar Republic," *Proceedings of the Royal Musical Association* 88 (1962): 193. In *Stravinsky: Chronicle of a Friendship, 1948–71* (New York, 1972), pp. 212–13, Robert Craft also noted the relationship between *Mahagonny* and *Lulu:* "Berg must have known *Mahagonny,* incidentally, and it seems to me that Lulu has a touch of Jenny, and Berg's Athlete more than a touch of Weill's. Perhaps even the choice of instruments in Berg's 'Garderobe' scene was influenced by the sax and banjo in Weill's jazz band and the zither in his glutton scene."

very obvious differences between their respective musical languages raise some important questions.

The musical language of *Lulu* is of a kind that Brecht would doubtlessly have regarded as being unacceptably elitist, esoteric, and sensual. It is the sort of music that, in the posthumously published essay "Über die Verwendung von Musik für ein episches Theater," Brecht described as "complicated music of a mainly psychological kind."[16] Brecht regarded a certain kind of music as being a prerequisite for the creation of epic theater, and we must, therefore, ask whether epic opera (at least in the narrowest sense of Brecht's after-the-fact description of the genre) is possible if allied to a different kind of music—whether, in fact, Brecht was correct in his assessment of the way in which music functioned within the epic model. The music of *Lulu* is indisputably sensual, and to claim that in the theater the work functions as an epic opera is necessarily to suggest that Brecht was wrong in assuming that the seductive power of music inevitably ensnares the spectator in the stage action and leads to the experiencing of emotions rather than to rational decisions for action.

In the essay mentioned at the beginning of this paper, Carl Dahlhaus summarized Brecht's and Weill's operatic reforms, although he mistakenly credits them primarily to Brecht and misrepresents the creative process of Weill and Brecht:

> Brecht did indeed change the relationship between text and music. But he left intact the public's habit of feeling more conventional musical responses in opera than at a concert; he even exploited this habit. Against the conception of a synthesis of the arts . . . Brecht posed the idea of a musical theater in which text, music, "gestics," and scenery mutually intercut and "alienate" each other. . . . When he takes a tune attesting fine emotions and joins it to a text betraying mean thought, Brecht seeks to demonstrate that the emotions, the universally human, are mere masks of selfish interest.[17]

This is not an adequate description either of the way in which Weill's music works in *Aufstieg und Fall der Stadt Mahagonny* and *Die Dreigroschenoper* or of the historical facts concerning the working relationship within the Weill-Brecht collaboration. The subtlety and strength of Weill's work comes not only from his simple joining together of musically fine emotions and mean texts but also from the music constantly questioning its own emotional gestures; from the contrast, the dialectic, between the "fine" and the "mean" embodied in the music itself—in the distinction, which Ian Kemp has pointed out, between the melody and the harmony; in the distinction between the lyrical vocal line and the flat, repetitive rhythmic accompaniment, between the yearning, romantic me-

16. Translated by John Willett in *Brecht on Theatre* (London, 1964), p. 86.
17. Dahlhaus, p. 68.

lodic gestures and the clean, acerbic textures of the orchestra to which these gestures are assigned.

Dahlhaus's view is, however, a fairly accurate description of one aspect of *Lulu*, as is the following passage by Brecht about *Die Dreigroschen-oper:*

> The tenderest and most moving love song in the play described the eternal, indestructible mutual attachment of a procurer and his girl. The lovers sang, not without nostalgia, of their little home, the brothel. In such a way the music, just because it took up a purely emotional attitude and spurned none of the stock narcotic attractions, became an active collaborator in the stripping bare of the middle-class corpus of ideas.[18]

Time after time in *Lulu* we become conscious of the disturbing difference between the emotional attitude adopted by the music and the nature of the text to which it is set. It is difficult when reading Brecht's description of the love duet in *Die Dreigroschenoper* not to think of the love duet and the hymn at the end of act 2 of *Lulu*, when the listener is most forcibly made aware of the distinction between the luxuriousness and overwhelming emotional intensity of the music, the unpleasantness of the dramatic situation (as Alwa declares his love for the woman who is at once his stepmother, stepsister, and the murderess of his father), and the absurdity of the text in which Alwa, the composer, compares parts of Lulu's anatomy to musical terms.

Many commentators on *Lulu* have been disturbed by and have been unable to account for this aspect of the opera. Almost thirty years ago Donald Mitchell suggested that Berg had unconsciously precipitated large-scale dramatic confusion because "what goes on in the orchestra pit and on the stage fail to match."[19] Reviewing the Paris premiere of the complete *Lulu*, composer Robin Holloway remarked that the dislocation of "one's sense of relationship between music and character" was such that "if one is concentrating on action and character, the music seems completely inappropriate."[20] More recently, Sir Colin Davis, the conductor of the Covent Garden *Lulu*, remarked about his experience with the work: "Sometimes I feel that there is almost no connection between what's happening on stage and what I am doing in the orchestra pit."[21] This dichotomy between music and action in *Lulu* cannot be accounted for if we consider the opera only in relation to *Wozzeck* and to the work of the Second Viennese School. If, however, we consider *Lulu* within the context of the theatrical works of Weill at the same time—if, for example, we

18. Translated in Willett, p. 85.
19. Donald Mitchell, "The Character of Lulu," *Music Review* 15 (November 1954): 268.
20. Robin Holloway, "The Complete *Lulu*," *Tempo* 129 (June 1979): 37.
21. *The Times* (London), 16 February 1981.

think of the way in which the music and the text sometimes work against one another in *Der Jasager,* in *Mahagonny,* or at the end of *Die Bürgschaft*—then we shall immediately understand what Berg is doing. Indeed, Robin Holloway came close to seeing this as the solution when (in the review quoted above) he observed that *Lulu* "contradicts its own intensity and undermines its listeners' obedience to emotive instructions" in what amounts to "a reversal of the expressionist aesthetic."[22]

Wedekind's two *Lulu* plays, with their lack of traditional characterization and their fragmentary narrative structure, already fulfill two requirements of epic theater. In transferring the plays to the opera house, Berg deliberately turned the absurdities of Wedekind's tortuous plot into what Brecht belatedly described *Mahagonny* to be—a conscious tribute to the senselessness of operatic form. "The intention was," said Brecht in his "Anmerkungen zur Oper *Aufstieg und Fall der Stadt Mahagonny,*" that "a certain unreality and irrationality should be introduced at the right moment."[23] The absurdity of *Lulu* is equally intentional, and it is an essential part of Berg's refusal to allow (at least until the final scene of the opera) the spectator to become involved emotionally in the stage action.[24] In this respect, we have only to think of the farcical comedy of act 2, scene 1 of the opera, during which Dr. Schön dies—a death that (like most of the other deaths in the work) goes almost unnoticed and certainly unlamented by the music, which does not even see fit to acknowledge the event to the extent of gracing it with the conventional diminuendo as life ebbs away.

In "Über die Verwendung von Musik für ein episches Theater," Brecht observed that the theme of his "culinary opera" *Mahagonny* is "the cooking process itself," although one of the functions of the opera is to change society. "It brings the cooking process under discussion; it attacks the society that needs opera of this sort."[25] The theme and the function of *Lulu* are precisely the same as those of *Mahagonny:* the opera not only attacks social hypocrisy, but it does so with reference to its own audience. At the beginning of *Lulu* the Animal Trainer invites us to step inside and

22. Holloway, p. 37.
23. Translated under the title "The Modern Theatre is the Epic Theatre" in Willett, p. 36. It must be emphasized that this essay was written without consultation with either Weill or Neher, and Brecht's statements contrast markedly with Weill's views.
24. In this respect, *Lulu* was anticipated by Weill's *Der Protagonist.* In his review of the premiere in Dresden, Maurice Abravanel summarized this *musical* technique of "emotional distancing": "Weill carefully avoids anything which could alter the clarity of the drama and lower its value. He neither weeps for the murder of the sister nor asks us to empathize with the despair of the hero. He is satisfied only to show them, but with such exactness that the audience is overcome. This is what gives the work its particular value. *Der Protagonist* is, as far as I know, the first successful attempt in opera at moving an audience without enlisting its sympathy" (trans. in Kowalke, p. 43).
25. Translated in Willett, p. 87.

see his animals: "real wild animals, not tame ones, like those in the orchestra stalls." In act 1, scene 3, set in Lulu's backstage dressing room, the operatic audience is equated with the offstage audience cheering Lulu's cabaret performance: "They sound like the animals at feeding time," comments Alwa.

The meaning of these comparisons becomes clear in the final scenes of the opera when the singers who had earlier played the roles of Lulu's husbands reappear as her clients. This doubling of roles has a number of important effects. On one level, it further destroys the illusion of reality by once more drawing attention to the artificiality of the medium; it carries the dislocation of character, action, and music one step further and thus reinforces our awareness that what we are witnessing is simply a stage production. On another level, the doubling of roles indicates the moral stance of the work by equating the respectable bourgeois figures of the first half of the opera with the sleazy, disreputable figures of the second. The respectable and the criminal worlds not only relate to but reflect one another. And because the different characters in the opera are interchangeable, Jack can step into the nightmare world of the last scene as the representative of all the characters in the opera and, by implication, as the representative of us, the "domesticated" animals in the audience. Having been denied the opportunity of becoming emotionally involved until this point, we are—as Brecht's model of epic theater requires—finally brought to a point of recognition and made to face our responsibility for the society in which such things can happen.

Brecht published a now-famous table showing those changes of emphasis which distinguish "epic" from "dramatic" theater. There is not, I believe, a single one of those features which Brecht regarded as characteristic of epic theater which is not also a feature of *Lulu*.[26] Whereas Brecht (and to some extent Weill, for a period of time) believed that the apparatus of commercial opera would inevitably control those who attempted to employ it and set about creating epic opera by dismantling the paraphernalia of traditional opera, *Lulu* attacks the form from within by simultaneously employing and containing within itself a criticism of the paraphernalia. If, as Brecht declared, *Mahagonny* includes innovations that show up the commercial character of the entertainment and the people entertained, *Lulu,* in the crucial third scene of act 1, draws a parallel between its own audience sitting in the opera house and the offstage audience titillated by the cheap cabaret. If *Mahagonny* pays tribute to the senselessness of opera by introducing a "certain irrationality," *Lulu* acknowledges its own irrationality by having the composer Alwa consider the possibility of writing an opera about Lulu and then reject the

26. Brecht, "Über die Verwendung von Musik für ein episches Theater."

idea because the plot of such an opera would be too absurd. In the event that Alwa had actually written his opera (the opera that we are seeing), it has a story line that even the characters find difficult to believe. If, in *Der Protagonist*, Weill's music condemns its central figure for his inability to distinguish between art and life, Berg is equally severe on Alwa for his ineffectiveness and artistic pretension—indeed, more severe, since Alwa is specifically identified as Berg. Alwa confuses art and reality to such an extent that he eventually succeeds in getting himself killed in the last scene of his own opera.

The musical language of *Lulu* bears little relationship to the musical language of Weill, and yet the ends to which this language is put seem to be totally Weillian. The extent to which *Lulu* reflects the ideals of epic theater is immediately apparent when one sees the work in the opera house, surrounded by (and part of) that respectable bourgeois society represented onstage in the first half of the work. *Lulu*, like *Mahagonny*, "may not taste particularly agreeable," and its effect in the opera house is deeply disturbing in a way that is comparable only to *Mahagonny*, *Die Bürgschaft*, and *Die sieben Todsünden*. Like *Die Bürgschaft* and *Mahagonny*, *Lulu* allows us no escape. There is no emotionally cleansing catharsis, as there is at the end of *Wozzeck*. Instead, we are forced, as in Brecht's epic model, to confront the facts which *Lulu* presents us, and, as with Weill's work, we must either acknowledge our responsibility or reject the piece outright. It is unfortunate that Weill, having hailed *Wozzeck* as the grandiose conclusion of the Wagnerian music drama, did not live to see the extent to which his own "new opera" was to influence Berg's second opera; that, having had his music so summarily dismissed by Schoenberg and Webern, Weill was never to know the extent to which his own ideas were to be accepted by at least one member of the Second Viennese School.

10

Most Unpleasant Things with *The Threepenny Opera:* Weill, Brecht, and Money
JOHN FUEGI

When Bertolt Brecht wrote his novel, "The Business Deals of Herr Julius Caesar" (unfinished at his death and first published in 1957), his objective was to reveal the mechanics of how Caesar worked behind the scenes to create an image for the world. "How," Brecht asked, "was this done?" What were the business deals that undergirded Herr Julius Caesar's staggering success? Were they sordid, were they manipulative, were they unethical? And if they were all of these things, what does this do to our perception of the great Caesar of stern visage and laureled brow? Given Brecht's careful cultivation of his own public persona, complete with uniform and props, one is prompted to direct the questions he asked of Julius Caesar back to himself. What about the business deals of Herr Bertolt Brecht?

We can see clearly from Günter Gläser's collection of carefully selected letters, published in 1981 by Suhrkamp and Aufbau as the *Brecht Briefe,* that it is very difficult to differentiate between the "business Brecht" and the "personal Brecht." For example, in the published *Briefe* there is only one letter from Brecht to Fritz Wreede, owner of Felix Bloch Erben, the large theatrical firm in Berlin. But there are many other letters between Brecht and Wreede in the files of the Brecht Archive, as Gläser himself indicates in the footnote-apparatus of his text. Yet the collection presents the one letter only, without its context; this is, of course, an enormous problem with the edition as a whole, and one sympathizes with the formidable obstacles Gläser faced here. Seldom, for example, are we told what prompted certain letters and what reply, if any, Brecht sent in response. This unfortunate editorial policy leaves unexplored the crucial questions of how often and on what particular subjects people wrote to Brecht and got no reply. Is there any discernible pattern, beyond the exigencies of life during Brecht's period of exile, which might account for replies or non-replies?

A proper scholarly examination of this whole nexus of problems would involve a systematic sifting of the thousands of pages of materials that were not included, for various reasons, in the *Brecht Briefe*. These unpublished letters outnumber by almost two to one the twelve hundred pages of published correspondence. Because so many of these letters and memoranda deal with contracts, hundreds of related documents in several languages must be examined in order to follow the threads of Brecht's business deals over decades in a multitude of countries. The lines cross and recross, tangle and bewilder; and always the border between business deals and personal relationships is blurred.

It is very clear, however, that an exhaustive examination of Brecht's business dealings with just one collaborator, such as Kurt Weill, would require a book-length study. Such a study, having tackled the scale and complexity of Brecht's business affairs, would shed a great deal of light on his relationships with those whose efforts made the construction of "the Brecht oeuvre" possible. If Valentin could speak of having an *Unsinn-fabrik*, and Erich Kästner a *Versfabrik*, then what kind of apparatus was necessary for Brecht to produce at the rate he did? How did such a "machine" run? How many "employees" (is that the right word even?) were required at all times to maintain production levels? Here again, was there a separation between the business-artistic strands and the personal strands of Brecht's life? Did his production method actually require the steady availability of several people (usually women), each willing to re-spond to his needs virtually at any time of night or day? What was the effect of these working conditions on the co-workers? For an understand-ing of Brecht's business relationships in general and of that with Weill in particular, it is helpful to survey first the way in which Brecht regularly dealt with contractual matters.

From the published accounts of his friends and/or lovers, there are numerous reports of Brecht insisting that a friendship, a love affair, or even a marriage be undergirded by a formal agreement (*Abkommen*). As Brecht scholarship moves beyond hagiography to actual biography, it is beginning to be recognized, at least in academic circles, that Brecht's practice throughout his adult life was to maintain multiple, simultaneous sexual liaisons.[1] During the period when Brecht moved back and forth frequently between his parents' home in Augsburg and various pads in Munich, besides several additional liaisons, he was having particularly intense affairs with Bie Banholzer (by whom he had already fathered a child in July 1919) and Marianne Zoff, a Viennese opera singer. After

---

1. Brecht himself is very frank about this (and in this particular area he is reasonably accurate) in his somewhat fictionalized *Diaries 1920–22*, trans. John Willett (London, 1979). Other good sources for the early period are the memoirs of Bie Banholzer and the fine anthology of interviews with people who knew the young Brecht, *Brecht in Augsburg*, a collection assembled by Werner Frisch and K. W. Obermeier (Berlin, 1975).

Bie (then in Augsburg) received a visit from a thwarted lover of Marianne who wanted Bie to break up Brecht's relationship with Marianne, the two women decided to confront Brecht together in a Munich café. They resolved to force him to declare his intentions and decide between them. But when they sat down with Brecht in the café and pointed out the incompatibility of the two intense liaisons and asked which one of them he *really* wanted to marry, he gave a disconcerting one-word answer: "Both!" He was not to be budged from this position. One can, I believe, extrapolate this one-word answer to explain a great deal of what happens in other areas of Brecht's life where his answer seems to have been almost invariably: "Both!"

After "answering" Marianne and Bie in this way, Brecht then negotiated simultaneous contracts with both women. He agreed to marry Marianne ("Ma") because she was again pregnant with what Brecht referred to in his diary as "a little Brecht," but the marriage contract was to have several subsidiary clauses. Ma was to agree that she would remain faithful to Brecht only, while Brecht's sexual independence was to be guaranteed because, as he put it, "Some things a wife has to accept as irrevocable."[2] Having established that any marriage contract must absolutely allow him to maintain as many other simultaneous liaisons as he wished, quite logically Brecht then set up a contract with Bie Banholzer. According to her own accounts, her contract specified that after Brecht had married Ma, as soon as the "little Brecht" was born and given Brecht's name, he would divorce Ma and marry Bie.[3] Brecht further recommended that Bie should begin to order her trousseau in anticipation of this blessed tertiary event. When Bie took her "contract" to a lawyer for an assessment of its legal merits, the lawyer declared that it offended all public morality, had no valid legal precedent, and would never hold up in court. Years later, after never marrying Bie but finally divorcing Ma, Brecht was simultaneously involved (with a view to marriage and not counting other minor affairs) with Marie-Luise Fleisser, Elisabeth Hauptmann, Helene Weigel, and Carola Neher. The traffic in mistresses was sufficiently brisk—and Brecht's requirement for dress and undress of "his" women so strict—that a Berlin tailor gave a discount on the custom-cut marengo wool coats that they were required to wear.[4] In the midst of all this, quite suddenly Brecht and Weigel entered a formal (i.e., state-sanctioned) marriage contract in Berlin. But again there were loopholes in the contract for Brecht. As he observed to Car-

2. Klaus Völker, *Bertolt Brecht* (Berlin and Vienna, 1979), p. 85.
3. Paula Banholzer, *Meine Zeit mit Bertolt Brecht* (Munich, 1981), pp. 87–88.
4. For this particular point, see Völker's biography or Marie-Luise Fleisser's long short story "Avantegarde."

ola Neher in April 1929 (on the day of his marriage to Weigel), and as he presented Neher with a handsome bouquet (surely it was not the re- cycled wedding bouquet of Weigel?), "It [the marriage] couldn't be avoided, but it doesn't mean a thing."[5] It meant enough to Fleisser that it would have an indelible effect on her life, and it meant enough to Elis- abeth Hauptmann that she attempted suicide.

But Brecht's personal Abkommen did not concern only the regula- tion of sexual relations. Hermann Kesten, in his wonderfully lively memoir, *Lauter Literaten,* reported:

> About 1935 in Paris Brecht called me up as he urgently needed to speak with me. Could I go to his place? He didn't feel well. He lived in a hotel on the Boulevard St. Germain, between the monuments to Danton and Diderot.
>
> As my wife and I entered Brecht's room he was saying good-bye to the philosopher Ernst Bloch, the film director Slatan Dudow, and one or two women co-workers. We had hardly exchanged a few words about health, Hitler, and the weather before he put down his cigar and declared to me in a friendly but threatening way: "We are going to make a contract" [Wir schliessen ein Abkommen].
>
> I smiled.
>
> Brecht remained serious: "A contract that we will become friends."
>
> "But," I said and laughed, "we get along fine together."
>
> "I hear," he said, not being led astray, "that quite regularly in all the literary salons and in the Paris cafés you make jokes about me and criticize my work. That has to stop."
>
> "Yes, I do make jokes in cafés," I said, "but I hardly ever enter literary salons."
>
> "Our contract," stipulated Brecht, "shall provide that everywhere you go, you speak well of me and of my work, and I'll do the same for you. I have contracts like this with Lion Feuchtwanger, Arnold Zweig, and Alfred Döblin."
>
> "I'm glad about that," I said, and unfortunately I had to laugh. "Your offer amuses me and does me honor. Why shouldn't we praise each other's work? But up to now I have managed to hang on to my literary friends without such contracts, and my friendships have even survived my jokes. From what I know of myself, I wouldn't be able to enter such a pact with a friend. Suddenly I would have an urge to make a joke. How would we be able to joke about our enemies, if we couldn't from time to time joke about our friends?"
>
> "I hear it from all sides that you laugh at me," Brecht declared. Not being led astray, "That cannot continue without consequences. When it is necessary, I'll climb over dead bodies to get my way. In Hessen there was a young director who opposed me. He ended up committing suicide."

5. Völker, p. 129.

I stood up. "On this point I can set your mind at rest, dear Brecht. On neither my father's nor my mother's side have there been suicides in my family."

"You are the literary advisor to the Allert de Lange Press," said Brecht, "where we are both authors. I must go to Mr. de Lange and say to him: 'It's either you or me.'"

"Why not?" I said. "Landshoff (former owner of the Kiepenheuer Press in Berlin) will be glad to choose one or the other of us. So I don't see problems for either of us there."

Brecht escorted my wife and me to the lift in the hotel.[6]

Given the fact that Brecht paid such strict attention to regulating personal relations on a contractual basis (and usually a very one-sided contractual basis at that), it should not surprise us that he was just as concerned with his own interest in his multiple business contracts. In December 1921 he noted in his diary that he was juggling potential business arrangements with Reinhardt, Warschauer, Oswald Films, and Terra Films, while also considering his options in draft contracts he had obtained from both Reiss and Kiepenheuer Verlag. By 23 December he had signed up with Reiss for 750 marks a month, he had collected another 1000 marks from his father, he had signed on with "The Untamed Stage" to sing his mesmeric ballads for 500 marks in a six-day engagement, and he was still in hot pursuit of various other contracts. His love life was not abating for a moment by 7 January 1922 when he renegotiated the Reiss contract. His diary entry for that day gives the current status of his love arrangements and then continues:

> First of all dealing with publishers. Reiss offered 750 Marks, Kiepenheuer 800. Both want stage rights too. I've already signed up with Reiss, but took the contract back in order to show it to Kasack (of Kiepenheuer). I also had to talk to Dreimasken. It seemed a good idea to ask them for 1000 a month for one year. I also pushed Kiepenheuer up to 1000. On top of that, I got Kiepenheuer to leave Dreimasken the stage rights for my next plays. Dreimasken wavered, offered 500. I hadn't brought *Garga* with me, as I didn't want to let them have it. But stuck out for the 1000. Finally they agreed after I had talked them into a stupor.[7]

These arrangements reward close examination. As contract negotiator, Brecht had moved within two weeks from one rather comprehensive contract for his work that yielded 750 marks a month to two fragmented contracts worth 1000 apiece and had kept one of his hottest properties, *Garga*, off the negotiating table entirely, so that he could negotiate for it separately. By skillfully playing off one publisher against

6. Hermann Kesten, *Lauter Literaten* (Munich, 1963), pp. 439–40.
7. Brecht, *Diaries*, p. 157.

another, he had obtained multiple contracts, all highly favorable to him and all subject to renegotiation at his discretion, while holding the other signatory implacably to every provision in his own favor. In effect, just as he had proposed to marry Bie and Ma, while keeping all other liaisons open for himself, he had now "divorced" Reiss and "married" both Kiepenheuer and Dreimasken and had contractually established his right to innumerable other liaisons. Brecht could now collect multiple salaries as a writer, also sign on later for a stipend as a dramaturg with Reinhardt, reserve the right to be a guest director at other theaters, keep the rights to all plays written with others, and invoke an escape clause if any censorship was attempted on his deliberately scatological and sacrilegious writings. To ensure that all these business enterprises were kept in good order and that he could produce on schedule, he later managed to add a little rider to the Kiepenheuer agreement, a rider that put Elisabeth Hauptmann on the Kiepenheuer payroll, even though she reported literally twenty-four hours a day exclusively to Bertolt Brecht. Later, when more favorable terms and greater freedom of expression were offered by Propyläen Verlag (a subsidiary of Ullstein), Brecht would cheerfully switch publishers while retaining the rights to works "written with others." As most of his work then was written at least *with* others, if not at times *by* others, in 1929 he could boast to the economist Fritz Sternberg that his was a rare case in which "Ullstein was exploited by an author" rather than vice versa.[8]

This was the person with whom Kurt Weill would deal in 1927. Although the artistic collaboration between Weill and Brecht started with enormous appreciation of each other's work, as they began to complete joint projects, enormous difficulties over contractual arrangements gradually developed. At the outset of their collaboration, Brecht was so inordinately skilled in contractual negotiations and Weill so relatively unskilled that it was quite predictable that their joint contracts would prove a lifelong nightmare for Weill and Lenya and a lifelong bonanza for Brecht and his heirs.

Weill's initial contract with Universal Edition, dated 22 April 1924, is stupefyingly straightforward in comparison with Brecht's deliberately entangled contractual relationships during the same period.[9] Weill simply agreed to give Universal Edition the rights to his work for eight years. Basically the contract was U. E.'s standard one, with substantial

8. Fritz Sternberg, *Der Dichter und die Ratio* (Göttingen, 1963), p. 20.

9. I am deeply indebted to the Kurt Weill Foundation for Music and the Weill/Lenya Archive at the Yale Music Library, the Brecht Archive, and Felix Bloch Erben for providing me with the correspondence and relevant contracts which provide the basis for this paper. All material relevant to Weill is quoted by permission of the Kurt Weill Foundation for Music.

portions unmodified on the printed form it used for all its young composers. The royalty arrangement was also standard. Weill even accepted
the clause in the contract that allowed Universal Edition to reduce his
royalties if he failed to live up to any of the other terms of the contract.
Weill's signing of this contract in April 1924 required no contractual
expertise whatsoever. He reserved no special rights for himself. As with
other artists of the same period, by signing his *Hauptvertrag* he relinquished both film and stage rights to the publisher. While the general
contract made no mention of ownership of Weill's autograph manuscripts, in the specific agreements for individual compositions he ceded
this property to the publisher too. Since Brecht usually reserved all kinds
of rights for himself in contracts from this same period (1924), when
Brecht and Weill began to sign contracts jointly in 1927, two radically
different styles came into genuine conflict.

These conflicts eventually grew so vast that they darkened Weill's
life until his death in 1950, tormented Lenya until her death in 1981,
and to this very day continue to enrich lawyers on both sides of the
Atlantic as heirs of the heirs now try to untangle a legal nightmare of
contracts and counter-contracts. Because the mere exposition of these
conflicts would require a volume unto itself, this article will make only
fleeting references to those contracts jointly signed by Weill and Brecht
for *Das Berliner Requiem, Der Jasager, Happy End,* the various versions of
the *Mahagonny* material, and *Der Lindberghflug.* Here the focus will be on
that basic agreement which produced the largest amount of income and
the largest amount of acrimony, the contractual arrangements for *Die
Dreigroschenoper.* But before turning to *Die Dreigroschenoper,* let us set the
scene for the atmosphere in which Brecht and Weill began their cooper-
ative work early in 1927.

If we look closely at Brecht's career in the years prior to his first
meeting with Weill, it is worth noting that Brecht was successful not so
much by reason of production of his plays but almost, startlingly
enough, in spite of the production of his plays. There is virtually no
production of one of his plays before he meets Weill that was an actual
box-office success. The Leipzig production of *Baal* in 1923, the one performance of *Baal* in Berlin during 1926, and the short-lived 1924 production of *Eduard II* in Munich are typical. Each of these productions led
to a wild outcry and mixed opinion at the premiere, and each was canceled after only a few performances.[10] But each production increased
Brecht's fame through extensive and intensive critical reviews. As
Brecht's friend Arnolt Bronnen was to observe with some puzzlement:
his own plays had *succeeded* in theaters but he had been *defeated,* while

10. See Sternberg's account of Brecht's "success," pp. 20–21.

Brecht's plays had *failed* but Brecht had *won*. From 1924 to 1927 Brecht actually completed only one play, *Mann ist Mann*, as most of his work as a playwright during this period remained unfinished. But despite a string of what many people might regard as failures, Brecht managed to project an image of extraordinary success, arrogance, and confidence. He was a one-man wave of the future. His short stories, poems, and advertising slogans kept him in the public eye, and his bitter attacks on Thomas Mann ensured him notoriety, if not fame. The failure of one of his works at the box office was a measure, said Brecht and his supporters, of the inadequacy of the public rather than the inadequacy of Brecht. Failure, dialectically was, in fact, success.

Apparently Kurt Weill was drawn to the playwright by the radio production (reviewed by Weill in *Der deutsche Rundfunk*) of the one completed play, *Mann ist Mann*, and some of the poems in Brecht's deliberately provocative and scatological collection, *Die Hauspostille*, particularly the group of poems on that mythological place or state-of-being called Mahagonny. Although the *Hauspostille* volume bore only Brecht's name on the cover, at least two, and perhaps more, of the five Mahagonny poems were almost certainly written by Brecht's "secretary," Elisabeth Hauptmann.[11] But this *is* and *is not* a side issue here. When Weill met with Brecht in 1927 and began collaboration on the Mahagonny materials, there is no evidence that Weill thought anyone but brash Bert Brecht had written the Mahagonny poems and *Mann ist Mann*.

When the joint work on the Mahagonny materials was well advanced, storm clouds began to gather about the actual staging of the *Songspiel* in Baden-Baden, as was usual with Brecht's work as a director in this period.[12] Everything was being manipulated to create Brecht's usual theatrical scandal. Although the boxing-ring set was accepted and used, Brecht's wish to have Lenya appear nude in the production was turned down by both Weill and the horrified management of the festival. But the production was still shocking enough to the gathering of musical elite that by the end of the performance the audience was on its

11. In the preface to his English-language edition of *Rise and Fall of the City of Mahagonny* (London, 1979), John Willett states flatly: "Elisabeth Hauptmann had studied English, and she wrote him the two English-language 'Mahagonny Songs,'" which have ever since figured among his poems." See also my essay "Whodunit: Brecht's Adaptation of Molière's *Don Juan*," in *Comparative Literature Studies* 11:2 (1974), pp. 159–72. Eric Bentley told me that, when he worked with Elisabeth Hauptmann in New York during the exile years, she, to Bentley's astonishment, would write "Brecht texts" without even showing them to Brecht.

12. A composite account of these events is provided by Ronald Sanders, *The Days Grow Short: The Life and Music of Kurt Weill* (New York, 1980), pp. 91–92. See also pp. 414–15, where Sanders provides details on the various sources for his description of the performance of the *Songspiel* in Baden-Baden. More information is included in my forthcoming *Brecht the Director: Chaos, According to Plan* (Cambridge, Eng., 1986).

feet, as some booed and whistled while others cheered and clapped. Knowing full well what the reaction would be, Brecht had provided the cast with whistles and placards so that he and the performers could respond to the audience's response. So far, it looked like just another of Brecht's openings, but after the performance in the hotel bar it became apparent to Lenya that something else had happened. When she entered the bar, Otto Klemperer slapped her on the back and asked (quoting Hauptmann's broken English of the "Benares Song"), "Is here no telephone?" The whole bar-crowd began to sing the *Mahagonny* songs. Whether Brecht and Weill recognized it or not, the combination of Weill's music, Hauptmann's English lyrics, and Lenya's singing had placed Brecht and Weill in the considerable danger of becoming a popular success. Even though the Baden-Baden *Mahagonny Songspiel* had been a one-shot affair before a specialized audience, Lenya knew instinctively that it had been a real hit. Almost by accident, it would seem, Brecht and Weill had created with their *Songs* something that could have enormous popular appeal. It was a first for both.

In 1928, Hauptmann, whose knowledge of English enabled her to teach the language, was preparing for Brecht, whose English was virtually non-existent at that time, a translation and adaptation of John Gay's eighteenth-century *Beggar's Opera,* which had been successfully revived in London.[13] Brecht was devoting himself mainly to something different, a play that he never finished called *Joe Fleischhacker.* Indeed, when Ernst Josef Aufricht approached Brecht in the spring of 1928 to ask if he had a play suitable for the opening of Aufricht's company at the Theater am Schiffbauerdamm, Brecht tried to sell him on *Joe Fleischhacker.* Only when Aufricht had rejected *Fleischhacker* and got up to leave did Brecht refer to a "secondary work," then called *Gesindel.* As Brecht described this work, Aufricht knew at once that this adaptation of John Gay smelled of theater. The very next day Hauptmann's fragmentary text was accepted by Aufricht.[14] He even provisionally acquiesced to the alarmingly avant-garde and, as far as he knew, totally inappropriate composer Kurt Weill as a necessary, if unwelcome, part of the deal.

No sooner had agreement been reached with Aufricht than the whole array of questions concerning publication, film rights, music rights, and so forth, had to be addressed. Weill, who had been receiving a meager monthly stipend from Universal Edition under the terms of his original

13. See John Willett and Ralph Mannheim, eds., *Brecht: Collected Plays* (New York, 1977), 2:xx, 343. "Nothing of this first script has come down to us, and there is no real evidence that Brecht himself had as yet taken any hand in it. The process of 'adaptation' credited to him by the original programme probably only started once the play itself and the principle of a collaboration with Weill had been accepted" (by Aufricht).
14. Ernst Josef Aufricht, *Erzähle, damit du dein Recht erweist* (Frankfurt, 1966), pp. 63–65.

all-inclusive contract of 1924 and who was obliged to give Universal all his new works, merely added the adaptation of Gay to his list of compositions with Universal under the standard provision which entrusted the publisher with virtually all rights to the piece. Meanwhile, Brecht was hard at work lining up a contract on *his* usual terms. In the spring of 1928, with large sections of the music and the libretto not yet written, Brecht and Weill went in to sign a contract with Felix Bloch Erben in Berlin. How Brecht persuaded Weill and Hauptmann to agree to the original terms is still a matter for further investigation, but the original *Dreigroschenoper* contract specified a division of royalties as follows: Brecht 62½ percent (net), Weill 25 percent (net), Hauptmann 12½ percent (net), with no provision for Klammer (K. L. Ammer), the German translator of Villon whose published versions of several poems would be patched into the text. Only after the critic Alfred Kerr spotted and publicized the unacknowledged use of the Villon verses was the contract slightly modified with Klammer then awarded 2½ percent of the total (subtracted from Brecht's share). In contrast to these terms, Weill had been awarded the traditional two-thirds of all royalties as composer of his two one-act operas with librettos by Georg Kaiser, who was the most famous expressionist playwright at the time. The contract with Bloch Erben, with its radically unequal division of royalties, was to remain in force until the late forties, when Brecht (ignoring Weill's rights) unilaterally canceled the contract and signed a new agreement with Suhrkamp that maintained the old percentages—without even telling Weill directly that he had done so.

But in the spring of 1928 the contract being negotiated was not, as far as anyone could then have suspected, for a world-wide success worth literally millions of marks in royalties over the years, but a contract for a half-finished and probably unsuccessful mishmash by the then unknown Elisabeth Hauptmann, by a certain Bertolt Brecht, who had never had a popular stage success, and by Kurt Weill, a composer with an alarming reputation as a far-from-popular modernist. For betting people in Berlin in the spring and summer of 1928, it was a poor gamble as to whether or not the work would open at all, never mind become one of the greatest successes in German theatrical history.

Behind the scenes during these months, Brecht was still working on contracts. The contract with Felix Bloch Erben needed to be reconciled with Weill's agreement with Universal Edition. In a letter dated 6 June 1928, signatories for Bloch Erben confirmed in writing the arrangements with Universal that had apparently been worked out by telephone. This letter agreement did not modify the original relationship of the Weill/Brecht/Hauptmann division of royalties, but only regulated the way in which Bloch and Universal would divide up their own relative *Vertriebsprovision*. This contract, countersigned by the officers of Universal, was promptly returned to Bloch Erben. Only after the play had been finished and the premiere on 31 August 1928 had assured sold-out houses for months to come did Bloch Erben notice that the firm had failed to secure access to the now extremely valuable film rights of the work. So, on 27 September 1928, Bloch Erben sent off a letter to Universal confirming another oral agreement that had been made by Hertzka for Universal and Wreede for Bloch. This rather curious document reads as follows:

> Very Honored Sirs!
> We confirm hereby the agreement that was reached today between Director Hertzka and Mr. Wreede: inasmuch as the film rights for the work, *Die Dreigroschenoper*, are not yet entirely clear, as, on the one hand, Mr. Brecht in his contract with us has retained the film rights for himself and, on the other hand, on the basis of your general contract with Mr. Weill, you hold the film rights for Mr. Weill's music, we have agreed to allow the two authors, beyond all doubt, to control the film rights themselves. It is immaterial which of us it will be who will succeed in owning the rights to represent, in whole or in part; or, to go further, it is also immaterial which of us accomplishes the sale [for filming] of the work, as long as we both have an equal share in that portion which the authors will give either to both of us or to one or the other of us.[15]

On the plus side for Weill, because Brecht insisted on retaining his film rights, Weill, in essence, was in a legally defensible position to do the same. But on the negative side, Brecht now apparently started to ask for a larger share of royalties for himself under Weill's contract with Universal for "print rights" of the music. In a contract revision dated 15 November 1929 (i.e., after the show had opened and was clearly a smash hit and a major money-maker), Weill allowed Brecht's share of the print royalties from Universal to be increased from 2 percent to 3 percent of net income. (In light of the huge income derived from the *Die Drei-groschenoper*, it is worth noting that Brecht established during this same period two other income-producing contracts with Felix Bloch Erben, one for *Happy End* and one for three as yet unwritten plays.) Early the next year, in a note dated 26 May 1930, Weill agreed to give up yet an additional 2 percent of his own royalty to Brecht, so that Brecht would now get 5 percent of the income from publications of music issued by Universal Edition. Weill's percentage was reduced to 13 percent, but it should be noted that income from sales of the piano-vocal score and individual songs through Universal was only a fraction of the income derived from license fees for performance rights and sales of the book version of the complete *Dreigroschenoper* collected by Felix Bloch Erben,

---

15. Document in the Weill-Lenya Research Center, New York. The original is in German; the translation is my own.

the latter of which Weill did not share in at all. While Brecht nibbled away at Weill's portion of the income from Universal, no compensatory modification of the Bloch contract was forthcoming. The net result of all this was that, although both Weill and Brecht were earning well from *Die Dreigroschenoper*, Brecht was earning at a vastly greater percentage rate than Weill. But it does not appear that this was as yet a source of irritation for either Kurt Weill or Lotte Lenya. Both continued to work with Brecht, and Weill completed the music for *Der Lindberghflug* and *Das Berliner Requiem*, both broadcast in 1929. However, in that same tumultuous year in Berlin the Weill/Brecht relationship was to be shaken severely by the events surrounding the unhappy ending of their work on *Happy End*.

Aufricht and others have described the *Happy End* project as an attempt to repeat in 1929 the extraordinary success of the previous year's *Dreigroschenoper*. The standard interpretation of the non-success of *Happy End* is that Brecht had moved sufficiently to the left in 1929 (following the shooting of workers by the police on 1 May 1929—an event he witnessed)[16] that he wanted nothing more to do with a piece planned by Aufricht as a commercial venture. This may well be true, but it is possible that personal and contractual events in Brecht's life may have had as much to do with the non-completion of *Happy End* as political events in Germany. If we are willing to accept the significant role of Elisabeth Hauptmann in the creation of *Mahagonny* and *Die Dreigroschenoper*, then let us look more closely at *Happy End*, a work prepared in the middle third of 1929. Why was the last act of the play never properly completed? Is it worth noting that on 10 April 1929 Brecht broke the agreements that Carola Neher, Elisabeth Hauptmann, and Marie-Luise Fleisser all thought they had with him when he suddenly married Helene Weigel? Hauptmann's reaction to the marriage was an attempted suicide. May we ask how enthusiastic she was in the summer of 1929 to return to work with Brecht? I think it highly probable that she (rather than Brecht) was the linchpin of the *Happy End* production and that she was the one who could not bring herself to complete it in those desperately unhappy months following Brecht's unexpected marriage.

In his fine book of memoirs, Aufricht described at length his ingenious attempts to get Brecht to finish the last act of the show.[17] These

16. See Sternberg, pp. 24–27.
17. Aufricht, pp. 98–101. The view that Aufricht expresses here was confirmed in November 1983 by his widow, Margot Aufricht, in a personal interview. However, when she heard the background evidence of Elisabeth Hauptmann's actual authorship of the text, Frau Aufricht agreed that the wrong author had been pursued in 1929. The original program credited the authorship of the play to "Dorothy Lane"; Brecht allowed the lyrics to be ascribed to him—at Weill's insistence.

attempts led to nothing, but it never seems to have dawned on Aufricht that he was pressuring the wrong person. He thought of Brecht as the author of the piece. After all, hadn't Brecht written *Die Dreigroschenoper* and *Mahagonny*? But, in fact, it is virtually certain that it was Elisabeth Hauptmann who was the real author of almost everything in *Happy End* except the song texts. She was the one who actually signed the principal contract for *Happy End* with Felix Bloch Erben, as that firm's records confirm unambiguously. In this case, she was the principal contractor and, in a sense, Weill and Brecht the sub-contractors on the project. Under her contract with Bloch Erben, Hauptmann was to receive one-third of the royalties as author of the play under the pseudonym "Dorothy Lane." In a recent letter to me, Manfred Wekwerth, the current Intendant of the Berliner Ensemble, who worked very closely with Hauptmann for a number of years, wrote:

> Elisabeth Hauptmann really did write *Happy End* and did so after a preliminary announcement that was made in a magazine of that period published by the Scherl Press (it was an entertainment magazine with a slightly indelicate tone). The topic of the Salvation Army always interested Elisabeth, right up to the end, and Brecht himself, at her suggestion, took up the topic again in *St. Joan of the Stockyards.* Of course, Brecht helped Elisabeth in writing out the story line of *Happy End* and later, after the failure at the premiere, they put together a new film version. Based on this new version, at first together with Elisabeth Hauptmann, I shot a film of it in 1976. After her death I wrote the script for it myself. Also, in the dialogue of the play *Happy End,* Elisabeth's diction is unmistakable. But it is also true that right up until the end she was more ashamed of the play than was necessary, so she told Brecht that her name should not be given but rather that of a certain Dorothy Lane. Without exception the texts of the songs are by Brecht. It is also true that Elisabeth Hauptmann argued in public that she had not written the play. That happened as an afterthought and, according to my view, out of false modesty.[18]

I offer this historical excursion here only as food for thought and will return to this subject in a later, more extensive and more *wissenschaftlich* essay on the subject of Elisabeth Hauptmann's contributions to "Brecht's plays" from the periods 1924–33 and 1948–56. Here, we must return to the fact of the *Happy End* fiasco rather than the reasons for it. By the time the curtain came down on *Happy End* in September 1929 after only three performances, it was abundantly clear to Lenya, Weill, and Aufricht that Bert Brecht's and his new wife's behavior had ensured the failure of the project. Aufricht reckoned his losses at 130,000 marks and, as he wrote, "At my theater, we had to take a breather from

---

18. The passage occurs in a personal letter to me dated 28 December 1984 on the stationery of the Berliner Ensemble. The original is in German; the translation is my own.

Brecht."[19] For Felix Bloch Erben, the failure of *Happy End* was a very serious blow because, in anticipation of other successful plays and songs from Brecht's "collective," they had signed their two new contracts for large sums of money for "Brecht" to produce what they thought would be a string of money-makers.

Despite the failure of *Happy End*, two more years elapsed before an open break between Weill and Brecht could be discerned publicly. Meanwhile, the opera *Aufstieg und Fall der Stadt Mahagonny* had been produced during March 1930 in Leipzig (and later in other opera houses) with only minimal involvement by Brecht. That year Weill also completed the music for *Der Jasager*, 80 percent of whose libretto Elisabeth Hauptmann claimed, in a personal interview with me, to have written.[20] Speedily, as we know, *Der Jasager* was complemented by a *Neinsager,* and Brecht's subsequent revisions of his original text (a customary practice throughout his life) were effected with no consideration for the music and without consultation with Weill. Brecht, it was clear, was going his own way and did not seem overly concerned whether Weill went with him or not. This becomes very clear with the lawsuit that swirled around the film version of *Die Dreigroschenoper* in the summer of 1930.

As far as I have been able to reconstruct events, Brecht's reworking of the stage material for the Nero film production was also accomplished in sovereign disregard for Weill's music. Weill seems to have joined the *Dreigroschenoper* lawsuit largely to ensure that his music be used in the film without interpolation of music by other composers. When Brecht's part of the lawsuit was settled in December 1930, the settlement document not only specified a payment of 16,000 marks, but, most important, the film rights for the work reverted to Brecht after only two years.[21] Not only is the two-year provision extraordinary in film contracts, but the settlement document gives *Brecht* (not Weill and Brecht) the right to make a new film version. It is extremely doubtful that either Nero or Brecht had any legal right whatsoever to settle "their" case on

19. Aufricht, p. 101.

20. Personal interview with Hauptmann conducted in her Berlin apartment, 9 November 1970. In another interview, this time with O. Schirmer (published as "Wie kam es zum 'Jasager' und zum 'Neinsager'?" in *Julia ohne Romeo* [Berlin and Weimar, 1977], pp. 175–76, Hauptmann answered the question, "You showed Brecht your translation of *Der Jasager* and he suggested that Kurt Weill compose it?" with the response: "No, in this case it was the other way around. Kurt Weill, who had worked with Brecht for several years, was looking at that time for a text for a *Schuloper,* which was to be premiered during 'New Music Berlin 1930.' When he read one day my translation of *Taniko,* he offered Brecht the adaptation. Brecht accepted Weill's offer, as Brecht too was very interested in the experiment of an opera for children."

21. Document in the Weill-Lenya Research Center.

these terms, but nevertheless settle they did. From now on, as one looks at the tangled history of the *Dreigroschenoper* contract through the exile years and into the postwar years, Brecht tends almost always to treat the work as something that he could unilaterally alter, sell, or reassign with little if any prior consultation with either of his collaborators, Weill or Hauptmann.

But before we follow these tangled threads through the post-1933 years, let us look briefly at the one time where the Brecht and Weill interests publicly diverged. In December 1931 Aufricht, despite the fiasco of *Happy End,* decided to mount an expensive commercial production of the full-length *Mahagonny* at the Theater am Kurfürstendamm. As Aufricht, Willett, and others have noted before, Brecht's behavior at the *Mahagonny* rehearsals was such that, in essence, Aufricht bought him off by agreeing to finance a simultaneous production of *Die Mutter.* Aufricht hoped that Brecht would be so involved in rehearsals of *Die Mutter* that he would keep his nose out of *Mahagonny.* Before Brecht went down to the cellar to rehearse *Die Mutter,* public fights between Weill and Brecht had become commonplace, and lawyers representing both parties shouted at one another during the chaotic rehearsals. Brecht knocked a camera out of the hands of a press photographer who wanted to photograph him with Weill. And Brecht, who was already a legend in German theatrical circles for his temper tantrums, shouted that he would throw Weill, "this phony Richard Strauss," down the stairs.[22] The Weill/Brecht collaboration looked to be very much at an end.

With both artists driven into exile by events in Germany in early 1933, the earning power of each was drastically curtailed, since much of their incomes had been derived from the German market. They both needed to look around at once for alternative sources of income outside Germany. When Weill immediately landed a contract for a ballet in Paris, he both shrewdly and magnanimously shared the commission with Brecht—after Cocteau had refused the offer; as a result, Weill held the contractual cards, as well as the artistic control, of *Die sieben Todsünden.* After two years in Paris and London, Weill crossed the Atlantic in September 1935, not to return again to Europe—and then for only a brief visit—until after the war. Brecht, however, stayed in Europe until 1941, and during this time he basically, as far as can now be determined, acted very much on his own in determining what happened to European contracts for *Die Dreigroschenoper* and other works written jointly with Weill and/or Hauptmann.

According to Brecht's correspondence, the owner of Felix Bloch Erben, Fritz Wreede, had been having second thoughts about Brecht's

22. The incident is described in Aufricht, p. 126.

contracts with the firm even before Brecht went into exile. Wreede had met with him in Munich during the summer of 1932 to propose changes in their agreements. In Wreede's view, Brecht had not properly fulfilled his contractual obligations.[23] The significant point here, as far as Brecht's relationship with Weill and the *Dreigroschenoper* contract is concerned, is that Weill was almost certainly unaware that Brecht was contesting his other contracts with Felix Bloch Erben and that this was having an effect on their joint *Dreigroschenoper* contract. According to Wreede, Felix Bloch Erben had committed to pay Brecht under a general contract (separate from the *Happy End* and *Dreigroschenoper* contracts) an advance of 1000 gold marks per month for seven years for the rights to several plays that Brecht was supposed to write and assign to the firm. A dispute arose because Brecht did not, in Wreede's view, deliver on time any plays that could be used by the firm to recover these advances of 1000 gold marks per month. When Brecht left Berlin, the controversy was still unresolved. It boiled down to this: did Felix Bloch Erben owe Brecht another three-and-one-half years of payments of 1000 gold marks per month, or was Brecht obligated to repay the three-and-a-half years of advance he had already received? Each claimed, in essence, that the *other* party owed 42,000 gold marks. Neither party was willing to budge from his position, and Wreede wrote to ask how Brecht planned to repay the firm.[24] Brecht, in turn, demanded to know why he was not continuing to receive his monthly advance for the remainder of the contractual period. If Wreede was correct in his interpretation of the situation, then one can understand why he wanted to use the money collected from theaters for performances of *Die Dreigroschenoper* as *his* only feasible source of recovery for the huge sum of money owed to him by Bert Brecht. But Brecht argued in his numerous letters to Wreede that he had, in fact, observed the terms of his contracts with Felix Bloch Erben, that his "pension" (he called his monthly sum "eine Rente") should be continued, and that he should also continue to get his royalties from *Die Dreigroschenoper* in full.[25]

23. Wreede's views are set forth at great length in a series of letters to Brecht commencing on 27 February 1933 (the historic date of the Reichstag fire) and petering out inconclusively in the late thirties. The correspondence can be seen either at the Brecht Archive in East Berlin or at Harvard University's Houghton Library (BBA 783).

24. In a letter dated 16 June 1933, Fritz Wreede is extremely blunt with Brecht. It is clear that he felt he had been tricked by Brecht, and in his anger he wrote to the playwright: "Reden wir doch ganz offen miteinander, lieber Herr Brecht, Sie haben sich auf unsere Kosten ein sehr luxuriöses Eigenleben gestattet" (BBA 783/49).

25. Although in all his letters to Wreede Brecht refers to his money from the firm as an earned Rente or pension and denies that it was an "advance" and hence repayable, when tax authorities had sought to collect income tax from Brecht during the period before he left Berlin, he refused to pay. He argued that he had earned no income; all he had received, so

While it is impossible to determine conclusively from the evidence at hand, it appears that Felix Bloch Erben failed to pay Weill any royalties after Hitler's accession to power in 1933. Obviously, if Wreede did pay Weill (with whom, presumably, he did not have a contractual dispute) during the thirties but did not pay Brecht, then Wreede's position would gain credibility. But if neither Brecht nor Weill nor Hauptmann was paid, as it now appears, then one must question the validity of Wreede's interpretation. Based on available evidence, it would appear that, although Brecht reported to Weill during the thirties that there were difficulties with royalty payments for *Die Dreigroschenoper*, Weill was led to believe that these difficulties were traceable exclusively to Nazi infiltration of Felix Bloch Erben. Weill may not have known that Brecht's *Dreigroschenoper* royalties had already been in dispute before the Nazis came to power. Brecht told anyone who would listen to him in Paris and other stations of exile that he was not getting his money from Felix Bloch Erben because of the Nazis; he neglected to mention that Felix Bloch Erben had tried to work out a new agreement with him before the Nazis came to power.[26]

If one looks in detail at the surviving records of Brecht's dealings with Felix Bloch Erben in the thirties, one sees that the situation was not clear-cut. However, it can now be shown that Brecht did, in fact, collect *some* money for *Die Dreigroschenoper* during the exile years and that this money was paid to him with the knowledge and cooperation of Felix Bloch Erben. I have managed to obtain a copy of a handwritten document in French, dated 16 May 1938 and signed by Brecht, acknowledging receipt from Dr. Alexandre Banyai of 4300 francs for performances of *L'Opéra de quat'sous* in France. In a letter dated 21 May 1938 from Dr. Banyai in Paris to Felix Bloch Erben in Berlin, we learn that Banyai received a total of 9300 francs as royalties for the play, that he had sent 5000 francs to Felix Bloch Erben in Berlin, and that he had remitted 4300 francs to Brecht (through Brecht's attorney, Martin Domke), with the express understanding that Brecht was to share this money with

---

he said to them, were advances or loans from publishers. Because Wreede never saw Brecht's reply to the tax authorities and the tax authorities never saw Brecht's correspondence with Wreede, neither party knew that the other was being told something diametrically opposite.

26. In Wreede's letter of 27 February 1933, he claims that he raised all these issues with Brecht as early as May 1932 and that Brecht kept promising Wreede that he would address the issues but somehow always was unavailable to do so. Wreede claimed that between 1 July 1929 and February 1933 Brecht had collected 44,000 marks under the General Contract, had also collected fairly substantial sums from Elisabeth Hauptmann for his part in her *Happy End* project, and had been paid about 80,000 marks for income derived from *Die Dreigroschenoper*.

Weill.[27] However, there is no extant evidence to suggest that Brecht did forward Weill a share of the royalties. Indeed, in a letter to Brecht dated 9 February 1939, Weill says explicitly that he has not seen one cent from the Paris production (or any other production) of *The Threepenny Opera*.[28] If he was correct here, and I am reasonably sure that he was, then Weill was not only failing to receive any payments from Felix Bloch Erben, but he was also being deprived of his share of the royalties that Brecht collected on behalf of both creators.

There is also very strong circumstantial evidence that in mid-March 1939 Brecht unilaterally accepted money for the sale of the film rights for the *Happy End* story or plot without, as far as I have been able to determine, mentioning this fact either to Weill or to Hauptmann, even though he was corresponding in his regular irregular way with both collaborators at this time. In a letter of 4 June 1939 to Weill, for instance, Brecht wrote about *Mahagonny*, but there is no mention whatsoever of *Happy End*.[29] And in his letter to Weill on 23 March 1939, Brecht discusses only the possibility of producing *Der gute Mensch von Sezuan* in America and says explicitly of royalties from Felix Bloch Erben: "It is a grotesque situation: anyone can see that the German firms can no longer carry out their obligations. *They can neither advertise our work nor give us our royalties*" (italics added).[30] Curiously, Brecht neglected to inform Weill that he had sold film rights for *Happy End* (remember that the original contract for *Happy End* with Felix Bloch Erben had been signed by Hauptmann, not Brecht!) and that he had collected at least some *Threepenny* royalties in Paris the year before.

It is, of course, quite possible that Weill might have allowed Brecht to keep all royalties collected in Europe if he had been informed of their existence and had been asked to donate them to the cause of Brecht's emigration from Europe. But as far as I know, Brecht never mentioned the money to Weill and never asked to be allowed to keep it. (In response

27. This document is one of the very few relevant to Brecht that have survived in the files of Felix Bloch Erben. The original was kindly made available to me by the present officers of the firm in Berlin. I have deposited a copy of the document in both the Weill-Lenya Research Center and the Brecht Archive.

28. A carbon copy of Weill's original letter is in the Weill-Lenya Research Center. Copies of all Brecht-Weill correspondence have been deposited at the Brecht Archive.

29. The 4 June 1939 letter is in the Weill-Lenya Research Center. The evidence for the sale of film rights to *Happy End* is contained in a letter from Brecht's attorney in Paris, Domke, to Ernst Josef Aufricht, dated 16 March 1939. Domke's letter points out to Aufricht, however, that if he has an interest in the songs from *Happy End* he should contact Kurt Weill directly. With documents concerning *Happy End* scattered from Berlin to New York, Louisville, and Los Angeles, I have not yet been able to determine if Aufricht followed up on Domke's suggestion.

30. The letter is in the Weill-Lenya Research Center.

to Elisabeth Hauptmann's plea in 1941 for funds to assist Brecht in coming to the United States, Weill sent a contribution of one hundred dollars.) For all Weill knew, Brecht too had received no income in Europe for the works under contract to Felix Bloch Erben, and Weill was certainly unaware that at least some money for Brecht had been authorized by Felix Bloch Erben and paid as late as 1938. It appears that, until his death in 1950, Weill assumed that his own collaborative works with Brecht were earning him absolutely nothing in Europe, and his outrage at this was directed solely at Felix Bloch Erben rather than at Brecht as well.

When Brecht and Weill did meet briefly on the American side of the Atlantic in 1935, Weill observed Brecht as he attempted to impose his iron will (by insisting absolutely on his own "rights") on the Theatre Union's production of *Mother* in New York. Here again Brecht was thrown out of the theater. Here again he wanted his own way regardless of what anyone else wanted. It is highly unlikely that Brecht's deliberately obnoxious behavior, behavior so reminiscent of the *Mahagonny* production in Berlin during December 1931, now prompted any nostalgia for their partnership from Weill, who was already trying to establish himself in the American theater. Brecht again returned to Europe, and by the time he emigrated to America in mid-1941, Kurt Weill had achieved fame with *Lady in the Dark*. During a trip to Hollywood in September–October 1942, Weill reported to Lenya on his first meeting with Brecht since 1935:

> Then I met Brecht. He was just as dirty and unshaved as ever, but somehow much nicer and rather pathetic. He wants badly to work with me and the way he talks about it sounds very reasonable—but you know how long that lasts. Anyhow, I will try to see him once more before I leave. . . . If I don't go in the army I think I will do a show with Brecht *for you*. He has enough money now for two years and could come to New York.[31]

But behind the scenes in California Brecht almost immediately again attempted to treat work he had done earlier with Weill as exclusively his own. Early in 1942 he tried to set up a California production of *The Threepenny Opera* in English with an all-black theatrical company. Weill had not been consulted in Brecht's preliminary negotiations with the producer, Clarence Muse. But when Weill first learned of the plans in a telegram on 5 March 1942, he responded immediately that he could reply only after discussing the matter with his agent and publisher. Meanwhile, Brecht and the producer enlisted both Paul Robeson and T. W.

---

31. Weill to Lenya, 1 October 1942. When the negotiations for the Brecht projects collapsed, Weill did compose a role for Lenya—the Duchess in *The Firebrand of Florence*—but it was not an effective showcase for her unique talents.

Adorno as intermediaries to convince Weill of the value of the project. On 31 March, Weill wrote the producer:

> Let me first tell you that I am very positive about the idea of a negro production of "Three Penny Opera." As a matter of fact, it is a very old idea of mine and I had worked on several negro versions of this show during the last years. Paul Robson [sic] seemed to have the notion that my score for the "Three Penny Opera" was for me a thing of the past and that I didn't care particularly what anybody would do with it now. But this is definitely not the case. I consider this score one of the most important things I have done and one of my most valuable "properties." . . . The importance which I attribute to this score and my experience with several attempts of a revival, make it necessary for me to have a number of questions settled before I could give you the "go ahead" signal on your production.[32]

Weill had not been shown the English translation of the work; he worried whether the words would fit the music and feared for the fate of his orchestrations. He recognized that a bad translation and/or production would ruin both the black theatrical company and the work's chances on Broadway. When the producer refused both to acquiesce in Weill's demand for approval over musical changes and to accept the terms of Weill's Dramatist Guild contract, Brecht pressed ahead unilaterally anyway, but the production never materialized.

Although insulted and privately outraged by Brecht's characteristic disregard for his rights, Weill maintained a public silence about the situation. In private, however, he was very explicit about his reaction; in a letter to Lenya, dated 8 April 1942, Weill wrote:

> I am sick and tired of this whole affair and I wrote him [Muse] I would be willing to make a contract for a production *in California only*, but that I won't allow it to be shown outside of Cal. unless I have seen and passed it. . . . If they don't accept this, to hell with them! But at least I have shown my good will. Muse writes me that Brecht had told him last summer he had written to me and I didn't answer. The good old swinish Brecht method. Well, I wrote Wiesengrund [Adorno] a letter which he won't forget for some time. I wrote him: It is a shame that a man of your intelligence should be so misinformed. Then I explained [to] him that the American theatre isn't as bad as he thinks and in the end I said: "maybe the main difference between the German and American theatre is the fact that there exist certain rules of 'fair play' in the American theatre. Three cheers for the American Theatre!"

Lenya replied by return mail:

---

32. All correspondence by Weill and Lenya is found in the Weill-Lenya Research Center and is quoted by the permission of the Kurt Weill Foundation for Music. The orthography of the originals has been kept. I am grateful to Kim Kowalke for guiding me to the relevant letters from the Weill-Lenya correspondence.

> The whole Brecht schit is just too funny for words. "Could you come to Hollywood?" Good God! Sounds like in the good old days when he tried to keep your name off the program. . . . You know what they will do, if you would give in. Cut the music to pieces and make the whole thing cheap and ridiculous. And this stupid Brecht, this chinese-augsburg *Hinterwäldler* [hick] philosopher. It's too much already, that letter from him, soil our mailbox.

In an undated letter from the same period, Lenya cautioned Weill about renewing any relationship with Brecht:

> I am very much against it, to send him money. I belief to a certain extent, what he writes about the procedure of that 3 penny opera project but I dont trust him at all. I never believe, that he ever can change his character, which is a selfish one and always will be. I am sure he went through a lot of unpleasant things, but not so unpleasant, that it would change him. I know Darling how easely you forget things but I do remember everything he ever did to you. And that was plenty. Of course, he wants to collaborate with you again. Nothing better could happen to him. But I am convinced after a few days, you would be disgusted with him, I just could write it down for you what would happen. . . . I always believed in dicency and a certain fairness. And Brecht hasn't got much of it. . . . "DIE SIEBEN WINTER UND DIE GROSSEN KALTEN" und die ganzen Gemeinheiten tauchen for mir auf. *Nein, nein.*

Given Lenya's and Weill's distrust for the business deals of Herr Bertolt Brecht, it is not surprising that Brecht's efforts to recruit Weill for the Schweyk and Sezuan projects came to naught. The loss of what these works might have been with Weill's collaboration is directly, if only partially, attributable to Brecht's previous betrayals of their contractual relationship. But the squabbles were far from finished. All through the Hitler years Weill had believed that Felix Bloch Erben had paid neither author any royalties. For Weill, simply to carry on with the contract after 1945 as though there had never been a Third Reich was impossible; whatever differences Weill and Brecht had, they were in agreement that it was necessary to take the *Dreigroschenoper* contract away from Bloch Erben. But once Brecht got back to Europe, he dealt with the property there just as he had dealt with it in California and in Europe before the war: unilaterally he began to talk of a new version of the text, to arrange for productions, to switch the contract to a new publisher, and to do all this without prior consultation with Weill.

On 2 September 1948, Universal Edition wrote an anguished letter to Brecht and a letter of inquiry to Weill. What, they asked, was going on with *Die Dreigroschenoper*? In his letter to Brecht, Alfred Schlee of Universal Edition wrote that he had read a newspaper article announcing that Brecht had written a new version of the opera. If this were true, continued Schlee, could they have the new text at once to forward to Weill in

case he wished to write any necessary new music? And finally, who held
the contract now? Was it still with Felix Bloch Erben? Later that month,
with no word from Brecht directly, a letter dated 9 September 1948
reached Weill in New York from an old friend during the Berlin days,
Jacob Geis, now with Bavaria Film in Munich and representing, so he said,
Bertolt Brecht.[33] The letter proposed breaking the Bloch Erben contract
but did not give any specifics for a new contract with a different publisher.
At precisely the time of Geis's letter, Weill's friend and attorney, Maurice
Speiser, died, so Weill was without legal counsel. Nevertheless, he wrote
back on 28 October 1948 to say he agreed that the contract must be taken
away from Bloch Erben. The letter ended as follows: "Before I do anything definite, however, I would like to know what we will do with *Die
Dreigroschenoper* if we do take it away from Bloch Erben." "Can you write
to me," he continued, "what Brecht has in mind, or, can you ask him to
write to me directly?"

Still having heard nothing from either Geis or Brecht (Brecht had
written a letter dated 6 December 1948 that must have crossed Weill's in
the mail), Weill wrote to Schlee at Universal on 11 December 1948 asking
for advice on how to stop unauthorized productions, such as one he had
heard about in Munich, where his music had reportedly been altered.
Replying to Brecht's 6 December 1948 letter, Weill pointed out in a letter
dated 20 December 1948 that he remained very concerned about alterations being made in either the text or the music of *Die Dreigroschenoper* and
that he wanted to see the altered text. By 17 January 1949 Weill had
received the alterations; he wrote to Brecht that he "honestly could not
understand what you have in mind with these alterations." On 28 January
Brecht wrote again to explain his point of view and to ask that Weill
refrain from making further objections to performances of *Die Dreigroschenoper*. Geis, said Brecht, would handle the royalties in Germany for
Weill. Weill replied on 14 February saying he did not want to do anything
until he had seen a very specific proposal for a new contract. On 16 March
1949, a Mr. Hartmann of Universal wrote plaintively to Weill in New
York: "Most unpleasant things are happening with *Die Dreigroschenoper*."
"Brecht," reported Hartmann, "is supposed to have said in Zurich that he
alone has a right to enter into contracts in foreign countries."

Meanwhile, without the knowledge of either Weill or Universal Edition, on 7 February 1949 Peter Suhrkamp and Brecht had already signed
an agency agreement by which Suhrkamp Verlag was entrusted with "the
licensing of public performances of Brecht's stage plays in all theaters in

---

33. All the materials cited in this section of my paper are in the Weill-Lenya Research
Center.

all zones of Germany." The list of works covered by the agreement included *Die Dreigroschenoper*. The contract also provided:

> Bertolt Brecht can entrust Mrs. Elisabeth Hauptmann-Dessau with the final drafting of the texts. Moreover, Mrs. Hauptmann-Dessau represents Bertolt Brecht in all transactions with the theaters. Suhrkamp Verlag will provide to Mrs. Hauptmann-Dessau a copy of all correspondence with theaters.

The agreement explicitly recognized that Brecht did not control the rights of his collaborators and stipulated that separate contracts with them must be negotiated by Brecht:

> Separate agreements between Bertolt Brecht and his co-lyricists as well as his musical collaborators will in each case be determined in writing and considered as constituent parts of this contract memorandum. They are to be confirmed in each instance by the signatures of Bertolt Brecht and the respective collaborator.

By May various European agents were involved in the fray. On 18 May, a certain M. Kantorowitz wrote to Universal from Zurich declaring, among other things, that "Bert Brecht has written a completely new text, and this will not be entrusted to any publisher, but will be handled by the author himself." Universal, in a letter signed by a Mr. Wieser and dated 16 May 1949, replied at once to Kantorowitz and sent a copy of the relevant correspondence to Weill. In part, Wieser stated: "Since the new text by Brecht is to be used, we cannot agree to such a performance before we obtain the consent of Mr. Weill." Several months before, on 7 January 1949, Bloch Erben had written to Weill saying he should understand that, in view of what Brecht was doing, "we cannot be held responsible for Mr. Brecht's violation of your interests." In a telegram Weill ordered that the Munich production be stopped. Hartmann at Universal wrote at once to Bloch Erben that no performances should be authorized until Weill could see the so-called new version, and he of course wanted to see a new contract also.

No new contract arrived, and Weill still did not know what was happening to his music. Hard at work on *Lost in the Stars*, he wrote a firm but polite and friendly letter dated 5 August 1949 to Universal forbidding any use of his *Dreigroschenoper* music until such time as he could get some direct word from Brecht on all these vexing matters. In November Universal wrote back to tell Weill that they thought the *Dreigroschenoper* stage rights had been transferred from Bloch to Suhrkamp. Meanwhile, a letter from Brecht himself had finally reached Weill indicating that Brecht wanted to take the play away from Bloch Erben and give it to Suhrkamp. Brecht did not mention anything about the situation concerning his other contracts with Felix Bloch Erben which had clouded the legality of any attempt to withdraw *Die Dreigroschenoper* from the firm. (Brecht himself was well aware of the complications: Jacob Geis had delineated them in a letter dated 25 May 1949, and Brecht's attorney, Wolf Schwarz, had done the same in a report sent from Zurich on 7 March. Schwarz and Geis recommended that, because Brecht's prospects for a favorable legal solution were in real doubt, he should try to work things out directly with the firm on "a friendly basis."[34]) Weill, in his reply to Brecht's letter and without knowledge either of Brecht's other contractual problems with Felix Bloch Erben or of Brecht's new agency agreement with Suhrkamp, said that he wanted a draft contract *before* anything was signed with Brecht's friend Peter Suhrkamp. No reply to this request seems to have come from either Brecht or Suhrkamp—only a letter from Brecht dated 17 July 1949 saying that he had now terminated the Felix Bloch Erben contract and switched it over to Suhrkamp Verlag. How this could have been done on his signature alone when both Weill and Brecht had signed the original contract remains a mystery to this day. In a letter dated 11 July 1949, Felix Bloch Erben expressed concern about Weill's rights and said that Ruth Berlau had spoken on Weill's behalf that he was in agreement with these changes. How Ruth Berlau, a long-time lover of Brecht, could have represented Weill is also not explained. In a letter dated 15 July 1949, Felix Bloch Erben simply confirmed to Weill that they had turned over everything concerning *Die Dreigroschenoper* to Brecht!

Weill's request to Brecht for news of the royalties from the 1949 performance in Munich also went unanswered. Finally, exasperated by the way he was being treated by Brecht, Weill wrote to Universal on 7 February 1950: "Unfortunately I have heard neither from Brecht nor from Suhrkamp in this matter, and all my letters to Brecht remain unanswered. Therefore, I have turned over this entire matter to my lawyers, especially since Bloch Erben—without having any authorization from me—submitted the entire royalty accounting for *Die Dreigroschenoper* in Germany to Brecht." Just as Weill was putting the matter in the hands of his lawyers, finally something did come, but it was an apologetic letter from Elisabeth Hauptmann, not Brecht. Hauptmann's letter mentioned Brecht's "antipathy to writing," repeated the terms of the second Bloch Erben contract (the one including the 2½ percent for Klammer), and coolly stated that Brecht had given all his plays to Suhrkamp.[35] Haupt-

34. A copy of the letter from Schwarz to Brecht turns up rather mysteriously in the Weill-Lenya Research Center, but I have found no copy of the letter in the files of the Brecht Archive as yet.

35. According to Dr. Christoph Köhler of Felix Bloch Erben in a conversation with me on 15 October 1984 in Berlin, Brecht managed to cancel the *Dreigroschenoper* contract with Felix Bloch Erben with the following stratagem: "When Brecht returned to Berlin after the war, he came in to see Frau Wreede, who was then the head of Felix Bloch Erben. He demanded

mann did not specify what percentage Weill was to get from the
Suhrkamp contract, but did complain that Brecht objected to the amount
Weill was getting from the Universal contract. That, as far as I have been
able to determine, is where matters stood for Weill at the time of his death
on 3 April 1950.

On 27 October 1950, Suhrkamp Verlag sent a copy of its agency
agreement with Brecht to Paul, Weiss, Rifkind, Wharton & Garrison in
response to the firm's letter of 2 October 1950 on behalf of Mrs. Karoline
Weill, executrix of the estate of Kurt Weill. The covering letter from Peter
Suhrkamp itemized the distribution of royalties among the authors—
"confirmed by Bertolt Brecht and Frau Elisabeth Hauptmann-Dessau"—
as follows:

> B. Brecht. 60%
> Karl Klammer. 2½%
> (For performances in the German language,
> otherwise Brecht's share)
> Mrs. Elisabeth Hauptmann. 12½%
> Universal Edition, Vienna, for Kurt Weill. 25%

The letter concluded: "There exists no contract with our agency on musical works by Kurt Weill. Our agency also handles the music of *Dreigroschenoper* only by order of Universal Edition, Vienna."

The letters and the lawyers and the arguments about contracts went
on and on and on. When Brecht died on 14 August 1956, he left behind a
tangle of contracts and a large group of widows. But one contract prevailed. Helene Weigel, on the very day of Brecht's death, had obtained
from him a little signed note in English which gave her *all* the rights to
collect royalties for his work.[36] Her will literally and figuratively pre-

---

to know why his royalties had been given to the Nazis rather than to him. (According to
Köhler, all royalties due to Jewish authors in the Nazi period had been paid directly to those
authors by the foreign theaters themselves to avoid the Nazi bookkeeper who had been
imposed on the Berlin firm. Once again according to Köhler, something went wrong with a
Threepenny production in Denmark, and the royalties were not given to the authors but sent
to Berlin and placed in a Nazi-controlled account.) Brecht began to shout at Frau Wreede
and said that they were all a bunch of old Nazis at Felix Bloch Erben. Insulted by this, Frau
Wreede asked an assistant to bring her Brecht's general contract with the firm and the
Dreigroschenoper contract. She threw the contracts at Brecht and said: 'There is the door,
young man!'" In light of the fact that no evidence has turned up so far to confirm Köhler's
view that royalties were regularly paid directly by foreign theaters to Weill, Brecht, and
Hauptmann (with the one exception of the 1938 Paris payment of 4300 francs to Brecht), it
is difficult to know how accurate his account of the encounter between Brecht and Frau
Wreede may be. Köhler was not with the firm at that time; his account is not firsthand. It is
possible that Frau Wreede, who now is a nursing-home resident in Munich, will be able to
verify this encounter.
36. BBA 655/59. This note has never been published by Brecht's heirs.

vailed, and she became heir to all royalties. A little later, Peter Suhrkamp, knowing of Elisabeth Hauptmann's contribution to Brecht's plays and poems, insisted on her being given a portion of this income. After a decade of protests from Lenya and her attorneys to Brecht's heirs, Suhrkamp, and Universal Edition, Peter Suhrkamp, fully aware that the unilateral *Dreigroschenoper* contract with Brecht should not be allowed to stand, used his good offices to change the contractual terms so that Weill's estate would receive 35 percent, and Brecht's estate (including Klammer and Hauptmann) 65 percent, of book and stage rights in certain territories, and that film rights be split fifty-fifty in Germany.

Some of the major *Threepenny Opera* battles ended there; others would drag on for decades more, to be taken up by the heirs of the heirs. But that is too long a story to be told here, and not all the battles are over yet. Suhrkamp and its sub-agents still license stage performances of *Die Dreigroschenoper* under an agreement with only the Brecht interest. In Germany one of Brecht's heirs continues to act unilaterally, prohibiting productions in West Berlin and elsewhere apparently on ideological or personal grounds.[37] In effect, Weill's stage rights for *Die Dreigroschenoper* in Germany, as he rather than Brecht defined them, have apparently not been represented since 1933. What seems clear in all this is that when Brecht wrote in May 1929 that he had a "grundsätzliche Laxheit in Fragen geistigen Eigentums,"[38] he meant that he had a basic laxity with regard to the intellectual property *of others*, but not to his own—not to "The Business Deals of Herr Bertolt Brecht." In these deals he permitted himself, as far as I have been able to determine, no laxity whatsoever.

37. Brecht's heirs have acted very disparately in their respective domains with regard to Brecht-scholarship. Stefan Brecht, for example, has always encouraged access to unpublished materials, as had, at least in my case, his mother, Helene Weigel.

38. Brecht originally made the comment in an article published in the *Berliner Börsen-Courier*, 5 June 1929.

11

"Suiting the Action to the Word": Some Observations on *Gestus* and *Gestische Musik*
MICHAEL MORLEY

In surveying the literature on the relationship between words and music, it is relatively easy to find discussions of what is *not* an effective marriage of poet and composer. It is more difficult to find analyses of how and why particular songs are effective in their combination of word and music, especially in a dramatic or, to use the Weill/Brecht term, "gestic" context. Nor, understandably enough, can one find anything that could be seen as a normative program for writing an effective song, and it is far from the intention of this article to propose that one can derive such an algorithm from Brecht's or Weill's statements.

The rather nebulous concepts of *Gestus* and *gestische Musik*, defined neither systematically nor succinctly by either Weill or Brecht, describe nothing more than a technique for writing pointedly and economically within a dramatic context. In Weill's case, it evolved by gradually stripping away the compositional excesses that Wagnerian and Straussian music drama had led to (even in some of Weill's own works) and concentrating on concise melodic and rhythmic cells to convey musically the underlying dramatic kernel of a scene. This is clear from his own remarks concerning *Aufstieg und Fall der Stadt Mahagonny* and *Die Dreigroschenoper*, but perhaps even clearer in the models of gestische Musik by earlier composers that he selected: scenes from *Die Zauberflöte* and *Fidelio*.[1] The situations in these two scenes are musically and dramatically analogous: one character or pair of characters is discharging a task and commenting

---

1. See Kurt Weill, "Über den gestischen Charakter der Musik," *Die Musik* 21 (March 1929): 419–23; reprinted in Kurt Weill, *Ausgewählte Schriften* (Frankfurt, 1975), pp. 40–45. For a discussion of the historical derivation of the term *Gestus* and a survey of various interpretations of its meaning, see Kim H. Kowalke, *Kurt Weill in Europe* (Ann Arbor, 1979), pp. 495–96.

on it while the other is reacting to both the situation and the other's words by stating his or her own position. In Brecht/Weill terms, the Gestus of the temple guardians in *Die Zauberflöte* (act 2 finale, no. 21: "Der, welcher wandert diese Strasse") could be seen as both instructional and cautionary, while Tamino's is assertive and deliberately confident. In *Fidelio* (Act 2, no. 12: "Nur hurtig fort, nur frisch gegraben"), Rocco's is work activity, the need to complete a task in time, while Leonora's is mastering her own emotional and physical resources for *other* purposes while at the same time outwardly assisting Rocco in his.

Stanislavski might have found much to respond to in the latter scene, for it stands as a neat example of one character's major action crossing another's without any verbal exchange between the participants.[2] While one might argue that the note values given to Rocco's words are eighth notes and hence brisker and more appropriate to activity than the quarter notes and dotted quarters of Leonora's line of internalized questioning, there is another aspect to the scene which removes it from the realm of the purely illustrative. It would perhaps have been more obvious for Beethoven to have suggested the activity with scurrying and bustling figures in the orchestra and occasional emphatic accents. But the scene is given a stylized, almost "distanced" quality by the musical delivery and dynamic level, which do not allow the singers and the music to rely on easy emotional associations by the audience, but rather impart to the scene a clearly defined tableau- or frieze-like character. The action is thereby suspended. While the previous scene has set up in dialogue the situation and provided the narrative detail, the duet now carries the scene forward in a different way by focusing on the *idea* of activity expressed with deceptively simple musical means. And it is these which, precisely because they *are* so simple, do not allow for excesses of emotional delivery or a soaring and overly dramatized declamation of the vocal line.

The concept of Gestus, both historically and critically, also encompasses the style of performance. If Gestus was, for Brecht, the clear and stylized presentation of the social behavior of human beings, a main concern must always be the question of *communication* and *delivery*, the *transmission* to an audience of an action, an emotion, a state of mind in gestic terms. For the librettist, this meant that the words as spoken had to convey the direction in which the speaker was aiming; they were not merely a vehicle for elegant expression of ideas and images. For the composer, it meant that the music required a rhythmic shape that embod-

---

2. The idea of a character's "major action" is a fundamental one for Stanislavski's approach to scene analysis. In this connection, another of his directorial concepts—that of the "subtext" to the written text—has prompted the drawing of parallels in the relationship between words and music in Weill's compositions. For further details, see Kim Kowalke's discussion of this point in *Kurt Weill in Europe*, pp. 130–31.

ied the ebb and flow of both speech patterns and the gist of thought itself. Once established, this shape should not be obscured by an overly ornate deployment of melodic devices which, though pleasing to the ear and sensibilities, might have little to do with the sense of the words.

To approach the topic from another angle, I now turn to two examples of unsuccessful (in gestic terms) marriages of word and music. The first example approaches the question from the composer's point of view, the second from the audience's and performers'; both represent, albeit in slightly exaggerated form, the sort of response that a performance of any of the works of Brecht and Weill is *not* calculated to produce. The first example by Dryden/Handel was cited by V. C. Clinton-Baddeley:

> In Handel's setting of Dryden's *Ode on St. Cecilia's Day,* the lines
>
> The TRUMPET shall be heard on high,
> The dead shall live, the living die,
> And MUSICK shall untune the Sky
>
> are prolonged throughout fourteen pages of an ordinary Novello score. Dryden's poem was deliberately written for music, but by the time Handel had finished with it he might just as well have set the words backwards.[3]

The second strikes a cautionary note for all—not only music critics; be assured that your Bernard Levinish sins will find you out:

> The other day I attended a concert consisting mainly of the Song Cycles of Debussy, setting the words of Verlaine. They were sung by an Armenian lady who had escaped from a Turkish harem and had had no musical training. She was a barbaric creature who uttered loud howls, and the effect was to me disagreeable in the extreme; all the same, the audience was large and enthusiastic and the most enlightened organ of musical opinion today spoke of the performance with a chastened enthusiasm. I happened to meet the writer of the notice in the course of the following afternoon, and I asked him what he really got for himself out of that singular collocation of sounds. He said airily: "Well, you see, one gets emotions!" I said: "Good God! What sort of emotions?" He answered, "Well, you see, if one shuts one's eyes one can imagine that one is eating strawberry jam and oysters in a house of ill-fame, and a cat is rushing violently up and down the keyboard of the piano with a cracker tied to its tail."[4]

Notwithstanding the above, a major problem facing both the historian and the critic is the question, beyond that of origin and evolution, of the meaning and significance of the terms *Gestus* and *gestische Musik* for performers. Although it is to Weill that we owe the first extended analysis

---

3. V. C. Clinton-Baddeley, *Words for Music* (Cambridge, 1941), p. 17. This brief study still stands as one of the clearest and most judicious examinations of the relationship between music and poetry.

4. *The Bodley Head Ford Madox Ford* (London, 1962), 1:351.

of the terms, I think it more likely that Brecht introduced the term *Gestus* to Weill rather than vice versa.[5] Given the former's fondness throughout his life for developing a quasi-scientific approach to the theater (and the vocabulary to go with it), together with his classical background—*Gestus* in Latin means both gesture *and* attitude/mien—it seems more feasible that Brecht, who was concerned from the beginning with developing a theater and a dramaturgy of gestures which expressed relationships between characters rather than a drama of psychological investigation, prompted Weill to his own application of the term to the language of music.

As early as September 1920, Brecht, in an important note, toyed with two notions which became characteristic of his mature drama and which are, in fact, essential to any discussion of Gestus: the idea of contradiction and opposition and the need to find a visible and theatrically effective way of expressing both opposites and the unity of these opposites:

> I'm beginning to feel a faint prejudice against binary divisions (stong-weak, big-small, happy-unhappy, ideal-not ideal). It only happens because people are unable to think of more than two things at once. That's all that will fit into a sparrow-sized brain. But the soundest policy is just to keep on tacking.
>
> . . . Doing everything with all one's body and soul. Never mind exactly what. Small or great: both. Not just politics, hope for the future, sunshine all the time. See that rain? drink it.
>
> . . . I want a gesture for all that, visible from the gallery, strong enough to smell and be carried away by, for Act 4 of *Drums*.[6] Where a man does something, then does something else (—but does it). Stirs up a whole city, drives deluded people to attack the newspaper offices, makes poor people drunk, fills them with speeches, decks them out with weapons, then goes home.
>
> Let them go to the newspaper offices, not him. He's no longer deluded, no longer poor. The main thing is the gesture with which he goes home, removes his tunic, tears off his tie, grips his throat with his hands, breathes deeply, says "It's all a bore" and goes off to bed with his woman.[7]

These are essentially primary dramatic ingredients, and what Brecht is looking for is the simple yet stylized rendition of these for an audience. Of course, at this stage the politicizing of these intrapersonal pieces of behav-

---

5. This contention is speculative. As far as can be ascertained at present, the first published use of the term occurs in Weill's essay of March 1929. For a discussion of this and related matters, see Susan Borwick, "Weill's and Brecht's Theories on Music in Drama," *Journal of Musicological Research* 4 (October 1982): 39–67. The reader should be cautioned, however, about Borwick's oversimplification of Weill's notion of Gestus.

6. Brecht is speaking of his 1919 "comedy" centered on the Spartacist uprisings, *Trommeln in der Nacht* (Drums in the Night).

7. Bertolt Brecht, *Diaries 1920–1922*, trans. John Willett (London, 1979), pp. 34–35.

ior was not part of his aim; that was to come with the commitment to Marxism after 1926. But social behavior was, from the beginning, a major concern of Brecht's drama, together with the search for its theatrical embodiment. Some impetus in this direction was provided first by the interest of the expressionist theater in gesture (one has only to look at expressionist cinema to find examples of this) and second by the interest that behaviorism had sparked among many writers at the time.

Weill's own writings prior to and subsequent to his first contact with Brecht also evince his interest in arriving at a simplified yet expressive musical language which would be dramatic without resorting to conventional and overly emotional poses and formulas. But whereas Brecht arrived at his ideas through his own practice and his fondness for the "lower" forms of theater—circuses, music hall, the cabaret—Weill seems to have come at it from another angle: through his own studies of and experiments with opera and the influence of his teacher, Busoni. Many of Weill's views on opera and on the relationship between music and theater echo some of Busoni's pronouncements on these issues. Both men saw in Mozart and Bach the ideal models of the composer in whose works theatrical and absolute music were indivisible—though oddly Busoni is less convincing in analyzing this paradox than Weill.[8] Busoni draws attention to some fairly self-evident points: the dramatic quality of the Evangelist's passages in the *St. Matthew Passion* and the notion of interchangeability in Mozart's works (how "every one of his operas is a pure symphonic score and there is something of an opera score in each quartet"[9]—a point he seeks to prove by adding words to an unidentified phrase, which turns out to be from the Piano Concerto in C major, K. 467; see ex. 1). Can one really maintain that this illustration helps in understanding what is theatrical about such moments? One might equally well suggest any number of alternative texts to ensure that what Busoni called Mozart's "exuberant interval of a sixth" attains its latent "dramatic completion."[10] What about "If you come tomorrow, we can go and have a meal"; or "Now we know the grim truth, let us string the villain up" (which has a rather Gilbertian ring to it); or "When you look into my eyes, my heart begins to beat"? What Busoni's example does show, however, is how even a fleeting phrase of Mozart's music takes on a shape which readily accommodates words, precisely because the rise and fall of the melodic line are close to the rise and fall of speech rhythms and even of breathing itself.

But aside from these musical models, Busoni also drew attention to

8. In this connection, see Busoni's observations in *The Essence of Music and Other Papers*, trans. Rosamund Ley (London, 1957), pp. 35–44.

9. Ibid., p. 3.

10. Ibid., pp. 73–74.

another aspect of the dramaturgy of opera which has direct bearing on Weill's later analysis of Gestus. This is his concept of the *Schlagwort*, the catchword or abridgment. Busoni's discussion of the term and his application of it to opera display some similarities with Weill's comments on the nature and function of Gestus and gestische Musik:

> Just as the abridgement can sum up the inner part of the text of an opera, it can be transferred in a changed form to the action in general. In relation to the music it serves to create a situation rather than to give the reasons for it logically. . . . Therefore the audience's counterpoint of attention should be simplified by allowing speech and music to retire where action has the chief role; . . . by putting music and action in the background when a thought is being communicated.[11]

But whereas Busoni's comments explore the question from a theoretical standpoint, Weill is more concerned with both the nature and the function of gestic music: how the composer can *assist* the performer to convey the appropriate attitude to any particular incident at any particular moment.

The concern with performance and delivery is common to both Weill's and Brecht's notions of Gestus, as is the conviction that it must articulate social behavior rather than internalized, personal psychological states. Needless to say, social and political thrust is integral to Brecht's later pronouncements; but the concern for capturing human behavior, for concentrating on interaction between individuals, is there in Weill's essay when he notes: "We find gestic music wherever an incident involving human interaction is depicted through a naive kind of musical language."[12] Compare this with Brecht's much later remark: "A Gestus delineates the relationships of human beings to one another."[13] Of course, solutions to the problem of conveying this Gestus then had to be sought by both men in different areas—Weill through music, Brecht through language, scenic effect, and character. But what is important is that initially at least—and in Brecht's case throughout his life—they approach the

---

11. Ibid., p. 13.

12. Weill, "Über den gestischen Charakter der Musik," p. 421. In Heinrich Strobel, "Situation der Oper: Gespräch mit Kurt Weill," *Melos* 10 (February 1931): 43–45, Weill articulated his own sociological bases for his aesthetic path: "Today, when a grand form of theater is once again emerging, a form that seeks with elevated language and heightened reality to incorporate ideas of the present with timeless ones, opera must then also find its sociological sphere. What is more, it can be assumed that this form of theater can by no means do without the gestic effect and stylizing power of music" (translated in Kowalke, p. 535).

13. Bertolt Brecht, "Gestik" (undated note, 194–?) in *Gesammelte Werke* 16:753. In two essays from 1932 Weill wrote of a theatrical form that recaptures the original purpose of theater: "representation of types of human behavior." See Kowalke, pp. 541–44.

problem from the same standpoint: from the point of view of performance, delivery, and the clarification of human behavior for the audience.

Two of Brecht's observations are relevant here. Looking back on his own early attempts to write both text and music, he stated, "It must be remembered that my main work was in the field of the theater: I was always thinking of actual delivery."[14] And from the 1940s comes the following interesting, if somewhat choleric, diary entry:

> A musician to whom I gave the *Courage* texts to compose, along with a few guidelines, did three settings, played them to his friends, heard that he was copying Weill and pulled out. In vain I explained to him that he had just retained a principle—a principle Weill hadn't discovered. (I told him how I'd come across Weill when he was a pupil of Schreker and Busoni, as the composer of atonal psychological operas, and how I'd whistled things to him bar by bar and above all performed them for him.)[15]

The most important point here is not the undoubtedly exaggerated picture of Brecht giving Weill musical dictation, but the emphasis on *actual delivery*. And it does tie in with Weill's own remarks—closer to the time— that Brecht's primitive setting of the "Alabama Song" was an attempt to fix both the rhythm and his own inimitable manner of delivery.[16]

This manner of delivery requires some description, since it is fundamental to any understanding of Gestus and how it functions. Brecht's own delivery has often been described as aggressive, even savage—a characterization that is not quite apt. Of course, his voice never prompted description as "cream poured over purple velvet." Rather than brutal or aggressive, however, it is more accurately characterized as exaggeratedly harsh and clear. It is this clarity and directness which also distinguish early, authentic performances by other singers—as in the selections from *Die Dreigroschenoper* recorded by members of the original cast. All these performers used a vocal and dramatic technique appropriate to Brecht's call for textual clarity and nonemotional delivery, yet in keeping with

14. Bertolt Brecht, "Über reimlose Lyrik mit unregelmässigen Rhythmen," *Das Wort* 3 (March 1939); reprinted in *Gesammelte Werke* 19:395–403.

15. *Bertolt Brechts Arbeitsjournal* (Frankfurt, 1973), p. 188. The implications of this later, somewhat colored account of Brecht's and Weill's working methods have been discussed by Kowalke in his study and in my own article "New Tunes for Old: Brecht, Weill and the Language of Music in Four Unpublished Songs," *German Life and Letters* (April 1982): 241–52. Weill never studied with Franz Schreker—he only considered doing so. [Editor's note: In an interview with Arnold Sundgaard on 14 September 1984 in Los Angeles, the librettist of *Down in the Valley* told me that when he and Weill worked together, he tried to hum for the composer certain tunes he'd envisioned for his lyrics. Weill cut him off: "I don't want to hear them. Brecht used to whistle his horrible tunes to me, and it just threw me off." K. K.]

16. See Weill, "Über den gestischen Charakter der Musik," p. 422.

Weill's melodic lines: that is, a very "forward" type of voice production linked with a style of performance in which the singer does not immerse him- or herself in the character or in the emotions of the song. Indeed, a fondness for this performing style led both Brecht and Weigel to admire Ethel Merman's—and, in Weigel's case, even to borrow a gesture from her for *Mother Courage*.

This manner of performance has become almost a paradigm of Brecht/Weill performance practice; insisted upon by Brecht and also by Eisler, it is not as revolutionary as it may appear, for it has a definite tradition. The neuroses of the operatic tenor had been cleverly satirized in Gilbert and Sullivan's "A tenor, all singers above," which opens Act 2 of *Utopia Limited*. At the same time, interpreters of Weill and Brecht might also use Fitzbattleaxe's complaints as a primer for performance:

> You can't do chromatics
> With proper emphatics
> When anguish your bosom is ringing. . . .
> One ought to be firm as a rock
> To venture a shake in *vibrato*
> When fervor's expected
> Keep cool and collected
> Or never attempt *agitato*.

More immediately relevant, however, is the following: "Moreover, he never permitted violent expression in a performance. The singer, as a rule, only relates the experiences and feelings of others and does not himself impersonate the characters whose emotions he describes." Not, as one might think, a report of guidelines Brecht, Weill, or Eisler gave to performers, but Sonnleithner's account of Schubert's suggestion for the correct delivery of his songs.[17]

It is, alas, all too easy to list famous opera singers with marvelous voices who deliver the text of a song or aria as if they were reading the telephone directory in Tibetan or as if they'd just emerged from a daydream and were unclear as to where to begin. (A famous Australian example immediately springs to mind.) At the same time, such singers manage to imply to the audience that any attempt to clarify the meaning through gesture—let alone acting—would be an insult. This is *not* the emotional detachment that Brecht and Weill sought; as Brecht put it in a fragmentary poem:

> The operating with definitive gestures
> Can alter your character
> Change it.

17. Quoted in Otto Erich Deutsch, *Schubert: Memoirs by His Friends*, trans. R. Ley and J. Nowell (London, 1958), p. 116.

If the feet are higher than the behind
The speech itself is different and the way of speaking
Changes the thought.
A certain violent
Movement of the hand with the back facing downwards
While the upper arm stays close to the body convinces
Not only others, but also you who are making the movement.
Leafing back while you read, literally drawing up a
scheme—[18]

Weill also implies some rudimentary, stylized gestural underlining in his comments on Tamino's aria from *Die Zauberflöte*, "Dies Bildnis ist bezaubernd schön," when he says that Tamino can hold the portrait in his left or his right hand, but it makes no difference because the Gestus is dictated by the music itself.[19] In this case, the Gestus establishes a certain quizzical response to the attractiveness of the unknown subject of the painting and combines this with reflection on his own reactions and an awareness of the resurgence of emotion.

Application to the present case of Brecht's dictum on the proof of the pudding being in the eating may be dangerous, but we leave this series of recipes to look at several songs as illustrations of some of the points already raised. The first thing to remember about all of them—whether set by Weill, Eisler, or Brecht himself—is that they present a dramatic situation *in nuce*. We must see and hear the singer as *singer* and as *persona* telling a story, commenting on it, and inviting the listener to share or to step back from the persona's attitudes. This sounds somewhat complicated and text-oriented, but music has an essential role to play in the process.

Take the "Barbarasong" from *Die Dreigroschenoper*, for example. The text of the stanza on the page might suggest that Brecht intended one attitude to be sustained until the refrain—an attitude which might be described as a performer taking a tough line saying: "You can't pull the wool over my eyes; I was starry-eyed once but I soon saw through life's illusions." Of course, this attitude is very much to the fore, but it is not the only one that needs to be presented. Rather than playing only that at-

---

18. Brecht, *Gesammelte Werke* 8:377. A similar view is expressed in the anecdote recounting the exchange between Keuner (an alter ego of Brecht's) and the professor of philosophy, who makes great play to Mr. Keuner of his wisdom: "After a time, Mr. Keuner said to him: 'You're uncomfortable sitting, you're uncomfortable speaking, you're uncomfortable thinking.' The Professor of Philosophy became angry and said: 'I did not want to learn something about myself, but about the content of what I was saying.' 'It has none,' said Mr. Keuner. 'I see you walking clumsily, and there is no goal for you to reach while I watch you walking. You speak obscurely and there is no brightness created by you while you speak. Seeing your attitude, I'm not interested in your goal'" (*Gesammelte Werke* 12:375).

19. Weill, "Über den gestischen Charakter der Musik," p. 422.

titude, the performer is guided by Weill's musical setting to show attitudes *in stages*. This procedure is very close to the notion of finding the "beats" in a character's speech that articulate a change in mood or intent. Thus, the song's opening section establishes the Gestus of the storyteller and with it an attitude of (perhaps forced) naiveté, which the audience is invited to share, not only through the "einst so wie du" but through the jaunty bounce of the music. This is offset by Weill's choice of the minor key, which in itself is an ironic comment. In this opening we can find a lucid illustration of what Weill meant when he wrote that "the gestic means are expressed first of all in a rhythmic fixing of the text."[20] It seems likely that this emphasis on rhythm dates from Weill's collaboration with Brecht—after all, he provided Weill with the texts—but rather than the question of who had the greater say, more interesting is the readiness on Weill's part to see the logic of this approach and to work with it. In the earlier setting of the song that Brecht worked on with Franz S. Bruinier, the rhythmic shape is similar to Weill's in many respects (see ex. 2).[21]

To return to the earlier point about "beats," it is significant that these are actually reflected in the musical settings—somewhat primitively and directly in the Brecht/Bruinier version, more subtly and, if you like, more gestically in Weill's. One of the most distinctive features of a Weill/Brecht song (but, to be sure, not only of theirs) is the fact that the text and music, rather than simply evolving organically, proceed in stages or episodes. One distinct section follows another rather than a whole emerging gradually from the flow of music and text together. (In some cases, of course, this structure corresponds to the verse/refrain pattern or a simple A+B+C+refrain form.) In the Brecht/Bruinier setting of the "Barbarasong," there are four clear episodes (marked A, B, C, D in example 2), although the sudden musical hiatuses are sometimes ill contrived. Weill's version manages to be more adroit with its juxtaposition of C- and F-minor and at the same time to catch the Gestus more faithfully. In this case, note the matter-of-fact sharing of a confidence with the audience and the suggestion that they and the singer have the same values—a suggestion, of course, shockingly dispelled by the sudden "No" and the sense of flying in the face of accepted attitudes and moving on to better things.

The refrain proper provides another illustration of how Weill could deploy the wide range of harmonic and melodic means at a genuine composer's disposal to develop what is present in only embryonic form in the original setting. Weill constructs an overly languid and

---

20. Ibid., p. 421.
21. Bertolt Brecht-Archiv 249/60. Permission to reproduce material from Mrs. Barbara Brecht-Schall for the Brecht Estate, and Suhrkamp Verlag, Frankfurt.

"emotional" melodic line to comment ironically on the unromantic, almost aggressive words in such a way that—just as in the "Alabama Song"—one responds both to the effectiveness of the melody and to the implied ironic comment on its banality. Or, as Brecht put it:

> [The performer] must perform everything, especially something dreadful, with enjoyment and show his enjoyment.[22]

> The manageability [it is significant that Brecht prefers this term to *intelligibility* or something analogous] of a description depends on whether it contains yes and no in it and whether the yes or no is sufficiently established in it.[23]

Unlike the Brecht/Bruinier setting, Weill's music does not merely chug along beside or beneath the text. His setting manages to be simple, even trivial, and at the same time a perfect example of musical irony. (This same approach, incidentally, is followed in the "Liebeslied" from *Die Dreigroschenoper,* where Weill combines a deliberately saccharine melody with the stilted rhythm of the hesitation waltz or "Boston.") In such cases the rhythm and the melody are simple, interdependent *musical* gests which indicate to the perceptive performer the way in which he or she might externalize through character-attitudes and physical behavior the *social* gests of the scenes.

It might be argued that thus far the attempt to give a concrete example of Gestus has adopted a rather tangential approach. The reasons are simple. Weill's analysis of the term is extremely compressed and refers to but one example from his own work. Brecht, rather than providing a series of notes for the performer, prefers to draw his or her attention to something analogous or to an example drawn from another work. Most annoying of all is Brecht's failure, in a commentary on *Aufstieg und Fall der Stadt Mahagonny,* to provide some precise negative reference points which might have helped the reader or critic to arrive by inference at the positive: "I should not like to leave unmentioned the fact that in my opinion Weill's music for this opera is not purely gestic: it does, however, contain many gestic sections, at least enough to seriously endanger the usual type of opera."[24] Which ones are and which ones are not? one asks with impatience, although an informed guess might single out "Herr Jakob Schmidt" (in the version for the 1931 Berlin production), "The Maiden's Prayer" scene, and "Moon of Alabama" as decidedly gestic.

22. Brecht, "Anweisung an den Schauspieler" (undated notes, 1935–41?), reprinted in *Gesammelte Werke* 15:411.
23. Brecht, "Das Ja-Nein," reprinted in *Gesammelte Werke* 15:413.
24. Brecht, "Über die Verwendung von Musik für ein episches Theater" (1935?), reprinted in *Gesammelte Werke* 15:476.

Given Weill's and Brecht's concurrence that the rhythmic fixing of a text is the starting point for a gestic setting, one of the more ambiguous arguments that Weill advanced in his essay on gestic music must be his comment that "one can interpret a sentence rhythmically in various ways and yet express the same *Gestus*."[25] If one compares Weill's two settings of "Lasst euch nicht verführen"[26] from *Aufstieg und Fall der Stadt Mahagonny* with Brecht's own early setting—where it was still entitled "Luzifers Abendlied"[27]—two points are immediately clear: the rhythm and meter (Brecht's 6/8 versus Weill's alla breve) are different, and the singers' attitudes are quite different. (See ex. 3.) Weill opts for the mock-solemn, portentous, somewhat threatening; Brecht aims at a combination of the insistent and the encouraging. But both subvert familiar expectations. After the E-minor opening and the arresting leap of an octave onto the significant word "euch" in Brecht's setting, one expects the exhortation to continue, but the shift to A major (on the words "Der Tag steht vor den Türen") provides a wry sweetness to offset the negative thrust of the lines. Presumably this is a Lucifer with a honeyed tongue and an engaging manner. Whereas Brecht finds this way of bringing out the Gestus of the anti-Christian credo, Weill's settings take the shape of an anti-chorale in which the usual diatonic progressions are replaced by more widely spaced melodic intervals and harsher harmonies. Weill's specifically *musical* parody is certainly more obvious, and it is used to comment in its way on the religious attitudes parodied in the text.

The difficulty in discussing the Brecht/Weill collaborations is the very difficulty over which they later fell out: the territorial imperative. There is little doubt that because of his own musical leanings and concern with the question of delivery, Brecht was of help to Weill. At the same time Weill was no unthinking "setter of words." As a composer with an understanding of theater, he shaped the form and content of Brecht's librettos according to musical precepts while still adhering to Brecht's attitudes—attitudes similar in their way to those expressed by William Butler Yeats when he wrote: "Music that wants of us nothing but images—that suggest sound cannot be our music. . . . Such music can but dislocate wherever there is syntax and elaborate rhythm. The poet . . . hears with derision most settings of his work. . . . And yet there are old songs which melt him into tears."[28] Although one must accept

25. Weill, "Über den gestischen Charakter der Musik," p. 421.

26. The two versions of the number appear in the piano-vocal score of *Aufstieg und Fall der Stadt Mahagonny* (UE #9851, ed. David Drew) on pp. 234–35 and 292–93.

27. Brecht's setting is in private hands, along with a number of early songs and simple guitar accompaniments. I am grateful to Walter Brecht for his permission to reproduce the setting.

28. Quoted in Clinton-Baddeley, p. 11.

that Weill could not have continued to collaborate with Brecht without even more room for independent or interdependent development, his settings of Brecht's texts written in the United States without consultation with the poet, "Nannas Lied" (1939) and "Und was bekam des Soldaten Weib?" (1943),[29] are a curious mélange of styles and approaches. They raise three somewhat contentious points of criticism:

1. These two songs aspire to the concert platform. Indeed, they come very close to a German equivalent of the much-maligned English art song. Not that the music is trite: "Nannas Lied" in particular, with its haunting melody and flowing line, might almost persuade the listener that the words and the music really *ought* to melt on the ear.
2. Linked with this, the rhythmic outline is much less determinate than in Weill's earlier settings of Brecht's texts. Of course there is a funeral march suggested by the punctuated quarter notes of the "Soldier's Wife," but this becomes hypnotic, almost numbing, rather than disturbing.
3. Perhaps because of his Broadway work and the need to take on the idiom of American popular music, Weill reacted by returning not to the German cabaret song for a model, but to a style midway between the French ballad and the German lied.

Both songs are "occasional pieces": "Nannas Lied" was a Christmas present for Lenya in 1939, and "Und was bekam des Soldaten Weib?" was intended for propagandistic use during the war. Weill had no hand in shaping the text of either song, as he often did during his direct collaborations with Brecht. Although neither of these settings was written with a theatrical production in mind, Weill's approach to Brecht's texts—which nevertheless can be seen as self-contained theatrical moments that embody the social and personal Gestus of a character and situation—is less obviously theatrical or "gestic" than his earlier settings of similar texts. Whereas many of Weill's earlier songs based on Brecht's poetry (and indeed Eisler's settings of the same texts) present characters in stages with an episodic juxtaposition and alternation of attitude and behavior that are reflected in the music, in these two later songs the words and attitudes of the singer become blurred by, and are absorbed into, the music itself. It seems that Weill returned to a more conventional approach to songwriting with mood settings concerned more with capturing in the music an overall, generalized attitude (in "Nannas Lied," a reflective, bittersweet melancholy) than with the contradictory aspects of

---

29. Both are published in *The Unknown Kurt Weill,* ed. Lys Symonette (European American Music Corp., 1982), pp. 1–4, 16–19, as recorded by Teresa Stratas (*The Unknown Kurt Weill*), Nonesuch D-79019.

the persona expressed in the words. Moreover, the overall musical shape is more regular and predictable; "Nannas Lied" is built on a periodic phrase structure, with the verse and refrain falling into a predictable 12+12 bar pattern.

Echoes of the German lied tradition are evident: the introductory figure of "Nannas Lied" suggests Schubert or perhaps Schumann, and where the earlier Weill might have pointed this ironically, these chords are, arguably, less ambiguous. One might suggest that the counter-melody, doubled at the octave, which spices the accompaniment to the third stanza, is an ironic echo of the Liszt "Liebestraum" (which Weill played as a youth). But when the left-hand chords are related to the ascending Lisztian progressions in the right hand and the rather bland harmonic palette, it seems that we have a case of a musician in search of an idiom rather than a composer juxtaposing the new with the old in such a way that one comments on the other. Eisler's setting—composed with a stage production of *Die Rundköpfe und die Spitzköpfe* in mind and far simpler, apart from the arresting jagged opening notes—comes closer to the implicit Gestus of the text in its theatrical context, which, from the poet's viewpoint, *must* be both social and psychological.[30]

Whereas Weill's flowing melodic line smoothes out the irregularities in Brecht's text and evolves continuously throughout the song, Eisler's primitive setting pays closer attention to speech inflections, draws attention to the episodic shape of the singer's account, and almost approaches montage. Rather than aspiring to the homogeneous texture adopted by Weill within each strophe, Eisler's song corresponds more to a recitative and aria pattern in its verse/refrain opposition for each stanza. The irregular speech inflections are reflected in the changing meter (4/4, 2/4, 3/4), and the vocal line of the verse is kept deliberately unadorned, following a basic chord progression of 9ths and 7ths. Weill's refrain effects a smooth transition from the verse and moves logically and inevitably toward its musical culmination on the word "Tränen," but Eisler's refrain, in keeping with the text, comes as more of a disruption, in which the prostitute's moment of reflection is offset by emotional detachment. Although Eisler allows Nanna human dimensions in the refrain (in contrast to the Blues of the verse in which the merchandization—or reification—is presented), the music is not emotionally charged. It has something of the naiveté and directness of a folk song, and this unsophisticated musical language is used to express by implication the singer's real feelings, which, far from being emphasized and heightened by the music, are kept, as it were, at arm's length. It is only in

30. Eisler's setting is readily accessible in the *Brecht-Eisler Songbook*, ed. Eric Bentley (New York, 1967), pp. 156–58.

the last bars of Eisler's refrain, with its final falling phrase in the vocal line (which mirrors the 7th-chord and falling phrase immediately before the refrain) and in the unresolved piano postlude that the listener is allowed to sense the gap between the matter-of-fact recital and the reality of the character's past and present situation.

Brecht's other text set by both Weill and Eisler allows similar comparisons to be drawn. Although not wishing to use Eisler as a stick with which to beat Weill, I would suggest that, although "more gestic" is not synonymous with "more effective" or "better composed," in this case Eisler's setting again may be more in keeping with the poet's intentions.[31] Weill's setting of "Und was bekam des Soldaten Weib?" opens with emphatic chords, characteristically vacillating between the major and the minor, to establish the mood of ominous foreboding which will dominate the song. This might be seen as revealing the outcome too early—even allowing for the paradoxical change to pure B major at the end to accompany the receipt of the widow's veil. The text suggests a simple folk song or round, and its recurrent linking of the names of cities with the gifts received suggests an up-tempo, briskly moving setting rather than the more deliberate and musically sophisticated idiom chosen by Weill. It might also be argued that he distorts the speech rhythms by choosing to emphasize the "-kam" of "bekam" at the expense of the more important "Was," which, when stressed, establishes the rhetorical and attention-grabbing Gestus which is so crucial to the song's opening—as if a salesman were displaying his wares or a *Bänkelsänger* drawing the crowd's attention to the various objects depicted on his screen.

The text's gestic elements are of the most basic theatrical type—question/answer/commentary—and they allow the performer the opportunity, in Brecht's terms, to show *and* to be. This linking of performance modes (the performer as both narrator and mime) is presented throughout the text: "Und was bekam des Soldaten Weib aus der Lichterstadt Paris? Aus Paris bekam sie das seidene Kleid, (narrator) zu der Nachbarin Neid das seidene Kleid" (which suggests an elementary piece of character portrayal/mimicry). Weill's setting, although it does differentiate in musical terms between question and answer, still follows the periodic phrase structure noted in "Nannas Lied." And rather than providing opposition and contradiction through gestic elements, it establishes from the beginning a type of generalized *Grundgestus* (which might be described as "it'll turn out bad in the end") that is simply reiterated throughout the song. Once again we find traces of an uneasy combination of lied elements with echoes of Broadway: in particular, the Schumann-

---

31. Ibid., pp. 183–85.

esque opening with its reminder of "Die beiden Grenadiere" and the ending with the typical Broadway melodic unit which can be found in any number of songs from the period.[32] Moreover, it is difficult to argue for the presence of any of that characteristic Weillian irony in this setting— irony which is so distinctive an element in earlier songs and which depends on the dialectic of word and music linked with what David Drew accurately summarizes as "ambiguities of structure and expression together with apparent anomalies of tone and idiom [which are] exploited with such merciless accuracy that no formal or emotional expectations are secure."[33]

Eisler's setting finds a more convincing musical equivalent for the episodic structure of the text, although it might be said that the shift to the minor and to extended note-values in the final stanza could be seen as merely reinforcing in musical terms the implied attitude of the text. Yet even the bleak close of the song provides a good example of how a basic Gestus of sadness is filled out by the addition of a call to witness and an implicit accusation. A song of lamentation is simply not enough; the sadness and horror of the final section leave a stronger impact precisely because they have been preceded by the jangling, bouncing, cheap, and even humorous music of the opening (although one might get into some difficulties with any attempt at a complicated explanation in gestic terms of the opening bars, which conform to a fairly common folk-song pattern of tonic-dominant progression). Finally, one might argue that Weill's rhythmic fixing of the text is not as responsive to the metrical pattern as Eisler's, especially given the breaks after "Weib"; perhaps he was simply unwilling to usurp blatantly—as Eisler did—Stephen Foster's "Camptown Races" for his opening idea! In both songs, Eisler seems to be more willing than Weill to sacrifice musical sophistication and compositional prerogatives for the "naive," gestic quality that Brecht probably envisioned.

Through comparisons such as these we can perhaps comprehend the admittedly nebulous notion of gestic music. But in the second section of one of his most extended and complex poems, "The Shoe of Empedocles,"[34] Brecht reflects on the question of how subsequent generations of scholars tended to mystify their teacher's disappearance, seeing his shoe—left behind before his leap into Mount Aetna—as an objective correlative for anything ranging from immortality and transcendent mystery to the intangible proof of their opposites. And the poet strikes a

32. The closing figure has become almost a cliché in popular song. For other examples, see "The Kid's Last Fight" and "It's Harry I'm Planning to Marry" from *Calamity Jane*.

33. David Drew, "Kurt Weill and His Critics," *Times Literary Supplement*, 3 October 1975, p. 1144.

34. Brecht, *Poems 1913–1956*, pp. 253–55.

cautionary note which could well apply to any overly confident interpretations of Gestus:

> We hasten to make obscurity
> More obscure and prefer to believe the absurd
> Rather than to seek for a sufficient cause.

and

> Scholars are busy scenting a mystery
> Developing profound metaphysics, in fact all too busy.

Any discussion of the meaning of this term prompts such thoughts, and I would not claim that the preceding comments are the honorable exception. Perhaps one or two of the illustrations might serve to clarify the issues, though ultimately we may still end up holding the Greek philosopher's leather sandal in some confusion, finding our elaborate interpretations gainsaid by its worn, unremarkable appearance. But at least in *that* case the Gestus will be appropriate.[35]

Examples

Example 1. Busoni's addition of words to Mozart's Concerto for Piano and Orchestra in C major, K. 467, mvt. I, mm. 128–29.

Example 2. Brecht/Bruinier: "Barbarasong."

35. John Willett's discussion of Brecht's musical collaborators ("Brecht and the Musicians," in *Brecht in Context* [London, 1984], pp. 151–77) also addresses some of the questions raised in this article. In particular, his comments on Brecht's attitudes toward the relationship between words and music and toward vocal delivery (pp. 173–77) are a valuable complement to the above discussion.

Example 2. Brecht/Bruinier: "Barbarasong" *continued*

Because no early draft of the song's text has survived, the underlay of text for the Brecht/Bruinier melody is conjectural in places. In some cases, the reconstruction suggests itself (e.g., the repetition of "dann sage" at mm. 21–24, although even here one might argue in favor of "dann sag' ich" followed by "dann sage ich."); in other cases, it is more problematic to arrive at a convincing underlay of text (e.g., mm. 18–21).

Lasst euch nicht ver - füh - ren! Es gibt kein Wie - der - kehr.

(Der) Tag steht in den Tü - ren; Ihr könnt schon Nacht-wind spü - ren. Es

kommt kein Mor - gen mehr.   (usw.)

Example 3. Brecht, "Luzifers Abendlied."

12

The Genesis of
Die sieben Todsünden
RONALD K. SHULL

To the thousands of people who have enjoyed *Die sieben Todsünden* in balletic, theatrical, concert, and recorded performances, it must come as a surprise to discover that to date this work has been largely ignored in the massive literature about Brecht and that only slightly more attention has been devoted to its background in the few major works of scholarship concerning Weill.[1] Considering the studies devoted to *Aufstieg und Fall der Stadt Mahagonny* (hereafter called *Aufstieg*), *Die Dreigroschenoper,* and even *Happy End,* it is particularly unfortunate that more light has not been shed on the genesis of *Die sieben Todsünden.* Not only is Weill's score "the crowning masterpiece of his European career,"[2] but *Die sieben Todsünden* is historically distinctive in a number of ways. It is, for example, the last work Weill completed in concert with Brecht and the first either completed after their emigration from Germany in 1933.[3] It also marked the

1. Characteristic of the position taken by Brecht scholars is John Willett's dismissal of *Die sieben Todsünden* as "a quite conscious regression on Brecht's part" and "a plain attempt to earn money." John Willett, *The Theatre of Bertolt Brecht: A Study from Eight Aspects,* 3d rev. ed. (New York, 1968), p. 136. See also Frederic Ewen, *Bertolt Brecht: His Life, His Art and His Times* (New York, 1967), p. 304; Werner Mittenzwei, *Bertolt Brecht: Von der "Massnahme" zu "Leben des Galilei"* (Berlin and Weimar, 1977), pp. 142–43.

In the literature on Weill, the most extensive historical account of the ballet is provided by Kim H. Kowalke, *Kurt Weill in Europe* (Ann Arbor, 1979), pp. 83–85. See also David Drew, Foreword to *Über Kurt Weill* (Frankfurt am Main, 1975), p. xvi; Jürgen Schebera, *Kurt Weill für Sie porträtiert* (Leipzig, 1980), p. 29; Gottfried Wagner, *Weill und Brecht: Das musikalische Zeittheater* (Munich, 1977), pp. 217–30.

This paper is based upon my remarks at the Kurt Weill Conference, but it has been substantially revised in light of new information provided by the Weill-Lenya Research Center and by David Drew, Kim H. Kowalke, and other conference participants.

2. Kim H. Kowalke, program notes, "The Seven Deadly Sins." Los Angeles Philharmonic, *Performing Arts* 16 (December 1982): 12.

3. In the 1940s, while Weill and Brecht were living in America, they attempted without success to collaborate on musical versions of *Der gute Mensch von Sezuan* and *Schweyk im Zweiten Weltkrieg.* After Brecht's return to Europe in 1947, he again tried to interest Weill in working on the *Schweyk* project, but nothing came of the attempt. (See Weill's letter to Brecht of 3 September 1947 in the Bertolt-Brecht-Archiv, No. 311/47. Hereafter, references to the

team's first major work together since its bitter disintegration over the production of *Aufstieg* in Berlin during December 1931. Finally, *Die sieben Todsünden* is the only libretto Brecht wrote for a ballet[4] and the last text he wrote specifically for Weill, under circumstances that allowed him the least influence over its realization in production.[5]

Weill's collaboration with Brecht began in March 1927 and reached its zenith even before the premiere of *Aufstieg* on 9 March 1930. The first performance of that opera was the fulfillment of an idea Brecht had held since at least 1924, and it concluded the project which had brought the two of them together.[6] It marked the beginning of the end of an era. Since 1927, Brecht had been searching for dramatic means which could express the social conflicts of industrial capitalism, and in 1929 he wrote the first of his didactic "learning plays," which were intended to help in altering society as well as critiquing it. At the same time, his musical tastes moved away from the ironic use of popular idioms toward the hard-edged and agitational melodies of mass songs and workers' choruses. For his part, by the time of the premiere of *Mahagonny*, Weill yearned to work with a more tractable librettist and to free his music from Brecht's increasingly rigid ideological precepts. The time was ripe for Brecht and Weill to follow their own paths.

The separation, however, did not occur immediately. Until the end of 1932, the two artists remained on polite terms professionally and even planned new projects. In the winter of 1929 Weill had sought a text to which he might compose a *Schuloper* or didactic opera. Elisabeth Hauptmann provided a translation of Arthur Waley's version of a Japanese Noh play, *Taniko,* which Brecht set into verse and altered only slightly. On the basis of this text, Weill completed *Der Jasager* in May 1930 and submitted it to Berlin's New Music Festival, where it was to be performed in June. Meanwhile, Brecht was working with Hanns Eisler and others to convert the *Jasager* materials into the revolutionary learning

---

Brecht-Archiv will be abbreviated "BBA" followed by the archival number.) Weill did complete the settings of Brecht's "Nannas Lied" and "Und was bekam des Soldaten Weib?" in America, but he did so without consultation with Brecht.

4. The original version of the *Badener Lehrstück vom Einverständnis* performed in 1929 included Karl Koch's film of a "Totentanz" by Valeska Gert in the section now entitled "Betrachtung der Toten." Brecht apparently liked the dance and insisted that the film be shown in later productions of the work. (See Brecht's contract provisions in his letter to Schott Verlag of 16 September 1929 in the Paul-Hindemith-Institut, Frankfurt am Main.)

5. Brecht was closely involved in the premiere productions of the *Mahagonny Songspiel, Die Dreigroschenoper, Der Lindberghflug,* and *Happy End.* He participated in a staging of *Der Jasager* shortly after that work's premiere.

6. Bertolt Brecht, *Tagebücher 1920–1922: Autobiographische Aufzeichnungen 1920–1954,* ed. Herta Ramthun (Frankfurt am Main, 1975), p. 202: dairy entry for July 1924.

play, *Die Massnahme,* also intended for the New Music Festival. When the festival's directors refused to allow performances of *Die Massnahme,* Weill supported the authors' protest against censorship by withdrawing *Der Jasager* from the festival.[7] Later that summer when Brecht first reworked the text of *Der Jasager,* Weill composed new music for two interpolations, but he was not involved in Brecht's later revisions and provided no music for *Der Neinsager.*[8]

Shortly before the New Music Festival, newspaper announcements stated that Brecht was working with Weill on *Der Brotladen* and implied that they were also planning an opera based on *The Good Soldier Schweyk.*[9] Nothing, however, came of these projects, and during the next twelve months the collaboration was limited to various revisions for *Aufstieg.* Brecht continued his work with Eisler on *Die Massnahme* and planned other learning plays, while Weill collaborated with Caspar Neher on their opera, *Die Bürgschaft.* In February 1931 Weill contributed incidental music for Brecht's production of *Mann ist Mann* at Berlin's Staatstheater,[10] and that summer the two of them prepared *Aufstieg* for its Berlin premiere. During rehearsals for that production, their relationship reached its crisis. Both collaborators wanted to dictate the artistic shape of the production. "Brecht fought for the priority of the word, Weill for that of the music."[11] The confrontation grew intense. Lawsuits and physical violence were threatened, bitter words were exchanged, and the collaboration seemed to have come to an irrevocable end. Even though the rift between Weill and Brecht at this point was deep, it did not yet preclude the possibility of future artistic work together, for, by the beginning of

7. See David Drew, "Weill's School Opera," *Musical Times* 106 (December 1965): 934; and Bertolt Brecht and Hanns Eisler, "Offener Brief an die künstlerische Leitung der Neuen Musik Berlin 1930, Heinrich Burkhard, Paul Hindemith, Georg Schünemann," *Bertolt Brecht: Gesammelte Werke in 20 Bänden: Werkausgabe Edition Suhrkamp* (Frankfurt am Main, 1967) 17:1029–30.

8. The autograph partitur for the two interpolations is in Universal Edition's archive in Vienna. See David Drew, *Kurt Weill: A Handbook* (Faber, forthcoming) for a full discussion. Neither Weill nor Lenya authorized performance of *Der Neinsager* utilizing Weill's music composed for *Der Jasager.*

9. The announcement appeared on 2 June 1930 in the *Wiesbadener Tageblatt* and on 4 June in the *Münchener Neuste Nachrichten* and the *Mainzer Anzeiger;* BBA 474/98, 134.

10. The production, codirected by Ernst Legal, opened on 6 February 1931. According to a program note, Weill provided three pieces of music, "Nachtmusik," "Schlachtmusik," and "Marschmusik" (BBA 1089/42). In his essay on stage music, Brecht mentions the first two pieces and "a song whose verses were sung during the unconcealed scene changes." Bertolt Brecht, *Gesammelte Werke* 15: 472–73. Weill's music for *Mann ist Mann* is presumably lost.

11. Ernst Josef Aufricht, *Erzähle, damit du dein Recht erweist* (Berlin, 1966), p. 126. See also Kowalke, *Kurt Weill in Europe,* p. 62.

1933, Weill was prepared to set Brecht's *Die Rundköpfe und die Spitzköpfe* to music as an operetta.[12]

The Nazi seizure of power in February 1933 drove Brecht and Weill into exile, separating them geographically as well as psychologically and artistically. On 28 February, the day after the Reichstag fire, Brecht and his family left Berlin for Prague. They spent a short time there and then went on to Vienna, where they found temporary refuge with Helene Weigel's family.[13] Although Brecht's movements during this period have not yet been precisely documented, it is clear that he remained in Vienna through 16 March, when he held a public reading from his *Lesebuch für Städtebewohner*.[14] A week after that reading, on 23 March, Weill arrived by car in Paris.[15]

Only a few months earlier, in December 1932, Weill had enjoyed immense success in Paris with a performance of an expanded version of the *Mahagonny Songspiel* and *Der Jasager*, attended and acclaimed by such leading artists as Cocteau, Gide, Honegger, Picasso, and Stravinsky.[16] He could be confident, then, of finding an initial welcome and some contacts who could expedite opportunities to work in Paris while waiting for the Nazi aberration to fade away. The opportunities came quickly, and within two weeks Weill accepted a commission to write a ballet for "Les Ballets 1933."[17] This company, newly founded by Boris Kochno, Diaghilev's former secretary, and George Balanchine, was financed by a young Englishman named Edward James. James had been present at Weill's triumph the previous December and now wanted him to write a ballet for his estranged wife, the ballerina Tilly Losch. Weill agreed to undertake the project "for a substantial fee" and approached Cocteau to write the libretto.[18] When he declined the offer, Weill turned once again to Brecht.

Looking for a less vulnerable home in exile than Austria could provide, Brecht had meanwhile moved to Switzerland. He spent a short time in Zurich and by 27 March had moved to a hotel in Lugano, where he could live less expensively.[19] There he met Kurt Kläber and his wife, Lisa

12. In a letter to me, David Drew has dated the beginning of Weill's interest in *Die Rundköpfe und die Spitzköpfe* as January 1933. In a letter inviting Brecht to the premiere of *Die sieben Todsünden* (BBA 911/47), Weill wrote that he had heard that Eisler was to write music for the play and informed Brecht that he was dropping the idea for an operetta.

13. Klaus Völker, *Brecht-Chronik: Daten zu Leben und Werk* (Munich, 1971), p. 55. Bertolt Brecht, *Briefe*, ed. Günther Gläser (Frankfurt am Main, 1981), letter no. 170, p. 164. See also Klaus Völker, *Brecht: A Biography*, trans. John Nowell (New York, 1978), pp. 173–78.

14. Günther Gläser, notes to letter no. 164, Bertolt Brecht, *Briefe*, p. 931.

15. Kowalke, *Kurt Weill in Europe*, p. 84.

16. Kowalke, program notes, "The Seven Deadly Sins," p. 11.

17. Ibid.

18. Ibid.

19. Brecht, *Briefe*, letter no. 166, p. 161.

Tetzner, who offered the Brechts and other artists a temporary home at their summer house in Carona.[20] A few days later, Brecht apparently accepted their offer and met his family in Carona. It was probably there that Brecht received Weill's invitation to write the libretto, and shortly thereafter he set off for Paris.

While waiting for Brecht to arrive, Weill and Les Ballets' producers decided on the formative idea of the piece. It was to be a "ballet chanté" centering on a woman whose personality was split into a singing half and a dancing half. This would allow Lotte Lenya, whose performance James had much admired in the December *Mahagonny*, to be called back from Vienna to perform opposite Losch, whom Lenya supposedly resembled. (She and Weill had been separated for more than a year and were awaiting finalization of their divorce.)[21] Thus, the basic outline for the ballet had been established before Brecht entered the picture.

The exact date of Brecht's arrival in Paris and the length of his collaboration with Weill are not yet certain. One of Brecht's letters shows that he was in Paris by 15 April,[22] the day before Weill began his score.[23] Presumably, then, Weill began drafting the music as soon as Brecht had supplied the text. Although Brecht later told Sergei Tretiakov that his stay in Paris lasted "a week,"[24] the collaboration probably took somewhat longer, for in a letter to Margot von Brentano Brecht noted that while in Paris he met Hanns Eisler,[25] who did not arrive there until "the end of April."[26] Certainly, it must have taken some time for Weill to convince Brecht that the Freudian sketch worked out by the ballet's producers could be transformed into an attack on capitalism.[27] Once Brecht had been won over, however, he must have thrown himself into the work with his customary energy and must have quickly drafted the necessary lyrics. A letter from Weill to Brecht indicates that Brecht had completed his

---

20. Ibid., letter nos. 167 and 168, pp. 162–63. See also Ernst and Renate Schumacher, *Leben Brechts in Wort und Bild* (Berlin, 1978), p. 114.

21. Kowalke, program notes, "The Seven Deadly Sins," p. 11. Weill had been toying with the notion of a "ballet with singing" since 1927, when Harry Kessler reported in his diary entry for 14 November that Weill proposed to write music for Kessler's ballet which "should be mainly *sung* from behind the scene, using only a very few instruments—flute, saxophone." See Harry Kessler, *In the Twenties: The Diaries of Harry Kessler,* trans. Charles Kessler (New York: 1971), p. 335.

22. BBA 783/32.

23. Weill's rehearsal score is held by the heirs of the Vicomtesse de Noailles and is dated at the end, "16 April–4 Mai 1933."

24. Brecht, *Briefe*, letter no. 170, pp. 164–65.

25. Ibid., letter no. 169, pp. 163–64.

26. Manfred Grabs, *Hanns Eisler—Werk und Edition: Eine Dokumentation*, "Arbeitsheft 28" of the Akademie der Künste der D.D.R., Berlin (1978), p. 90.

27. See Kowalke, program notes, "The Seven Deadly Sins."

libretto and left Paris before Weill finished five of the musical numbers.[28] In the same letter, Weill wrote that James was "completely enchanted" by the libretto and would soon send Brecht's payment to him. Obviously, Brecht had completed his part of the bargain to everyone's satisfaction. On 4 May Weill finished his piano score.

Since the score and text had been completed, there seems to be no compelling reason for Brecht to have returned to Paris in May, as some scholars have speculated.[29] Further work on the lyrics at that time would have led to musical changes and, consequently, changes in choreography and staging. The delays occasioned by such changes would surely have reopened the old wounds in Brecht and Weill's relationship, and it is improbable that either was willing to risk another confrontation during the already insecure first days of their exile. For the same reason, it seems implausible that Brecht returned to Paris to have a hand in staging the ballet, a genre in which he had no previous experience and no particular interest. Furthermore, a second trip to Paris would have cost Brecht money that he needed during a time when he and his family were in uncertain financial circumstances and contemplating an expensive relocation to Denmark.[30] In fact, Weill was so aware of Brecht's financial situation that, in a letter inviting him to the premiere of *Die sieben Todsünden*, the composer was moved to promise Brecht one thousand francs to pay for the trip.[31] In that same letter, written the week before the premiere, Weill's description of preparations for the production indicates that earlier in May Brecht had not been involved in plans for the design or choreography. Actually the text of *Die sieben Todsünden* itself, as David Drew points out, "contains nothing to indicate that it was intended for the stage, [although] it resembles the 'Mahagonny-Gesänge' in that its descriptions of actions and reactions develop a certain narrative momentum." The scenario Balanchine used for the choreography in 1933 has acquired quasi-official status and has frequently been misattributed to Brecht. In fact, it was written by Edward James and Boris Kochno without consultation with Brecht.[32]

Brecht accepted Weill's invitation and traveled to Paris for the bal-

28. BBA 911/46. In the undated letter Weill wrote that he was working "like a horse" and had completed five numbers.

29. See Völker, *Brecht-Chronik*, p. 56.

30. Regarding Brecht's financial situation, see Brecht, *Briefe*, letter no. 167, p. 162; Schumacher, *Leben Brechts*, p. 116; Völker, *Brecht: A Biography*, pp. 173, 178.

31. BBA 911/47. The letter is dated only with "Donnerstag" (Thursday), but the wording of the invitation makes clear that it was written during the week before the premiere.

32. David Drew, *Kurt Weill: A Handbook.* When the libretto was first published by Suhrkamp in 1959, a German translation of the James/Kochno scenario was included, uncredited. A carbon copy of the original typescript of the scenario is in the Weill/Lenya Archive at Yale University.

let's premiere on 7 June. A few days later he sent a postcard to Helene Weigel describing the production as "completely lovely but not all that important."[33] On 1 July the ballet opened under the title *Anna-Anna* for a two-week run at London's Savoy Theatre with the original cast, presented in a hasty English translation by James and Weill after the first performance. Thereafter, the collaborators seemed to lose interest in the fate of their work. On 12 November 1936, *Die sieben Todsünden* was staged at the Royal Theater in Copenhagen near Brecht's home in exile, but there is no evidence that he took part in the preparations for the production.[34] After 1936 neither Brecht nor Weill made any move to produce or to publish *Die sieben Todsünden*. Aside from the program insert for the premiere and a copyist's piano-vocal score duplicated for the use of Les Ballets 1933,[35] neither the original German text nor Weill's music appeared in print until the score was published privately in 1955 by Lotte Lenya.[36] Brecht's text was not included in any of the sanctioned collected editions of his works published during his lifetime, but in 1959 Suhrkamp posthumously published a "revised" text under the spurious, extended title *Die sieben Todsünden der Kleinbürger*.[37]

One of the most surprising facts about the history of *Die sieben Todsünden* is that its generative idea, Anna's split personality, was provided by Weill and James, for Brecht had been toying with this motif for a number of years. Brecht's concern with the fragility of human personality and its vulnerability to social forces goes back at least as far as *Trommeln in der*

33. Brecht, *Briefe,* letter no. 172, p. 165.

34. Engberg's claim that the Danish producers worked together with Brecht and Weill to prepare for the production has not been substantiated. Inasmuch as Weill had already arrived in America by that time, it is certain that he did not participate in the Danish production. See Herald Engberg, *Brecht auf Fünen: Exil in Dänemark 1933–1939,* trans. Heinz Kulas (Wuppertal, 1974), p. 160.

35. David Drew, *Kurt Weill: A Handbook.*

36. Kowalke, *Kurt Weill in Europe,* p. 447. The vocal score published privately by Lenya in 1955 was a piano reduction by Wilhelm Brückner-Rüggeberg, who had transposed the score down to accommodate the lower range of the 57-year-old Lenya. Because there was no indication to the contrary, it was widely assumed that the lower version was the original. In fact, Lenya had sung in the higher keys in 1933; the first performance of the original version after 1936 was by the BBC Symphony under Colin Davis with Evelyn Lear in 1968. The original score was not released on recording until 1983 (EMI-Angel Digital DS-37981; City of Birmingham Symphony Orchestra, Simon Rattle, conductor; Elise Ross, Anna I).

37. Bertolt Brecht, *Die sieben Todsünden der Kleinbürger* (Frankfurt am Main, 1959). When Brecht revised and retitled the piece is uncertain, but Weill was never consulted. Apparently Helene Weigel proposed the revised title to Suhrkamp, and Brecht's heirs have insisted that it be retained in subsequent publications. Only two typescripts with this title, both undated, are held in the Brecht archive (BBA 50/1–21 and 41–60). The 1959 contract among B. Schott's Söhne, Helene Weigel, and Lotte Lenya refers to the work only as *Die sieben Todsünden;* "der Kleinbürger" did not appear in Schott's published vocal score until 1972, when it was added without Lenya's consent.

Nacht (1919), *Im Dickicht der Städte* (1923) and, most explicitly, *Mann ist Mann* (1920–25). In these plays Brecht portrays human personality as completely malleable, subject to the social forces which impinge upon human needs and desires. He also demonstrates that those forces can be rigged to take advantage of human needs, so as to produce whatever type of personality one wants. In *Im Dickicht der Städte,* for example, Schlink shapes Garga's world until he must become the kind of opponent Schlink needs. In *Mann ist Mann* Galy Gay is transformed from a peaceful dockworker into "the human fighting machine" through control of his environment and manipulation of his needs. In these early treatments of personality Brecht takes perverse delight in showing human beings as machines which can be retooled to serve any function.

When he began his Marxist studies in 1926, Brecht came to view personality as a product of socioeconomic processes and human beings as the victims of capitalism's control of those processes. In industrialized capitalism workers produce goods from which they do not directly benefit. Indeed, some of those goods can be turned against their producers and used to hold workers in a subservient state. The worker, then, is "alienated" from that which she or he produces, in Brecht's view. Worse, workers are alienated from their own labor, because that which they create by their labor no longer bears a direct relation to their needs and desires. Both labor and the goods it produces are the property of the capitalist, and workers are forced to negotiate in order to recover any real value from their creations. Workers must depersonalize their labor in order to sell it as a commodity to the capitalist. For this they receive whatever wage the capitalist is prepared to pay, and with their wages they then must buy back the very products they have created. In order to survive in capitalistic society, according to Marxist theory, the individual has to adopt a set of businesslike behaviors which are often in direct contradiction to his or her most human needs. The worker is asked to exploit him- or herself, acting as both producer and seller. In other words, workers are forced to adopt a societally induced "split personality."

Around 1927 Brecht set out to explore this self-alienation in a dramatic piece to be called "Fanny Kress oder der Huren einziger Freund," in which a prostitute disguises herself as a male cigar merchant in order to help her fellow prostitutes.[38] This plan marks the introduction into Brecht's works of a character who maintains two distinct, simultaneous personalities, one of them loving and ready to help others, the second businesslike and able to secure the means of help. Around 1930 Brecht

---

38. Werner Hecht, ed., *Materialien zu Bertolt Brechts "Der gute Mensch von Sezuan"* (Frankfurt am Main, 1976), p. 17.

returned to this idea for *Die Ware Liebe*, a play which was to explore more fully the socioeconomic elements of the split-personality motif.[39] In this fragmentary piece, on which *Der gute Mensch von Sezuan* is based, a young prostitute again disguises herself as a businessman. The businessman is effectively able to handle the prostitute's business affairs, but his presence requires the increasing repression of her original personality. Although Brecht did not continue work on *Die Ware Liebe*, in 1929 he incorporated the Faustian dimension of this bipartite personality into the character of Mauler in *Die heilige Johanna der Schlachthöfe*. His interest in dual personalities may also have resurfaced shortly before his exile. In February 1933 Brecht requested from Felix Bloch Erben the rental material for Charles LeCoq's operetta *Giroflé-Girofla*,[40] a piece centering on identical twin sisters (both played by the same actress) and the complication of their marriage plans. Brecht emigrated before receiving the rental materials.

Inasmuch as Brecht had already been seeking a way of incorporating a "split personality" into his drama, Weill's suggestion for *Die sieben Todsünden* must have appeared at least a little serendipitous. Weill offered Brecht a chance to try out the split-personality motif before an audience. At the same time, the Freudian overtones inherent in the motif surely gave Brecht pause and caused him some frustration. He was being given the chance to create a significant emblem of the human condition under capitalism but could not hope to control all the circumstances under which his vision was to be presented. Over that vision hung the specter of the "psychologizing" music which Brecht ascribed to Weill and which he loathed.[41] Given this situation, Brecht did what he could to rescue the opportunity for his own purposes. He quickly drafted texts exploring the "split" and incorporating other ideas culled from his recent past.

The most immediate, but as yet unexplored (and surely subconscious), source of Anna's dual personality and her journey is the split between Weill and Brecht and their emigration from Germany. The victim of divided personality in *Die sieben Todsünden* is an artist. In Brecht's other attempts to handle this motif the division occurs within a business person—a porter in *Mann ist Mann*, a speculator in commodities in *Die heilige Johanna*, a landowner in *Herr Puntila und sein Knecht Matti*, and a

---

39. Ibid., pp. 17–18.

40. The letter of response from Felix Bloch Erben is uncatalogued in the BBA. This information was passed along to me by Joachim Lucchesi in a letter of 25 May 1983. Alexander Tairov's spectacular production of the operetta had toured to Berlin in 1923, and knowledge of this production may have helped spark Brecht's interest in the piece.

41. See Brecht, "Über die Verwendung von Musik für ein episches Theater," *Gesammelte Werke* 15:474; and "Anmerkungen zur Oper *Aufstieg und Fall der Stadt Mahagonny*," *Gesammelte Werke* 17:1011; Bertolt Brecht, *Arbeitsjournal 1938–1955*, ed. Werner Hecht (Berlin, 1977), entry of 16 October 1940, p. 124.

prostitute in "Fanny Kress," *Die Ware Liebe,* and *Der gute Mensch von Sezuan.* That Anna is an artist may point to parallels between the two artistic "sisters" and the "sister arts" of music and theater represented by Weill and Brecht. Like Anna, Brecht and Weill formed the simultaneously complementary and antagonistic elements of a single creative team, the separate personalities of a successful artistic entity. Anna I's description of her dancing sister as "beautiful" but "somewhat mad"[42] seems in retrospect to embody Brecht's view that Weill was the practitioner of a lovely but irrational art to which his texts provided the "rational," "practical" antidote,[43] much as Anna I's verbality contrasts with her sister's nonverbal dancing. Similarly, the "culinary" appeal of Weill's music made the team's works "marketable commodities," which Brecht through his words sought to save from the "sin" of irrelevance. Conversely, the "marketability" of Weill's melodies made it possible for the team to earn a living in spite of Brecht's artistic and political "pride," a notion alluded to in scene 2.[44]

The journey which takes Anna from her Louisiana home to six cities reminds one that *Die sieben Todsünden* was begun during the first weeks of the collaborators' emigration.[45] Like Anna's journey, Brecht's emigration had already taken him to several cities—to Prague, Vienna, Zurich, Lugano, and Carona. The purpose of both journeys was to provide security for the principal actor and his/her family, and in both cases the traveling artist must sell his/her art to obtain that security. Brecht's peculiar familial situation underscores this parallel. In addition to earning money for his current wife, Helene Weigel, and their two children, Brecht was also helping to support two families who remained in Germany: his former lover Paula (Bie) Banholzer and her son by Brecht, and his ex-wife Marianne Zoff and her daughter by Brecht.

The other elements Brecht used in the ballet have a longer history. Randolph Goodman has noted that Theodore Dreiser's *An American Tragedy* may have provided some of the material for *Die sieben Todsünden.*[46] This novel appeared in Berlin in 1927,[47] and shortly thereafter

42. Kurt Weill, *Die sieben Todsünden der Kleinbürger/The Seven Deadly Sins: Ballet Chanté,* Text Bert Brecht. Vocal score edited by Wilhelm Brückner-Rüggeberg (Mainz: B. Schott's Söhne, 1972), p. 7.

43. See Brecht, *Gesammelte Werke* 15:474; and Weill, *Die sieben Todsünden,* vocal score, pp. 7–8.

44. Weill, *Die sieben Todsünden,* vocal score, pp. 20–30.

45. At the beginning of *Die sieben Todsünden* Anna has been on the road for four weeks (vocal score, p. 6). This may be an unconscious allusion to the length of Brecht's travels before arriving in Paris (see Brecht, *Briefe,* letter no. 170, p. 164).

46. Randolph Goodman, ed., *From Script to Stage: Eight Modern Plays* (San Francisco, 1971), pp. 496–97.

47. The first German edition of the novel was published in Berlin in 1927 by P. Zsolnay. See Hugh C. Atkinson, *Theodore Dreiser: A Checklist* (Kent, Ohio, 1971), p. 2.

Erwin Piscator and Lena Goldschmidt began adapting it for the stage.[48] At that time Brecht was a member of Piscator's dramaturgical collective working on the stage version of *Schweyk,* and both he and Weill surely knew of the *American Tragedy* project. Brecht probably also knew of Piscator's attempts in 1930 to arrange a filming of the novel in Moscow and of the renewed work on the stage adaptation, which continued through April 1931.[49] One can also speculate that both Brecht and Weill had seen von Sternberg's film version of the novel, which was a great hit throughout Europe that fall.[50] In any case, Brecht had ample opportunity to become familiar with Dreiser's story, and he may well have recalled it in developing *Die sieben Todsünden.*

Goodman points out the parallels between the two works. Both *An American Tragedy* and *Die sieben Todsünden,* of course, encapsulate the basic elements of the American "success story," and both upset the traditional story development to provide social criticism. Piscator's stage adaptation was to have sharpened this criticism by emphasizing the "seven deadly sins" committed by the protagonist, Clyde, and was to have played up the role of Clyde's alter ego, Gilbert. Furthermore, the adaptation was to dwell on the destructive role of religion and the family, as well as the depiction of class conflict. A residue of these elements may have been in Brecht's mind when he began drafting the lyrics for Anna's "success story."

The sources of other elements in the ballet are more positively traced. The seven deadly (or cardinal) sins were introduced to Brecht in his childhood religious training, and he had examples of their dramatic uses in medieval morality plays, scholastic theater, and emblematic theater of the Baroque.[51] Hofmannsthal's *Jedermann* (1912), which commenced yearly performances at the Salzburg Festival in 1920, provided a more contemporary source. Brecht borrowed the notion of inverting the traditional *topos* as a means of critiquing social conditions from Bernard de Mandeville's *Fable of the Bees, or Private Vices, Public Benefits,* which Brecht knew by way of his Marxist studies.[52]

Thematically, the choice of the inverted medieval *topos* allowed Brecht to free the core idea of the ballet from its psychological implications and to set it in a moral and social realm. Structurally, the choice

48. Goodman, *From Script to Stage,* p. 496.

49. John Willett, *The Theatre of Erwin Piscator* (New York, 1979), pp. 81–82.

50. Herman G. Weinberg, *Josef von Sternberg: A Critical Study* (New York, 1967), pp. 59, 237.

51. This element of the ballet is discussed by Steven Paul Scher, "Brecht's *Die sieben Todsünden der Kleinbürger:* Emblematic Structure as Epic Spectacle," *Studies in the German Drama: A Festschrift in Honor of Walter Silz,* ed. Donald H. Crosby and George C. Schoolfield (Chapel Hill, 1974), pp. 235–52.

52. Helfried Seliger, *Das Amerikabild Bertolt Brechts* (Bonn, 1974), pp. 192–93.

solved two problems. First, it allowed the story to unfold in a series of discrete tableaux without the need for troublesome exposition and excessive plotting. Since the story was to be sung and danced, it was important that the plot be economically conveyed without traditional dramatic dialogue or action. Second, the episodic structure accommodated a series of self-contained song texts, leaving the composer free to develop the continuity and consistency of the piece by musical means. One can only suppose that Weill was grateful for this freedom.

To "socialize" further the split-personality motif, Brecht returned to other thematic concerns which had surfaced in his earlier plays and poems. He first of all called into service one of the favored "alienation effects" of his earlier works by setting *Die sieben Todsünden* in an ironically romanticized American landscape.[53] The effect of this setting is to remove Anna from consideration as a psychologically "real" human being; the obviously artificial backdrop emphasizes the contours of her behavior, not of her psyche. Having recently read from his *Lesebuch für Städtebewohner,* Brecht also incorporated into the ballet his fascination with large cities and their effect on human behavior. This fascination had been with him since about 1921,[54] and he and Weill had already exploited it in the Mahagonny projects and the *Berliner Requiem.*[55] In *Die sieben Todsünden* the cities lure Anna with their promises of economic potential, while the human conditions in each both feed and frustrate her quest for "success"—until, that is, she "learns" to give in to metropolitan morality.[56] The lure of the cities also provides a structural device which keeps Anna and Weill's music on the move, while Brecht's texts proffer static recapitulations of moral lessons.

That Brecht returned to many of the themes and motifs he had already used in his work is certainly due in part to the limited amount of time he had to draft the texts for *Die sieben Todsünden,* but the historical and thematic background of the ballet may also throw a somewhat different light upon the working relationship between Brecht and Weill. An earlier view of Weill as a complacent musical arranger for Brechtian ideas

---

53. Ibid., passim.

54. The development of Brecht's interest in cities is discussed by Klaus Schuhmann, *Der Lyriker Bertolt Brecht 1913–1933,* rev. ed. (Munich, 1971), pp. 114–30, 213–37.

55. In his prefatory note to *Das Berliner Requiem,* Weill stated that the piece was an attempt "to express that which metropolitan man feels about death." Kurt Weill, *Das Berliner Requiem: Kleine Kantate für Tenor, Bariton, Männerchor (oder drei Männerstimmen) und Blasorchester,* nach Texten von Bertolt Brecht, full score, ed. David Drew (Vienna: Universal Edition, 1967 [UE 16630]), p. ii.

56. Brecht had already pursued this theme around 1926–27 in his poem "Lied einer Familie aus der Savannah," in which the family leaves their farm to seek the "good life" in city after city. In the end they are left stranded in Chicago and worse off than ever. Brecht, *Gesammelte Werke* 8: 144–45.

has recently been replaced in many circles by the more plausible picture of Weill and Brecht sharing enough points of ideological and artistic agreement that for a time each found the other useful.[57] This "revisionist" picture also portrays Brecht as a master manipulator who was usually able to badger or cajole his colleagues into adapting their contributions to suit his ideological ends, while Weill appears as the shy genius who only seemed to acquiesce quietly to Brecht's ideas before selectively weaving them for his own purposes into his own artistic fabric.[58] The outdated picture of a worldly, politically active Brecht dominating the passive, ivory-tower Weill may reflect to some extent a limited period of their collaboration, but it does not do justice to the Weill who won the battle of Berlin over *Mahagonny,* and it does not account for *Die sieben Todsünden.*

Had such a picture been taken in the spring of 1933, it might show Weill as an artist who had learned to arrange circumstances in such a way that the plan for the ballet could be made to appeal to Brecht. It would certainly show the composer in contractual and economic control of the situation in which Brecht's lyrics were written. By that March, Weill surely knew what subjects interested Brecht and, therefore, knew how to lure him into accepting the commission for a ballet libretto. Thus, I suspect that the idea to center the ballet around a "split personality" arose not only out of James's desire to unite Losch and Lenya on stage, but also out of Weill's knowledge that Brecht had been toying with the idea since 1927. I also suspect that the appearance of other motifs favored by Brecht may be as much due to Weill as to good fortune or the brevity of the period of collaboration. Weill was armed not only with a lucrative offer for Brecht but also with the knowledge of Brecht's projects since 1927. Both these weapons helped Weill to win his troublesome librettist to a project which must have seemed to Brecht both unlikely and unproductive. Meanwhile, his commission from Les Ballets 1933 gave Weill firm control over the ideological and artistic latitude customarily demanded (if not actually usurped) by his librettist in most of their earlier projects. It also allowed him to compose a symphonic score far removed from the song style of *Die Dreigroschenoper* or *Happy End.*

If this picture is correct, then *Die sieben Todsünden* may represent something more than a brief, anachronistic return to the success of the earlier Weill-Brecht partnership. It may, in fact, mark the historical point at which Weill succeeded in establishing his dominance over his alter ego, his Anna I, and in setting his own ground rules for further collaborations with Brecht. This is the position Weill held during his American years,

57. See Drew, Foreward to *Über Kurt Weill,* p. xvi.

58. See Lotte Lenya-Weill, "Das waren Zeiten!" in *Bertolt Brechts Dreigroschenbuch: Texte, Materialien, Dokumente,* ed. Siegfried Unseld (Frankfurt am Main, 1973), 1:330.

and it is one of the reasons that Brecht was unable to negotiate him into the completion of another project. In this sense, *Die sieben Todsünden* represents the watershed between Weill's German years within Brecht's circle and his independence in the American theater, and this is not the least of the ballet's distinctions.

13

Reflections on the Last Years: *Der Kuhhandel* as a Key Work
DAVID DREW

for Christopher Shaw

The eulogy spoken by Maxwell Anderson at a memorial concert of Weill's music in the summer of 1950 and the obituary published by T.W. Adorno in the 15 April 1950 edition of the *Frankfurter Rundschau* are diametrically opposed in both spirit and content. Each is informed by highly personal feelings; but only in Anderson's case are they manifest:

> I find these words difficult to write, difficult to say. Kurt Weill was not only my friend and neighbor. We had worked so closely together, had exchanged ideas and criticism so constantly, that in losing him *I* am crippled and lost. Something has gone out of this spring for me, and out of this year, that will not return. There is only one thought that comforts me at all. I have sometimes thought I would like to have known great men of genius whose work I especially admired. I would have liked to have known John Keats or Franz Schubert, and many others. Well, for fifteen years I have had a very great man for my neighbor and friend. How helpful and how loving and keen he was as a person, the world will never know. That goes when a man dies and cannot be recaptured. But how great Kurt Weill was as a composer of music, the world will slowly discover—for he was a much greater musician than anyone now imagines. It takes decades and scores of years and centuries to sift things out, but it's done in time—and Kurt will emerge as one of the very few who wrote great music. I wish you could have known him—for his wit, his gentleness, and the swift intuition that took him to the heart of every subject. That is no longer possible. But he left his music for us, and his music will keep his name and his spirit alive. It will not console us who have lost him; but it will live—long, long after we are forgotten, along with our grief.[1]

Anderson's testimony to Weill's human qualities reflects his experience of the last fifteen years of Weill's life, and yet it is strikingly consistent with

---

1. Maxwell Anderson's untitled and undated typescript is in the Maxwell Anderson Collection of the Humanities Research Center at the University of Texas in Austin. A carbon copy is in the Weill/Lenya Archive of the Yale University Music Library.

that of Heinrich Strobel,[2] whose contacts with Weill had been confined to the ten years previous to Anderson's. We need, perhaps, to remind ourselves of the great affection in which Weill was held by many people in many walks of life; for the quality of the man does indeed have some bearing on the quality of the music. But Anderson's path between man and music was, of course, his own private one, through the woods of South Mountain Road, and private it should remain.

Adorno, for his part, chose a public forum and wrote as a public figure par excellence: behind him, the Frankfurt School's long-awaited homecoming, ahead a successful career in the Federal Republic. Although his personal acquaintance with Weill went as far back as 1928, there is no mention of it; nor is there any trace of the extraordinary insights that had distinguished his account of Weill's music during the years of their closest acquaintance—that is, from 1928 to 1931. The obituary's function is strictly occlusive:

> The profile of this composer, who died in America, is scarcely touched by the concept of a composer as such. His gift, like his influence, resides much less in musical capacities . . . than in an extraordinary and original feeling for the function of music in the theater. Not that his gifts were dramatic, as, for instance, Verdi's were. On the contrary: the interpolatory character of his numbers, which stopped the action rather than carried it forward, and his espousal of the idea of "epic theater" challenge the traditional view of the dramatic.
>
> Weill was a pupil of Busoni. The lack of real craftsmanship, from the simplest harmonization to the construction of large forms, was his inheritance from a school which was more aesthetic than strictly technical. That may account for a certain monotony in his style, despite all the versatility: music can only develop properly from the problems of the métier. On the other hand, he brought to bear, from the outset, a literary taste that freed him from the naiveté of "good musicians," . . . The collaboration with Brecht not only determined his outward success. He owed to Brecht the intellectual authority for the initiation of his work; but also, and above all, he owed to him a method that ran counter to every kind of artistic consolidation and at the same time unceasingly submitted every bar to the demands of the performance.
>
> He . . . tried to write grand opera. The most pretentious was *Die Bürgschaft*. He no doubt realized the inadequacy of that and yielded to the constrictions and enticements of exile, without fully counting the cost. . . . Little remained of the surrealistic; with a shy and crafty innocence that was disarming, he became a Broadway composer modeled on Cole Porter and talked as if concession to the commercial field were no concession, but only a

---

2. Heinrich Strobel, "Erinnerung an Kurt Weill," *Melos* 17 (May 1950): 133–36; reprinted in David Drew, ed., *Über Kurt Weill* (Frankfurt, 1975), pp. 146–51.

pure test of "skill" which made everything possible even within standardized boundaries.

Weill believed himself to be a kind of Offenbach of his century, and as
far as swiftness of social-aesthetic reaction and lack of real substance go,
the analogy is not without foundation. But the model was not repeatable.
The grimness of reality has become too overwhelming for a parody to
measure up to it. . . . What seemed to him the expression of his time was
for the most part only the admittedly troubled and hence all the truer echo
of its progress. But perhaps he had something of the genius of those who
lead the great fashion houses. He had the ability to find melodies appropriate to the annual shows; and this supremely ephemeral thing in him
may last. [my translation]

So urbane is the tone that the destructive force of the content could
almost be overlooked. Readers more familiar with Weill's music than
with the labyrinthine workings of Adorno's mind might well dismiss the
obituary as lightly as Weill himself seems to be dismissed. They would be
ill advised to do so.

In the immediate background of Adorno's obituary is the *Philosophie der neuen Musik,* published in 1949, less than a year before Weill's
death. Perhaps because the tactical weapons used in the obituary are
different in kind as well as in size from the strategic ones with which
Adorno attempted in the *Philosophie* to demolish the neo-classical
Stravinsky, they seem relatively harmless. No Freudian searchlights are
trained on Weill's work (though they usefully could be); no complicity
with authoritarian tendencies is hinted at (though it might be). With
such skill does Adorno observe the diplomatic niceties proper to the occasion that it is hard to believe that his intentions are in any way aggressive. What, for instance, could be more "disarming" than the "shy
and crafty innocence" with which he inserts the name of Offenbach,
apparently on Weill's own authority?

In Adorno's commentary on Weill from 1928–31, the name invoked is Mahler's, not Offenbach's. Times changed, however, and so, of
course, did Weill. On the assumption that Adorno knew or had at least
heard about some of Weill's post-1933 work, the conclusion he reaches
can be fairly put to the test by selecting for special consideration the
work that seems best qualified to support Weill's alleged view of himself
as a modern Offenbach. Without doubt, that work is the operetta *Der
Kuhhandel* of 1934. Its German libretto—a most remarkable one—is the
work of the Hungarian-born Robert Vambery,[3] who had been Auf-

---

3. Robert Vambery was born in Budapest in 1907 and now lives in Los Angeles. In 1927
Ernst Josef Aufricht engaged him as dramaturge at the Theater am Schiffbauerdamm. For
Aufricht's music theater enterprise, Vambery made German versions of Donizetti's *La Fille*

richt's *Chefdramaturg* at the Theater am Schiffbauerdamm from 1927 until 1933. The greater part of the score was drafted in Louveciennes in 1934. With the conclusion early in 1935 of an agreement for a first production in London, *Der Kuhhandel*—by then nearing completion in voice-and-piano score but still with vital aspects of its operetta form unresolved—was swiftly converted into the likeness of an English musical comedy and blessed with the irrelevantly royalist title, *A Kingdom for a Cow*. Several important numbers from *Der Kuhhandel* were discarded unorchestrated; other numbers in more popular style were inserted in their place and elsewhere.[4] *A Kingdom for a Cow* duly opened at the Savoy Theatre, London—the home of Gilbert and Sullivan's Savoy operas—on 28 June 1935. It was well received by the press, but shunned by the public. The production closed after three weeks. The end of *A Kingdom for a Cow* was also the end of *Der Kuhhandel*, for Weill never returned to the German-language version. But it is that, rather than the London travesty, which mainly concerns us here. The only number said to have been written and composed for London yet consistent with the style and structure of the German version is the choral prologue.

The prologue tells of an island that was once inhabited by a "simple and happy race." In 1497, the Spaniards landed on the east shore, shot the menfolk, ravished the women, burnt the crops, and started "a new and better government." Later that year the Portuguese landed on the west shore and did likewise. Such were the origins of today's republics of Ucqua and Santa Maria, to which the Waterkeyn Armaments Corporation of Cleveland, Ohio, has now sent its chief salesman, Leslie Jones. When the curtain rises, Jones has already paid an abortive visit to Ucqua.

---

du Régiment and (in February 1933) Gilbert and Sullivan's *The Pirates of Penzance. Der Kuhhandel* was his first independent venture into the theater, and it has remained his last. As a cultural commentator, Vambery contributed to *Die Weltbühne* and other journals. After settling in America in the late 1930s, he taught for a time at Columbia University, where he was associated with the world premiere in 1941 of Britten and Auden's "operetta," *Paul Bunyan.*

4. The history of *Der Kuhhandel* and the circumstances and reception of *A Kingdom for a Cow* are examined in detail in my forthcoming *Kurt Weill: A Documentary Biography* (Faber & Faber); the bibliographic aspects and musical problems are treated in my forthcoming *Kurt Weill: A Handbook*. The appendix lists the numbers in the two versions of the work and indicates the relationship between them. The copyright in *Der Kuhhandel* was assigned to Heugel et Cie. (Paris) in 1934 under the terms of Weill's general agreement and was reassigned to Schott (Mainz) in 1978. No published edition is yet in view. *A Kingdom for a Cow* was covered by a sub-publishing agreement of 1935 between Heugel and Chappell (London), which published two putative hit songs in sheet-music form ("Two Hearts" and "As Long As I Love") and announced a book of piano-vocal selections that, in fact, did not appear. The entire holograph material for the two versions, with the exception of a few minor items, is now in the Weill/Lenya Archive.

On his arrival in Santa Maria he is ordered by Waterkeyn to buy the national newspaper, publish reports of a massive arms purchase by Ucqua, and then proceed to the office of the Santa Marian president, an ex–university professor of staunchly liberal and pacifist views and there-fore—Waterkeyn concludes—undoubtedly a fool and probably venal as well. Sure enough, Jones easily traps the president into accepting an ill-concealed bribe and ordering munitions which the impoverished nation cannot afford and which (to his credit) he has no intention of using.

When Jones presses for payment, the president institutes a Public Welfare Tax, which has to be levied twice in order to pay the "commis-sion" demanded by General Conchas, Santa Maria's dreaded war minis-ter and leader of the paramilitary "Strong Hand Fellowship." In a des-perate attempt to keep Jones happy without entirely betraying his own principles, the president allows Conchas to exercise his newly con-scripted army close to the Ucquan frontier and then calls a peace con-ference which will end with a gala dinner for the Ucquan delegation (Act 1 finale). Jones swiftly organizes and subsidizes a coup d'etat by General Conchas, who seizes power while the gala dinner is in full swing, insults the Ucquan delegation, and vows to defend the national honor against the "traditional enemy."

The effect these mighty events have on the lives of ordinary people is illustrated by the star-crossed romance of two simple villagers, Juan and Juanita. Juan's sole means of livelihood is an obliging milk-cow from which, however, he is twice separated by the bailiff, who distrains upon it in lieu of the two installments of the Public Welfare Tax which Juan has scorned to pay. After a short spell as a railway porter, Juan finds himself conscripted into the general's brave new army. As luck would have it, he is selected by Ximenes, the minister of information, as the nation's rep-resentative in a "symbolic referendum" designed to convince foreign bankers that the general and his policies enjoy full democratic support. Trained to say "Yes" to every question which General Conchas puts to him, Juan decides on another course, and, when the great moment comes, gives the general a resounding box on the ears. He is saved from the firing squad, and Santa Maria from war, by the discovery that none of the weaponry supplied by Waterkeyn is in working order. General Conchas promptly proclaims to the defenseless Santa Marians the vir-tues of peaceful coexistence and, amidst popular rejoicing, pardons Juan and gives a vote-winning blessing to the happy couple.

Der Kuhhandel is the first of Weill's stage works to contain an ele-ment of sociopolitical journalism. It belongs to the tradition founded by Offenbach and his colleagues and revived during the 1920s by Karl Kraus in his revisions of Offenbach's librettos. Kraus, indeed, is the spir-itual father of *Der Kuhhandel*. Although he and Weill might have conceived such a work in 1932 (the year of their brief collaboration in Berlin),[5] *Der Kuhhandel* itself could only have been written after March 1933. Its reflections on the subjects of dictatorship and war belong to the European era that began with the Nazi seizure of power.

Santa Maria is much less remote from that event than from the never-never lands traditionally colonized by operetta. Echoing as it does the title of Kleist's novella, *Die Verlobung in St. Domingo,* Weill and Vambery's subtitle, "Die Verlobung von Santa Maria," points directly to the island of Hispaniola in the West Indies and hence to the Republic of Haiti and the Dominican Republic (whose capital is Santo Domingo). The settlers—established on the western shore by Columbus when he discovered Hispaniola on his first voyage in 1492 and then on the eastern shore when he returned a year later—had shown as little concern for the welfare of the natives as the prologue of *Der Kuhhandel* suggests (with some poetic license); and it was in their manly spirit that General Molino Trujillo of Dominica staged a successful "revolution" just three years before Hitler's. Trujillo appointed himself president and was to remain in that office until relieved of it by an assassin's bullet in 1961. His notoriously unjust, corrupt, and incompetent regime made much of its aggressive designs on Haiti and would not have survived but for regular injections of American capital.[6]

While the Caribbean background provided Weill and Vambery with the exotic color upon which operetta thrives, the European foreground would have been unmanageable in operetta terms without the kind of reductio ad absurdum afforded by Caribbean politics. On that level the frame of General Conchas is ample enough to contain both Mussolini and Goering, and Ximenes can prove an apt pupil of Goebbels

5. At the Breitkopf Hall in Berlin on 11 January 1932, Karl Kraus gave a recital whose first part comprised selections from Raimund, Wedekind, and Peter Altenberg; the second half was devoted to excerpts from the *Mahagonny* opera, with Weill at the piano. This was the furthest Weill went in accommodating himself to the matchmaking ambitions of Universal Edition and its opera chief, Hans Heinsheimer. From a Viennese point of view, and indeed from Heinsheimer's broader one, a creative collaboration with Kraus would have been highly opportune, now that the collaboration with Brecht had apparently come to an end. The rapport with Kraus established by Schoenberg and his circle had already been inherited by the younger generation in the person of Krenek, whose flirtations with operetta in the late 1920s (notably in his one-act opera *Schwergewicht,* of which there are echoes in *Mahagonny*) owed as much to Kraus in one sense as his Kraus song cycle, *Durch die Nacht,* of 1931—his first tentatively dodecaphonic work—did in another. But neither in his investigations of Kraus's writings nor in his work with the great man himself did Weill find what he was looking for. There is no record of any contacts subsequent to the 1932 recital.

6. The first critical account of the influence of American capital on Latin American politics is a work that clearly had a direct influence on *Der Kuhhandel:* Joseph Freeman and Scott Neary's *Dollar Diplomacy: A Study of American Imperialism* (New York: 1925).

long before he apes that master of public relations by applying to the general's seizure of power the term "nationale Erhebung" (national rebellion), which Goebbels had coined for Hitler's. Previously Ximenes and the general had established an "understanding" with the president, who embodies the less admirable traits of the Social Democratic leadership in the Weimar era, and seems—amidst the Wilhelmstrasse pomp and ceremony of the Act 1 finale—to be well on the way toward exchanging the role of Friedrich Ebert with that of the aging Hindenburg. As for the ruling classes, they applaud with equal fervor the president at the start of the first finale and the newly emerged dictator at the close. When the crowds emerge in the second finale to watch the parades that Ximenes has organized in the general's honor—much as Goebbels had organized the so-called "Day of Potsdam" for Hitler in March 1933— they are apparently at one with the regime and certainly incapable of identifying themselves with the unexpected result of the "symbolic referendum."

Since there is no collective will to support Juan's individual gesture of resistance to tyranny, the general can only be defeated by a deus ex machina whose absurdity is commensurate with his own. As a means of averting bloodshed and preserving the conventions of operetta, the rusted weaponry supplied by the Waterkeyn Corporation is serviceable enough. Comparison with the manner in which Richard Strauss and Josef Gregor contrived a happy ending for their tentatively antiwar opera *Friedenstag*—the outline of which was sketched by Stefan Zweig in August 1934, only a few months after the inception of *Der Kuhhandel*— reveals a direct parallel and an important difference. In both works the final crisis is resolved by a timely stroke of fortune rather than by a structural development; and "peace" is then restored and celebrated amidst a flourish of C major. But whereas in *Friedenstag* some form of deus ex machina was indispensable to a drama that had no ideological or dialectical basis, in *Der Kuhhandel* it was merely a tactical rather than strategic device, and the central argument is unscarred by it. The argument is not so much about militarism or authoritarianism as about the problem of effectively opposing both without in some sense becoming tainted by either. Rejecting as ineffective (or at least as idealistic and impractical) the concept of passive resistance advanced by the judge in *Die Bürgschaft* (Act 2, new scene), *Der Kuhhandel* satirizes the armaments trade in order to introduce the question of disarmament and relate to it the need for security in a dangerous world.

In 1921, a League of Nations commission on disarmament reported that munitions firms had sought to control and influence the press and public opinion and to spread alarmist reports about military and naval programs.[7] During the 1914–18 war there had been collusion between representatives of the armaments industry on the two sides, and the American branch of the industry had traded impartially with both sides until the United States itself entered the war. An "observer" was dispatched by three American firms to the Geneva Naval Conference in 1927 with instructions to use every means, including falsified press reports, to block or inhibit impending disarmament agreements. Covert links between armaments and newspaper interests continued to be influential after the first International Disarmament Conference convened in Geneva in February 1932. That conference, and its successor which opened in October 1933 and adjourned eight months later, achieved little. Germany resigned from the conference—and from the League of Nations—in October 1933, and the third disarmament conference, which met in May 1934, was the last. Germany had already published military estimates for the first phase of the rearmament cycle and in March 1935 announced the reintroduction of conscription. On 21 May, however, Hitler delivered a "peace speech" whose imagery of "rivers of blood" and general air of humanitarian concern would have gladdened the heart of the president of Santa Maria.

The year of the Nazi seizure of power, 1933, was also the year when the Nobel Peace Prize was awarded to Sir Norman Angell, whose standard work, *The Great Illusion* (1910), was reprinted that year and dominated pacifist thinking until the end of the decade. Other notable publications during 1933 were Fenner Brockway's *The Bloody Traffic* and Beverley Nichols's *Cry Havoc!*, which opened with a skillful exposure of the armaments industry and all its works. (Nichols was later approached to undertake the English adaptation of *Der Kuhhandel*, but he declined.)

---

7. Most of the sources for the present account of inter-war disarmament politics would have been accessible to Vambery and Weill in 1934–35. Beverly Nichols's *Cry Havoc!* (London, 1933) was an international best seller; its principal source was *The Secret International*, a documentation published in London in 1932 by the Union of Democratic Control. 1932 saw the publication in Paris of Jean Huteau's *Les Industries de Mort*, which was followed two years later by Jean Galtière-Bossière and René Lefebvre's *Les Marchands de Canons*. In England the campaigning publisher Victor Gollancz initiated a series of books on the armaments question with Fenner Brockway's *The Bloody Traffic* (1933); Routledge followed suit in 1934 with H. C. Engelbrecht and F. C. Hanighen's *Merchants of Death*. Phillip Noel-Baker's *The Private Manufacturers of Arms* (London, 1936) appeared too late to influence *Der Kuhhandel*, but it is representative of the climate of opinion, as are the *Hearings of the Special Committee Investigating the Armaments Industry*, 73d Congress of the United States (Washington, 1934–35) and the *Minutes of Evidence Taken before the Royal Commission on the Private Manufacturing of and Trading in Armaments* (London, 1936). The techniques employed by the Waterkeyn Company and its representative in *Der Kuhhandel* are unmistakably modeled on those of Sir Basil Zaharoff; see Donald McCormick, *Pedlar of Death: The Life of Sir Basil Zaharoff* (London, 1965).

It was in the spring of 1934—just when *Der Kuhhandel* was beginning to take shape—that the armaments industry, in open defiance of international agreements, intervened in Bolivia's and Paraguay's dispute over the Gran Chaco territory and supplied both sides with the modern weapons they lacked. On 25 May 1934 many thousands died in Gran Chaco.

By then armaments salesmen had won their place in the popular demonology of the time. While cartoonists in the bourgeois press showed salesmen counting their profits from the carnage in Grand Chaco and major publishing houses were issuing such inflammatory titles as *Les Industries de Mort* and *Merchants of Death*, the Left had no need to exert itself in publicizing the notion that Marx's "werewolf capital" was abroad again. Nationalization of the industry—to which Leon Blum's Popular Front government finally resorted in 1936—was already being prepared by some of the more liberal advocates of capitalism. In 1933, Sir Arthur Salter had remarked: "Peace can exist under capitalism provided that no section of the industry can get into a position in which it can dictate the public policy. This danger exists in the armaments industry."[8]

In *Der Kuhhandel*, the business of selling arms is inseparable from the business of funding political reaction: Jones pays the general's debts just as the Ruhr industrialists paid the bankrupt Nazi Party's debts in 1932. In "The Ballad of Pharaoh," sung by Juan and his fellow workers in a railway freight-yard, an implied critique of capitalism serves as the functional link between the work's otherwise uneasily related indictments of dictatorship and rearmament. Since the workers are not aware that the unlabeled crates contain armaments, their militancy requires an objective value: whatever they carry on their backs is immaterial to their perception of labor conditions in Santa Maria. The first part of the two-part "Ballad of Pharaoh" begins as a call for deliverance, led by Juan, but becomes, in effect, a call for strike action. In his mediating arietta, "Seit ich in diese Stadt gekommen bin," Juan renounces urban industrial society and ends by declaring that he will return to the village where, thanks to the obliging cow, he is self-supporting. Then follows the second and intensified half of the ballad which effects the transition from class politics to national and (in Biblical guise) racist politics.

The fundamental difference between *Der Kuhhandel* and *A Kingdom for a Cow* is epitomized by the replacement of "The Ballad of Pharaoh"

---

8. Quoted by Sir Norman Angel, *The Great Illusion*, rev. ed. (London, 1933), p. 190. Sir (James) Arthur Salter (1881–1975), economist and statesman, held many positions within the British government but first won prominence during World War I as the organizer of world shipping. From 1922 until 1931 he directed the Economic and Finance Section of the League of Nations. Appointed professor of political theory and institutions at Oxford in 1934, he was elected to Parliament in 1937.

in the latter by a cheerful ditty entitled "San Salvatore" and by the removal of the introductory dialogue in which the workers complain about their miserly wages. The railway workers in *A Kingdom for a Cow* seem altogether content as they blithely whistle the refrain that links the verses of "San Salvatore."

In the most cogent section of his notes on the *Mahagonny* opera, Brecht said of the culture and entertainment industry that it is "conditioned by the society of the day, and only accepts what keeps it going in that society. We are free to discuss any innovations which do not threaten its social function—that of providing an evening's entertainment."[9] To have ignored the fact that an evening's entertainment had always been the primary social function of operetta was hardly the kind of intellectual folly to which the authors of *Die Dreigroschenoper* would have subscribed. The "innovations" discussed by Weill and Vambery were not, in fact, incompatible with "an evening's entertainment" in, say, the Paris or Prague of 1934. What ensured that *Der Kuhhandel* would be unacceptable to a West End management in London without the excisions and additions that converted it into *A Kingdom for a Cow* was not so much the restoration of Offenbach's subversiveness (after its highly ingenious diffusion by Gilbert and Sullivan) as the consolidation, on the dark side, of that which Offenbach had found in the revolutionary Mozart. Together with the humane irony which, in the Weill of these and earlier years, invariably rescues satire from cynicism and therefore allows cynicism itself to be satirized, there goes an acute sense of the present perilousness of every ideal and endeavor. Music and text together proclaim not only that the war jokes of Johann Strauss's *Der lustige Krieg* or Offenbach's *La Grande Duchesse de Gérolstein* have lost their license, but also that the paths of true love can no longer convincingly be shown to lead to some last-minute revelation that will enable the impoverished lovers to live sumptuously ever after. The wedding of Juan and Juanita depends on only ten *duros*. But even that has to be earned, and there is no reason to suppose that the economic hazards that bedevilled the courtship will cease with the sound of wedding bells. In the world of *Der Kuhhandel* (but no longer in *A Kingdom for a Cow*), great and small alike are visibly and audibly living on the edge of disaster.

Yet *Der Kuhhandel* is Weill's first attempt to write "light music" as the man in the street understood it (until that particular street turned out to be a cul-de-sac). Within the strophic numbers, extreme contrasts of character or tonality are rare. Most of the music is firmly diatonic, with the

9. Bertolt Brecht and Peter Suhrkamp, "Anmerkungen zur Oper *Aufstieg und Fall der Stadt Mahagonny*," *Versuche* 2 (Berlin, 1930); trans. by John Willett in *Brecht on Theatre* as "The Modern Theatre is the Epic Theatre" (New York, 1964), p. 34.

major mode predominating and the relative minor as the favored contrasting area. All the numbers in medium and fast tempo are based on
popular rhythms: traditional (Offenbachian) waltzes, marches, and can-
cans are balanced by Latin American rhythms appropriate to the milieu—
a fandango for the general, a tango-refrain for the "Ballad of the Robber
Esteban," a calypso-cum-rhumba for the betrothal rite, and several
zarzuela-like passages in the finale. (In *A Kingdom for a Cow* the balance
was tipped toward the Latin American side by the last-minute insertion in
the second finale of the tango from *Marie galante*.)

In *Der Kuhhandel* the influence of European jazz idioms is confined
to the bailiff's song and the lover's Boston, "Auf Wiederseh'n." Since this
was a dangerously meager ration in relation to the demands of the entertainment industry, it was doubled in *A Kingdom for a Cow*, where "San
Salvatore" has a jazzy ground rhythm, and the new version of "The Song
of the Cow" is a Left Bank Blues (and so it still sounds when transformed
into "The Song of the Guns" in *Johnny Johnson*). Entirely missing from *Der
Kuhhandel*, at the stage when Weill interrupted work on the German
version and turned his thoughts to London, was any kind of popular song
in the commercial sense. It was surely for that reason rather than for any
artistic one that Weill arranged "Le Roi d'Aquitaine" from *Marie galante*
as a duet and cobbled it on to the end of the opening scene, to which it
manifestly bears no musical relationship. With that as his precedent he
then composed two new or partly new numbers: "As Long As I Love"
(whose lyrics by Desmond Carter have the memorable second-line rhyme
"I live for my love") and the "Ballad of the Robber Esteban." Both are
solos for Juanita—the first in a monochrome musical-comedy idiom
flecked by a single Weillish chromaticism at every recurrence of the refrain's dominant harmony, the second a would-be *Schlager* that fails to
match the precision of Vambery's pastiche folk song but faithfully reflects
the platitudes of the English adaptation. The fact that these are the only
extant solos for Juanita emphasizes their lack of any real relationship to
the musical and aesthetic premises of *Der Kuhhandel*. Excrescences from
Weill's commercial work of 1934, they are quite distinct from any of the
numbers that were written before *A Kingdom for a Cow* was thought of.

The style and language of the original *Kuhhandel* numbers are new
in the sense that neither is a "natural" development from the works of
1930–33, and yet both are organic in the sense that they have their roots
in those works. Thus, the duet "Auf Wiederseh'n" begins in the C-minor
manner of *Die sieben Todsünden*, but develops from its opening material a
refrain in G major whose melodic/harmonic substance and wayward
phraseology have no precedent in Weill. An analogous feat is accomplished in the tonally related quartet "O trüber Tag!" From an idea in C
minor reminiscent of the Commissar's motif in *Die Bürgschaft*, Weill devel-

ops a refrain in G major unlike anything in that opera or indeed elsewhere in his music. Yet the voice is unmistakably Weill's, both in the expressive ambiguity of the dominant "resolution" and in the concomitant destructiveness of the final B-flat minor cadence—an event so alien to the world of musical comedy that it seems to encapsulate the reasons why the entire quartet was excluded from *A Kingdom for a Cow*.

More extensive evidence of Weill's self-renewal is provided by the two interlinked numbers sung by Juan and his fellow workers in the railway depot—"The Ballad of Pharaoh" and Juan's arietta. The *martellato* rhythm and open fifths that initiate "The Ballad of Pharaoh" stem from the *Konjunktur* music of 1927, while the harmonic extensions through third-related triads again recall *Die Bürgschaft*. But the force that binds them together is a new type of melody, one that proudly displays its Jewish origins (see ex. 1). The developments are neo-Handelian, but the shadows of *Die Bürgschaft* are soon dispelled by the resounding confidence of the ballad's triadic harmony. Metaphorically as well as literally, the major triad has a dominant function throughout the ballad: it persistently opposes the negative forces derived from the minor third stresses of *Die Bürgschaft* and finally overwhelms them. It seems that by identifying himself with the Jewish rather than with the German people, Weill in 1934 could reach the militant conclusion he had withheld from *Die Bürgschaft* in 1931.

The two parts of the ballad are bridged and illuminated by Juan's arietta, whose *molto cantabile* line and continuously developing single-span form contrast with the abrupt phrases and graphically repetitive movements of the work song. As a sequel to the first part of the ballad, the arietta expresses Juan's joy at his own imminent freedom from the labor market, a joy tempered by regret that his comrades will be left behind; as a prelude to the second part it explains why he renounces class war in favor of Tolstoyan verities. Its musical kinship with The Mother's arioso in D minor from *Der Jasager* and Jenny's "Havanna Lied" in *Mahagonny* may reflect the fact that the text incorporates domestic and maternal images comparable to theirs. But the basic musical idea and feeling could only have arisen from *Der Kuhhandel*. Like the betrothal rite, the arietta is in E major, a key traditionally associated, in opera and in lied, with spiritual or emotional havens, real or imaginary. When David Orth at the end of *Die Bürgschaft* has assured Mattes that he is being carried away to safety, the tonality reaches the threshhold of E major, only to withdraw by way of a cadence as deceptive as Orth. In the achieved E major of the arietta, Weill recalls the Schubertian accompanimental rhythm of the Orth-Mattes duet, as if paradoxically to underline the genuineness of the values represented by Juan's village home; but in the development he averts any latent threat of sentimentality by means of a tonal shift to the flat side, which alerts the listener to a tension between anticipated or recollected consolations and present dangers. The closing reaffirmation of E major does not suggest any permanence in the village idyll to which Juan is returning.

The level at which irony operates here is deep enough to allow the arietta to be accepted at face value as a directly appealing lyrical number. That, surely, is why it was admitted to *A Kingdom for a Cow*, while its counterpart, Juan's wry meditation on the theme of guns before butter, suffered the same fate as "The Ballad of Pharaoh" and had to give way to an inferior substitute. Brief though it is, the "Song of the Cow" has many fresh things to say about the "relative" values of E-flat major and C minor—of butter and guns. The harmonic shading, the tonal balance, and the orchestral texture created by grumbling basses and high-lying, night-sky counterpoints—all these are of a much finer imaginative order than anything in the second version, which keeps to a blues-tinged C minor and aspires no higher than an easily apprehensible and somewhat Pucciniesque pathos.

Such were the limits of seriousness in *A Kingdom for a Cow*. The theater that rejected certain elements on purely musical grounds demanded others that Weill would clearly have preferred to do without. Nothing in the incomplete *Kuhhandel* score, not even "The Ballad of Pharaoh" or "O trüber Tag," would have been quite so alarming to his prospective backers in London as the parsimonious and eccentric dispensations of romantic ingredients. Operetta, disqualified by its nature from appealing to the piety or religiosity of its time, traditionally had to content itself with advertising the divine and redemptive power of "romantic love"—"Die Liebe ist eine Himmelsmacht," as *Der Zigeunerbaron* declares. Since Weill had paid his last creative tribute to the ideals of romantic love in the period leading up to his studies with Busoni, the fact that Juanita's love songs are inferior to Juan's social ones is due to more than a quirk of inspiration. Juan is singing of circumstances and contingency, which for Weill are fundamental topics, whereas Juanita is left with folksy or commercialized affirmations of love's omnipotence.

Just how little the authors cared for the love songs is confirmed by the character and history of the opening scene by the trout stream. After the courtship has been presented symbolically—Juan's trout-fishing and the catch that Juanita rejects—there is a brief and conventional marriage proposal, whereupon the German libretto notes that "a duet will follow." But no organic continuation ever evolved. Weill's voice-and-piano sketch is firm until the marriage proposal, but then loses itself in meretricious chromatic sequences suggesting a bridge to a refrain but having no clear tonal destination. There the sketch ends. When Weill returned to it at the time of negotiations for the London production, he merely extended the bridge and attached to it a duet arrangement, in F major, of the D-flat major ballad "Le Roi d'Aquitaine," which he had meanwhile composed for the heroine of *Marie galante* to sing as she watches over an old and dying Negro. Although this sweet-scented pastiche of a *café-concert* waltz may have charmed potential backers of *A Kingdom for a Cow*, it makes no musical sense as a sequel to the freshly imagined and classically poised setting of the trout-fishing scene. Here, with imagery developed from *Der Silbersee* and *Die sieben Todsünden*, Weill recaptures a springtime mood absent from his music since the days of *Frauentanz*. A bright stream of waltz figures issues from a B-flat major source, pursues its tonally unpredictable course (with occasional pauses, as if at some pool) until at last it arrives at the remotest possible key, E major, which is later to be that of the betrothal rite (and, later still, as we have seen, of Juan's homeward-looking arietta). So striking is this curtain-raiser, and so effectively does its impressionistic *allegro giusto* movement contrast with the narrative pacing of the choral prologue, that its *Marie galante* appendage seems to cripple the whole work. Fortunately—and it is not the only good fortune of this kind—Weill's unpublished manuscripts contain material for an extended waltz-duet whose character and proportions are exactly those of the remainder of the scene.[10] With that as its conclusion, the whole scene is in balance with its structural counterpart, "Der Mädchenraub," the betrothal rite.

In "Der Mädchenraub" Weill accomplishes a doubly unexpected feat: first, in creating a frankly popular number with climax and coda fulsome enough for *Das Land des Lächelns;* second, in reconciling this with something of the classical restraint of *Der Jasager*. It is almost as if the formalities and stern exactions of the betrothal rite were being interpreted as aspects of Noh-theater. Indeed, after the lover has abducted his beloved and defied her parents, the subservience he demands of her is

10. In the sense that it seems to epitomize the structural problems left unsolved or actually aggravated by *A Kingdom for a Cow*, the opening scene of *Der Kuhhandel* was the starting point for the performing edition of the score that I prepared in 1970–72 in collaboration with Christopher Shaw, who was responsible for orchestrating—with exemplary fidelity to Weill—not only the important numbers left unorchestrated (some seventy pages of full score) but also the "new" first-scene duet and various shorter numbers (another fifty pages of full score). The material for the latter had been culled from sketches dating from the period 1935–37 that either related directly to *Der Kuhhandel* or had clear musical affinities with it. The musical aspects of the performing edition were, of course, inseparable from dramaturgic and textual considerations; but the tentative revision of the text on which Josef Heinzelmann and I collaborated and which we submitted to Robert Vambery with a view toward production in a West German municipal theater did not meet with Vambery's approval either in principle or in substance. All materials relating to the Shaw-Drew "performing edition" and to the tentative revision of the text were therefore withdrawn. Subsequent attempts to establish a performing edition agreeable to all parties have so far been fruitless.

defined by a catechism curiously analogous to that of The Teacher and
The Boy in *Der Jasager* and is granted in that same mode of *Einverständnis:*

> *Juan:* Will you leave your father?
> *Juanita:* I will leave him.
> *Juan:* And forget your friends?
> *Juanita:* I will forget them.
> *Juan:* And none know but me?
> *Juanita:* None but you.[11]

The terseness of this is already anticipated by the ensemble's abrupt start
(see ex. 2). The same motif recurs when Juan first suggests they spend the
night together (see ex. 3). The contrasting music is in feminine character
and a more popular style (with major-minor harmony, added sixths, and
leading-note suspensions). But when the lovers join together in a duet,
their music—begun by Juan—denies them the rosy illusions of operetta,
for the bass tritone (see ex. 4) seems rooted in the realism of Juan's
obdurate questions:

> Will you live with me in a single hut?
> Will you eat with me from a single plate?
> Will you lie with me on a single couch?

In *A Kingdom for a Cow,* this became:

> Simple is my fortune, but will you share it?
> Humble is my dwelling, but will you share it?

Poverty and concupiscence were evidently not considered suitable topics
for a London audience in 1935. The fact that there are no explicit declara-
tions of love in the original scene contributes to its strange atmosphere
and also to its sense; for it allows the emphasis to fall on the social rather
than the romantic significance of the ritual, so that the tenderness and
passion with which the music is nonetheless informed seem already to
have survived adversity and been strengthened by it.

Juan and Juanita declare their love for the first and last time when
they are separated and then only in the anguished coda to their "letter
duet" in the Act 1 finale. The duet itself mainly concerns the nature and
circumstances of their separation. It takes the romantic relationship for
granted and concentrates on the social one in which Juan and Juanita
appear as sole representatives of the common people whose destinies are

---

11. "Der Mädchenraub," holograph rehearsal score, pp. 14–15; the text (my translation)
as set by Weill differs slightly from that in the original libretto (untitled photocopy in the
Weill-Lenya Research Center with pages numbered 5–115; "Der Mädchenraub" is on pp.
31–34).

being decided by the events at the state banquet. Exemplary as the simplicity of their gravely tranquil music sounds when it is first juxtaposed with the banquet music, its effect is greatly enhanced when the two musics are combined. The crowning stroke is reserved for the close of the first finale, long after the lovers have faded from view. As the banquet guests applaud the coup d'etat in a *pomposo* chorus ("Die starke Hand hat Gott gesandt"), the orchestra replies with a *fortissimo* reprise of the "letter music." This reminder of what is at stake in ordinary human terms raises the finale to a level to which neither Offenbach nor Johann Strauss had cause to aspire, and yet it remains true to their formal conventions. At the close of a predominantly ironic and parodistic structure, Weill has contrived to refer to the reality of political oppression with a gesture so simple that one is surprised at its moving effect until one notes the dignity and complexity of the feeling behind it.

The divergence from Offenbach is always most striking in those passages where the political background or foreground seems to call for satire. The music for Santa Maria's Prussianizing national anthem is a notable example, for it is first heard in an orchestral version as preface to the choral prologue. Without the rampant folly of its text it reveals no satirical intent but evokes the patriotic matter of early Wagner to such (mock-) serious effect that the final scene of *Lohengrin* seems about to be replayed with some latter-day German leader acknowledging the acclaim of his liegemen and summoning them to battle against the enemies of the Reich.

Too "good" to be parody of something so deplorable, the introductory version of the anthem relates in spirit to the two *recitativo* speeches delivered by the president. In the first, the old muddler declares his sacred obligation to the cause of peace with such passionate conviction that his music's recollection of the Pilgrims' Chorus in *Tannhäuser* seems spontaneous rather than parodistic; in the second he concludes his announcement of a Public Welfare Tax with a musical reference, via the so-called "Johannistag" motif, to Pogner's Address in *Die Meistersinger*. Conceptually, the device of comparing the president's view of public welfare to Pogner's fulfills all the requirements of Offenbachian satire. Musically, however, its effect is transformed by a lyricism which grows out of Wagner's as if of its own accord, and it ends by indicating the humane sense behind the president's hypocrisy.

For obvious reasons, Weill seems to have found the general harder to approach than the president. Of the surviving attempts at his blood-and-thunder entry song, the one that finally reached *A Kingdom for a Cow* is certainly the most convincing in its fusion of the sinister and the comic. Were the original setting of the German lyrics not missing, it might clarify Weill's attitude toward a figure whose representative significance had the most direct bearing on his own predicament. There is perhaps a trace of hostility in his second (fandango) setting of the general's drinking song in Act 2, but none at all in the number entitled "Das Erlebnis im Café," a brilliantly successful Offenbachiade which only Weill could have written. The pleasure he had in composing it is so much a part of what the song conveys that he might almost be suspected of having momentarily forgotten that the general is not the buccaneering bon vivant he would like to be taken for.

In fact, Weill can well afford to be charitable: with great cunning, he has reserved for the relatively insignificant person of the bailiff all the opprobrium which, according to the antifascist conventions of the day, should have been heaped on the general. By tackling the phenomenon of authoritarianism at the level of petty officialdom rather than at the summit, he is able to achieve his ends without destroying the operetta conventions. Like the Lottery Agent in *Der Silbersee*, the bailiff has only one number; and it, too, is all-important.

"The Song of the Bailiff" is political cabaret self-inflated into operetta for satirical purposes and raised to a higher power by the quality and critical efficacy of its composition. The four bars of arrogantly strutting harmonies which open the song (see ex. 5) are sufficient to expose the insolence of the refrain (see ex. 6a) and the cheapness of its oily chromaticism. It so happens that a very similar refrain (see ex. 6b) was concocted in 1929 by the Berlin Agitprop troupe Kolonne Links for a song satirizing politically biased film censors. The fact that the resemblance is explained by a common resemblance to Yellen and Ager's 1927 hit, "Ain't She Sweet?", tells us everything about the aims of the Agitprop song but nothing about the bailiff's song that has not already been unmasked by example 5. In that sense it is wholly characteristic that the bailiff's first mention of his official role is associated with a transposition and harmonic "ennoblement" (intensification) of his chromatic motif. For a moment, the dignity of his office has got the better of his sense of personal outrage. But as soon as he reminds himself that Juan's threats of physical violence are, in effect, threats both to the state itself and to the civil and military powers at its command, his music throws dignity to the winds and breaks into a *stringendo, poco a poco* jazz development of the chromatic motif which culminates, *allegro molto*, in a fanfaronade of blue thirds as the bailiff gives warning of what will befall anyone who dares to raise a hand against him.

The villagers' choric reiteration of his warning gives the bailiff time to regain his composure. Drawing himself to his full height—and 5'1" would be ideal for the part—he concludes with a brief homily about his fatherland and the common weal. The effect of the words alone is ludicrously sentimental; but Weill recognizes in them a reflection of a universal feeling, if not of his own loss, and, with a generosity that transcends all caricature, allows that the bailiff too is a human being—no worse, perhaps, than Juan's schoolmaster father, a die-hard conservative nationalist who believes what he reads and reads what he believes. The *molto espressivo* character of the bailiff's peroration is a victory of heart and mind over justified prejudice. Snatched from the tight grip of mockery, it sounds genuine and is convincing for purely musical reasons: the substance for it is derived, astonishingly, from the song's opening material. The feat of composition is precisely matched to the depth of understanding. Cabaret, operetta, and indeed Offenbach are left far behind.

A brief orchestral coda reinstates the song's critical functions and dismisses the bailiff from the scene. The anger contained in it is part of the essence and the genius of the song, and it is not, in principle, disproportionate to the dramatic situation. There is, however, a further reason why Weill invested so much in this, the only number of a "minor" character. During the last two winters of the Weimar Republic, Germany's rural economy suffered appallingly from the effects of the world crisis. As distraint orders and compulsory land auctions became the order of the day, and both the national and the *Länder* governments failed to fulfill their welfare obligations, commentators from left and right warned of an incipient peasants' revolt. One of the earliest and most widely reported incidents occurred in the state of Baden, where the Weill family had its roots. In November 1931 an impoverished allotment farmer named Baetz shot and killed the local bailiff who had arrived with a distraint order upon his only cow. Baetz was charged with murder and committed to a mental institution. Bailiffs now took to carrying arms and often had to be given police protection. Friedrich Wolf's play *Bauer Baetz*, with music by Hanns Eisler, was written in 1932 to promote the KPD's (Kommunistische Partei Deutschland) United Front policy for revolutionary workers and peasants. After its first performance in December of that year, no one in the literary and intellectual circles with which Weill was familiar could for long have remained ignorant of the fatal meeting between Baetz and the bailiff.

Everything the bailiff's song has to say about the role of *Beamtentum* in furthering the interests of authority irrespective of its legitimacy is applicable to the Prussian tradition as a whole. Perhaps because that tradition had so often been reviewed by Weill's music in the Weimar years, the Weill of the antimilitarist "Song of the Cow" is contemplative rather than aggressive. Even the "O trübe Tag" quartet is circumspect until its fierce cadence. The main thrust is reserved for the work's conclusion—the second finale, an extended structure that merits detailed consideration in light of its potentially "overwhelming" subject matter.

The music that begins the second finale is like a breath of the old

Berliner Luft from the last golden summers of the pre-1914 era. As one column after the other marches into the town square, Weill observes the simple-minded melodic sequences with amused affection and gives no hint of danger, whether past, present, or future. There is a slight darkening of tone when General Conchas arrives singing the refrain of his entry song from Act 1, but it is not sustained; as soon as he begins his (unpitched but rhythmically notated) militarist harangue, the holiday mood is restored by a vamped accompaniment in E-flat major. To conclude the initial stage of the finale, the general announces the one-man referendum to the music of the ex-president's Wagnerian recitative—last heard as a peace speech at the gala dinner in Act 1 and still sounding amiable enough despite the new scoring for trombones, tuba, and harp.

Weill's musico-dramatic plan for the second finale has two reciprocal functions. On the one hand, a traditional form of light music is interposed like a scrim between the scene itself and its ugly contemporary background in order to make possible a denouement strictly within the chosen operetta framework; on the other, a consistently cheerful opening not only creates tension through contradiction of the expectations aroused by the previous scene (in which Juan and Juanita's feelings about the general and his referendum are expressed in an angry duet in D minor) but also ensures that when the crisis comes, an elementary musical contrast will—if properly composed—provide the necessary emphasis. And so it does. Juan's act of rebellion is presented in musical terms strong enough to ensure that its symbolic significance is protected from the low comedy, yet light enough not to distort the more precarious balance of the operetta form. After a sustained open fifth has underpinned the fateful question, Juan boxes the general's ears on a *fortissimo* downbeat which momentarily suggests the earlier "oompah" accompaniment but then reels back in slow and thunderstruck waltz time—*diminuendo a pp*. These eight bars establish the key of C minor and prepare the way for a strangely hallucinatory choral waltz in which the populace wonders how best to react to the untoward result of the referendum.

C minor—hitherto associated only with "O trüber Tag" and some incidental music for the military maneuvers at the start of Act 2—now replaces E-flat major as the principal key of the second finale. It is not, however, intended to convey a tragic feeling, either at this time or later on. By reducing the rate of harmonic change (with the aid of prolonged pedal points), lowering the dynamic norm to *piano,* and adopting an exotic (*zigeuner*) melodic idiom, Weill contrives to shift the action into a dream-world where all emotions seem unreal and questions of probability irrelevant. The change is achieved with so light a touch that one may overlook its importance. In fact, it is the first move toward providing a structural and imaginative justification for the otherwise unprepared trick with the defective weapons. The clinching move is the setting (in the major of the new tonic) of the pleas for clemency sung in the name of the virgins of Santa Maria by Mme. Odette's whores as they emerge from her nearby establishment dressed in bridal white and bearing garlands (see ex. 7). The display of C-major innocence is so outrageous that henceforth nothing can safely be taken on trust. It even allows for games to be played with Juanita's "Ballad of Esteban": having been reminded of the ballad by Juanita, the general obligingly sings it in counterpoint to the music of example 7. But then, as if to show what rubbish the ballad is, he ends by brusquely repeating the order for Juan's immediate execution.

While the firing squad goes to collect the rifles from the arsenal, Juan and Juanita begin a farewell duet in C minor whose music does not take itself as seriously as they do. Despite the swooping lines and weeping appoggiaturas, an air of unreality is suggested by the close harmonic relationship with the previous waltz chorus. The monotone interjections of two dignitaries who are worried about missing their siesta are another sign that the tears will soon be over. Sure enough, a grief-laden series of falling sequences leads to F major and a lively mock-fugal chorus (in four dummy parts) for the members of the firing squad as they return from the arsenal brandishing their useless rifles.

The subject of the disarmament "fugue" (see ex. 8) belongs to the same simple-minded family as the sequential parading tune at the start of the finale. Although the counterpoint is hardly intended to bear examination, the effect it creates in the context is perfectly judged. After the tearful C minor, the tonal and textural contrast is comic enough in purely musical terms to supply what is necessarily missing from the libretto; and, like all local solutions that are truly inspired, it has long-term consequences. Having devised a countersubject that introduces a new and, for the moment, unexplained quality of skittishness, Weill turns to the comic pathos of men whose symbols of virility have suddenly failed them and gives them the remaining vocal entries a *cantabile* accompaniment which extracts the maximum plangency from a harmonic emphasis on the submediant and supertonic elements in the underlying root progression (I–VI–II–V). Finally, there arises from that modal emphasis a *fortissimo* climax in which Juan and Juanita conclude their farewell duet as if now in D minor, while the soldiers in unison roar out their F major "fugue" subject and Mme. Odette's young ladies do their utmost on behalf of the skittish countersubject. A codetta brings this amazing ensemble quietly to rest in G major, with the combined chorus reiterating the words which began it—"Excellenz, es ist fatal."

Although Weill saved the whole rifle episode from becoming "fatal" in quite another sense, the danger is not yet over. A work that sprang from a fundamentally serious concern with reality has now been forced to escape into a storybook realm of playful fantasy; and there it promises to end, without further thought of its original obligations, yet faithful to the code of traditional operetta. Given the choice of genre, one could argue that any other kind of conclusion would be inappropriate; and it is certainly true that after the rifle episode, and at this late stage in the libretto, no explicit restatement of the work's serious themes is artistically practicable. Nevertheless, the music is still free to express its own thoughts and, hence, to remind us that the questions of war and peace in Santa Maria are not altogether divorced from those in the world outside. There is, however, some delay before Weill can take advantage of that freedom.

Structurally, the firing squad's hushed cadence in G major seems to lean toward an immediate conclusion in C major. But what actually follows—after a few spoken lines and the general's return to the platform for his second speech—is a literal repeat of the E-flat major vamped figure. As a mere signpost indicating the hollowness of the general's sudden espousal of peace and goodwill, the reprise serves its dramatic purpose. Musically, however, it marks a temporary break in the flow of Weill's invention. Apart from the appropriately unctuous setting of the words with which the general pardons Juan, there are no fresh ideas for some while. The effect of scrappiness, especially on the tonal level, is confirmed by the ensuing reprise, in its original E major, of the love duet (example 4) from the betrothal rite. If, as seems likely, Weill would have preferred to ignore the conventional and indeed commercial need for such a reprise, that could well explain the awkwardness of the whole passage following the firing squad's cadence in G major and the unseemly haste with which the music of the enraptured lovers is dismissed by the orchestra, which bursts in on their final cadence, establishes a new *vivace* tempo, and then hurtles down to the long-awaited key of C major.

The sense of release is immediate, and the dramatic reason for it confirmed as the soldiers sing that they now have neither weapons nor honor nor security, but at least they are *happy* (see ex. 9). The skittishness of the "countersubject" in the disarmament fugue is now explained; and the melancholy, which also was there, has apparently disappeared. With a neatly prepared leap to the flat submediant key—whose own flat submediant *harmony* pretends to provide a retrospective enharmonic justification for the E major of the previous "romantic" reprise—the lovers take the stage again and jubilantly proclaim that they each have five *duros*, making the ten they need for a new cow. As if to remind them that Santa Marian fiscal policies are always liable to upset such calculations, Weill abruptly divides the metrical scheme into irregular twos and threes that never add up to more than seven. It is only when the threes are ousted that the lovers are allowed to conclude with a triumphant ten-bar phrase.

The phrase moves back to C major (closing on a prolonged dominant seventh) and seems to promise an immediate return to the frivolities of example 8. But at the very point where the finale would thus have become irrevocably trapped on the level of entertainment, Weill re-establishes the essential connections and does so by the most radical means available to him: he reverts to a much earlier idea whose function had been satirical and transforms it into something that proves strong enough to sustain and bring to an unexpectedly moving conclusion everything that is fundamental to the work's serious purposes. The passage gives final and conclusive evidence of the way his inner feelings have tended throughout the work to neutralize his anti-German intentions.

The theme of the closing passage is a variant of the one that dominated the mock-Prussian parade at the start of the finale. In that context and setting, its raison d'être was the comic discrepancy between its aspirations and its technical capacity. Flat-footed, short-winded, and yet—through sheer obtuseness—invincibly and touchingly proud of itself, it knew of no other way to halt its descending sequences than to start them again a fourth higher. Thus, a single 4-bar phrase was made to grow like some diminutive stage-army whose soldiers no sooner reach the wings on one side than they must run around to join the end of the column before it comes into view on the other side. The possibility of making an endless loop was evident from the start (see ex. 10). The tune had seemed unfit for anything but its original purpose of cheerfully mocking the general's "Day of National Uprising"; and having served that purpose well, it had been discarded. That it should now reappear, in C major, as the immediate sequel to the lovers' "10 *duro*" duet, is already surprising; that it should do so in an augmented and reharmonized form which conveys the parting words of the general with such quiet and touching dignity that they sound like some quixotic farewell to arms—though on paper they merely express disappointment at the turn of events—is something that has to be heard to be believed, and heard, moreover, in the formal context of the entire finale. For instance, the new harmonization arises from the same I–VI–II–V root progression that lent so strange a poignancy to the soldiers' fugal complaints about their useless weapons; and the similar feeling in the general's music is enhanced by the ruminations of the violins, high above the vocal part and its soberly walking bass. If the music evokes the world of example 10, it is only to hint (as the text does not) that the general has already begun to see beyond it and may yet prove worthy of better things. Satire that refuses to destroy the destructible adversary is characteristic of *Der Kuhhandel* and worthy of Weill. (And how typical of *A Kingdom for a Cow* that this chivalrous gesture toward the general was omitted.)

The process of transforming and reorienting the idea in example 10 culminates in a choral hymn. Its subject is not "peace" but "joy," not

"Friede" (by now a discredited word) but "Freude." While the new variant of example 10 is taken over by the orchestra in an ampler and structurally different harmonization, the chorus of townspeople reaffirms the words of example 9 in a fresh setting: "We have no honor, guns or security, but we do have (an immense) joy." The fact that the new setting sounds notably more sagacious than example 9 is partly due to the breadth and demeanor of the accompanying music; but the decisive element is the one implicit in its own melodic and dynamic structure, which lays equal emphasis upon the losses of weapons and military honor while reserving the main stress for the consequent lack of security. The climax is reached at the word "Sicherheit" (security) in the third 8-bar phrase of what still promises to be a 32-bar variation on the march music in example 10. The climax not only emphasizes the word itself but also engulfs the joyful march tune and its striding bass and precipitates an immediate flight from the "security" of the home key, the major mode, and the 32-bar unit. As example 11 shows, the tension produced by associating the word "Freude" (joy) with a falling phrase that lands on a minor triad is then increased by the melodic/harmonic clash in the second falling phrase and is not resolved until the final phrase—again a falling one—which leads back to example 8's chirpy C major. The slip of the pen in the holograph vocal score that has the townspeople singing "*keine*" instead of "*eine* Riesenfreud'" seems true to the music's expressive sense, for the unmistakable implication of the whole passage is that, whereas the soldiers are indeed "immensely joyful," the now defenseless civilians are rather less so.

By stressing the loss of security with such firmness that for a moment the rejoicings collapse, Weill at one stroke dissociated *Der Kuhhandel* from the ostrich attitudes of so many peace campaigners of the day and ensured that the finale could fulfill its obligations for the work's fundamental seriousness of purpose. The effect is already apparent when the merry strains of example 9 are resumed by the entire company at the end of example 11. What had originally seemed to be a form of musical make-believe appropriate to the toy-town armies of traditional operetta has now acquired a critical context and a human dimension. Example 11's warnings about the future delimit the merriment of example 9 in such a way that Weill can now with good conscience allow the civilians to take part in it; whatever their doubts about the general's "true and lasting peace," they have at least been saved from the immediate threat of war.

In that sense a rumbustious conclusion on the theme of example 9 would have been an artistically justifiable response to the requirements of operetta. But Weill goes on to complete the thematic symmetry indicated by example 9's return and gives it a wholly serious function; his closing paragraph reaffirms the C major "hymn to joy" which example 11 had prematurely interrupted and this time sustains it to the very end: not by eliminating the previous stresses, but by redistributing them so as to suggest that a balance had been struck between natural high spirits and reasonable doubts. In place of the expected harmonic crisis at the word "Sicherheit," a slight but still sufficient stress is exerted by contrapuntal means, whereupon the melodic line slowly ascends, instead of falling swiftly as it had in example 11. Meanwhile, the bass line has been restricted to marking the changes of harmony every four bars, thus emphasizing the fact that the root progression, I–VI–II–V, is identical with the one that had already compared the general's *pianissimo* "farewell to arms" with that strange moment of sadness in the firing squad's fugato; and it is the general we are particularly reminded of now, since it is "his" instrument, the tuba, that gives the bass line its distinctive color.

The slow ascent of the melodic line after the harmonically secure setting of "Sicherheit" coincides with the dominant stage in the I–VI–II–V progression; and since the words are by now as familiar as the harmony and since the phrase is marked *crescendo* throughout, it is reasonable to expect an "immense" tonic downbeat on the very last word, "Riesenfreud'." But having removed one kind of stress from "security," Weill places another kind on "joy" (see ex. 12). The flat submediant interpolation has the effect of recalling the lovers and their jubilant A-flat major duet and thus suggesting that theirs is a truly "immense" joy of the sort that can safely be celebrated by everyone (including even the general, or so the tuba's merry runs suggest). It is left to the orchestra to confirm C major with a vehemence that reminds us how ambiguous, by comparison, were the closing festivities of the Second Symphony and how self-questioning the gentle affirmation of hope at the end of *Der Silbersee*. It is indeed the most exuberant ending to any of Weill's works since the early 1920s; one has to go back as far as the *Sinfonia Sacra* and its closing "Hymnus" to find anything remotely comparable in that respect. Even so, the joy it expresses is not, as we have seen, unqualified. Moreover, the conventions of a "happy end," as operetta traditionally sees it, have been complied with only up to the point where a powerful expressive need asserts itself and is answered. Without such a need, structural integration of the kind Weill finally achieved would have been beyond his or any other composer's reach.

Comparison with the closing chorale of *Die Dreigroschenoper* shows that in the operetta's "hymn to joy" any residual irony has been subordinated. Whereas the structure of the chorale is decisively influenced by the irony it conveys, that of the hymn is designed to restore the symmetry which irony had previously disturbed. The differing degrees and levels of integration do not, however, indicate differences of expressive intensity; and they are only partly attributable to the structural consequences of the irony, since the chorale's comprehensive motivic organization would have been incompatible with the more relaxed and traditional melodic structures of *Der Kuhhandel*. In any case, it is not through motivic working that the chorale's irony is first revealed. The salient features are tonal: first the chorale's C-major answer to Peachum's C-minor admonitions, and then the undermining cadential retreat to the subdominant.

A similar tonal procedure and expressive effect could well have figured in *Der Kuhhandel*, but not at the end and especially not via C major. In *Die Dreigroschenoper*, that most "just" and homely of keys had from the start been robbed of its moral connotations and forced to become a neutral and vagrant observer of human frailties. Since there was insufficient dramatic or philosophical justification for its apparent recovery of righteousness at the start of the final chorale, it was only by pointedly retreating from it that Weill could indicate the absence of those reassurances with which many classical and romantic composers had associated it. But in *Der Kuhhandel*, C major undergoes a fundamental change. When first established by the trio, "Schlafe, Santa Maria," it seems even more lethal than it did in *Die sieben Todsünden* and much further removed from its traditional associations. In homage to the Offenbach of *Hoffmann* rather than the operettas, but for purposes that are strictly political, Weill uses the convention of the lullaby to strip C major of any honorable intentions. As the president, his domestic advisor, and his war minister sing, in close imitation, of their need for the nation's trust—which only a moment before they shamelessly betrayed—and as their *berceuse* for Santa Maria and its democratic institutions wafts through the night air, the music's lyricism is wholly charming yet purely Mephistophelean. The only outward sign of evil intent is a stealthy move from C major to C-sharp minor and back again; but in case the listener should overlook it and be puzzled by the music's apparent blandness, a brief orchestral ritornello evokes Brecht's image of the sharks by citing the opening motif of the "Moritat." Although the substance of the lullaby-trio is very different from that of the "Moritat," the quotation indicates the type of audience Weill was thinking of in 1934, since it would have been noticed only by audiences familiar with the stage, film, or recorded versions of *Die Dreigroschenoper*. (The "Moritat" did not begin a life of its own until 1955.)

So perversely fascinating is the effect of the lullaby that it almost seems to account for the harmonic impotence of the subsequent "Ballad of Esteban," which uses or misuses C major as an emblem of the innocence and *Volkstümlichkeit* that the general longs to be reminded of. So it is no wonder that the next we hear of C major is from Mme. Odette's whores (ex. 7). The wonder is that they prove to be its salvation. For their pretense of innocence is oddly and humorously childlike; and from that to the frank naiveté of example 8 is only a short step. With the final episodes, C major at last wins back its traditional strength and virtue.

It says much for Weill's character that such a conclusion was reached at a time when he might forgivably have despaired of the world around him and of his own situation in it. In the context of his German works it represents a fulfillment of the fleeting C major passages in *Die Bürgschaft* (Act 1 finale) and *Der Silbersee* (Fennimore's entry) and thus a safe crossing to the opposite and happier side of the latter's symbolically frozen waters. Within *Der Kuhhandel* itself, the story of C major epitomizes the whole drama; and its conclusion confirms that *Der Kuhhandel* was—in its essence—an expression of artistic and intellectual convictions.

The same could hardly be said of the *Kingdom for a Cow* numbers (except for the choral prologue, whose origins are in any case rather obscure).[12] In a qualitative and chronological sense, they are successors to the purely popular numbers Weill had written for *Marie galante* after completing the main part of the *Kuhhandel* draft. If his financial circumstances had allowed him to complete every detail of *Der Kuhhandel* before they forced him to embark on *Marie galante*, and if a German-language production of *Der Kuhhandel* had materialized in, say, Zurich or Prague, he would, at worst, have been none the poorer, and posterity would have been the richer.

A Kingdom for a Cow was the unhappy result of an attempt to superpose the conventions of modern musical comedy on an incomplete formal structure that had been designed according to the quite distinct if related conventions of operetta. For the very reasons that had ensured the decline of operetta and the rise of the musical, the two sets of conventions were incompatible. There was never any hope of success for *A Kingdom for a Cow*—especially in the London of Noel Coward and Ivor Novello—so long as the pacing and the greater part of the structure of *Der Kuhhandel* were retained. Meanwhile, the adoring public that continued to support the D'Oyly Carte Company's monopoly of Gilbert and Sullivan was open to approaches only from composers and librettists who obeyed the strict rules of Savoy opera but were clever enough to turn them to their own advantage. The last composer to accomplish that feat was Walter Leigh (1905–1942), who wrote his first "comic opera," *The Pride of the Regiment,* in 1931, shortly after returning to England from three years' study in Berlin with Hindemith. Of that background there is no trace: with a forgetfulness of recent events typical of the English musical theater of its day, *The Pride of the Regiment* harks back to the Crimean War and interweaves its romance of the upper-middle classes and harmless politicomilitary comedy about General Sir Joshua Blazes, his prime minister, and a villainous traitor to the Russians. Such were the frontiers that *A Kingdom for a Cow* breached. In his second and more celebrated comic opera, *Jolly*

---

12. The problematic origin of the choral prologue is discussed in my forthcoming *Kurt Weill: A Handbook.*

Roger, which was produced at the Savoy Theater two years before *A Kingdom for a Cow,* Leigh and his librettists retreated to seventeenth-century Jamaica for a pirate comedy very much simpler than Gilbert and Sullivan's and more "modern" only because of some echoes from the recently revived and hugely successful *Beggar's Opera.* The scene is a model of British decorum and gives not the slightest hint that its composer might have chanced upon *Die Dreigroschenoper* during his wanderings in Berlin.

An English adaptation of *Der Kuhhandel* that emulated the homespun virtues of *The Pride of the Regiment* and *Jolly Roger,* and treated the political content accordingly, would have been easier to accomplish than a wholesale popularization and would perhaps have stood a better chance of success with the Savoy Theater public. The only audience in London for anything resembling the original *Kuhhandel* was the one created in the shadow of the world crisis, the one for which Ashley Dukes had adapted and staged plays by Kaiser, Toller, and Feuchtwanger at his little Mercury Theater (opened in 1933) and which now, in 1935, supported Rupert Doone's Group Theater and its first Auden-Isherwood production, *The Dog beneath the Skin.*

For such a public in 1935, sets in the approved Piscator style, with blow-ups and projections of topical news photographs, were no longer a novelty. But the photo-montages which Hein Heckroth—a gifted associate of Caspar Neher—incorporated in his original set designs for *A Kingdom for a Cow* so alarmed the management of the Savoy Theater and the representatives of the celebrated couturier Schiaparelli (who was providing the financial backing and the costumes) that Heckroth was obliged to redesign the sets in conventional style. For the same reasons, the original idea that the part of General Conchas should be played as a parody of Goering was dropped in favor of broad comedy. The tendency of the production, especially toward the end of the rehearsal period (when the original director was replaced), was reflected in the advance publicity, which might have been expressly devised to ensure that the "serious" public stayed away.

As a mere by-product, already faulty in itself and then made doubly so by faulty marketing, *A Kingdom for a Cow* was unprecedented in Weill's career. The production process that gave it an appearance of completeness left it without some of the structural supports that ensure the survival, against all odds, of the unfinished *Kuhhandel*—a "work-in-progress," but a work for all that. In its incompleteness and also in what it nevertheless completed, *Der Kuhhandel* was the unquiet resting place between the old way and the new. From *Die Bürgschaft* it inherited part of its underlying thesis about the relationship between authority and violence; to *Johnny Johnson* and *Knickerbocker Holiday* it handed over the task of developing this line of discussion in an American context. When the possibility of continuing such developments was, in effect, preempted by the outbreak of the Second World War, the only implications of *Der Kuhhandel* that could still be worked out were formal and generic. For that purpose the fantasy world of *Lady in the Dark* proved ideal: its through-composed dream sequences provided opportunities for sustained invention in popular idioms which had not been available since *Der Kuhhandel*, while the compositional experiment with irrational continuities substituted for the missing level of sociopolitical reality.

In that sense *Lady in the Dark* was literally a tour de force and could not be repeated. Once Weill had assessed the professional consequences of its success, it was to the Offenbach tradition that he returned. A "Nell Gwyn" operetta with political overtones was one of his favored projects;[13] and another, based on F. Anstey's novella, *The Tinted Venus,* had begun to develop as a "European" operetta before it came to grief and was swiftly reconstituted as the all-American *One Touch of Venus*—a putatively conventional "musical" whose subversive and anarchic elements were so skillfully packaged that they went almost unnoticed. Formally speaking, Weill's evident longing for a return to Offenbachian principles remained unassuaged by *One Touch of Venus:* hence the Columbus escapade in *Where Do We Go from Here?* and hence *The Firebrand of Florence.* It was in *The Firebrand,* written and staged well before the end of the Second World War, that Weill ventured a brief but highly significant reaffirmation of the unsoldierly sentiments which had informed so many of his European works and the first of his American ones; and yet it was there that he allowed the sorry history of *A Kingdom for a Cow* to repeat itself, with peculiarly painful variations.

The period between January 1941 and February 1945—that is, between the triumph of *Lady in the Dark* and the disaster of *The Firebrand*—was the latest and longest of the three periods in which Weill might conceivably have risked coupling Offenbach's name with his own (and the risk would have been doubled in the presence of Adorno or of someone known to him). That he would at any time have described himself as "the Offenbach of his century" is beyond the bounds of credibility unless the words were exclaimed with ironic bravado after his first year in France—which was the time of *Der Kuhhandel.* The only known instance of the collocation is, however, in a letter of 1928 from Weill to his publisher in which he objected to a critic's thesis on "Weill als Humperdinck" and proposed "Weill als Offenbach" in its stead.[14] His admiration for Offen-

---

13. The "Nell Gwyn" project originated in September 1942; see also note 18.
14. Weill to Universal Edition, 17 October 1928.

bach is frequently attested in his critical writings from 1925 on;[15] but this particular expression of it seems calculated to disarm rather than persuade. Hostile as he must have been to any exposure of his musical origins by association with so passionate a Wagnerian as Humperdinck, he adduced an obviously heterodox figure, regardless of the fact that his own creative connections with Offenbach (unlike those he once had, and was to have again, with Humperdinck) were extremely tenuous. Aside from the can-can in *Zaubernacht* and some snapshots in *Der Zar lässt sich photographieren*, there was nothing for Weill to point to but an arguably "Offenbachian" attitude, far behind the actual notes, in parts of *Die Dreigroschenoper*. Nor were the connections strengthened during his remaining years in Germany. Indeed, except for one or two passages in *Der Silbersee*, everything that followed *Die Dreigroschenoper*—from *Das Berliner Requiem* to the Second Symphony—tended increasingly to contradict what little sense there had been in Weill's counterthesis. By February 1933, "Weill als Offenbach" was sufficiently devoid of meaning to recommend itself only as a crudely racist jibe.

Such was the background from which the tribute to Offenbach in *Der Kuhhandel* derived its psychological necessity and its moral justification. It was only in the precise circumstances of Weill's awakening to the realities of exile, in France and in the year 1934, that a work of this type and this bearing was conceivable. Adorno was, of course, right to remark that the Offenbach model was unrepeatable (though incomprehensibly wrong in his prior reference to "lack of real substance"). The Weill of *Der Kuhhandel* understood this, just as the Weill of *Der Zar* had understood what Walter Benjamin, in his great essay on Karl Kraus,[16] defined as the "secret" of Offenbach: "how in the deep nonsense of public discipline— whether it be of the upper ten thousand, a dance floor, or a military state—the deep sense of private licentiousness opens a dreamy eye." The Anatolian Venus whom Weill at last brought to musical life in 1943 embodied that same subversive secret and was knowingly the agent of its anarchic consequences. But except for a brief respite in Mme. Odette's establishment, the villains of *Der Kuhhandel* have not time to spare for venery; they are fully occupied with meaner and more dangerous pursuits, and their sense of life's urgencies is of quite another order.

Viewed from its Offenbachian side, *Der Kuhhandel* seems to have been tailor-made for the dummy that used to be wheeled out whenever Weill's name was mentioned in the presence of the young and impres-

---

15. See Kurt Weill, *Ausgewählte Schriften,* ed. David Drew (Frankfurt, 1975), pp. 42, 84, 146–47, 152, 156–57.

16. "Karl Kraus," in Walter Benjamin, *Reflections: Essays, Aphorisms, Autobiographical Writings,* trans. Edmund Jephcott (New York: 1978), pp. 239–73.

sionable. Topical and political in exactly the way that his German works were once reputed to be but never are, it lends substance to the favorite illusion of his false admirers in that it is, up to a point, indisputably parodistic. And yet every musical idea that is dispatched to the playing fields where parody traditionally lays its booby traps finds itself rerouted toward the front-line trenches and sooner or later is mown down— whether by a sense of the hostile realities it is consciously confronting, or by an unseen adversary from behind the lines, who is none other than Weill himself, instinctively defending the German heritage he is trying to disavow.

As if fearing that *A Kingdom for a Cow* might somehow be annexed by his "German" works, via the German origins of *Der Kuhhandel*, Weill began a tunneling operation as soon as he arrived in the United States and extended it, inch by inch, for the next ten years. Musical materials extracted from *A Kingdom for a Cow* are to be found in every one of his Broadway scores before *Street Scene* and also in two of his three film scores.[17] The fact that none of the *Kuhhandel* material excluded from *A Kingdom for a Cow* was ever drawn upon in this way is certainly no coincidence. Even if the reasons are purely stylistic, they emphasize on the one hand the conclusive nature of *Der Kuhhandel* and on the other the transitional functions Weill retrospectively discovered in *A Kingdom for a Cow*.

While *Lady in the Dark* was built on the formal experience of the two *Kingdom for a Cow* finales (and used one of the waltz melodies from the first of them), *One Touch of Venus* (which used a waltz tune from the second finale) abandoned the formal conventions of operetta but played the parody game for all it was worth as cabaret. Although Broadway's and Hollywood's love affair with the singer Grace Moore had led to a brief rehabilitation of European operetta in the early 1940s, and indeed to Weill's brief involvement with *La belle Hélène* and the Nell Gwyn project, the Weill of 1942 found Offenbach sadly "dated" (or so he told the producer Russell Lewis)[18] and seems to have acted accordingly in the up-to-

---

17. The main borrowings are listed in my *Kurt Weill: A Handbook*.

18. During summer 1942 the Broadway producer Russell Lewis invited Weill to undertake a reorchestration and elaboration of Offenbach's *La belle Hélène* for a production starring Grace Moore. Weill, who was then working on the first version of *One Touch of Venus*, declined the orchestration commission and successfully recommended Darius Milhaud in his stead. The possibility that he might nevertheless write one or two additional "hits" for *La belle Hélène* continued to be discussed, and for Weill, this was a means of mentioning his own operetta projects: *Venus* in passing, and then a Nell Gwyn project of his own, outlined in detail in a letter addressed "Dear Russel" [*sic*] and written from Beverly Hills on 30 September 1942. (In the Weill/Lenya Archive this letter is misfiled under Russell Crouse, another Broadway producer with whom Weill had been corresponding since 1938.) On 14 November 1942 Weill wrote to Russell Lewis: "I saw *La Vie Parisienne* and was quite shocked how stale and dated the Offenbach music sounded. It will take a great deal of musical

the-minute style and tempo of *One Touch of Venus.* This is surely the period in which Weill is most likely to have coupled his name with Offenbach's within the hearing of Adorno, and it lasted until *The Firebrand* failed so signally to reestablish the very type of operetta against which *Der Kuhhandel* had marched and Karl Kraus had railed. Apart from their indebtedness to *A Kingdom for a Cow,* the one thing *Lady in the Dark, One Touch of Venus,* and *The Firebrand of Florence* had in common was the avoidance of any topic that threatened to be "too overwhelming" for parody.

Karl Kraus's image of the tragedy of mankind played by the characters from an operetta had been inspired by the first act of that tragedy and suited it perfectly. He did not live to witness the second, but the entr'acte gave him a foretaste of it, and it was enough for him. He died in July 1936 a broken man. The previous November he had chosen the operetta *La Créole* for his last Offenbach "reading" in public. Although he added a satirical verse about Hitler, it was perhaps only a gesture of valedictory defiance. In an issue of *Die Fackel* published while Weill and Vambery were at work on *Der Kuhhandel,* Kraus had remarked that, while the spirit of Offenbach's music is immortal, in the world of Hitler and Stalin it was no longer possible to update his texts.[19]

By 1934 the questions so lightly brushed aside by Offenbach's *Brigands* and Peachum's beggars had become the questions of mankind's survival. It was surely the experiences of the previous year that compelled Weill to accept, for the first time in any dramatic work, the necessity of a protagonist who was not only unambiguously committed to ideals of freedom and justice (as Kaiser's Czar had been) but also prepared to defend them "heroically." The prologue's apparently satirical apposition of noble savage and ignorant conqueror allows the innocence of the opening scene by the trout stream to have a normative function in relation to the entire work, while the entry of the serpentine arms salesman is clearly seen for what it is. Not until *Love Life* (1948) and its opening evocation of Mayville, New England in 1791 did Weill attempt a comparable image of prelapsarian harmony at the start of a dramatic work. The serpent in the Thoreauesque Eden of *Love Life* has the same instincts as in *Der Kuhhandel* but is altogether more experienced. As soon as it reveals itself—in the guise of nineteenth-century capitalism—the values established at the start

---

showmanship to revitalize this music." A Grace Moore/Russell Lewis *belle Hélène,* orchestrated by Milhaud, conducted by Efrem Kurtz, with a new book and lyrics by Edward Eager and Alfred Drake, was duly announced in the press (clippings dated 12 December 1942 and 2 January 1943 from unattributed sources are in the Library of the Performing Arts at Lincoln Center, New York), but the production itself never materialized; neither did Weill's promised contributions nor his Nell Gwyn project.

19. See Paul Schick, *Karl Kraus* (Reinbek bei Hamburg, 1965), pp. 133–36.

are abruptly called into question. From then on, the decline is continuous and increasingly precipitous, so that the final tentative reminder of the principles established at the start figures only as a hope against hope. If *Love Life* were not so despairingly in earnest, it could be mistaken for a parody of Noel Coward's *Cavalcade* in the baleful light of Adorno's negative dialectics.

Although its musical substance is indefensible from Adorno's post-Schoenbergian standpoint, *Love Life* is the only creation of Weill's American years to exhibit, in however primitive or compromised a form, any of the characteristics Adorno had admired in *Die Dreigroschenoper*, *Happy End*, and *Mahagonny* during the three years when he was observing Weill at close hand and with a freshly discovered sympathy. The nature of that sympathy is peculiar to Adorno and scarcely discernible if his writings on Weill in the period 1928–31 are read as music criticism rather than as signs and signals of his own development in the relevant areas of philosophy, politics, sociology, and Benjaminian cultural criticism. In the 1950 obituary, however, the only hint of personal involvement is the reference to Offenbach.

At first reading it is impossible to determine whether the obituary's frosty sparkle is merely a surface effect designed to attract the readership of the *Frankfurter Allgemeine*, or whether the subsoil, too, is frozen. Certainly there is no evidence of that warmth which in later years was characteristic of Adorno's obituary tributes to such men as Eduard Steuermann or Winfried Zillig. But unless we refuse to grant that Adorno might in the circumstances have had as much reason to be cryptic about Weill as had Maxwell Anderson to bare his heart, any quotation from the obituary that is allowed to stand without reference to the suppressed background must, in the different light of today, misrepresent his reticence as a form of subterfuge. Insofar as the obituary prompts investigation of *Der Kuhhandel*, so does it merit further consideration in the light of it.

The period bounded at the one end by the world premiere of *Die Dreigroschenoper* and at the other by the Berlin premiere of the *Mahagonny* opera had been as crucial for Adorno as for Weill.[20] After three years'

20. As yet, there is no definitive biography of Adorno. Gerhard P. Knapp's *Theodor W. Adorno* (Berlin, 1980) gives the fullest account of his career available at present, but it is none too precisely documented; as far as dates and other details are concerned, it should be compared with the shorter outlines in Gillian Rose, *The Melancholy Science: An Introduction to the Thought of Theodor W. Adorno* (London, 1978) and Martin Jay, *Adorno* (London, 1984). Thomas Mann's famous tribute to Adorno in his study of the genesis of *Doktor Faustus* (Mann, *The Story of a Novel* [New York, 1961], p. 43) begins with a biographical note which incorrectly states that Adorno was for some years the editor of Universal Edition's modern-music monthly *Anbruch*—an error reproduced in most of the literature on Adorno. The history of Adorno's relations with Weill has yet to be recounted and remains nebulous between 1933 and 1942. Adorno himself—in conversation with me in 1960—was evidently

study in Vienna with Alban Berg, Adorno returned to the University of
Frankfurt, where in 1924 (at the age of 21) he had earned his doctorate
with a dissertation on Husserl. A second dissertation, combining neo-
Kantian and Freudian disciplines, had been started in Vienna and was
completed in Frankfurt. Having duly submitted it to the university as his
inaugural dissertation, he withdrew it on the advice of his mentor.

The decisive shift toward Hegel, Marx, and sociology which Adorno
accomplished in 1928 was his reaction to new associations that developed
first in his native Frankfurt, both at the university and at the Institute for
Social Research, where his lifelong collaboration with Max Horkheimer
was established. The intellectual and artistic links between Frankfurt and
Berlin in Weimar Germany were such that his extramusical interests
would have been sufficient to make him a regular visitor to the German
capital even if his musical responsibilities had not obliged him to establish
a second base there.

---

disinclined to revive memories of unhappy meetings in the U.S. after his arrival in 1938. A
two-page typescript letter to Weill, dated 31 March 1942 and written from Adorno's address
in Brentwood Heights, Los Angeles (but using the official letterhead of the Office of Radio
Research in New York), begins: "Lieber Weill, es wird Sie erstaunen nach so langer Zeit und
einem verunglückten New Yorker Rendez-vous mit einem Mal von mir zu hören." ("Dear
Weill, you will be astonished to hear from me all of a sudden after so long a time and an ill-
fated rendezvous in New York.") The letter, which is now in the Weill/Lenya Archive, was
prompted by Brecht's predicament in California and his hopes for an all-black production of
Die Dreigroschenoper. Adorno makes a case not only for the production but also for a "refunctioning" (*Umfunktionierung*) of the music. In a subsequent letter to Lenya, Weill described
Adorno's pleas as "completely idiotic" and stated that he had sent a reply that Adorno "will
not forget in a hurry." No copy of Weill's letter to Adorno has yet been traced, nor is there
any record of further contact during Weill's lifetime. Yet the words with which Adorno
ended his 31 March 1942 letter—"Ihnen und der Lenja alles Liebe/Ihr alter/Theodor W.
Adorno"—were certainly no empty formality. Whatever wounded pride there may have
been behind Adorno's 1950 obituary, his attempt to make amends in the article he wrote for
the program book of the 1955 production of *Street Scene* in Düsseldorf is touching and wholly
honorable; the article, entitled "Nach einem Vierteljahrhundert," is in fact a "refunctioning" of the obituary that is intellectually consistent with the original yet altogether warmer in
tone and more positive in tendency. The dexterity with which Adorno skates across the
American years without even mentioning *Street Scene* did not go unnoticed by the young
theater and ballet critic Horst Koegler, who, in the face of the almost unanimous hostility of
the German press, bravely sprang to the defense of *Street Scene* and identified Adorno as the
arch-enemy. (See Koegler, "Der Vortrupp der Musicals," *Der Monat* [January 1956]: 68–71.)
The typescript of Adorno's masterly reply, "Vortrupp und Avantgarde," is in the
Weill/Lenya Archive at Yale. Whether Adorno actually heard and saw the Düsseldorf production of *Street Scene* is not revealed and is, in fact, immaterial. (If he did, his reactions may
perhaps be gauged from those of Caspar Neher, who designed the production but nevertheless gave Lenya to understand that the music was wholly alien to him.) In the sense of
Adorno's envoi of March 1942, it is revealing that he and his wife were most gracious to
Lenya on her visits to Germany in the 1950s and that Adorno's distinguished pupil Carla
Henius was one of the first academically trained singers to take on the role of Anna I in *Die
sieben Todsünden*.

Berlin, for Adorno in 1928, was epitomized on the one hand by Schoenberg and his masterclass at the Prussian Academy of Arts, on the other by a group of variously unorthodox Marxists, most of whom had academic or literary links with Frankfurt. The senior member of the group was the philosopher Ernst Bloch (1885–1977),[21] who was at the time living in Walter Benjamin's apartment, while Benjamin[22]—a distant relative of Adorno, though they did not become closely acquainted until 1928—lodged with his parents at their home in the Grünewald. Benjamin had first met Bloch in Switzerland in 1919, shortly after the publication of Bloch's first major philosophical work, *Geist der Utopie*. To a friend he had written that the book was remarkable, but its author much more so. If that somewhat artificial distinction helped preserve their close friendship until Benjamin's death, it was only in the sense that music—as integral a part of Bloch's philosophy as of Schopenhauer's—was the one art to which Benjamin's unique critical intelligence and imagination had no ready access. A so-called "philosophy of music"—more properly, a philosophy *through* music—forms the central and largest section of *Geist der Utopie*. It was that which earned Bloch the lifelong friendship and admiration of Otto Klemperer[23] and that which must have excited the eighteen-year-old Adorno when he first read *Geist der Utopie* in 1921.[24]

The 1918 edition of *Geist der Utopie* is to German philosophy what Kurt Pinthus's historic anthology, *Menschheitsdämmerung* (1920), is to German poetry—"a document of expressionism." In its revolutionary and

21. Except in academic circles, Bloch remains largely unknown in the English-speaking world, where the dearth of adequate translations is today as crippling for Bloch as it was for Adorno twenty years ago. The first full-length book on Bloch, however, is in English: Wayne Hudson, *The Marxist Philosophy of Ernst Bloch* (London, 1982). Apart from the biographical outline, this is a highly technical work intended for the specialized reader. Two short monographs published in Germany—the first by Ernst Bahr (Berlin, 1974) and the second by Sylvia Markun (Reinbek bei Hamburg, 1977)—are expressly intended for the general reader. A selection of Bloch's musical writings, entitled *The Philosophy of Music* and with an introduction by me, was published by Cambridge University Press in 1985.

22. Walter Benjamin (1892–1940) won posthumous fame in the 1960s and is today widely accepted as one of the major critical minds of the twentieth century. In the copious literature on Benjamin there are no significant references to Weill; yet their mutual friends and acquaintances were too numerous for there not to have been some contacts between them in the period from 1929 (when they were almost certainly together in Le Lavandou with the Brechts during the summer when *Happy End* was uncomfortably gestating) until perhaps as late as 1933, when Benjamin was in Paris.

23. Klemperer's first reading of *Geist der Utopie* and his introduction to Bloch through Furtwängler are described by Peter Heyworth in *Otto Klemperer: His Life and Times*, Vol. 1: 1885–1933 (Cambridge, 1983), pp. 111–12.

24. Adorno described his early experiences of Bloch in "Henkel, Krug und frühe Erfahrung," an essay included in Siegfried Unseld, ed., *Ernst Bloch zu ehren* (Frankfurt, 1965); Bloch's informal recollections of Adorno are in Arno Münster, ed., *Tagträume vom aufrechten Gang* (Frankfurt, 1977), pp. 50–51.

quasi-Christian socialism it is a direct forebear of the first edition (1921) of Johannes R. Becher's pageant, *Arbeiter, Bauern, Soldaten,* from which Weill selected the motto of his First Symphony. But whereas Becher in his 1923 revision of the pageant removed the entire metaphysical superstructure and attempted a strictly Marxist-Leninist version of the remainder, the equally "revolutionary" Bloch retained in his 1923 edition of *Geist der Utopie* everything essential to the original version and merely elaborated or developed it.

That inclusiveness was predicated on Bloch's definition of "the spirit of Utopia" as harbinger of socially progressive tendencies at all times and in all cultures—a version of that "dream of a thing" about which Marx wrote to his friend Ruge in 1843.[25] Within the framework of his unwavering atheism Bloch included a large part of the heritage of Christianity and elements from other religions, among which Judaism was prominent although not preponderant. Bloch's heretical development of a form of Marxist metaphysics was coordinated with an equally unorthodox and "open" form of aesthetics that comprises manifold variations on the social and cultural dichotomies he first experienced during his formative years in industrial, plebeian Ludwigshafen and across the river in patrician Mannheim. The fascination Bloch had for genuinely popular culture and also for *Kitsch* was as foreign to Adorno as his penchant for theological debate. Yet Bloch remains at the back of Adorno's mind from 1928 onward, just as surely as Benjamin remains at the front, challenging, urging, and exemplifying. It was most probably Adorno who introduced Bloch to the pages of Universal Edition's *Anbruch,* the journal of modern music edited in Vienna by Paul Stefan. Bloch's first essay, "Wagner's Rettung durch Karl May" (again, Mannheim versus Ludwigshafen), appeared in January 1929. The second, on the "Lied der Seeräuber-Jenny," followed two months later; it was dedicated to Weill and Lenya.

Die Dreigroschenoper and its success were together responsible for altering relationships and redefining aims within the left-wing intelligentsia in Germany and Austria. The enthusiasm of Otto Klemperer (who had famously embraced Lenya and Weill a year before Bloch met them) was representative as far as the musical world was concerned; and there was more than a symbolic significance in the fact that he first encountered Karl Kraus at one of the many performances of *Die Dreigroschenoper* which he attended during its first season. The meeting may not have had any direct bearing on the Kroll Opera's revolutionary 1930 production of Offenbach's *Les Contes d'Hoffmann* (for which Bloch wrote

---

25. Karl Marx, *Die Frühschriften,* ed. Siegfried Kröner (Stuttgart, 1978), p. 171. Bloch's references to the September letter are numerous; see, for example, *Atheismus in Christentum* (Frankfurt, 1968), pp. 344–48, where a whole chapter is developed from it.

the introductory essay). But it was certainly the origin of the later Kroll production of *La Périchole* in Kraus's own updated version; and the introductory essay for that was provided by Benjamin. Was it not somewhere on the well-trodden route between the Theater am Schiffbauerdamm and the Kroll that the notion of "Weill als Offenbach" first began to take shape? To Kraus's way of thinking (not to mention that of Vambery, his young admirer at the Schiffbauerdamm)—it would have been wholly acceptable. For Bloch and Benjamin it might have had at least a passing attraction.

Although the triangular relationship among Bloch, Benjamin, and Adorno was based on the linear one between the two older men, Adorno's role was by far the most intense and complex. The intervention of Brecht in 1929, and the profound intellectual friendship which then sprang up between him and Benjamin, had far-reaching effects on Adorno and certainly influenced his attitude toward Brecht, and hence toward Weill, for the remainder of his life. Adumbrated in his first notice of *Die Dreigroschenoper* and completed by his writings on *Mahagonny,* his defense of Weill is inseparable from his commitment to the Schoenbergian revolution and his lifelong belief that the exhaustion of the tonal system, parallel to the exhaustion of bourgeois society and the capitalist system, had determined the historic necessity of atonality (which in turn justified the "atonal" structure of his own philosophy, as he saw it). Acceptance of *Die Dreigroschenoper, Happy End,* and *Mahagonny* in the context of his passionate rejection of Hindemithian and Stravinskian neoclassicism was grounded on exclusively negative inferences: for him the philosophical and sociological value of Weill's work lay in its exposure of the senselessness of continuing to compose in a tonal idiom. His lofty scorn in later years for Sibelius and Britten is only to be understood in that polemic sense—a sense that *seems* to be lacking from his 1950 obituary of Weill, with the result that his reference to "the lack of real craftsmanship, from the simplest harmonization to the construction of larger forms" is altogether baffling until one recognizes it for what it is: an empty and long-discarded shell in which, if one puts one's ear to it, one can hear the minuscule reverberations of a marvelously clear and fruitful thesis that had been exploded two decades before by Weill's obstinate refusal to follow the dialectical course Adorno had prescribed for him.

By then the thesis had already fulfilled its revelatory and germinating functions on the highest levels—above all, in relation to Bloch. If Benjamin's is the name most often cited by Adorno in his post-1928 work, Bloch's is the one that holds sway between the lines. The practice begins in Adorno's writings on *Die Dreigroschenoper,* which presuppose, make room for, and render indispensable, those of Bloch. The contrast is impressive. Fully aware of the significance of Schoenberg, but untroubled by a need to justify himself in the eyes of any camp or party, Bloch entered the field as an inspired amateur. His musical intentions, like Schopenhauer's, belonged to the antennal system of his philosophy and could neither obstruct it nor be inhibited by it: spontaneity of reaction, which increasingly eluded Adorno, was always characteristic of Bloch. Unmindful though Bloch sometimes was of the risks inherent in free-wheeling imagination, the rewards can be great, and where Weill is concerned they are beyond compare. Already in his essay on "Pirate-Jenny" Bloch diverged from the triumphantly one-sided Adorno and established for the first time and with a minimum of fuss the essential fact that the dynamics of Weill's art depend on certain extreme polarities and are characterized by rapid oscillations between them. Although the insights deriving from this perception are inevitably very different from Adorno's, it is significant that he did not tackle the topic of *Mahagonny* until after Adorno's death.[26]

It was, however, in their reactions to *Die Bürgschaft* that Bloch and Adorno first parted company, though surely in a friendly way and quite without the hard feelings of later years in very different contexts. Adorno was to have written the first article on the work for *Anbruch*, but, like its promised predecessor on *Der Jasager* (musically the forerunner of *Die Bürgschaft*), it did not materialize, for reasons clearly discernible in the 1950 obituary. Instead, there appeared in *Anbruch* Bloch's "Fragen in Weills *Bürgschaft*,"[27] perhaps the single most important contribution to the understanding of Weill that was published during his lifetime and certainly far removed from anything that Adorno could or would have written about the work from the Existentialist-Marxist-Schoenbergian standpoint he had by then made his own.

The "secret" Bloch penetrated was at the furthest possible remove from the one that Benjamin, and Siegfried Kracauer after him,[28] had gleaned from Offenbach. Weill, who was as secretive in the philosophical areas as he was candid in the erotic one, had inserted it on the long-lost title page of the First Symphony but did not disclose it again until the

26. Bloch lectured on *Mahagonny* in Tübingen in the 1960s. There are many references in his writings—most notably, as far as the present topic is concerned, in "Etwas fehlt . . . Über die Widersprüche der utopischen Sehnsucht. Ein Gespräch mit Theodor W. Adorno," in Rainer Traub and Harald Wieser, eds., *Gespräche mit Ernst Bloch* (Frankfurt, 1975), pp. 58–77.

27. "Fragen in Weills *Bürgschaft*," *Anbruch* 14 (November-December 1932): 207; reprinted in Drew, *Über Kurt Weill*, pp. 82–84. A slightly different version of the article appeared in the program book for the 1932 production of *Die Bürgschaft* in Düsseldorf that was conducted by Jascha Horenstein.

28. Siegfried Kracauer, *Jacques Offenbach und das Paris seiner Zeit* (Amsterdam, 1937). Kracauer (1889–1966) was an important link between Bloch and Adorno, and, as sociologist, essayist, and editor, he was an influential figure in the intellectual life of Weimar Germany. Weill owned the first edition of his book about Offenbach.

events of 1933 drove him into an isolation more nearly complete than any he had previously experienced. As a form of self-therapy and creative renewal after the crisis, *Der Kuhhandel* necessarily unlocks several doors.

The largest of them is the one that opens onto the railroad freight-yard scene. Here are assembled the hopes and intentions that had fought their way through every major work and most of the minor ones for the previous thirteen years. As the two complementary halves of "The Ballad of Pharaoh" turn on the axis of the arietta like a revolving stage through 180 degrees, the trompe l'oeil backcloth that had been concealing (even in *Der neue Orpheus*) Weill's promised land ever since 1921 is momentarily removed, and the young Marx who was creating his own form of exodus theology is reunited with his Pentateuchal archetype. In his magnum opus, *Das Prinzip Hoffnung,* drafted in the United States during the Second World War, Bloch wrote: "The intervention of Moses changes the substance of the salvation that had made up the external, wholly achieved goal of the pagan religions, the astral mythical ones in particular. Now, instead of the achieved goal a promised one appears . . . and instead of the visible nature-God there appears an invisible one of justice, and of the kingdom of justice."[29] From the vantage point of Werfel and Weill's *Der Weg der Verheissung,*[30] "The Ballad of Pharaoh" might seem prophetic in another sense. But in *Der Kuhhandel* there is no latent theology; the hopes it contains are restricted to this world.

Der Kuhhandel even discounts the pacifist utopia. The deus ex machina, like the leaders of yesterday and today, makes a farce of disarmament. It is only the music which protests that the question must nevertheless be taken seriously—and in principle no less seriously in 1935 than in 1945. If, for Adorno, Auschwitz was the nadir in the decline of the West and the determinant of his postwar philosophy and aesthetics, Hiroshima, which casts far fewer shadows both in Adorno's Kierkegaardian hell and in Bloch's future earthly paradise, is no less the consequence of events whose grimness had become "too overwhelming for parody." That *Der Kuhhandel* survives even such an enormity is a tribute to its authors' prescient recourse to the absurd.

Like the open ends of *Der neue Orpheus* and *Der Silbersee,* the final cadence of *Der Kuhhandel* insists upon a possible future, despite and because of the demonstrated failure of all panaceas. Neither sentimental nor cynical, but concrete, realistic, and observant, it proclaims, with all the power its tonality can muster, the necessity of persevering with the strug-

---

29. Ernst Bloch, *Das Prinzip Hoffnung* (Frankfurt, 1959), p. 1454; the present translation is slightly adapted from that in Hudson, *The Marxist Philosophy of Ernst Bloch,* p. 188.

30. *Der Weg der Verheissung,* written and composed in 1934–35, is the original version of *The Eternal Road* and stands in the same relationship to it as *Der Kuhhandel* does to *A Kingdom for a Cow.*

gle for those age-old ideals which the stage picture is displaying in such manifestly imperfect and transitory forms. The energies latent in that cadence and the perceptions that helped generate them are surely a truer measure of Weill's achievement in the coming years than any that Offenbach could provide.

Examples

Example 1. Der Kuhhandel, no. 7: "Die Ballade vom Pharao," part 1, opening.

Example 2. Der Kuhhandel, no. 5: "Der Mädchenraub," mm. 1–4.

Example 3. *Der Kuhhandel*, no. 5: "Der Mädchenraub," mm. 138–46.

Example 4. Der Kuhhandel, no. 5: "Der Mädchenraub," mm. 211–14.

Example 5. Der Kuhhandel, no. 12: "Triffst du mich Abends in der Schenke" (Song of the Bailiff), opening.

a.

Triffst du mich a - bends in der Schen - ke, Dann kannst du

mich ver - hau'n mein Sohn.

b.

[beschnitten wird . . .]

Het - ze ge-gen den Staat, was ro - te Ten-den-zen

hat, wo zum Streik man hetzt, wer die Kir - che ver-ketzt,

Example 6.
a. *Der Kuhhandel,* no. 12, mm. 6–10.
b. "Hetze gegen den staat" from Ludwig Hoffmann and Daniel Hoffmann-Ost-wald, *Deutsches Arbeitertheater, 1918–1933: Eine Dokumentation* (Berlin, 1961), no. 15.

Example 7. Der Kuhhandel, no. 24: Finale II.

Example 8. Der Kuhhandel, no. 24: Finale II ("disarmament fugue").

Example 9. Der Kuhhandel, no. 24: Finale II.

Example 10. Der Kuhhandel, no. 24: Finale II, "alla marcia," mm. 28–35.

Example 11. Der Kuhhandel, no. 24: Finale II.

Example 11. continued

Example 12. Der Kuhhandel, no. 24: Finale II.

Appendix

Der Kuhhandel	*A Kingdom for a Cow*
ACT 1	
1a. Siehst du keine?	1. Prologue
	1a. Fishing Scene
	1b. Duet, "Two Hearts"
1b. Denn Einer ist Kleiner	
2a. Wenn der Husar zu Pferde sitzt	
2. Friedensrede	*2. Peace Speech
3. Leise, nur leise	3. Trio, "Hush, Not a Word"
4. Schockschwerenot!	
4a. Die Wohlfahrtssteur	*3a. The Public Welfare Tax
	*4. General Conchas's Song, replaced by:
	4. A Military Man
5. Der Mädchenraub	5. Wedding Scene
6. Auf Wiederseh'n	6. "Goodbye My Love"
	7. "San Salvatore"
7. Die Ballade vom Pharao, 1. Teil: "Lass das Volk jetzt frei!"—Arbeitslied	
8. "Seit ich in diese Stadt gekommen bin"	8. Arietta, "Since First I Left My Home"
9. Die Ballade vom Pharao, 2. Teil	
10. Das Erlebnis im Café: "Heute abend ging ich ins Café"	
11. "Schlafe, Santa Maria"	9. "Sleep on, Santa Maria"
12. "Triffst du mich abends in der Schenke"	10. "If You Should Meet Me"
13. "O trüber Tag"	
14. "Es zog zu Salomon"	11. "As Long As I Love"
15. I. Finale	12. First Finale
ACT 2	
16. Soldatenmarsch and Zwischenspiel	13. Soldier's March (shortened)
17. "Wehe über Land und Meere"	

18. Ballade vom Räuber Esteban, "Wenn der Wind geht"

19. "Schön war die erste Flasche"—Fandango
20. National Hymn (reprise)
21. "Ich habe eine Kuh gehabt"
22. "In der Zeitung steht geschrieben"
23. "Fünf hab ich und fünf hast Du"
24. II. Finale

14. Ballad of the Robber Esteban
15. "A Jones Is a Jones"
16. "Life Is Too Sad"
16a. Fandango and Tango

17. "A Year Ago I Had a Cow"

18. Second Finale

*Denotes that the number was completed in rehearsal score but not orchestrated.

14

The Road to
The Eternal Road
GUY STERN

Kurt Weill and Franz Werfel's musical drama *The Eternal Road*[1]—especially its genesis—mirrors and illuminates all the vagaries, difficulties, and heartbreak of a work written in actual or impending exile. The letters and telegrams that scurried back and forth between the three great European collaborators, Weill, Werfel, and Reinhardt—beyond reflecting concerns about a very unaccommodating work in collaboration, its staging, and publication—provide in an occasional aside or coded aperçus a reflection of the disquieting times and circumstances under which it was written and, preternaturally, an augury of the far worse ones to follow. The letters and documents concerning *The Eternal Road* emanate, on Weill's part, initially from Paris and London, include a hasty but significant (and all but forgotten) interview from England, and continue to flow from New York, Bridgeport, Connecticut, and Hollywood, California. Werfel writes from Austria and New York, Reinhardt from all of these. In addition, he fires off a perturbed telegram from aboard ship, in transit from Paris to New York.

Equally symptomatic of the anomalies of exile are the publishing history of Weill's composition (in brief, only a few passages have been published in piano-vocal arrangements) and the correspondence that surrounds the work's germination. As was the case with Werfel's later drama *Jacobowsky and the Colonel*[2] (which, after his death, inspired a libretto for an opera by Giselher Klebe and the musical *The Grand Tour*), some of the most important letters documenting the premiere of *The Eternal Road* were first published as part of an American college textbook, a

---

1. The English title was originally *The Road of Promise*. This title appears as letterhead and in the correspondence as late as November 1935. See *The Eternal Road* folder at the Performing Arts Research Center at the New York Public Library. References to the original German version are to *Der Weg der Verheissung*, published in *Die Dramen* 2 (Frankfurt, 1959): 91–177.

2. See Werfel, *Jacobowsky und der Oberst. Komödie einer Tragödie*, ed. by Gustave Otto Arlt (New York, 1945).

reader by Gustave Mathieu and myself for students of German, entitled *Brieflich erzählt*.[3]

The road to *The Eternal Road*, which at times appeared more like a *via dolorosa* with its overwhelming artistic success and its financial failure after a relatively short run, can perhaps be best understood if we hypothesize for a moment that its year of birth had come at a more propitious time. Let us suppose that Reinhardt had still been in complete command of his Berlin theater-in-a-tent, the famous Circus Reinhardt, that he, Weill, and Werfel had not been deprived of their hard-earned popularity in Germany; and that they and Oskar Strnad, a famous stage designer, had all collaborated on a Berlin production of *Der Weg der Verheissung*. Such a musical drama might have become an institution in Berlin analogous to Reinhardt's annual staging of Hofmannsthal's *Everyman* in Salzburg. The themes of the two plays are equally universal, timeless, and majestic. In *The Eternal Road* a community of Jewish Everymen is huddled in a synagogue; fear of a pogrom has brought them together. To allay their fears and to refute doubters, apostates, and a detractor, the rabbi reads his congregants stories from the Bible, which come alive on the multi-level stage. At the conclusion of the drama the community is expelled from the city, but its faith is restored, as its members walk *their* mile on Israel's eternal road. In a different milieu this drama, with its timeless theme of perseverance and survival and its implicit invocation of the myth of the Wandering Jew, might have become a perennial.[4]

But having indulged this hypothesis for a moment, it is time to discard it. For in all likelihood, without the gathering storm in Europe, without actual or threatening persecution and exile, *The Eternal Road* would probably never have been written. Clearly its inception rested on two time-contingent premises. One of them was the idealistic and compassionate vision of a neophyte American producer. Meyer Weisgal, later the president of the Chaim Weizman Institute but then an indigent, unestablished producer, considered an outsider and rank amateur by the theatrical world, had achieved only one fledgling success with a previous Jewish-historical pageant-play, *Romance of a People*. Though eager for a second success via a Jewish theme, he was even more impelled by the

---

3. (New York, 1956), Ch. 21: "Ein Broadwaydrama wird geboren"; and *In Briefen erzählt* (München, 1965), pp. 134–40.

4. The potential of *The Eternal Road* as a pageant play was recognized even before its opening. On 16 February 1936 Lion Feuchtwanger wrote to Brecht (not without a liberal tinge of sarcasm): "By the way, I was asked originally to write the text for that Jewish-American Oberammergau. But I refused. No doubt Werfel and Reinhardt feel a greater inner urge [*innere Sendung*] for such a work." See Lion Feuchtwanger, "Briefe an die Freunde," *Sinn und Form* 11 (1959): 12.

conviction that the Bible could provide Jews with a rallying point in troubled times, or could, in his words, "constitute a stirring commentary on current events." He therefore approached Max Reinhardt in Paris with the request to direct and coordinate the creation of an original musical drama, yet to be written and composed.[5]

The second time-induced reason is more abstract but reified in the draft of a speech by Max Reinhardt: "Always when the Jews (forgive me these harsh words), when the Jews were in dire need," Reinhardt wrote, "they took, even in ancient times, the Holy Writ out of the shrine and thereby uplifted themselves for the future."[6] He might have been speaking in propria persona—as well as for his collaborators. Prior to the Nazi takeover, his preoccupation with Old Testament subjects had been minimal. Weill, the son of a cantor, had, like his father, composed liturgical music in his youth, but he then turned away from Jewish subjects.[7] Werfel, hovering eternally between Catholicism and Judaism, had never addressed himself to the Old Testament before and in his gnostic search had leaned since 1911 more toward Christianity as the true religion than toward Judaism.[8]

These, then, may be considered the main impulses that led to the first step on the road to *The Eternal Road*. When Reinhardt consented, on a rainy day in November 1933, to shepherd such a drama—taking on an unforeseen four years of preparatory work—he did not proceed as impetuously as his usual work-mode (or as Weisgal's account of it) leads us to believe.[9] When several weeks later (on 1 December 1933) Weill provided Manfred Georg, a well-known journalist and editor, with a description of his works-in-progress, he made no mention of *The Eternal*

---

5. Weisgal chronicled the genesis of *The Eternal Road* at least twice. See his "Beginnings of *The Eternal Road*" in the Souvenir Program, pp. 7 and 30. The program is included in the *Eternal Road* folder, New York Library for the Performing Arts; also see his *So Far: An Autobiography* (New York: 1971), Ch. 11.

6. Printed in Edda Fuhrich-Leisler and Gisela Prossnitz, *Max Reinhardt in Amerika* (Salzburg, 1976), pp. 138–39; henceforth cited as Fuhrich-Leisler.

7. Obviously Weill did not *reject* his Jewish heritage, even when it lay dormant. See Horst Koegler, "Ein Verdi der Armen, ein Händel der Amerikaner," *Stuttgarter Zeitung*, 28 May 1981, p. 50. Koegler speaks of "the increasing impact of Weill's Jewish origins" and "the unbroken development" emanating from his origin as the son of a cantor.

8. Werner Braselmann, *Franz Werfel* (Wuppertal-Barmen, 1960), p. 65; Braselmann reinforces this interpretation by analyzing the figure of the apostate's son as a self-projection of Werfel: "According to his biography, he is precisely such a son whose eyes are opened to the mystery of his people during this, the hour of their need." See also Lore B. Foltin and John M. Spalek, "Franz Werfel" in Spalek and Strelka, eds., *Deutsche Exilliteratur seit 1933*. *I. Kalifornien* (Bern and Munich, 1976), p. 644: "Werfel had written this Biblical play as an answer to the flood of lies and hatred which, emanating from Germany, flooded the world."

9. See Weisgal, "Beginnings," p. 7.

Road. Since the letter (to be found in the archives of the Deutsche Liter-atur-Archiv in Marbach) obviously aims at completeness, it very likely predates any contact from Reinhardt concerning the proposed biblical drama:

> Today I can tell you only this much about my planned work: at the mo-ment I am composing a symphonic work for orchestra that will be per-formed this spring in the house of the Princess [Edmonde de] Polignac and which will be published (as will all my works from now on) by the large French music publisher HEUGEL. For the theater I am preparing a grand opera and a musical comedy, but I have not as yet progressed far enough to say anything about the subjects. I am writing these works in German, but they will appear immediately in French and English.[10]

Why did Reinhardt procrastinate at the beginning and at various stages during the genesis of the production? His son, Gottfried Reinhardt, assumes (in his memoirs) that his father harbored throughout an inner resistance against the entire product. "If I postulate that my father sabo-taged Weisgal's project a bit, either consciously or unconsciously, that thought is by no means as outlandish as it may appear to an ingenuous observer." He then explains that Reinhardt resisted a new professional career in America (for a variety of reasons, for example, he did not wish to be identified with the maelstrom of refugees) at the very moment he needed it most.[11] Perhaps so. But what can reasonably be assumed, certainly with equal plausibility, is the hypothesis that Reinhardt was at times intimidated by his own initial boldness, as he faced the reality of his new American venture.

At any rate, by mid-December planning had begun in earnest.

---

10. The letter's greeting, addressed ambiguously to "Lieber Herr Dr.," has caused it to be miscatalogued in Marbach as a letter from Weill to Reinhardt. The letter was found among the posthumous papers of Manfred Georg and sold to Marbach. I am grateful to Kim Kowalke for sharing with me a photocopy of the letter made by Georg's child, Renée O'Sullivan, before its sale to Marbach. The "symphonic work for orchestra" was Weill's Second Symphony, completed in February 1934. The "grand opera" most probably refers to his plans for a Faust opera with Cocteau, whereas the outlines of a musical comedy were being sketched with Robert Vambery, the eventual librettist for the operetta *Der Kuhhandel.* Weill had been released from his contract with Universal Edition in October 1933 and signed the agreement with Heugel on 31 October. All of Weill's letters are quoted by permission of the Kurt Weill Foundation for Music. Unless otherwise noted, all transla-tions of German texts are my own.

11. Gottfried Reinhardt, *Der Liebhaber: Erinnerung seines Sohnes Gottfried Reinhardt an Max Reinhardt* (Munich and Zurich, 1973), pp. 212–13. The book's fascinating summary of the history of *The Eternal Road* advances two further arguments: that the artistic collab-orators were basically incompatible, and this alone doomed the production; and that the drama's artistic merits stemmed from neither Weill nor Werfel, but from Reinhardt. These assumptions (not supported by other expert opinions) are decidedly not shared by me.

Meyer Weisgal's original and seminal idea of producing the work "as a means of raising funds for the victims of Nazi persecution" (as reported by David Drew) and "to [begin] its world tour at the Albert Hall at London," was quickly abandoned.[12] As early as 17 December 1933 Weill reported to Lenya that he "almost journeyed to America for the sake of a large-scale Jewish theater production [*Theatersache*]."[13] But Weill's initial concept of the work was quite different from the composition that ultimately came to fruition. According to Drew, who studied the Weill-Lenya correspondence and interviewed Lenya, what Weill "had in mind during the early stages of composition was not opera, as Reinhardt supposed, but popular oratorio in the nineteenth-century sense—Mendelssohn of course, but also, perhaps, Gounod. Yet it was a twentieth-century work that offered him the closest precedent—the oratorio *Le roi David* by [his friend] Arthur Honegger."[14]

From here on, the visible milestones, the detours, and roadblocks on the path to *The Eternal Road* have been mapped in some detail, largely through Meyer Weisgal's autobiography, a documented study of Reinhardt in America, the previously mentioned textbook by Mathieu and myself, and extensive articles in journals.[15] Before supplementing this chronicle with some less visible landmarks—the major purpose of this paper—it will prove useful to recall briefly some of the more manifest way stations.

1. In May 1934 Werfel had completed the first draft of *Der Weg der Verheissung* and held a reading of it at Castle Leopoldskron, Reinhardt's luxurious residence near Salzburg, with Weisgal, Weill, and Rudolf Kommer (a friend and collaborator of Reinhardt) in attendance. The reading reportedly brought tears to the eyes of his listeners.[16] A second meeting of Reinhardt, Weill, and Werfel took place one month later in Venice, where Reinhardt was directing a production of *The Merchant of Venice*. At this meeting they essentially outlined the future course of their artistic collaboration.

2. Weill reported to Reinhardt on 6 October 1934 that he had solved the structural problems of the composition, especially the intermingling of strictly musical passages, background music, and spoken sections. He had finished half the composition and was beginning to

---

12. David Drew, *Kurt Weill: A Handbook* (forthcoming), entry for *Der Weg der Verheissung*.
13. The letter from Weill to Lenya is in the Weill-Lenya Research Center.
14. Drew, *Kurt Weill: A Handbook*, entry for *Der Weg der Verheissung*.
15. See my notes 3, 5, and 6. For a particularly interesting magazine article (since it is written from the perspective of Norman Bel Geddes), see Geoffrey Hellman, "Profiles: Designs for Living, II," *The New Yorker*, 15 February 1941, pp. 22–26.
16. Weisgal, "Beginnings," p. 7.

think of the casting: he accepted the notion of a cast of singing actors, but requested operatic singers for some of the recurring roles.[17]

3. In October and November 1934 Weill enthusiastically described his progress both as to the composition for the latter parts of the drama and his orchestration of the earlier parts.[18]

4. In the summer of 1935 Reinhardt made a fateful decision. When Oskar Strnad, Reinhardt's first choice as a stage designer, fell ill, he replaced him with the American Norman Bel Geddes, his former collaborator on the American production of *The Miracle*.[19] Bel Geddes, as gifted a stage designer as he was grandiose (if not megalomanic), designed sets that necessitated the complete rebuilding of a theater, endless postponements (at one time, he, like Moses, struck water beneath the theater's foundation), and the tearing out of rows of expensive orchestra seats. He precipitated a race between fund-raising and bankruptcy, all before opening night.[20] The production's artistic success and financial failure—it ran large deficits despite respectable attendance throughout and not infrequent full houses—is attributable to the fact that Reinhardt and Bel Geddes, who should have served as checks on one another, reinforced each other's tendency toward extravagance.[21]

5. The chief miracle worker, conjuring up new financial backers time and again (for instance, Maurice Levin of Hearn's Department Stores) and impoverishing himself and his far-flung family in the process, was Meyer Weisgal.[22]

6. With even the orchestra pit falling victim to Bel Geddes' spectacular designs, a decision was reached after the controversy between Bel Geddes, Weill, and Reinhardt that had prompted Reinhardt to fire

17. Letter from Weill to Reinhardt, dated 6 October 1934 (copy in Weill-Lenya Research Center). On 16 August 1934 Weill had written to his cantor father requesting him to send genuine, traditional liturgical Jewish music for use as preparatory study for the composition of *Der Weg der Verheissung* (letter in Weill-Lenya Research Center).

18. Letters from Weill to Reinhardt of 23 October and 13 November 1934, respectively; reprinted in Fuhrich-Leisler, p. 143.

19. Ibid., p. 144. Another important source becomes available after Bel Geddes joins the production: the specialty collection at the Humanities Research Center of the University of Texas at Austin. See Frederick J. Hunter, comp., *Catalog of the Norman Bel Geddes Theatre Collection* (Boston, 1973), pp. 95–100.

20. As detailed by Weisgal, *So Far*, pp. 126–33.

21. See Leopold Zahn, *Franz Werfel* (Berlin, 1966), p. 43. Although relying too much on the autobiography of Alma Mahler Werfel, Zahn's otherwise well-documented study reaches essentially the same conclusion.

22. "Weisgal . . . was on the whole indomitable." See Hellman, "Profile," p. 26. In an interview held jointly with Reinhardt, Weisgal also named Alfred A. Streisin, head of the Reliance Advertising Agency, as a heavy investor. See "Reinhardt Here for Opening of *Eternal Road*," *New York Herald Tribune*, 14 December 1936, p. 8.

off his shipboard telegram. The decision was to prerecord the music and synchronize the recordings with the stage action.[23] Bel Geddes, who was designing his sets in a multi-level structure (consistent with Werfel's stage directions) treated the factor of visibility from the various parts of the theater cavalierly. As reported by *The New Yorker* (and recently confirmed by David Farneth's and my interview of August 1983 with Mr. David Lipsky, then a very young press agent for the production), Bel Geddes deliberately tricked Reinhardt. When the director, skeptical of a clear line of vision from the audience to Bel Geddes's basement-level stage sets, tested it from various parts of the balcony, Bel Geddes climbed on tables or ladders, thus misleading Reinhardt into believing that the actors performing at the lowest point of the set would be visible.[24]

7. The monetary and architectural difficulties—Bel Geddes ultimately ripped out all but the outer walls of the theater—forced a one-year postponement of opening night. Originally planned for 23 December 1935, the play did not open until 7 January 1937. In the meantime, Norman Bel Geddes, though nominally still with the production, had been replaced by his more practical assistant, Harry Horner.[25] Werfel, deeply grieving and aggrieved, had returned to Austria, and Meyer Weisgal, to placate the theatrical establishment and to attract yet

23. As the telegram, dated 9 September 1935, reveals, Reinhardt was at first opposed to replacing the orchestra by prerecordings. A letter of 13 August 1983 from Miles Krueger, president of the Institute of the American Musical, Inc., to David Farneth, archivist of the Kurt Weill Foundation for Music, sheds some amusing sidelights on this early (if not earliest) experiment with prerecorded music on Broadway. (Mr. Krueger had interviewed the actor Michael Wager, whose real name is Mendy Weisgal, the son of Meyer Weisgal): "We [i.e., Wager and Krueger] often saw each other, and he was the one who revealed to me that because Norman Bel Geddes's setting occupied the orchestra pit at the Manhattan Opera House, it was necessary to pre-record the score. This was done by the RCA Photophone sound-on-film system, the same system that Disney used in recording *Fantasia*. As *The Eternal Road* opened in early 1937, I have to assume that its recording came first, for I believe that *Fantasia* was not recorded until some time during 1937 at the Academy of Music in Philadelphia with Stokowski conducting. . . . Mendy added that a few live musicians did appear at each performance and were perched on tiny platforms behind the proscenium. There, they hovered precipitously bowing or tooting away with the fear that at any moment they might topple onto the stage below."

24. See Hellman, pp. 25–26.

25. See Fuhrich-Leisler, p. 172; see also pp. 172ff. for a more detailed letter from Harry Horner to Max Reinhardt, dated 22 November 1936. According to *Variety* ("*Eternal Road* World's Most Costly Show," 13 January 1937, p. 54), Bel Geddes briefly returned just before the opening: "Geddes did not participate during this winter's activity to ready *Road* until several days before the actual debut. There had been differences of opinion between him and the management, but he responded to a last minute call for help and corrected the lighting faults, and many other technical difficulties, which others could not cope with."

another set of backers, engaged an established and respected, though token, coproducer, Mr. Crosby Gaige.[26]

8. In the interim, the cast, given the short rehearsal period after the complete alteration of the theater and Reinhardt's martinet habit of rehearsing far into the night, had reached a point of near-exhaustion. Some of the production staff, for example, the main publicity agent, quit because of nonpayment, while other publicity agents concocted unprecedented promotional schemes. Mr. Lipsky succeeded in establishing ticket sales at all Pennsylvania Railroad stations between Philadelphia and New York and in getting dispensation for Catholics from the diocese to attend theatrical performances during Lent.[27]

9. Opening night was an artistic triumph. All the papers with a morning deadline gave the show fervently enthusiastic reviews. The drama critics, although disclaiming musical expertise, admitted to being enthralled with Weill's music.[28] Subsequent reviews, however, were sharply critical of the ending. In the unceasing struggle of the collaborators to curtail the length of the drama (which had led to a previous flare-up between Weill and Reinhardt),[29] the final and possibly best scene of the drama, Werfel's Messianic vision and Weill's rousing evocation of it, was cropped off after an opening night that had run to 3 A.M.[30]

10. The play closed because of deficits on 17 May 1937. Sets, costumes, and properties were subsequently sold at auction to satisfy the creditors, including Weill, Reinhardt, Werfel, and Bel Geddes themselves. Rescue attempts prior to the sale through the launching of road shows failed, in large part because of the unwieldiness of the sets and the

26. About Werfel's deep disappointment, which caused him to break out in tears of despair, see Alma Mahler Werfel, in collaboration with E. B. Ashton, *And the Bridge Is Love* (New York, 1958), pp. 228ff. About Gaige's engagement, see Weisgal, *So Far*, p. 132.

27. See "*Eternal Road* Approved in Lent," *New York Times*, 22 February 1937, p. 13.

28. A few examples will illustrate the point. "You will listen with pleasure to Kurt Weill's music," promised John Mason Brown in the *New York Post* on 8 January. Douglas Gilbert, in the *New York World-Telegraph* of the same day, found the play monotonous but lauded "the lovely score by Mr. Weill." Burns Mantle, in the *Daily News* of 8 January, summarized: "For Kurt Weill, who composed the incidental score, it must stand as the most expansive of his musical creations to date." "Kurt Weill," wrote Arthur Pollock in the *Brooklyn Daily Eagle* on 8 January, "has written the music—fine, clear, sweeping music."

29. Weill's letter, in which he protested the possibility of having his large and complex forms destroyed by cuts, was dated 27 November 1935. Reinhardt's partially firm, partially conciliatory, and also hand-delivered letter carries the same date. Both letters are in the Weill/Lenya Archive at Yale and are quoted at greater length later in this article.

30. See "A Noted Critic Reminisces. Brooks Atkinson" in Henry Marx, ed., *Weill-Lenya* (New York, 1976). Atkinson recalled: "On its opening night *The Eternal Road* ran until 3 o'clock the next morning. . . . But the management cut the show in half the next evening."

size of the production.[31] The orchestra parts have apparently been lost, but the full orchestral score has survived. The play has never been revived.

Now that past and my present research has clearly adduced this sequence of outward events, it is essential to ask why this drama or oratorio—some have compared it to Handel's *Messiah*[32]—briefly succeeded so well and then submerged so completely. To my mind all the reasons can be subsumed under the previously mentioned postulate: works originating in exile endure unique birth pangs. These are noticeable in at least three major areas of this collaborative work. From any reasonable perspective the three European collaborators were ideally suited for the task at hand. Moreover, there is evidence of Weill's very early affinity for Werfel. In a passage which appears all but prophetic in the light of their subsequent collaboration, Weill, upon his first reading of Werfel's poetry, recognized its quality and toyed with the idea of setting Werfel's poems to music. These thoughts surfaced in a letter of 1917 to his brother Hanns (a photocopy of the letter is in the collection of the Weill-Lenya Research Center), in which he states: "The poems of Fr. Werfel (is he Jewish?) are truly excellent. Bing [Weill's theory and composition teacher at the time], advises me, to be sure, against setting them to music. Nonetheless, I would like to try it; it might become my first philosophical composition *à la Palestrina*."[33]

Thus, Weill and Werfel's collaboration was surprising only in that it occurred as late as 1933. Every aspect of Werfel's work, from the title of his poems and novels (so often using word composites with "song," "cantata," or "hymn") to the acoustically perceived rhythm and rhyme of his poetry, to his preoccupation with composers in his Verdi novel, he was, in the words of Adolf Klarmann, "a pantheist of music," or, as Johannes Mittenzwei put it, a searcher for a "musical *unio mystica*."[34] Time and again he espoused in his writings the free spirit of music over the captive

31. See Fuhrich-Leisler, pp. 178ff. Two "serious offers" for road shows are mentioned. One came from the Chicago Opera, the other from the Association of Public Auditoriums, which was considering a forty-week tour through North America.

32. See Koegler, "Ein Verdi der Armen, ein Händel der Amerikaner."

33. Weill was obviously referring to one of the collections of Werfel's poetry—possibly the most recently published one at that time, i.e., 1917. See Franz Werfel, *Gesänge aus den drei Reichen* in *Ausgewählte Gedichte*, 2d ed. (Leipzig, 1917).

34. See Werfel, *Verdi: Roman der Oper* (Berlin, 1924). Also see Klarmann, "Musikalität bei Werfel" (Ph.D. dissertation, University of Pennsylvania, 1931), p. 78. Klarmann further defines Werfel's view of the world as an "entire cosmos suffused with music [in which] God is the exalted musician." For Mittenzwei, see his *Das Musikalische in der Literatur* (Halle, 1962), p. 299. Valuable insights also occur in Friedrich Torberg, "Gottes Kind und Gottes Sänger: Persönliche Anmerkungen zu Franz Werfel," *Welt und Wort* 11 (1956): 147–48.

concepts of words. A passage from one of his poems will exemplify this espousal:

> O stünde ich am Dirigentenpult,
> die nun gelassenen Arme zu entketten!
> Die Leidenschaft in Rhythmen hinzubetten!
> Hah! alla breve Takt voll Ungeduld!

> Oh if I stood at the conductor's stand,
> from idle arms my chain would fall!
> My passions I'd bed in rhythms all!
> Ha! In alla breve time, full of impatience![35]

It seems almost inconceivable that such a poet, who perceived music in almost metaphysical terms, should arrive so late in life at a collaboration with a composer.[36]

Conversely, Weill, as is well known, came to the collaboration with abundant experience in working with librettists, from Bertolt Brecht to Georg Kaiser to Iwan Goll to Caspar Neher. Weill's own skill in the writing of lyrics—for example, for the song "Berlin im Licht" and (as is often assumed, quite reasonably) for some verses in *Die Dreigroschenoper*[37]— and the structuring of large-scale works of musical theater stood him in good stead in the writing of *The Eternal Road*. As can be gleaned from the piano-vocal score now in the Weill/Lenya Archive at Yale University, Weill occasionally had to supply an English text or a more singable phrase in supplementing the quite serviceable translation by Ludwig Lewisohn.[38] Here he managed to stay very close to the spirit of Werfel's German original.

35. The poem, entitled "Grosse Oper," appears in Werfel's earliest collection of poems, *Der Weltfreund: Erste Gedichte* (Munich, 1911), p. 61.

36. Werfel's drama *Juarez and Maximilian* (1924) had, of course, been reshaped as the libretto for an opera by Darius Milhaud as early as 1930, but according to the composer's autobiography, *Notes without Music,* trans. Donald Evans (New York, 1953), pp. 210ff., Werfel only gave directions: "As he [Werfel] spoke only German and I was unable to do so, our interview was brief. . . . The very next day he sent me a French translation of his play. . . . With a few alterations it could be used as a basis for a libretto. We worked in collaboration. Dr. Hoffman, a specialist in his [Werfel's] direction, and Lunel agreed to make a free adaptation of the German text. He preserved the order of the scenes and the broad dramatic outline, but pruned the text and enlivened the dialogue by interpolating arias and duets on traditional operatic lines." For an excellent critique of libretto and music see Paul Collaer, *Darius Milhaud* (Antwerp, 1947), pp. 190ff.

37. Weill's "Berlin-im-Licht-Song" has recently been republished in *The Unknown Kurt Weill* song album (Totowa, N.J.: European American Music, 1982) and recorded on Teresa Stratas's *The Unknown Kurt Weill*, Nonesuch D79019. For the song's earlier publishing history, see Kim H. Kowalke, *Kurt Weill in Europe* (Ann Arbor, 1979), p. 418.

38. Werfel, *The Eternal Road,* trans. Ludwig Lewisohn (New York, 1936). I am most grateful to Lys Symonette for pointing out Weill's emendations of Lewisohn's translation.

Yet, with all the reciprocal appreciation of each other's art, the potential conflict between librettist and composer was clearly visible from the start. Had the two been in close contact, this difficulty could have been nipped at an early stage. As it was, it centered on two factors: the length of the piece and the nature of the musical setting for it. Having finished his drama, Werfel must have had misgivings about its length (even without music) from the very start, because in one of his earliest letters to Weill, dated 15 September 1934, he elaborated several times on his own concision: "For the sake of brevity . . . I have deleted a hundred beautiful ideas." He wrote of his repeated incisions, which he compares to a process of "burnishing out" and "dehydration." Invoking the different audience of a New York he had never seen, he then enjoined Weill to confine himself to "melodies, melodies, melodies," in order to avoid liturgical monotony and excessive recitatives, especially in the readings of the rabbi. All this leads up to an outright entreaty in a postscript to the letter: "*The most essential cardinal point of all* [!] For God's sake, the playing time *per se* must not exceed 3½ hours by a single breath of air. With intermissions that would make it a 3¾ to 4-hour performance."[39] To oversimplify the content of Werfel's letter: music, yes, but it must not protract the evening to the point where I, the dramatist, must further pare my text.

This interpretation of Werfel's letter gains in plausibility in light of another unpublished one to the Berlin theater critic Julius Bab, dated 28 August, less than a month earlier. It was written in the illusory hope that a drama so elaborate could be staged by the modest theater of the Jewish Cultural Club (*Kulturbund*) in Berlin. More central, however, is Werfel's description of *his* (italics mine) Bible drama. He outlines it in broad strokes, called it an "epic-dramatic form, scarcely ever tried before," but did not mention by one word that it was meant as a musical drama. In short, in assessing the length of his drama, he took only intermittent cognizance of the inevitably expansive effect of the music.[40]

Weill, on the other hand, as a widely experienced composer of operas, operettas, plays with music, and even musicals, knew that music in a modern musical drama must be integral. Contrary to Werfel, he felt that the text itself (as its reading convinced him) stood in danger of dissolving and that only music could provide it with a firm scaffolding. He shared this conviction with Max Reinhardt in a letter of 6 October 1934, in which he added that he found Werfel's play, to be sure, "magnificent," but his attitude "steadily more puzzling":

> Now that I know the entire book and the more I involve myself with it, the more puzzling it appears to me, how Werfel can conceive of it as a 'spoken

39. Unpublished letter in Weill-Lenya Research Center.
40. Letter at Leo Baeck Institute, New York.

drama.' Quite apart from the large stage which would swallow up every spoken word, the drama would be unperformable even in such theaters, because there is scarcely a page which does not decidedly cry out for music. I am devoting myself at this time only to those parts which, in my opinion, absolutely must be sung. But I am certain that also in those [passages] I leave untouched you will find many [passages] you will want to have set to music.[41]

This conflict was never resolved, not even in dress rehearsals. Reinhardt, in fact, never timed an entire run-though.[42] As for Werfel, he did not understand the function of the music, nor did he become reconciled to it even when, after arriving in New York, he saw the play in rehearsal. As Meyer Weisgal recalled: "Werfel was not at all happy with the production. 'Why all the scenery, why all the music?' he wanted to know."[43] Had Weill and Werfel been able to work together concertedly, not with Weill in his American asylum and Werfel in an Austria which he perceived, especially after the Spanish Civil War, as a doomed republic, this difference might have been capable of resolution.[44]

Weill's resolve, on the other hand, comes out clearly. In an all but forgotten interview that was somehow permitted to appear in a German-Jewish newspaper a full year after Weill had been forced to flee, he gave a summary of his compositional intent.[45] While he was to elaborate on some of the essential points in later publications, our resurrection of this early statement will serve to document his immediate comprehension of the task before him. It will also show how unwaveringly he adhered to it. Weill's response, after speaking in general terms about opera and musical drama as genres and of their respective missions, defined his views of the present-day musical theater and made, essentially, two key points: A musical drama, as Weill then perceived it, takes on the character of epic theater (in the Brechtian sense), that is, it reports and narrates how man, how whole groups of people make their way through life. But the broad events, the action of people, must be focal, not the psychological motivation that prompts them. Hence, as Weill had previously opined, the role

41. Letter in the Weill/Lenya Archive. Translation by Lys Symonette.

42. See Fuhrich-Leisler, p. 178: "During the premiere the necessity to shorten the performance became manifest, especially in the concluding parts which, because of shortness of time, had never been rehearsed properly and therefore had grown too long and imprecise."

43. Weisgal, *So Far*, p. 137.

44. Werfel, in a letter to Weill of 6 September 1936, firmly agreed with Weill's decision not to return to Europe, "where one will barely be able to save one's very life. Since the Spanish Civil War there is truly the smell of a conflagration in the air." Weill/Lenya Archive, Yale University.

45. See Mosco Carner, "Die Musik zu Werfel's Bibeldrama: Ein Gespräch mit Kurt Weill," *Jüdische Rundschau*, 22 February 1935, p. 9.

of music is no longer to propel the plot line, tighten transitions, provide background, or intensify passions. Rather the music, going its own way, ought to intrude at static points in the plot. If the plot line is clearly delineated, epic-theater fashion, the music can retain its *concertante* character and does not serve as the interpreter but as the objective coequal of the text. *Der Weg der Verheissung* was to exemplify this partnership of text and music. "If we are to speak as musicians," Carner paraphrased Weill, "[*Der Weg der Verheissung*] represents in its form a fusion of elements taken from drama, opera, and dramatized oratorio—elements which become unified by the dictates of artistic necessity; hence [they fuse] organically. Still they do not surrender their individual effect within the total work."

Mosco Carner also supplied, undoubtedly with Weill's consent, a detailed description of the music and text of *Der Weg der Verheissung* (as it was still titled), which to his mind represented anything but a conventional drama with music. Carner held it to be consistent with the concept of modern musical theater, as Reinhardt had begun to champion it. Also Carner singled out from the score some of its most striking features: the four through-composed act-ending finales where the dramatic and musical climaxes coalesce; large-scale solo and choral sections; the lyric parts, exemplified in the antiphony between Jacob and Rachel; the masterful use of such themes as the marchlike "wandering theme" and the theme of God's promise, as well as an opera-within-the-opera (or oratorio) in the form of the Book of Ruth. Carner also recognized that the work required, especially in the main portions, singers who could act rather than singing actors. Finally, he commented on the originality of the work which only occasionally drew on traditional liturgy or on the recitatives common in oratorios, or on the well-known Hebrew *nigunim.* And he reserved special praise for the (subsequently hacked off) ending of the drama: "The musical symbol of eternal wandering and moving on . . . in part four, when all persons of the drama advance toward the apparition of the angel, closes the drama in the form of an apotheosis."

We know that Weill never wavered from this initial conceptualization of his composition or of the work in its entirety. When he, misunderstanding Reinhardt's intention for shortening the play—or perhaps understanding it only too well—responded in a letter of 25 November 1935, he asserted once more his basic conviction about his artistic task:

> I have been led to believe that I was not to write just incidental music, but music in which singing—that is, a new sort of loosely connected singing—should play an important part. Not only my music has been constructed upon this basic concept but Werfel's poem as well—the play's accelerations always leading into music in such a way that cutting of music would also mean cutting into highlights of the play.
> Having considered yours and Werfel's requests, these musical climaxes—

after continuous work on my part—have become entities within a definite musical form with which one cannot tamper without destroying them. I consider this very form not only the most substantial part of my artistic labor, but also the most important factor for success; during my entire career I have observed that always I have failed wherever I had given license to a destruction of my musical form. The Sacrifice and Liberation of Isaac, the Farewell and Death of Moses, the Book of Ruth, the Building of the Temple—with Solomon's Consecration of the Temple—and the Jubilee Choirs: all of them are based on artistic structures formed according to musical and theatrical laws which simply would be robbed of their effects, if they were to be dissected.[46]

Given Werfel's and Weill's divergent points of view, it clearly was Reinhardt's responsibility to resolve them. And, had Werfel, Reinhardt, and Weill been together during the entire preparatory period, this would have been relatively easy in view of the generally cordial relationship of author and composer and their basic empathy for each other's artistic medium. But an ocean, not mere differences of theoretical views, had separated them, with Weill finding refuge in America and Werfel, despite his misgivings, still clinging to his homeland. Actually there was only one way, to my mind, to resolve the conflict: despite Werfel's assertions to the contrary, the plot of his drama was still inflated. I suspect that people were frightened away from the theater—and Weill (unlike Weisgal) was the only one to admit to the empty theater seats in the weeks following opening night[47]—by the sheer length of the performance. Other spectators at early performances might have complained, word-of-mouth fashion, of the inorganic truncating of the play following the 3 A.M. debacle of opening night. Here, too, Werfel and Weill were victims of the impediments imposed by the times. The separation of the two collaborators proved to be a serious detriment to the play's success.

So did their ignorance of the American theatrical world or, more precisely, their lack of power to affect it. Both Weill and Werfel immediately recognized the dangers that Bel Geddes's extravagant designs posed for the success of the play. On 3 August 1936 Weill wrote to Werfel:

> In order to give the show a chance of success, Reinhardt will have to insist that Bel Geddes make the necessary changes. He must create a durable synagogue, easier set changes, and better costumes. Personally, I am of the opinion that we will again have the same difficulties with Bel Geddes (and there is nobody who does not share my opinion except Reinhardt and Dr.

46. Translation by Lys Symonette.
47. In a letter of 1 March 1937 Weill wrote to Alma Mahler Werfel: "It was assumed that the theater, following the successful premiere, would be sold out for weeks. That, unfortunately, did not happen. The first weeks were very slow-moving [flau]." Copy of letter in Weill-Lenya Research Center.

Kommer). Once more he will spend a fortune in his inability to be realistic, and nobody will be around who is able to stop him. But I have said this so often that it is beginning to bore me.

Werfel, as it turned out, was in full agreement with Weill. In his reply from Vienna of 8 September 1936 he speculated that even Reinhardt must now begin to have second thoughts about Bel Geddes: "I assume that he has the same fears as you and I: that the carrying out of Geddes's plans for stage decorations can lead to one last debacle, eternally irrevocable."[48]

My final point, frankly speculative, is based on one further disagreement between Weill and Werfel which was resolved in favor of the latter, but, at the least, should have been argued at greater length, as it would have been had the circumstances been different. If in such a prolongation of the argument Weill's opinion had prevailed, a work might have resulted with an even greater appeal to an American audience. In the aforementioned letter of 3 August 1936 Weill initiated a plan for some revisions of the play, based on his newly acquired knowledge of the American public:

> I do believe that we too will have to do some work on the show. I have been here for almost a year now and have studied the American theater and its public very carefully. After all I have seen and learned, I believe we should strive to construct the synagogue scenes as one unit of suspenseful action— the way we started the first scene. Throughout the entire play we should keep the Bible scenes strongly tied together—more than is the case now. I have talked about this in detail with Reinhardt and I am sure he will discuss it with you.

But Werfel, in his response of 8 September 1936, appeared unconvinced. He feared a major revision—which would avail nothing.

> I cannot entirely share your view that we should convert the events in the synagogue into a unified suspenseful drama. Since it was and is our task to bring the entire Bible to life, the balance and pathos of the entire giant panorama would be shifted in favor of a realistic drama, as people have seen it before a hundred times (an Eastern pogrom drama). This would not greatly enhance interest, I believe. Moreover, as you know very well, of course, we would have to create, in the course of restructuring, a new piece with new figures. That surely is not part of either your or my intention. I am sure that the form and characters, as we have jointly fashioned them, will arouse sufficient empathy and that we do not have to shake more realistic pepper into our strong boullion in deference to an American public.

48. Both letters are in the Weill/Lenya Archive. These and the following translations are by Lys Symonette.

In my opinion, the rewriting would have been less demanding than Werfel claimed. Judging by Weill's later success with the American public, it is not such a wild hypothesis that he was right about his adopted homeland and its theatrical audience.

But the play, as it now stands, is nonetheless a landmark in the development of the modern musical drama. And Weill's music, as Richard Cockridge, one of the first-night critics, put it (in the *New York Sun* of 6 January 1937), might well merit superlatives: "If I were a musical critic," Lockridge wrote "I would risk superlatives on Herr Weill's music, so powerful did it seem in its design and effect, so continuously alive and vital in its accent." Perhaps American taste has evolved since then. Other biblical musicals have prepared this evolution. As so often happens, epigonic works may have paved the way for the reemergence of the earlier, far more daring and pioneering forerunner. And thus this essay should end with a question: With Weill and Werfel having beaten out a new form—and their American exile—to paraphrase Thomas Wolfe, isn't it time for a revival of *The Eternal Road?*

15

Weill in America:
The Problem of Revival
MATTHEW SCOTT

When *Lost in the Stars* closed on 1 July 1950 with $45,000 of its original cost unrecouped, an occasion such as the 1983 Kurt Weill Conference at Yale University would have been unthinkable, perhaps unimaginable. To Weill himself it might have seemed subversive. For by that time he had finally established himself in the public mind as an American songwriter: a good one certainly, and for some, a great one, on a par with Gershwin, Kern, Porter, and Berlin. "September Song," "My Ship," "That's Him," "Speak Low," and "Lost in the Stars" were indisputable credentials certifying his status in American popular music. But in 1950, few, if any, of his European works were known in the United States outside a very limited, erudite circle: by the time of Weill's death, *The Threepenny Opera* had run for a total of only twelve performances in New York, in a phenomenally unsuccessful production back in 1933. In America Weill himself had played a primary role in suppressing interest in productions of the European works. Of the various obituaries that appeared in the American press when he died in 1950, only those by Virgil Thomson and Brooks Atkinson attempted to give a picture of his work on both sides of the Atlantic, which he had recrossed on only one occasion following his departure from Europe in 1935.

Today Weill's music is performed more widely than at any time except, perhaps, the twelve months immediately following the premiere of *Die Dreigroschenoper*. In the United States, *Street Scene, Lost in the Stars, Die Dreigroschenoper*, and *Silverlake* entered the repertory of the New York City Opera; *Mahagonny* solemnly achieved belated legitimacy at the Metropolitan Opera. Weill's forgotten concert works have been recorded, expanding his current discography to more than twenty-five compositions. In England the 1983–84 season witnessed two television productions of *Die sieben Todsünden*, a television film of *Down in the Valley*, and the first complete performance of *Street Scene* in Great Britain—thirty-seven years after its premiere. On the Continent Weill has become a staple of theater companies. But aside from a few scattered stock and amateur productions in the United States each year, Weill's Broadway works, specifically composed for and shaped by a populist aesthetic, have traded places in the obscurity that had claimed his European works at the time of his death. None of his American works is currently available on records in its entirety. Not one has been successfully revived by the commercial theater in New York for which it was written. This ironic situation wherein the works most "commercial" at the time of their creation have become the least susceptible to resuscitation is symptomatic not only of their specificity, which dates them within a genre dominated by "period pieces," but also of the confusion in the process by which they might be revived. Just as he did during the disparate periods of his career, Weill is posthumously searching for a new audience.

"Revival" is by definition an anabolic process, one parallel to that of creation itself, one in which the component parts of an object or being are arranged from an earlier incarnation to one in which that object or being may be pronounced yet again alive. This applies as much to a Broadway show as to the victim of a freeway accident. And yet most revivals result from an empirical, almost accidental process, with little or no agreement "in the business" about the logical path that such a process should follow. With a Broadway show, it is seldom enough merely to reassemble the parts of the original production with the aid of xerography and plastic tape and to re-present the patient—groggy, covered with sticking plaster, and very unsteady on its feet—to a public which supposedly awaits eagerly beyond the frosted doors of the theater's foyer. A revival must aim to bring a piece back to life in every sense; the result must have the reflexes and the spirit of the original, as well as its structure and vocabulary. To do this, the process of revival must accurately reflect the process of creation.

Not all musical theater works can be revived. Some have vital organs that are simply worn out; others can't survive in a new cultural environment. When is the patient worth reviving? To have a reasonable chance at survival after the costly operation, the piece in question should fulfill one, some, or all of the following criteria. It might be a major work of art, timeless and unflawed, an indisputable success in its own time, and as relevant and commercially capable of survival in the present as it was originally. Statistically more probable, it may be a flawed period piece of historical and academic interest which still holds appeal within sufficient markets to ensure that the gesture of its revival will not be a quixotic one. It may be of interest because it is a rarely seen link in the work of an established craftsman, which would at the same time entertain and promote interest in the composer's work beyond that already established in the public eye and ear. Maybe it was "ahead of its time," more atune with the current cultural setting and present trends; as such, it could and would be recognized as a major contribution to the new scene. In a repertory that has depended historically on the "star" personality to a large extent, the piece may offer a plum role for a current celebrity. Lastly and probably most relevantly, it may have the potential to make money, a critical factor overriding all the criteria mentioned above. Virtually all of Weill's works for the American theater meet one or more of these criteria. But the nature of his American output makes Weill a risky composer to "average out" in the commercial sense. Of the six works that he wrote after *Knickerbocker Holiday* (still European in many aspects of idiom and structure), *Lady in the Dark* and *One Touch of Venus* were massive commercial successes, *Love Life* enjoyed a "respectable" run, *The Firebrand of Florence* was a disaster, and although it took great efforts to get them onstage, *Street Scene* and *Lost in the Stars* only partially repaid their investors' faith.

   Lady in the Dark established Weill's position in the American musical theater. It was a milestone in his life and work, the point of no return in the American transformation. The composer's voice had changed, and with this change, he scored, by accident or design, a great success with major implications. Severing his already tenuous connections with the world of "serious" music, *Lady in the Dark* also irrevocably detached Weill from his only alternative to Broadway, the socially or politically conscious "fringe" theater in America. The philosophical outlook and political priorities of the Group Theatre and the Federal Theatre Project could not have been more removed from those of Moss Hart, Ira Gershwin, and producer Sam Harris. If Weill had any doubts about his choice of options, the success of *Lady in the Dark* was certainly a persuasive, if temporary, bulwark against any second-guessing of his new *Linie*. As a tireless experimenter to the end of his life, Weill could also take pride in the fact that he had received a first-class education in the art of the Broadway musical from his collaborators.

   Fortunately for the study of this period in Weill's career, two happy coincidences occurred. Ira Gershwin was loath to leave his home in Beverly Hills to work in New York (other than directly with Weill alone) and hence, after the working draft had been finished, Weill had to report changes made in the script and score of the show to Gershwin in letters which have survived and are collected in the Library of Congress as part of Ira Gershwin's bequest of 1967. Second, and linked with this, the collective experience of the writing and production teams means that most of the changes that were made to the show were accomplished before rehearsals began rather than during the out-of-town tryouts, a happy accident for Weill, since some of his later shows, notably *Street Scene,* scarcely survived eleventh-hour alterations. All the changes that Hart made as both author and director during the period from August to October 1940, when rehearsals began, were faithfully passed on to Gershwin by Weill. The residuary letters form an important set of documents which charts the course of Weill's American transformation with great accuracy. These letters chronicle the confrontation between an imaginative and adventurous mind and a complicated and established theatrical system. They describe in detail the techniques and attitudes Weill was learning in a more unequivocally articulate form than the music to which they refer.

From Hart, Weill learned that the expediencies demanded by the nature of a production on Broadway had to be inextricably built into a collaborative work intended for that outlet. Maxwell Anderson's dramas had often appeared on Broadway, it is true, but he was in no sense a son of that theatrical system in the same way that Hart was. With *Lady in the Dark,* Weill profited from the opportunity of watching one of Broadway's master craftsmen tailor a show to fit the boards. Virtually every one of the letters that Weill wrote to Ira Gershwin reports at least one major change to script or score by Hart. As Hart's draft play, *I Am Listening,* evolved into *Lady in the Dark,* the single childhood song which Liza Elliott had only hummed in the former flowered into five separate dream sequences in the latter. Yet, in the course of the Weill-Gershwin correspondence, one dream was cut altogether (along with two scenes from the script), four extended musical items—three songs and a long dance—were removed from the other dreams, and a new number was substituted as the climax of another dream. It is not surprising, therefore, that *Lady in the Dark* is the last Broadway show for which Weill, in the European tradition, used a bound sketchbook; from this time on his sketches and drafts are written entirely on unbound single sheets.

When the script and score were in a condition he deemed satisfactory, Hart focused his attention on the scenic design for the show. One of his reasons for cutting an entire dream (which was to have been set in Hollywood, a favorite target of Hart's satires) was to keep the initial investment at less than $100,000 (already extravagant at the time). Weill had composed and orchestrated three numbers for the sequence when the "Hollywood Dream" was deleted. The same financial considerations led Hart to reject the first scenic designs, which required four revolving stages (twice the number that had ever been used before) and would have demanded an investment of $130,000. They were also so cumbersome and complicated that touring the show would have been impossible. Weill wrote to Gershwin: "We were all convinced it would have been the most beautiful way to do the show."[1] But the designer and production assistant were

1. Letter from Weill to Ira Gershwin, 2 September 1940, Library of Congress. Weill's letters are quoted by permission of the Kurt Weill Foundation for Music.

dispatched to find a cheaper and simpler solution, and Weill learned a system of priorities that was to shape his work and his outlook for the rest of his life.

Before he collaborated with Weill, Moss Hart had written the books for five musical comedies, but they had all been in the form of "sketch-shows" rather than librettos in which music played a structural role. In his comedy with George S. Kaufman, *The Man Who Came to Dinner*, there is a song, "What Am I to Do?" by Cole Porter, sung as an affectionate but unmistakable lampoon to Noel Coward, but in the rest of Hart's "straight plays" before *Lady in the Dark* there is no significant use of music. Through his collaboration with Weill, Hart may be said to have been converted, at least to a modest extent, to the use of music. For the rest of his life he searched unsuccessfully for an idea equivalent to *Lady in the Dark*, but found nothing which interested him as a playwright.[2] Indeed, until *Lady in the Dark*, Hart had been known professionally as a specifically anti-musical author. In his autobiography, he recalled that, on his first meeting with the Sam Harris office (which was to produce so many hits for him in the future), Hart, then an unknown playwright, had refused to adapt *Once in a Lifetime* as a musical with Irving Berlin. He was, Hart told Harris, a playwright, and he did not write scripts for musical comedies.

Ironically, Hart became Weill's entrée into this commercial but rigorously crafted vein of theater, and for the remainder of his life in America Weill's name was linked socially and professionally with some of the most prestigious playwrights of his generation. In 1946, following the resignation of S. N. Behrman, Weill was elected to membership of the Playwrights' Company, "the holy of holies," as Gertrude Lawrence referred to it in a letter to Weill.[3] The very few surviving letters between Weill and fellow composers (other than those whom he had known or befriended in Europe) are dwarfed by a mountain of correspondence between Weill and distinguished playwrights ranging from Brecht to George Kaufman. From Ira Gershwin, with whom he again collaborated on *The Firebrand of Florence* and whom he represented in New York during the period between the writing and rehearsal of *Lady in the Dark*, Weill learned that the fundamental requirements of the American musical did not necessarily include either distinguished poetry or inspired drama-turgy: "Since lyrics in this lodgment were arrived at by fitting the words mosaically to music already composed," wrote Gershwin in the preface to

2. Although only three of the eight plays Kaufman and Hart wrote together were musicals, both directed major works in the musical theater later in their lives: Hart directed the first production of *My Fair Lady*, and Kaufman, the first production of *Guys and Dolls*.
3. Letter from Gertrude Lawrence to Weill, 26 September 1946, Weill/Lenya Archive, Yale University.

his book, *Lyrics on Several Occasions,* "any resemblance to actual poetry, living or dead, is highly improbable."[4] And in a letter to Ira Gershwin informing him of Virgil Thomson's attack on the score for *Lady in the Dark,* Weill wrote: "It was all very personal and his main point was that I am no good any more since I stopped working with Brecht and that I am 'constantly avoiding' collaborating with 'major poets.'"[5] Weill's commentary on Thomson's judgment—"a rather bold statement, don't you think so?"—hardly contradicts it. If he thought he was collaborating with major poets, Weill clearly did not place Ira Gershwin among them.

Ira Gershwin was neither an ignorant nor a prosaic man, but he was a writer whose skills were directed toward the froth rather than the wave of literature. He was a showman who had shared only marginally in the major artistic achievements of his brother. He had been enlisted to help DuBose Heyward with the lyrics of *Porgy and Bess,* but a brief examination of the play on which that work was based shows that Ira Gershwin's contribution, although increasingly important toward the end of the opera, was not crucial. He had supplied only theatrical finesse, and it is therefore not surprising that during the course of their collaboration he showed little interest in Weill's previous works. He knew, however, the score of *Die Dreigroschenoper,* which he had seen in Berlin, but only referred to it in letters to Weill when a bizarre effect, rather than a specifically musical one, was needed in *Lady in the Dark.* Gershwin's ignorance in these matters of "high art" was not important to the work in hand, except that it may have denied us any primary evidence of what the changes that Weill was undergoing in his theatrical music might have wrought in his concert music of the time. Gershwin showed no interest, and his silence caused Weill either to cease writing the material or at least to keep news of it to himself. "I have written some orchestra music," he told Gershwin in a letter, "but I threw it away. It seems so silly just to write music at a time like this. But I hope that one of my show projects will work out."[6] And in a later letter: "I am also working on an orchestral piece. It might grow into my Second Symphony."[7] This is the last Weill writes of his concert music, and it is the last mention of any music other than the immediate show project in his correspondence with Gershwin, which had begun just fourteen months earlier with Gershwin's musical advice to Weill, who was just

4. Ira Gershwin, *Lyrics on Several Occasions* (London, 1977), p. iii.

5. Letter from Weill to Ira Gershwin, 8 March 1941, Library of Congress.

6. Letter from Weill to Gershwin, 28 May 1941, Library of Congress. Weill is referring to the appalling situation in Europe: "It seems silly to write music at a time like this."

7. Letter from Weill to Gershwin, 9 September 1941, Library of Congress. Weill did not acknowledge his "Berliner Symphony" of 1921 with a number; he referred to the Symphony of 1934 as no. 1 (now known as Symphony no. 2). No material from this orchestral project has survived.

starting on the score for *Lady in the Dark*. "What we want to do," he had told Weill, "is turn out one hell of a score with at least four or five publishable numbers."[8]

Although Weill gleaned much from his more experienced collaborators, *Lady in the Dark* provided other rewards. He learned the healing power of money. For the first time in ten years, he had in Brook House a permanent home, purchased with his share of the record-breaking price paid for the film rights by Paramount.[9] He could also buy a Buick convertible and enjoy an annual income approximately twelve times the national average at the time. That *Lady in the Dark* allowed him finally to replace everything he had lost in the material sense in his flight from Europe was a lesson Weill never forgot. In that sense, *Lady in the Dark* was his American *Dreigroschenoper*. For the second time in his career—the first again being *Die Dreigroschenoper*—Weill had reached a point of artistic no-return by virtue of an unprecedented, if unexpected, popular success. As in 1928, he again had to choose between a "serious" and a "vernacular" future.

In choosing the latter in America, Kurt Weill could not afford to look back. Whatever he thought of his new voice (and he had many reasons to be delighted with it, since he had, in denying himself a "yester" voice only to replace it with a different but equally mature one, achieved a first in musical history), Weill must have been swayed to some extent in his choice of options by the press battle which raged around him following the success of *Lady in the Dark*. It was an unequal struggle between the show-business/theatrical press, which took him to their hearts as vehemently as the other side, the musical press, thrust him from their ranks in reviling his recent work.[10] *Lady in the Dark* provoked from that quarter the first specifically musical attack on Weill since he had left France. The fact that he could console himself with a very impressive press-book from the theatrical arena must have forced his hand to some extent as to the direction in which he was to go in the years remaining to him.

Whether or not it was only a rationalization for his choice, Weill now viewed his American career as a continuation of what he had achieved in Europe. It *was* indeed possible to interest major American playwrights in the musical theater, a branch of writing in which they had either been previously disinterested (Maxwell Anderson), or, in the case of Moss Hart, against which they were philosophically opposed. This image—the

8. Letter from Gershwin to Weill, 20 March 1940, Library of Congress. Gershwin's letters are quoted by permission of his Estate.

9. Weill purchased a charming three-story house, known as Brook House because a trout stream flowed through the property, in New City, New York, only a short walk through the woods to Maxwell Anderson's estate.

10. See S. L. M. Barlow, review of *Lady in the Dark*, *Modern Music* 18 (March/April 1941). See also Virgil Thomson, "Plays with Music," *New York Herald Tribune*, 23 February 1941.

playwrights' composer—is crucial to the way in which the American press represented Weill in his last years, and he himself contributed to the maintenance of that image: "Ever since I made up my mind that my special field of activity would be the theater," he wrote in the sleeve notes to the original cast album of *Street Scene*, "one of the first decisions I made was to get the leading dramatists of our time interested in the problems of the musical theater. The list of my collaborators reads like a good selection of contemporary playwrights of different countries; Georg Kaiser and Bert Brecht in Germany, Jacques Deval in France, Franz Werfel, Paul Green, Maxwell Anderson, Moss Hart, and Elmer Rice in America."[11] Alan Jay Lerner, who collaborated with Weill only once but was in the planning stages of a second work when Weill died, has stressed the importance of this decision on Weill's outlook: "In the twenties, he had lured serious dramatists and poets . . . into the musical theater to collaborate with him. When he came to America he did the same. Instead of looking for a partner among the steady practitioners, he turned to the dramatists."[12] In so doing, Weill was lengthening the odds against his scoring a commercial success, let alone another *Lady in the Dark*. He was building a wall against which he was pressed by the other acquired taste he had brought with him from Europe: public approval.

Lady in the Dark marks a shift for Weill which brought this taste for approval from the edges of his outlook to its center to form the central plank on which the remainder of his life and work was to be based. *Lady in the Dark* was a spectacular achievement both technically and artistically in this respect, but Weill's decision to enter the mainstream of Broadway musical theater brought with it a major problem. From now on, there were increasing numbers of people holding stakes in his decisions: backers wanted to hear show tunes which were exploitable as potential hits outside of any theatrical vehicle; performers wanted roles which were both demanding and convincing; and collaborators demanded both of the above, together with whatever limited degree of self-expression they permitted themselves. Dramatic works whose form and content could withstand demands from so many conflicting directions were rare, but Weill kept looking for them, and it became an increasingly desperate search. He explored many different strata of theater in search of promising collaborators, and he took under consideration many plays and adaptations, as the vast collection of his extant project notes demonstrates. The solutions he eventually found attest to the wide range of works that he considered: *One Touch of Venus* was transformed from its satirical origins into a simple escapist fantasy; *The Firebrand of Florence* was a period piece,

11. Kurt Weill, Notes to the recording of *Street Scene* (CBS 4139).
12. Alan Jay Lerner, *The Street Where I Live* (London, 1978), p. 42.

a mistimed attempt at Broadway operetta that gradually degenerated into an unwieldy costume drama; *Love Life* (in the format of a vaudeville) was an initiative in the direction of naturalistic cabaret, the only work (apart from *Lady in the Dark*) in which characters had a logical and legitimate theatrical reason to break into song; *Street Scene* defies any categorization, because it wanders unhappily through the course of the show among areas already mentioned; and *Lost in the Stars* is a stylized pageant, a neo-classical form derived from the traditions of Greek tragedy and mystery play.

The works form a bewildering lot, unconnected and academically imponderable; a series of experiments, some good, some bad, some successful, some less so, some glittering, some lackluster. Where then does the case for revival begin, and what criteria should apply? The works under discussion are *old*—the last of them, *Lost in the Stars*, closed thirty-five years ago. The theater, as opposed to the opera house, is consumingly "now": today's rehearsal, tomorrow's run-through, next week's opening night, the next day's closing. Combined with the psychological disadvantage at which they are placed, possible revivals of the works are victims of the consequences of the system for which they were written: authentic performance materials are difficult to obtain and seldom convey the actual intentions of the creators. Sadly, the piano reductions of Weill's scores up to and including *Der Silbersee* which were not the work of the composer are more accurate and less misleading than the reductions of subsequent works made by the composer himself with an eye toward consumption as "singles."

Of the six works under consideration, only two, *Lady in the Dark* and *One Touch of Venus*, were proven commercial successes. The experimental nature of all of Weill's works for the American stage makes it impossible to "sell" one in terms of another. The revival of one work, only moderately successful in its first production, cannot be justified by the success of another, as has been the case, for instance, in the revival of some of the lesser successes of the Kern-Bolton-Wodehosue series of musicals for the Princess Theater, *On Your Toes*, or the Gershwin compilation, *My One and Only*. Such a compilation in Weill's case would be impossible, since with few exceptions the musical numbers cannot be patched into a new dramatic situation and structure. Furthermore, Weill himself headed a committee set up by the Dramatists Guild in 1948 to investigate ways of curtailing the escalating production and running costs of Broadway shows. His own works span a period of immense cost inflation, especially after the Second World War, that also reflects a longer period of caution which began with the stock market shocks of 1929 and continued throughout the 1930s, dethroning many of the independent producers who had dominated Broadway theater before the war. P. G. Wodehouse,

returning to New York in 1946 after an absence of ten years, thought the
new system weaker: "Today what happens is that some complete novice
gets hold of a play and then passes the hat round in the hope of raising
enough money to produce it. When it fails, he goes back into the suit and
cloak trade. How anybody ever does raise the money beats me."[13] At the
same time as Wodehouse was writing, Weill himself was playing a major
part in the drive to raise the necessary money to ensure that *Street Scene*
reached the boards, and it was only through a great deal of idealism on the
part of many backers that either *Street Scene* or *Lost in the Stars* ever reached
Broadway. Weill's death marked the end of lavish musicals.

The obvious conclusion to draw from all this would be that Weill's
work can no longer compete in the markets for which he wrote them and
that his work belongs in the subsidized rather than the commercial theater. That conclusion in itself proves that Weill's American scores have
shifted away from the market he addressed. In February 1940, shortly
after he had begun his collaboration with Moss Hart, Weill told an interviewer from the *New York Times:* "I've made that theater which exists
without subsidy my life work."[14] Yet the various revivals of his European
works, with a few notable exceptions, have been exclusively within the
subsidized theater. As set pieces, products of a unique artistic climate, the
European works seem to have aged better than their supposedly less
respectable cousins written in America.

The restoration of the American works to their original market
through revival, not to mention their dissemination for the first time
elsewhere, demands a radically different approach from that which has
successfully reinstated many of the works written in Europe. The American musicals must be restored to their own contexts; that is, they must be
recognized as experiments—musical, orchestral, and literary—and be
treated as such. The single-minded protection of the integrity of a whole
show—either as the composer originally envisioned it or as it emerged in
non-definitive form from the collaborative compromises of first production—can often be a disservice to a piece designed to work primarily in a
specialized performance setting. "When a composer's idea is greater than
its embodiment," wrote Marc Blitzstein in an article published six months
after Weill had arrived in the United States, "the idea itself runs the
severe risk of deteriorating, since followers have to feed on theories
rather than on music."[15] Is academic reconstruction of the American
pieces then a disservice to those works, as one might suppose from the

13. P. G. Wodehouse, "Send in the Girls," *The Performing Flea* (London, 1981), p. 391.
14. Kurt Weill in untitled interview, *New York Times*, 3 February 1940.
15. Marc Blitzstein, "Coming—The Mass Audience," *Modern Music* 13 (May/June 1936):
27.

logical extension of Blitzstein's argument? Some of the ideas are larger than others, but the embodiment is always "small."

Development by a composer within the genre of the Broadway musical is generally possible only when an artistic team has been established. Now, as at the time when Weill was writing, this is an economic rather than an artistic point; more risks may be taken when the audience has come to see the most recent show of a proven author/composer/lyricist team. Such a collaboration requires a lengthy period of incubation, the right "mix," and a rare willingness by all to compromise. Apart from Maxwell Anderson, Weill never worked with a playwright twice during his American years, but it was not for lack of trying. When Weill died, Alan Jay Lerner was planning a second show with him. Works by Moss Hart, S. J. Perelman, and Elmer Rice turn up frequently in Weill's project lists and in his correspondence, but no projected collaborations resulted in a renewal of any of the partnerships that Weill had formed in America. His professed approach, that of continuing to develop an American operatic form (which he felt he had attained in *Street Scene*), denied Weill the only path that might have led to the higher form of *musical* which was more realistically the proper vehicle for his plans from the beginning to the end of his Broadway career. A regular partner, a playwright so self-effacing as to serve in this mission, would be tantamount to a contradiction in terms, and no such person was to be found.

The stony path which Virgil Thomson described in his obituary ("Every work was a new model, a new shape, a new solution of dramatic problems")[16] was the alternative. But why that path took the meandering course that it did remains to be explained. That Weill's correspondence is now available for research is probably the most constructive accident to fall across the troubled path of scholarship in this area. The correspondence surrounding *Lady in the Dark* contains only the first stirrings of the mental battery which Weill forced himself to develop in America, and a deeper understanding of this new psyche is germane to a secure future for these flawed pieces. Close examination of processes at work in the European output is too empirical an approach to adapt for Weill's works for Broadway, since wider cultural decisions contradict and override musical ones at every turn. Chronicling alone is not enough: to represent the American Kurt Weill, scholarship must be enlisted to re-present his work. Experiments, even successful experiments, remain experiments.

16. Virgil Thomson, untitled obituary for Kurt Weill, *New York Herald Tribune*, 9 April 1950.

16

Musical Dialects in
Down in the Valley
JOHN GRAZIANO

The strategic decision to premiere *Down in the Valley* at Indiana University during its summer program in 1948 with a cast of students (except for *Brigadoon* star Marion Bell) was surely intended to emphasize the populist aesthetic that had characterized the project from its inception. Hoping to find a home for an American opera in colleges and universities rather than on Broadway, Weill wanted to demonstrate that "it can be performed wherever a chorus, a few singers, and a few actors are available. The physical production can be as simple as a dramatic concert performance. Scenery and lighting can be just as elaborate as equipment allows. The leading parts should provide training for the specific type of singing actor who has become such an important asset of the musical theater in America."[1] His strategy worked. Three weeks after the premiere at Indiana University, NBC broadcast nationally a performance at the University of Michigan. Within two years the publisher of the opera could advertise its success as "the most explosive of any contemporary opera."[2] G. Schirmer's promotional campaign, including the reprint of Grandma Moses's "The Spring in Evening" on the cover of the piano-vocal score, could claim as much credit as the intrinsic attributes of the work—its engaging scenario, pervasive tunefulness, and modest production requirements. By 1950 Schirmer claimed nearly three hundred productions "in high schools and colleges, in universities and churches, in summer camps and studios, on the radio and on television."[3] *Down in the Valley* had already been staged in England, Germany, Switzerland, and Scandinavia; productions in Israel, Australia, and India were being prepared. In the first nine years of its existence, the opera received over 1,600 productions and some 6,000 performances.[4] Only *Die Dreigroschenoper*

1. Quoted by H. W. Heinsheimer, "Right Kind of Opera Has Market in America," *New York Times*, 30 May 1949.
2. H. W. Heinsheimer, "Opera for All the Valleys," *Educational Music Magazine* (March/April 1950): 25.
3. Ibid.
4. Douglas Jarman, *Kurt Weill: An Illustrated Biography* (Bloomington, 1982), p. 135.

may have surpassed that record within Weill's catalogue, and even today *Down in the Valley* is perhaps Weill's second-most-often performed stage work in the United States.

Although the opera succeeded spectacularly with its targeted amateur theatrical groups, it was not originally conceived by Weill and his librettist, Arnold Sundgaard, for that purpose. During the summer of 1945, Weill had been asked by Olin Downes, music critic of the *New York Times,* to join him in a musical project designed for radio broadcast. Weill described the show's evolution several years later: "In 1945, Olin Downes acquainted me with his concept of finding a new artistic form through which American composers might evolve a native art by the utilization for dramatic purposes of the American folk song. . . . I suggested as a basic form for this radio program a weekly dramatization of a specific folk song and this formula was accepted."[5] For Weill, it was a return to the kind of project with which he had been involved many years earlier in Germany: an attempt to find a broad audience for contemporary music through the medium of radio.[6] Now he was drawn to the project with visions of long-term involvement. In a letter written in 1945 to theatrical agent Irving "Swifty" Lazar, Weill commented on his piano audition of *Down in the Valley* for fellow composer Jule Styne: "The radio show . . . is generally regarded as the most exciting and freshest combination of drama and music for radio. . . . If the concept sells, I will have to write or supervise a program every week, for which I am part owner of the program with a very good salary."[7] Unfortunately for Weill, prospective sponsors could not be persuaded to underwrite such a series. An audition recording of *Down in the Valley* with full orchestra had been submitted to the sponsors, who were "frightened by the idea that they might be accused of submitting an *opera* to the public. It seemed that our project for radio advertisers was somewhat ahead of its time."[8] *Down in the Valley* was temporarily shelved. In 1947, however, Weill was asked by Hans Heinsheimer at Schirmer to recommend an opera appropriate for a school production; with characteristic sensitivity to the potential of a new market, Weill and Sundgaard revised their dormant radio play to make it suitable for a college opera-workshop production.

5. Letter to the Music Editor, *New York Times,* 5 June 1949. For an additional account of the genesis of *Down in the Valley,* see Arnold Sundgaard, "Portrait of the Librettist as a Silenced Composer," *The Dramatists Guild Quarterly* 16 (Winter 1980): 24–30.

6. Weill had written successfully for radio in the 1920s; his most important surviving works for this medium are *Das Berliner Requiem* (1928) and *Der Lindberghflug* (1929). For additional information on these works and their reception, see Kim H. Kowalke, *Kurt Weill in Europe* (Ann Arbor, 1979), pp. 70–74, and Jarman, pp. 49–50.

7. Letter to Irving "Swifty" Lazar, 28 November 1945; copy at the Weill-Lenya Research Center.

8. Weill, in a letter to the Music Editor, *New York Times,* 5 June 1949.

Weill articulated his specific approach to musical theater in an article published in the *New York Times* in 1947. Although his comments there concerned the genesis of *Street Scene,* they can be viewed in a more general aesthetic context and thereby apply to *Down in the Valley* as well as to his earlier musicals:

> The special brand of musical entertainment in which I have been interested from the start is a sort of "dramatic musical," a simple, strong story told in musical terms, interweaving the spoken word and the sung word so that the singing takes over naturally whenever the emotion of the spoken word reaches a point where music can "speak" with greater effect.
>
> This form of theater has its special attraction for the composer, because it allows him to use a great variety of musical idioms, to write music that is both serious and light, operatic and popular, emotional and sophisticated, orchestral and vocal. Each show of this type has to create its own style, its own texture, its own relationship between words and music, because music becomes a truly integral part of the play—it helps to deepen the emotions and clarify the structure.[9]

Once he had decided to revise his two-year-old radio opera, Weill set about changing it into a new type of "dramatic musical"—a folk opera for amateur groups.

In the original version for radio, there had been a number of passages of spoken dialogue. In the new version, those passages were changed in a variety of ways; texts are spoken over thematic background music, interwoven with sung passages, or set in their entirety as recitatives.[10] Although the "school opera" *Down in the Valley* has sometimes been likened to Weill's *Schuloper Der Jasager* in terms of function, aesthetic intent, and instant popularity, its origins argue against that interpretation. The apparent simplicity of the stage version of *Down in the Valley* is probably a vestige of Weill's practical estimation of the limited rehearsal time available for a weekly radio show, a restriction that fortuitously served the new market for the revised work as well. The fact that his 1947 revision expanded on the original by adding solo pieces for Brack and Jennie, recitatives in place of the existing spoken dialogue, and new passages for the chorus adds weight to the argument that Weill, who seldom turned down a potentially lucrative offer, merely seized the opportunity of the moment to get a performance and publication of an unperformed radio opera.[11] The new genre which *Down in the Valley* inaugurated was

9. Weill, "*Street Scene* Becomes a 'Dramatic Musical,'" *New York Times,* 5 January 1947.
10. See the appendix for a comparison of the two versions.
11. Throughout his career, Weill revised and recast his compositions when new performance opportunities appeared. *Der Lindberghflug,* for example, originally set jointly by Weill and Hindemith, was recast by Weill himself into a "forty-minute, fifteen-movement 'didactic cantata'" (Kowalke, *Kurt Weill in Europe,* p. 73). Although the revised work was intended for performance in schools, it was heard most often in concert performances.

essentially the offshoot of an earlier attempt to find new outlets for contemporary opera.

While *Down in the Valley* is not the first of Weill's works to utilize folk
songs as part of its compositional fabric, it is certainly his only major work
to use them so extensively. In fact, the folk song idiom so infuses this "folk
opera" that Weill's newly composed song for Jennie, "Brack Weaver, My
True Love," approaches the "folk authenticity" of the preexistent tunes.
Although the premise of the projected radio series had been that each
show was to be based on a story generated from a single folk song, *Down in
the Valley* departs from that guideline by using no less than five.[12] Three of
the songs, "Hop Up, My Ladies," "Sourwood Mountain," and "The Little
Black Train," each appear once as set pieces; their melodies and texts
serve as foci for their respective scenes. Weill's use of "The Lonesome
Dove" is more complicated; the song appears twice, initially at the end of
the first part and then again just before the final scene. There, through a
combination of Weill's chromatic harmonization of the diatonic melody
and Sundgaard's new text, the reworked song symbolizes an eternal love
which will endure in spite of its temporal doom.

Most interesting, however, is Weill's repeated use of a brief and
almost too familiar folk song, "Down in the Valley." That Weill was aware
of its limitations is evident from his correspondence with Irving L.
Sablosky, a Chicago critic, author, and composer: "You are definitely
right when you say that the title tune is a bastard one. But in connection
with the words, the idea behind it and just the hillbilly connections you are
talking about, it seemed to me perfectly suited to the purpose. Sure, it is

12. Kurt Weill's personal library, now housed at the Weill-Lenya Research Center, con-
tains several anthologies of folk songs. Sundgaard has described how he introduced Weill
to various tunes once the premise for the radio opera had been established ("Portrait of the
Librettist"). The following anthologies contain versions of the tunes used in *Down in the
Valley:* Carl Sandberg, *The American Songbag* (New York, 1927); John A. Lomax and Alan
Lomax, *Our Singing Country* (New York, 1934); Jean Thomas and Joseph A. Leader, *The
Singin' Gatherin'* (New York, 1939) and B. A. Botkin, ed., *A Treasury of American Folklore*
(New York, 1944). "Down in the Valley" is present in all four sources, but with a surprising
degree of variation. Of the many varying stanzas found in these sources, those used by
Sundgaard correlate most closely with the ones in *A Treasury of American Folklore*, while
Weill's tune itself is most similar to that in *The American Songbag*. "The Lonesome Dove" is
found only in *The American Songbag;* Sundgaard's text utilizes stanzas 1, 4, and 3, respectively, of the version presented in the *Songbag*. Weill's version of the tune differs in several
minor details. "The Little Black Train" is based on the version in *Our Singing Country*. The
text utilizes the chorus and stanzas 1 and 3, with a new text by Sundgaard interpolated.
The tune is unchanged in Weill's setting. Another version is found in *A Treasury*, but it does
not correspond musically or textually to the Weill-Sundgaard version. "Sourwood Mountain" appears in *The American Songbag* and *A Treasury*. The text for the second verse is
newly written by Sundgaard. "Hop Up, My Ladies" is found only in *Our Singing Country;*
the Weill-Sundgaard version does not differ substantially from the printed version.

somewhat more 'corny' than other folktunes (it seems to me a sort of German-type tune) and it is certainly not a first-class melody—but its very limitations as musical material seemed attractive to me for this piece."[13] Apparently, Weill was not troubled by its seeming slightness. In fact, he explained to Sablosky:

> My teacher, Busoni, at the end of his life, hammered into me one basic truth which [he] had arrived at after fifty years of pure aestheticism: the fear of triviality is the greatest handicap of the modern artist. . . . Instead of worrying about the material of music, the theory behind it, the opinions of other musicians, my main concern is to find the purest expression in music for what I want to say, with enough trust in my instinct, my taste and my talent to always write "good" music, regardless of the style I am writing in.[14]

Weill's style in his German works might best be described as eclectic, in the most positive sense of that term.[15] The style of his American works, however, has been viewed with some disdain by many critics as "consciously American."[16] More than any other work, *Down in the Valley* has been associated with Weill's obviously "commercial" style and often unfavorably compared with his European output. Perhaps the folk melodies themselves have prompted more sympathetic commentators to see *Down in the Valley* as Weill's archetypal American work, as his clearest attempt to reach out to a new and larger public through utilization of an indigenous musical source. As early as 1950, Virgil Thomson stated that *Down in the Valley* "speaks an American musical dialect that Americans can accept."[17] Close examination of the score, however, must question that view, because Weill's music for *Down in the Valley*, in my estimation, appears to "speak" in a number of distinctly different "dialects." From the Cello Sonata of 1920 through *Lost in the Stars*, Weill variously combined many traditional melodic and harmonic idioms to create his own distinctive musical language. Although the syntax, vocabulary, and stresses of the musical language changed from work to work, the fundamental stylistic identity of the composer did not. *Down in the Valley* attempts to synthesize, as do Weill's other American works, the somewhat slick but distinctively American harmonies of Tin Pan Alley with the neo-Romantic idiom so successfully exploited by Schreker, Korngold, and Zemlinsky. One finds the whole-tone scale used side-by-side with unresolved ninth chords *à la*

13. Letter to Irving L. Sablosky, 24 July 1948; copy at the Weill-Lenya Research Center.
14. Ibid.
15. For a full discussion of Weill's synthesis of various musical styles, see Kowalke, *Kurt Weill in Europe*, pp. 281–310; and Jarman, *Kurt Weill*, pp. 92–93 and 104ff.
16. An analysis of the perceived negative qualities of Weill's American music is presented in Jarman, pp. 135–38; and Ronald Sanders, *The Days Grow Short* (New York, 1980), pp. 367–68.
17. Weill's obituary notice, *New York Herald Tribune*, 9 April 1950.

Gershwin and harmonic progressions deriving from "serious" music of the first three decades of our century. Although the dramaturgy of *Down in the Valley* has little in common with Weill's celebrated works with Brecht and the musical raw material is unambiguously American, the style, technique, and structure of the opera are a sophisticated blend of the European and American "Weills."

Down in the Valley exhibits a variety of idiosyncratic Weillian devices—the mixing of major and minor modes, lengthy harmonic pedals and frequent ostinatos, the "double tonic" chord, and pervasive chromatic linear motion—all of which are heard in conjunction with the title tune that appears no fewer than nineteen times in the course of this forty-five-minute work. "Down in the Valley" occupies almost a fourth of the total number of measures in the opera. In spite of its persistence, the tune doesn't seem to wear out its welcome. With each appearance, it takes on a new variational guise—sometimes with its melody changed, sometimes in the minor mode, sometimes with the harmonies altered. Because the tune occupies only eight measures in most of its appearances, Weill's subtle harmonic alterations tend to go by unnoticed. *Down in the Valley* seems to have been conceived by Weill as a connected series of miniatures; through his use of the theme-and-variation principle, its final form is significantly different from the "Broadway operas" which surround it. Unlike *Street Scene* and *Lost in the Stars*, which exhibit many of the conventions of the number opera, *Down in the Valley* is basically constructed according to through-composed principles, while at the same time it exploits the strophic implications of theme-and-variations. Whatever one thinks of it as a work of art, *Down in the Valley* is a compositional tour de force, for it shows Weill's inventiveness and skill in finding new ways to make a brief, rather modest tune sound both fresh and "artless" at the same time. His varied harmonizations give evidence that he had synthesized in a remarkable amalgam the vernacular of late nineteenth-century harmonic language, the twentieth-century innovations which characterize compositions from his formative years, and the harmonic formulas so typical of American musical theater in the 1930s and 1940s. This essay explores the harmonic and melodic alterations to which the title tune was subjected by Weill, and their relationship to the different "dialects" of his earlier music.

On the largest scale, *Down in the Valley* divides into five sections; the first and last are devoted solely to the title tune (see appendix). The tune itself is used by Weill in two forms: an eight measure antecedent-consequent construction, A, A_1, which corresponds to the original format of the tune, and an expanded A, A, B, A_1, which ranges in length from twelve to thirty-two measures and includes newly composed music for the B section. The larger form of the opening portion of the opera, as detailed in the following chart, seems to function aurally as a rondo. With the exception of the Introduction and Interlude, the music of both the A and B sections in this opening scene is based on the two versions of the title tune detailed above; each statement is characteristically subjected to a different harmonic and textural treatment. The melodic alteration and changes in tempo generate a clear form, even though Weill's sequence of tonal areas does not follow any traditional structural pattern. The Interlude which interrupts the narrative and represents a passing train utilizes the whole-tone scale as its basis.

Section 1 of *Down in the Valley*

mm. 1–7	8–17	18–24
Introduction	A	A
Largo	Moderato	— — — —
♩ = 69	♩. = 58	
Chromatic descent to:	F major-minor	A♭ major

mm. 25–49	50–57	58–84
B	A	B
Allegro animato	Tempo I°	Allegro animato
♩. = 120	♩. = 58	♩. = 120
E major	A major	D major

mm. 85–101	102–116	117–124
Interlude	A	A
Molto agitato	Moderato assai	Poco meno mosso
♩ = 120	♩. = 60	[♩. = 58?]
whole tone	B minor	G major

Following the Introduction, the opera opens with a lullaby-like accompaniment, in which a gentle undulation, repeated over a tonic pedal, is hummed by the tenors and basses of the chorus (see ex. 1). Through the reiteration of D-flat on the second beat of each measure, Weill suggests the minor mode; its presence, however, is quickly contradicted by the tune, which is clearly in F major. Although Weill had used modal juxtaposition in his earlier works,[18] they more often occur consecutively rather than simultaneously. In No. 11 ("Das Lied von der harten Nuss") from *Happy End*, for example, Weill merely alternates E-major and E-minor triads to heighten the text. In example 1 from *Down in the Valley*, however, the juxtaposition is simultaneous; the major-minor conflict presents the tune in a vacillating harmonic context which belies its fundamental innocence. Without modulation, Weill jumps to the relative major, A-flat, for the second statement. Chromatic alteration of the tonic harmony is introduced here: the opening augmented triad, which begins

18. Weill's compositional use of a mixed major-minor mode is a technique which can be found in many of his German works. See Kowalke, pp. 168ff.

All excerpts and harmonic reductions in the musical examples are from *Down in the Valley*.

Example 1.

Example 2.

both the antecedent and consequent phrases, would normally function as a passing chord; in this context, however, it is presented as a tonic substitute (see ex. 2). An A-diminished-seventh chord (VII$_2$ of V of V) is heard on the final beat of those measures; in the antecedent phrase, it is followed for two measures, in best late-Romantic fashion, by the dominant-seventh chord (E-flat) in inversion, which resolves as expected to the unaltered tonic triad. In the consequent phrase, Weill substitutes a new harmonic progression for the two measures of dominant harmony heard earlier. Harmonic motion is accelerated by the use of a different chord on each beat of measure 7; the progression subtly amplifies the opening measure's diminished chord. Here it is preceded by an F-seventh chord (V of V of V) and followed by the traditional II$_6$–V$_7$–I cadence (see ex. 3).

Example 3.

After the introduction of the expanded version of the tune, which will be discussed shortly, the third statement of the original version occurs, this time in A major (see ex. 4). Weill continues to divide the tune into its now-familiar antecedent-consequent configuration. Although the harmonization of the first phrase is tonally unambiguous because it is limited to only the tonic and dominant chords, complexity is introduced by a treble triple-pedal built from perfect fourths (an incomplete V$_9$ chord?) and prolonged throughout the first six measures of the state-

mm. 51-54

Example 4.

mm. 56-58

Example 5.

ment.[19] The second phrase begins as the first did; however, in the third measure of this phrase (measure 7), Weill substitutes a linear cadential progression that includes two more ninth chords (see ex. 5). Another harmonization of the expanded tune is followed by an orchestral embellishment of the tune, now for the first time in the minor mode (see ex. 6). Over a pulsing dominant pedal, the tune takes on a decidedly dark and poignant character.[20] The opening scene ends with one more statement of the original tune.

mm. 102-104

Example 6.

19. This chord complex can also be analyzed as a fifth-derived chord, similar to those used in the German period. See Kowalke, pp. 261ff.

20. The use of the pedal tone is a structural device which recurs throughout Weill's career. See Kowalke, pp. 261ff.

mm. 117–124

Example 7.

This time, Weill avoids the previously featured antecedent-consequent division of the tune. Instead, he builds upon the preceding versions
by using nonfunctional seventh and ninth chords that call to mind color-
istic effects of early twentieth-century musical language. As seen in example 7, measure 1 brings the listener to a new interpretation of the opening
phrase, as it is harmonized by a G-seventh chord. Measures 2 through 5
follow no expected harmonic progression; measures 6 through 8, however, close the rondo form by utilizing the cadential pattern heard before in
versions two and three, here expanded by the addition of G-natural (the
eleventh?) in the penultimate dominant chord. E and A thus expand
the final G-major tonic chord. The inclusion of nonharmonic tones at
the cadence once again provides a link to procedures used by Weill in
his earlier music; see, for example, the closing measures of No. 5 in *Die
Bürgschaft* or the final measures of the Cello Sonata.

　　Five times during the opera—when the Leader takes up the narrative—Weill substitutes the expanded version of "Down in the Valley,"
for the original eight-measure folk song. The melodic alterations here are
subtle but very significant (see ex. 8 a–e). Although the tune is always
recognizable, for dramatic purposes and without regard for the harmonic
mode of the setting, Weill varies the interval which closes the first phrase;
the first and fourth statements descend the expected minor sixth, the
second and third statements a minor seventh, and the final statement, an
ominous major sixth. The harmonization of these five narratives covers a
wide variety of musical styles. The first and second of the narratives,
which serve respectively as the two B sections of the rondolike opening
scene, suggest a style of performance reminiscent of the songs recorded

Example 8. Weill's melodic alterations to the original folk song "Down in the Valley."

Example 9.

in the early 1940s by various "cowboy entertainers." That Weill had that rendition in mind is evident from the performance of Tom Scott on the acetates from the audition recording.[21] Harmonically, the repeated A section of the first statement, in E major, is constructed from a simple progression which uses only the tonic, dominant, and an embellishing diminished chord (see ex. 9). The harmonization of the second narrative is more complex. Weill mixes major and minor modes once again, through the introduction within a D-major context of B-flat in measures 1

21. The acetates are now held by the Weill-Lenya Research Center.

mm. 62–69

Example 10.

mm. 43–46

Example 11.

and 7 and C-natural in measure 2 (see ex. 10). The new music that comprises the B sections of the first two narratives centers on the relative minors of their respective keys; they are each four measures long and feature a progression of third-related chords (see ex. 11). The final four bars of both versions are similarly constructed; they are cadential in design and strongly support traditional harmonic motion to the tonic.

The third occurrence of the expanded "narrative" version of the tune (see ex. 12), which is heard immediately after Brack's escape from jail, harkens back harmonically and rhythmically to Weill's European

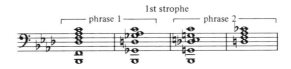

Example 12. Harmonization of the expanded "narrative" version of "Down in the Valley."

mm. 223–225

Example 13.

works. Of all the variants of "Down in the Valley" appearing in the course of the opera, this one most openly recalls techniques used by Weill in his pre-American works. Although the key is ultimately revealed to be F minor, a B-flat pedal controls the first two-thirds of the A section.[22] Weill's use of repeated ninth chords as an ostinato in this passage reflects the intensity of the situation facing Jennie as she realizes that Brack will be executed the next morning. Rhythmic ostinatos similar to the one heard here appear in works as dissimilar as the "Alabama-Song" from the *Mahagonny Songspiel,* No. 5 from *Der Jasager,* or mm. 179–200 from the last movement of the Cello Sonata. The opening phrase is harmonized by the minor subdominant, a B-flat ninth chord, and a whole-tone arpeggio; the second phrase follows with the dominant chord (C ninth chord), which cadences deceptively to a D diminished chord. The second strophe follows the same pattern until the cadence, when it resolves, as expected, to F minor. The tonic chord continues into the B section; while a new melodic strain is heard twice, the tonic harmony alternates with a flat-VII, half-diminished chord (see ex. 13). The final four measures again imply a II–V_7–I cadence, though in this version the resolution is deceptive in that Weill substitutes a ninth chord on E for the tonic.

The fourth and fifth occurrences are shifted from duple to triple meter. The first of these, presented in example 14, depicts a tense situation by harmonically pitting the tonic triad, G minor, against a dominant open fifth, D–A; the listener's perception of a weak tonic is further eroded by the cross relationship of F-sharp in the vocal part and F-natural in the orchestral accompaniment.[23] The B section indulges in some obvious word painting for "Danger around," as the chorus sings canonically (see ex. 15). In the closing measures Weill substitutes the submediant VI for his original II chord.

22. This chord complex can also be analyzed as a fifth-derived chord. Its use at this point in conjunction with the rhythmic ostinato provides a clear link with Weill's pre-American works.

23. Weill's use of ambiguous tonality to heighten tension is one of his characteristic devices. Jarman (p. 119) notes its use in *Mahagonny.*

Example 14. Mm. 325–28.

Example 15. Mm. 337–38.

Example 16.

    A reduction of the starkly dramatic final occurrence of the ex-
panded tune, which occupies only twelve measures, is given in example
16. The setting is in C minor, and Weill utilizes a deceptively simple
chromatic linear progression over a C pedal; harmonic ambiguity is
achieved by a reinterpretation of the first pitch of the tune as a tonic
rather than a dominant pickup. The final occurrence of the B section is
narrowed melodically here to a diminished fifth. The unadorned tritone
calls attention to the impending separation of Brack and Jennie (see ex.
17). Weill's cadence to this final version of the expanded tune continues to
exploit the tonal ambiguity heard ten measures earlier. A D-flat slips into
the melody and propels the listener toward F minor; when the tune comes

mm. 884–885

A - way   and he   died.

Example 17.

mm. 238–243

sun - shine, vio - lets love   dew.   An - gels in

Hea - ven know I love you.

Example 18.

to rest on F, however, Weill maintains an open fifth, C-G, in the orchestra that causes another harmonic clash between tonic and dominant.

Although he usually maintains the major or minor mode of the tune throughout each variant, at one critical point in the story—the only time that Jennie sings "Down in the Valley" and the only vocal presentation of the tune where the antecedent is heard without the consequent phrase— Weill mixes modes within the tune itself (see ex. 18). The statement starts in A major, but changes to A minor for the second phrase; the tune then continues in minor in the orchestra in a sequence that is quite similar to the B minor interlude heard earlier in the opening rondo.

The finale to the first version of *Down in the Valley* comprised only two statements of the folk tune, both retained in the 1947 revision, but with the second statement altered and augmented by the addition of new material. The revised finale presents the tune four times;[24] the statements are united by the prevalence of the dirgelike ostinato present in the first version. The first statement, which is presented in part in example 19, was newly composed in the revision. Surely inspired by the "blowing wind" (shades of *Rigoletto!*), the parallel minor thirds floating over the

---

24. Weill's revised finale provides *Down in the Valley* with a closing section which formally complements the "rondo" of the opening. Harmonically, the four statements become increasingly complex as Weill mirrors the intensity of the moment. Tonal uncertainty, similar to that in his German works, as well as in *Street Scene*, becomes more prevalent as the chorus's lines come into conflict with the orchestral ostinato (mm. 925–39). Weill's use of counterpoint at the climax is another hallmark; this passage most readily recalls the music of *Recordare* (see Kowalke, pp. 258–60).

Example 19. Mm. 917–20.

ostinato are only decorative. In the second segment, which Weill transferred unchanged from his earlier version, the tune is transposed to G major, although the ostinato continues in C. Harmonic clashes of conflicting sonorities occur in most measures. The third statement (see ex. 20) returns to C major; it is an incomplete version of the tune, with only the first six measures appearing. This passage is the most overtly "polytonal" of any in this work, as Weill again superimposes tonic and dominant chords (see especially mm. 3–4).

For the 1947 revision, Weill introduced a new contrapuntal episode for the chorus to sing; it temporarily replaces the last two measures of the tune. This musical expansion, which provides a more satisfying culmination to the opera than was initially conceived, brings the chorus back to its position of primacy. As the tune comes to rest on a G-seventh chord in measure 6, Weill unexpectedly interjects seven measures of free counterpoint. As the music increases in intensity, the "Down in the Valley" tune returns one last time. It is intoned by the tenor section (marked "ff marc." in the score) as the contrapuntal fabric around it slowly disintegrates into homophonic texture in a concluding gesture.[25] Although this closing

25. The final chord of the opera (mm. 954ff) presents an analytic problem; the A can be viewed as a tone within a "double tonic" complex—that is, the superimposition of the C major and A minor triads as a "resolution" to both tonalities. However, the A is more often deemed (because of its contrapuntal context) an added sixth. I believe that in *Down in the Valley*, Weill was reinterpreting one of the harmonic devices which permeates his German music where it descended from Wagner and Mahler; in its new American guise, although the *sound* was the same as before, the A *functioned* as American audiences expected it would, adding an extra brightness to the major chord.

Example 20. Mm. 932–38.

passage is clearly C major, Weill's use of chromatic alterations, suspensions, and seventh-chords almost camouflages C's tonic function. Example 21 presents a two-stage harmonic reduction of these closing measures.

Although Weill has been criticized by some commentators for his

Example 21. Harmonic reduction of the closing measures of *Down in the Valley*.

"unnatural" harmonizations of the folk tunes in *Down in the Valley*, in his letter to Sablosky, he anticipated and answered any objections: "It is your right as a composer to say that you would give folk tunes a less sophisticated treatment, but it would be wrong to develop this feeling into a general theory. The treatment I have used is not based on any musical theory but on the necessity for the particular moment within the musical-dramatic construction. Besides, what seems sophisticated to you might seem over-simplified to another composer."[26] Although Weill's move to the United States was reflected in his musical language, it is surprising how many remnants of his European procedures remained deeply embedded in the later music. To this amalgam, Weill added one more element in *Down in the Valley*—the American folk song. Given the clearly articulated aesthetic which governed his musical thoughts, his intuitive approach to each work, and the actual music he composed in the 1940s, we should not be surprised that Weill used a varied and sophisticated harmonic approach in setting these essentially diatonic folk songs. Perhaps one can question the validity of Weill's complex harmonizations, but his settings are no more idiosyncratic in their way than those of Aaron Copland, Virgil Thomson, or Roy Harris.[27] In some significant ways, his settings remind one of Charles Wakefield Cadman's turn-of-the-century settings of American Indian melodies.

Dispassionate judgments of the music of our century are hazardous at best, particularly for works like *Down in the Valley* which attempt to mesh diverse styles of music into a unified whole for a new market.[28] While certain critics have debated whether some of Weill's settings of the folk tunes are too sentimental, too sophisticated, or too "Hollywood," *Down in the Valley* appears to succeed on an artistic level appropriate for its intended audience despite any objections. It tells its simple story directly, but nevertheless uses a sophisticated dramatic device, the flashback, and music that camouflages its cleverness in folklike simplicity. *Down in the Valley* stands alone among Weill's American musico-dramatic works; it is neither a Broadway musical nor an opera in the traditional sense. Although it was

26. Letter to Sablosky, 24 July 1948.
27. This issue is a knotty one, to be sure; Weill is certainly not the only composer to incorporate preexistent tunes into a new piece. Alban Berg, for example, surrounded the chorale tune, "Es ist genug!" in his *Violinkonzert* with complex non-tonal counterpoint within a twelve-tone context. Weill's neo-Romantic settings in *Down in the Valley* are problematic to some critics because, while implying traditional tonality, they avoid many of the standard progressions associated with the tonal tradition and acquire a sophisticated veneer that seems at odds with folk material.
28. Weill's other American operas, *Street Scene* and *Lost in the Stars*, as well as works like Loesser's *The Most Happy Fella* or Gershwin's *Porgy and Bess*, are difficult to assess for the same reasons. See, for example, Lawrence Starr, "Toward a Reevaluation of Gershwin's *Porgy and Bess*," *American Music* 2 (Summer 1984): 25–37.

not originally intended as such, it has become the prototype for the American version of "school" opera, which has flourished as a genre since its premiere. Despite all its differences from his other works, *Down in the Valley* is quintessential Weill; it is a work which displays his considerable compositional and dramaturgical skills while simultaneously corroborating the validity of his strongly articulated aesthetic.

Appendix

Weill's revision of *Down in the Valley* in 1947 is summarized below. Measure numbers and tempo indications correspond to the published piano-
vocal score (G. Schirmer). Except for the addition of new text for the
new musical segments of the revision, Sundgaard's text remained essentially unchanged.

Measure numbers (Tempo indication)	*Comment/Explanation of changes*
SECTION 1	
1–7 (Largo)	This introduction, which has no thematic relationship to the remainder of *Down in the Valley,* was evidently designed by Weill to serve as theme music for the projected weekly radio series. In its original form it is 18 measures.
8–17 (Moderato)	Newly composed for the revision.
18–25	No change.
25–50 (Allegro animato)	No change.
50–58 (Tempo I°)	No change.
58–85 (Allegro animato)	No change.
85–101 (Molto agitato)	No change.
102–16 (Moderato assai)	Instrumental portion unchanged. Recitative (mm. 108–12) replaces rhythmically spoken dialogue.
116–24 (Poco meno mosso)	Originally a solo for Brack. The revision (for chorus) starts as a unison, expands at the third line to 5-part harmony, but then returns to a unison for the final line of the strophe.
SECTION 2	
124–67 (Tranquillo)	Newly composed for the revision. Version 1 goes directly from m. 123 to m. 168; Weill's original harmonic scheme ended Section 1 deceptively—a d_{11} chord resolved to an *e*-flat chord in first inversion. The revision cadences normally (*d* to *g*); however, the concluding chord of the new section is *a*-

	added sixth, which has a tritone relationship with the *e*-flat continuation.
168–86 (Allegro non troppo)	Instrumental portion unchanged. Recitative (mm. 179–83) replaces rhythmically spoken dialogue.
187–98 (Vivace assai)	Expanded by 2 measures.
199–233	Minor alterations; for example, the rhythmic setting of "Brack Weaver will die" has been altered from $\frac{6}{8}$ ♩. | ♩. ♪♪ | ♩. to $\frac{6}{8}$ ♩. | ♩. ♩♪ | ♩.
233–38	Originally 8 measures.
238–45 (Meno mosso)	One change, which at first glance does not seem too significant: Weill substitutes *c*-natural for *c*-sharp (m. 242) at the text " . . . know I love you." This change of mode within the strophe creates a subtle moment of poignancy, as Jennie's thoughts reflect a premonition of hopelessness.
246–55	Newly composed for the revision; the original text was spoken.
256–323 (Andantino semplice)	Newly composed for the revision.
324–39 (Allegro assai)	Minor alterations.
339–52 (Meno mosso)	No change.
353–82 (Agitato)	Music added under original spoken dialogue.
383–93 (Un poco tenuto)	No change.
394–405 (Moderato assai)	No change.
406–21 (Tranquillo)	No change.
421–26 (Vivace)	No change.
427–46 (Moderato assai)	No change.
447–57 (Andante sostenuto)	Newly composed for the revision. Based on motive used in the introduction (mm. 1–7).

SECTION 3

458–526 (Allegretto quasi andantino)	In addition to minor changes, Weill's expansion of the original version includes a longer introduction (7 measures instead of 4), a developmental episode (mm. 469–

	88) and a longer coda (mm. 505– 19).
527–38 (Meno mosso)	No change.
539–49 (Andante espressivo)	No change.
550–57 (Allegro non troppo)	No change.
558–605	No change.
606–21 (Tranquillo)	Music added under original spoken dialogue.
622–42 (Quasi lento, Poco piu mosso)	No change.
643–65 (Tranquillo)	Music added under original spoken dialogue.

SECTION 4

666–871 (Allegro vivace)	Various alterations: 2nd strophe moved back to occur before the dance music (mm. 733–49); new music (mm. 766–84); two 4-measure interpolations (mm. 817–20 and 825–28); and some minor changes in choral parts.
872–86 (Andante sostenuto)	No change.
887–95 (Piu mosso)	Music expanded by 2 measures under dialogue.
896–910 (Moderato assai)	No change.
911–15 (Piu mosso)	No change.

SECTION 5

916–24 (Andante sostenuto)	Newly composed for the revision.
925–32	No change.
933–38	No change.
939–51	Newly composed for the revision.
952–58	No change, except for the final two measures.

17

Street Scene
and the Enigma
of Broadway Opera
LARRY STEMPEL

"There is nobody like me when it comes to discovering new grounds," Kurt Weill quipped late in his career.[1] Though at the time he was referring to a specific type of movie musical he called "film-opera," the statement about *discovering new grounds* suggests an approach to the full course of his career. The term *film-opera* itself originally appeared in Weill's vocabulary much earlier, in an essay he had written in Germany,[2] but it was only one of the many terms used by the composer to describe the various "new grounds" of musico-dramatic forms he seems perpetually to have been bent on discovering. *Die Dreigroschenoper,* for example, he called "an utter revolution of the entire operetta 'industry'," in effect, altogether "a new genre of musical theater";[3] *Der Jasager* was, in his words, a didactic opera or *Schuloper;*[4] the "little" *Mahagonny,* a "Songspiel," and the big *Mahagonny,* an "epic opera"—*epic,* that is, not in any Homeric sense, but in the new sense given the word by the theater of Piscator and Brecht.[5]

Not just new grounds, therefore, but the discovery of new names as

1. Letter dated 28 November 1945 to Irving "Swifty" Lazar; copy in the Weill-Lenya Research Center, New York. All such correspondence is quoted by permission of the Kurt Weill Foundation for Music.

2. This essay, "Tonfilm, Opernfilm, Filmoper," appeared in the *Frankfurter Zeitung,* 24 May 1930; it is reprinted in *Kurt Weill: Ausgewählte Schriften,* ed. David Drew (Frankfurt/Main, 1975), pp. 181–85.

3. Letter to Universal Edition dated 10 September 1928, Wiener Stadt- und Landesbibliothek, Musik Abteilung (Mappe III/415). "Korrespondenz über *Dreigroschenoper,*" *Anbruch* (January 1929): 24–25; translated in Kim H. Kowalke, *Kurt Weill in Europe* (Ann Arbor, 1979), p. 488.

4. "Über meine Schuloper *Der Jasager,*" *Die Szene* 20 (August 1930): 232–33; translated in Kowalke, p. 530.

5. "Anmerkungen zu meiner Oper *Mahagonny,*" *Die Musik* 22 (March 1930): 440–41; translated in Kowalke, p. 517. (Weill's usage of "Songspiel" predates his collaboration with Brecht.) "Situation der Oper," *Melos* 10 (February 1931): 43–45; translated in Kowalke, p. 532.

well had a special attraction for Weill. The practice grew out of the composer's conviction that each of his works was something sui generis, a
unique undertaking which had to "create its own style, its own texture, its
own relationship between words and music."[6] And to emphasize that
uniqueness Weill demonstrated a knack for coining names which corre-
sponded to the "sui generis-ness" of each of his works. It was a knack,
moreover, which he apparently did not lose upon immigrating to the
United States, even when he chose to work in the commercial theater,
whose constraints were normative and notoriously unfavorable to the
development of both new grounds and new names. If we can safely assume that Weill was the primary author of the generic subtitles of his
American works, he was remarkably accurate. *Lady in the Dark*, for instance, appeared under the heading of a "musical play," a designation as
appropriate to its content as was calling *Lost in the Stars* a "musical tragedy"[7] or *One Touch of Venus* a "musical comedy." Only when it came to
Street Scene did the sureness of Weill's sense for names appear to falter, for
he christened that work twice: first as a "dramatic musical" and then as a
"Broadway opera." Thus, more than his other works, *Street Scene*, by its
dual nomenclature, appears sufficiently enigmatic to make us pause.
Weill's "sui-generosity" in this regard especially piques our interest because it resonates with an ambivalence that may also reflect the show's
content. Why two designations for one work, after all, and what "new
grounds" did each of them imply?

On the one hand, in his public statements about the show, Weill
described *Street Scene* as a "dramatic musical." "I am not calling my work
an opera," he told an interviewer prior to *Street Scene*'s Philadelphia
tryout. "I would rather term it a dramatic musical. There are certain
things one usually expects from opera which cannot be done in a Broadway production. For instance, . . . in order to preserve the realism, I cannot tell my whole story in music but must weave the spoken word with
song for a blending of these effects. . . . I cannot deal in fantasy, because
the people in the play are the people we know—with whom we rub
shoulders every day of our lives—and one distortion would throw the
entire seriousness of the situation out of the window."[8] In other words,
while opera (at least in the public mind) told everything in music, a dramatic musical divided its story between music and spoken dialogue and
presented these two elements either successively, as in the separate "numbers" of musical comedy, or simultaneously, as in the melodrama or un-
derscoring of operetta and film. What governed which of these ap-

6. Kurt Weill, "Score for a Play: *Street Scene* Becomes a 'Dramatic Musical,'" *New York Times*, 5 January 1947, sec. 2, p. 3.

7. See Ronald Sanders, *The Days Grow Short* (New York, 1980), p. 378.

8. Kurt Weill (as told to Edward J. Smith), "Broadway Opera: Our Composers' Hope for the Future," *Musical Digest* 28 (December 1946): 42.

proaches would prevail at any given moment, however, was a new sense of musical dramaturgy which (unlike the usual practice in traditional musical comedy, operetta, or even opera) tried to preserve the theatrical realism of the play on which the dramatic musical was based.

That put the dramatic musical squarely in the camp of the new school of musical comedy of the 1940s: it used the genre of musical comedy to serious theatrical effect and was thus essentially "dramatic musical comedy"—a paradoxical formulation wisely avoided by all concerned in the endeavor. The old school of musical comedy, although it had reached its peak a decade or more earlier, was still well represented on Broadway at the time, and its approach boiled down to variations on a single plot (boy–meets–girl . . .), interspersed with show-stopping musical numbers (discrete in structure though often indiscreet in style). The genre was legion, and to it the 1940s contributed such eminently forgotten examples as *Something for the Boys, The Girl from Nantucket,* and *Toplitzky of Notre Dame.*

The new school of musical comedy, however, was most closely associated with the names of Richard Rodgers and Oscar Hammerstein II, whose unprecedented success with their first professional collaboration, *Oklahoma!,* established the commercial viability of the new approach that had eluded a work like *Pal Joey. (Oklahoma!,* in fact, was still running on Broadway some four years after its premiere—at the time *Street Scene* opened at the Adelphi Theatre on 9 January 1947—and it continued to do so for another year after *Street Scene* closed.) By way of contrast with older musical comedies, Hammerstein preferred to call his shows "musical plays," indicating that their "books" relinquished none of the dramatic integrity of the spoken theater and that their music did nothing to violate that sense of integrity, but actually participated in its creation:

> The musician is just as much an author as the man who writes the words. He expresses the story in his medium just as the librettist expresses the story in his. Or, more accurately, they weld their two crafts and two kinds of talent into a single expression. This is the great secret of the well-integrated musical play. It is not so much a method as a state of mind, or rather a state for two minds, an attitude of unity. Musical plays, then, are not "books" written by an author with songs later inserted by a composer and a lyric writer.[9]

The hallmark of the musical play was its attempt to integrate words and music right from the start; and after the impact of *Oklahoma!,* Rodgers recalled, "everyone suddenly became 'integration'-conscious, as if the idea of welding together song, story, and dance had never been thought of before."[10]

In so many words, this was the approach Weill had described as basic

9. Oscar Hammerstein II, *Lyrics* (New York, 1949), p. 15.
10. Richard Rodgers, *Musical Stages: An Autobiography* (New York, 1975), p. 229.

to *Street Scene,* his "dramatic musical"; and it *had* been thought of before. Weill, in fact, had been working toward it at least as far back as his own "musical play" of 1941, *Lady in the Dark*—that is, before the *Oklahoma!* project first brought Hammerstein and Rodgers together and thus initiated the partnership most influential in determining the course of popular musical theater after the Second World War. Weill was rather jealous, perhaps not so much of the popularity of Rodgers and Hammerstein (though that surely must have played its part) as of the success they were reaping in the field which he felt he had sown—that "vast, unexploited field," as he put it, "between grand opera and musical comedy."[11] And when the second Rodgers and Hammerstein show, *Carousel,* opened in April 1945, the critical acclaim accorded it as a work signaling a new direction in the American musical theater rankled Weill all the more, coming as it did less than a month after the opening of *The Firebrand of Florence,* the most disastrous of Weill's box-office failures. He wrote to Lenya, "So Rodgers 'is defining a new directive for musical comedy.' I had always thought I've been doing that—but I must have been mistaken. Rodgers has certainly won the first round in that race between him and me. But I suppose there will be a second and a third round."[12] In some sense Weill must have regarded *Street Scene,* the next major theater piece he undertook after *Firebrand,* as the beginning of that next round. In-

11. Kurt Weill, Notes for the original cast recording of *Street Scene* (Columbia OL-4139). Weill could hardly have known that already in the 1920s Hammerstein and Rodgers separately had attempted writing integrated shows (e.g., *Rose-Marie* and *Chee-Chee,* respectively), or that in a 1925 article in *Theatre Magazine* Hammerstein had asked, "Is there a form of musical play . . . which could attain the heights of grand opera and still keep sufficiently human to be entertaining?" (cited in Gerald Bordman, *American Musical Theatre: A Chronicle* [New York, 1978], p. 392).

12. From a letter dated 18 May 1945 to Lotte Lenya, now in the Weill-Lenya Research Center. I have been unable to determine the precise source of Weill's citation, though it presumably derives from a drama critic of the day; for example, Louis Kronenberger, reviewing *Carousel* on opening night, compared it to *Oklahoma!:* "Though it may not run for years and years, it may yet seem more of a milestone in the years to come" ("A Famous Team Scores Again," *PM,* 20 April 1945).

Carousel's success must have been particularly frustrating for Weill because he had attempted to obtain the rights to adapt *Liliom* as a musical from Ferenc Molnár in 1937. The *New York Times* reported that everything had been settled between Weill and the Theater Guild and that Weill "had done a good deal of preliminary work on it, along the lines of *The Threepenny Opera,*" but "Molnár does not want his play set to music and that is that" (see Kowalke, p. 337).

Among George Davis's unpublished notes for his projected biography of Weill (now in possession of the Weill-Lenya Research Center) is a summary of an interview with Alan Jay Lerner that contains the following remark: "At times Kurt seemed obsessed with the hope of having a Rodgers-and-Hammerstein-type success, and yet he would always resist the type of show that would have given it to him—like *The King and I,* which Alan suggested, and Kurt said, 'Leave that to somebody else.'"

deed, as a "dramatic musical," *Street Scene* would have been in direct competition with Rodgers's own "musical plays," though by 1947 these could hardly have provided an example of "new grounds" for Weill to discover.

On the other hand, as a "Broadway opera," *Street Scene* would have meant upping the musical ante in "that race" Weill envisioned between Rodgers and himself, while at the same time allowing Weill singularly to lay claim to the discovery of new grounds in the commercial theater. For no one had yet worked both consistently and successfully in an operatic medium that did not exclude either the musical or the theatrical values of Broadway. The few who had tried, according to Weill, had erred either on the side of theater (*Song of Norway*, "a kind of *Dreimäderlhaus* about the life of Edward Grieg, . . . has all the elements of the theater which I despise")[13] or on the musical side ("I found only one fault with *Porgy and Bess*, that being the tendency to tell everything in music").[14] A Broadway *opera*, as Weill conceived it, would indeed amount to "a new directive" in the musical theater, and apparently Weill had few misgivings about his ability to achieve it. "The new form of entertainment which *Street Scene* has started," he confided shortly after the show opened, "already has made theater history."[15] Weill's exuberance over the ultimate significance of the work ("Seventy-five years from now, *Street Scene* will be remembered as my major work")[16]—even before the course of history could bear him out—was not wholly unfounded. Whatever its merits as a work in its own right, *Street Scene* has come to occupy the keystone in the conceptual arch which connects such American operas that followed it to Broadway as *Regina* (1949) and *The Saint of Bleecker Street* (1954) with such Broadway "musicals" as *The Most Happy Fella* (1956) and *West Side Story* (1957).[17]

Curiously, Weill seems first to have invoked with any regularity the "Broadway opera" catchword not for *Street Scene* but for *The Firebrand of Florence*, of all his American stage works surely the most traditionally European.[18] Furthermore, he cited such *pasticcio* operettas as *Song of*

13. Letter dated 1 July 1944 to Lenya; Weill-Lenya Research Center.
14. Weill, "Broadway Opera," p. 42.
15. Letter dated 14 February 1947 to Arthur Lyons; Weill-Lenya Research Center.
16. Weill quoted by Arnold Sundgaard, "Portrait of the Librettist as Silenced Composer," *Dramatists Guild Quarterly* 16 (Winter 1980): 26.
17. *Street Scene* gets short shrift—and even no *Schrift*—in the major discussions of the whole Broadway-opera phenomenon. See, for example, Herbert Graf, *Opera for the People* (Minneapolis, 1951; reprint, New York: Da Capo Press, 1973); or Lehman Engel, *The American Musical Theater*, rev. ed. (New York, 1975).
18. See, for example, Weill's letters to Lenya dated 12 July and 14 July 1944; Weill-Lenya Research Center. In a letter to his parents in Israel written from the Bel-Air Hotel in Los Angeles on 30 April 1945, Weill described his reaction to the failure of *Firebrand:* "This time

Norway (based on Grieg's music) and *Polonaise* (based on Chopin's) among
Street Scene's immediate musical forebears.[19] One might suspect that what
was operatic in Weill's notion of "Broadway opera" not only involved the
structural integration of word and music, which he talked about, but also
extended to something *stylistic*, which he did not. He never intended his
brand of "Broadway opera" to abandon the musical rhetoric associated
with traditions of opera, operetta, and concert music in Europe. Whatever he may have understood by "Broadway," "opera" in Weill's present
formulation clearly meant the kind of musical conventions more at home
at the Metropolitan than at the Adelphi Theatre.[20] Indeed, Weill considered several numbers in *Street Scene* to be arias (labeled explicitly as such in
the published score), and he even took one of these to be the touchstone of
what he was trying to achieve in the work as a whole. "If that aria doesn't
work," he told Billy Rose, who had suggested shortening Anna Maurrant's seven-minute solo in the first act, "then I haven't written the opera I
wanted to write. I will not change a note of it."[21]

To compare Anna's "Aria" with Billy Bigelow's "Soliloquy" in *Carousel*—not only a similarly "operatic" moment but one which also exercised an analogous centrality in Rodgers's whole conception of that
show[22]—is to clarify to what extent Weill's musical conception derived

it was especially difficult because the dramatist who wrote the book was a total disaster, and I
feel especially responsible because it was a very big and expensive show and, of course, also
because Lenya played in it. Musically it was the best thing I've written in years, a real opera,
with big choruses and ensemble numbers, full of melodic invention, utilizing all the knowledge of my trade that I've accumulated through the years. . . . Apart from the momentary
unpleasantness and aggravation, which is always tied up with these things, the meager
success of *The Firebrand of Florence* has not bothered me very much, and it shouldn't cause
you any headaches either. Long ago I got used to the up-and-down curve of success, and I've
been aware for a long time that, after the two gigantic successes I've had in recent years, a
setback was again due. Somehow, I'm even content that I am not falling into the routine of a
homogeneously successful career. As long as I am trying something new with each piece,
something that in many cases is ahead of my time, I must make allowances for such set-
backs—which, of course, is much easier since I can hold out financially quite well" (Weill-
Lenya Research Center).

    19. Weill, "Broadway Opera," p. 42. On *Carousel*'s own indebtedness to *Song of Norway*,
see Richard Traubner, *Operetta: A Theatrical History* (Garden City, New York, 1983), p. 428.

    20. Europeans were particularly sensitive to this aspect; the European premiere of *Street
Scene* in Düsseldorf in November 1955 prompted one critic to detect musical "formulas"
from Wagner to Lehár (Alfons Neukirchen, *Düsseldorfer Nachrichten*) and another to hear
quotations from *Turandot* in the score (G. Sch. [Günter Schab?], *Die Welt*). Weill himself had
earlier indicated a more general affinity between *Street Scene* and Puccini's works. Appearing
on the "Opera News" feature of the radio broadcast of *Madama Butterfly* from the Metropolitan Opera (8 February 1947), Weill stated, "I'm mighty glad that Puccini did not have the
chance to see *Street Scene* [the play], because he might have beaten me to it." Transcript in the
Weill-Lenya Research Center.

    21. Lotte Lenya cited in Joseph Horowitz, "Lotte Lenya Recalls Weill's *Street Scene*," *New
York Times*, 26 October 1979.

    22. Rodgers, p. 238.

from opera and diverged from Broadway, even Broadway at its most serious and most musical. Anna's moment in *Street Scene* is lyrical in that she reveals herself to the audience by reflecting on her past, while Billy's in *Carousel* is dramatic because the decision he makes during the course of the soliloquy motivates the future action of the show. Though both numbers incorporate substructures which derive from the pop-song patterns of the period (the verse-chorus setups in the one, the A-A-B-A relationships in the other), the lyrical presentation allows the music to provide its overall structure and effect, while the dramatic presentation tends to favor the word (see ex. 1). When Anna's initial F-minor refrain, "Somehow I never could believe," recurs with the same words at the end of the aria, it makes its emotional point in purely musical terms, climaxing on the high A-natural and asserting F major with a freshness not heard before in the aria (see ex. 2).[23] The only comparable *musical* recurrence in Billy's "Soliloquy" is "Verse No. 1" which serves to introduce both principal songs: "My Boy, Bill!" at the beginning and "My Little Girl" at the end (see ex. 3). But whereas Anna's words remain the same while her *music* indicates a basic change of attitude from despair to hope, it is Billy's music which remains the same when it returns while his *words* indicate the basic emotional change he undergoes in thinking about being a father.

The "Soliloquy" is a continuous musical scene only in the quantitative sense. Although it too amounts to some seven minutes of uninterrupted singing from beginning to end, its logical continuity is supplied by the structure of the lyrics. Its musical structure, however, is quite discontinuous, amounting to a brilliant patchwork of individual songs and sketches for songs, almost any one of which, given the right circumstances, could stand on its own. By contrast, the sections which make up the "Aria" are indeed espisodic, but connected in a qualitative sense by means of music which is repeated, transformed, and developed. As in traditional opera, musical logic creates a continuity which expresses itself in terms of "classical" techniques, from the overall unity of tonal organization (see ex. 1) to such piecemeal devices as the transformation of a theme independent of the vocal part (see ex. 4) and the development of a long legato vocal line by means of motivic foreshortening and harmonic sequencing (see ex. 5). All these features are characteristically lacking in the "Soliloquy." If Anna's music, in turn, lacks the dance-derived rhythmic impetus which informs Billy's throughout, that too may characteristically have something to do with Weill's approach to "a real opera . . . on Broadway"[24] rather than "a real *Broadway* opera."[25] In short, to judge by Anna's "Aria" (in accordance with the composer's intentions), musical

23. Its transformation in the act 2 "Choral Lament" is the musical coup of the opera.
24. Letter dated 7 December 1946 from Weill to his parents, Weill-Lenya Research Center: "This time it's a real opera—and that, for sure, is risky business on Broadway."
25. Weill, Notes to *Street Scene* recording (my italics).

assumptions of opera, European-style, are what determine the stylistic as well as structural underpinnings of the "American Opera"—as *Street Scene* is labeled in the published score—that Weill wanted to write.

In the face of such operatic evidence then, why did Weill publicize *Street Scene* as a "dramatic musical" and insist upon "not calling my work an opera," even as he wrote to his parents, "Es ist ja diesmal eine richtige Oper—und das ist natürlich sehr gewagt am 'Broadway' "? Considering that he had no difficulty in publicly reconciling the discrepancy in nomenclature once the show had closed—"my dramatic musical (it really is an opera)"[26]—there seems to have been no real ambivalence on Weill's part after all when he resorted to two names for *Street Scene* during its run, one evoking the musical show he touted in public, one evoking the opera he admitted to in private. The ploy appears to have been a deliberate effort to minimize the riskiness of his venture on Broadway and to mollify producers who felt that a good part of *Street Scene*'s potential audience would be scared away from the box office by means of a discouraging five-letter word. That this was a legitimate concern was perhaps best summarized by Hammerstein's maxim: "Opera was a way people lost money."[27]

If commercial considerations plausibly explain the dual nomenclature surrounding *Street Scene,* they are not sufficient to account for the profound ambivalence which permeates the work itself. What was to make this work unique, after all, was the Broadway component that was to constitute the breaking of new grounds in the operatic domain (and not the other way around, as Hammerstein viewed it). Yet for Weill, the function of the Broadway component in "Broadway opera" was more theatrical by far than it was musical. "I'm all in favor of the Metropolitan as a museum to play the classical opera," he said, "but to start a movement of an American musical theater, you cannot go to the Metropolitan. They haven't got the means to do it and they haven't got the audience."[28] These, he felt, could be found only on Broadway, "because Broadway represents the living theater in this country, and an American opera, as I imagined it, should be part of the living theater."[29] Broadway meant a *theatrical liberation* from the conventions of the opera house rather than (what had to be for a composer of Weill's background and training) the kind of *musical limitations* usually associated with that street. Weill would speak of his American opera being "on Broadway," "for Broadway," and

26. From a press release of the Playwrights' Company in connection with the opening of *Lost in the Stars* (24 August 1949), p. 2; Weill-Lenya Research Center.
27. Oscar Hammerstein II, *Carmen Jones* (New York, 1945), p. xiii.
28. Kurt Weill, cited in Shana Ager, "Broadway's First Real Opera," *PM,* 9 February 1947.
29. Weill, Notes to *Street Scene* recording.

"in a Broadway production" as if it were possible to achieve success in the theatrical domain of musical comedy (dramatic musical comedy, to be sure) without the corresponding presence of musical-comedy music.

But there *are* musical-comedy numbers in *Street Scene*, both in form and function. Their presence may well have resulted from compromises demanded by the collaborative process that shapes the Broadway musical to a degree few opera-house operatic composers would tolerate.[30] Elmer Rice, the original playwright of *Street Scene*, had turned librettist for the occasion and tended to chafe at the musical-comedy *forms* he felt were "out of harmony with the overall realistic tone"[31] of the play. As "he began to 'mother' his dramatic script in the course of the collaboration,"[32] it became clear he had little intention of letting music exceed its dramatically subordinated musical-comedy *functions* either. Unmindful of the Hammersteinian principle that musical plays "are not 'books' written by an author with songs later inserted," Rice not only insisted that "we should adhere closely to the original play, merely reducing the number of characters and condensing the dialogue,"[33] but as lyricist Langston Hughes saw it, "Elmer really resisted making a musical out of his wonderful old play"[34] altogether. That was a rather odd posture for a librettist to adopt, particularly when working with a composer whose musical demands were as strong as Weill's. Hughes, for his part, also apparently had his difficulties with Weill,[35] who at times virtually dictated the kind of texts he wanted his lyricist to write[36]—unlike the working arrangement between Rodgers and Hammerstein but not unlike that between, say, Verdi and Piave, or even Weill himself and Brecht. Of all the collab-

30. Even before *Street Scene*, Weill's view of the composer's role in collaboration with others was less Broadway-like than operatic. He wrote to Lenya on 12 August 1944: "It seems that I have become so sure now of my craftsmanship, of my theater knowledge and of my taste that I would take a dominating position in almost any [collaboration]. . . . I am sure that Verdi or Offenbach or Mozart contributed as much to their libretti as I do without getting credit for it. This is part of a theater composer's job to create for himself the vehicle he needs for his music" (Weill-Lenya Research Center).

31. Elmer Rice, *Minority Report: An Autobiography* (New York, 1963), p. 412.

32. John F. Wharton, *Life among the Playwrights: Being Mostly the Story of the Playwrights' Producing Company* (New York, 1974), p. 153.

33. Rice, p. 411.

34. Langston Hughes on *Recollections of Kurt Weill* (RCA Victor LL-201), side 1.

35. The suggestion is taken from Faith Berry, *Langston Hughes: Before and beyond Harlem* (Westport, Connecticut, 1983), p. 314, which alludes to an unpublished essay by Hughes about Weill entitled "My Collaborator." I have not been allowed to examine this essay and cannot therefore determine whether or how it relates to Hughes's "Meine Zusammenarbeit mit Weill," published in *Über Kurt Weill*, ed. David Drew (Frankfurt am Main, 1975), pp. 141–44.

36. See, for example, Weill's letters to Hughes of 22 January and 20 September 1946; Weill-Lenya Research Center.

orators, however, director Charles Friedman seems to have brought
along the keenest taste for outright musical-comedy numbers, especially
those in the manner of Rodgers and Hammerstein. It was he who insisted
on inserting another Rose-Sam duet, "We'll Go Away Together," into Act
2 (which eventually replaced the Rose-Lippo duet, "Italy in Technicolor")
and on including an ensemble in Act 1, "Wrapped in a Ribbon and Tied in
a Bow" (which led to the deletion of the Act 2 ensemble, "That's Where
Our Horoscopes Lie").[37] The upshot of all this give-and-take was that
Weill, as a Broadway composer, may not have been solely responsible (as
an operatic composer would have been) for the gallimaufry of musical
styles that *Street Scene* ultimately became.

But Weill cannot be let off the hook so easily, for he felt and acted as
if he *were* the operatic composer and thus ultimately responsible for the
fact that in his "Broadway opera" the Broadway elements and the operatic elements were working at cross-purposes. (Nor did he merely capitulate
to the personal and practical demands of his collaborators, for when it was
his vision of the work that was on the line he could stand up and insist, "I
will not change a note of it," as he did when it came to Anna's "Aria.")
Indeed, Weill even went so far as to embrace the contradiction at the heart
of his "Broadway opera" concept as if it were something purposeful; and
the grounds he suggested to account for it—because they contain their
grain of truth—remain somehow plausible as causes even as their effects
have continued to confuse.

Weill maintained that one reason for the *strategic* tension between
the "Broadway" and the "opera" ingredients in *Street Scene* was the work's
role in the continuation and even culmination of what he had started in
Europe. His "Broadway opera" was nothing less than "the fulfillment
of . . . [a] dream of a special brand of musical theater" which had begun
with *Die Dreigroschenoper* and for which "all the theatrical works I have
written since then have been stepping stones."[38] To put Weill's claim for
continuity to the test, consider only the matter of songs—a characteristic
feature which his European and American theatrical works share. In the
1940s the musical language which the American theater spoke was predicated on the popular musical idiom of the day. Popular songs were perfectly at home on Broadway (though that may be putting the proverbial
cart before its horse), and the only consistent difference between the pop

37. All four numbers are still listed in the program of the Schubert Theatre in Philadelphia (December 1946), though "Horoscope" is called "She's a Gemini Girl." The deleted
numbers are extant in piano-vocal format on onion skins in the Kurt Weill/Lotte Lenya
Archive, Music Library, Yale University (Box 31: Folder 31/436). The information about
Friedman comes from an interview with Lys Symonette, rehearsal pianist for the original
production of *Street Scene*.
38. Weill, Notes to *Street Scene* recording.

"hit" and the theater tune was that the latter tended to be crafted better. But in the 1920s, against the backdrop of the cultivated tradition of nineteenth-century music still prevalent in Europe, adopting the sound of popular entertainment under the aegis of art amounted to an all-out assault on the stylistic norms on which operatic utterance as such was predicated. Weill's use of popular song style in his epic theater pieces, however, went beyond much of the primitivist chic of the 1920s because it was not exclusively aesthetic in purpose. In order to serve social and ethical ends, it was intended rather as a bid for comprehensibility among a wider public than opera had traditionally attracted. Banality, in other words, was a means, not an end in itself; and irony was the method for drawing the distinction. Here is Weill on the subject in 1929:

> In no case is it the purpose of [our] efforts to enter into combat with the composer of "hit-tunes" but rather merely to bring our music to the masses. . . . Under no circumstances should the impression be created that we want to renounce the intellectual bearing of the serious musician in order to be able to compete fully with producers of lighter market wares. . . .
> With the use of elements of jazz, simple, easily comprehensible melodies originate which superficially produce a more or less strong resemblance to the melodies of "light" music. In the process the observer all too often overlooks that the effect of this music is not catchy, but instead rousing; that the intellectual bearing of this music is thoroughly serious, bitter, accusing, and, in the most pleasant cases still ironic; that neither the poetry of this music nor the form of the music itself would be conceivable without the vast background of an ethical or social nature on which it is based.[39]

It would be futile to look for these qualities in the show tunes of *Street Scene*. With the possible exception of the "Lullaby" and its ironic word-music relationship,[40] these songs no longer merely resemble "the melodies of 'light' music" but, by abandoning any irony, they have become such melodies themselves. "What Good Would the Moon Be?" (despite the "cavatina" label) has all the earmarks of a popular ballad with its standardized lyric imagery and song-form tailored for commercial extraction from the show. "Wrapped in a Ribbon and Tied in a Bow" even goes so far as "to enter into combat with the composer of 'hit-tunes'" by

39. "Die Oper—Wohin?", translated in Kowalke, pp. 506–07; originally published in *Berliner Tageblatt*, 31 October 1929.

40. *Street Scene*'s "Lullaby" closely fits Weill's earlier description of how the irony in the "Zuhälterballade" from *Die Dreigroschenoper* works: "The piece fascinates precisely because a rather unseemly lyric (which incidentally is not so offensive as many an operetta lyric) is set to music which is tender and endearing." ["Der Reiz des Stückes besteht eben darin, dass ein etwas saftiger Text (der übrigens nicht so anstössig ist wie viele Operettentexte) in zarter, angenehmer Weise komponiert ist."] Letter dated 10 September 1928 to Universal Edition, cited in note 3.

imitating Richard Rodgers outright, in effect competing in what Weill felt was "that race" with Rodgers on Rodgers's terms. And "Moon-faced, Starry-eyed" is such a far cry from something like *Mahagonny*'s moon in the "Alabama Song" that, instead of orchestrating the number himself, as he would have done in Europe and as he generally took pride in doing in America, Weill adopted the stance of a Broadway tunesmith and handed the task over to someone else (Ted Royal). Popular songs, simply by their presence in *Street Scene*, may be taken as an indication of the continuity with the European operas that Weill asserted, but there can be little doubt that such songs, their purposes, and the attitudes that inform them really represent something quite different.[41]

Another reason Weill gave for *Street Scene*'s conflicting use of "different forms of expression, from popular songs to operatic ensembles," was that "the play lent itself to a great variety of music, just as the streets of New York themselves embrace the music of many lands and many people."[42] It is a truism, of course, that the form of a work should suit its content; and considering that *Street Scene* represents an urban "melting pot" presented in "realistic" terms, a multiplicity of musical styles reflecting the ethnic diversity would seem appropriate, though the number and order of such examples would hardly matter. As it turned out, this diversity took the form of show-song pastiches to match the ethnic stereotypes in sound—or to mismatch, as in the case of the rhumba rhythm to "Italy in Technicolor," one of the songs cut in Philadelphia. And it is clear from the discarded sketches that Weill contemplated populating the score with even more such numbers than it now contains—"It's the Irish," "Buon Giorno, Signore," etc.—creating, in effect, in the words of "The Kids in School" (another discarded number), "a regular Noah's ark" of popular songs.[43] But *Street Scene* is not simply a musical revue of ethnically interrelated numbers, nor are such Broadway "forms of expression" the structural principle behind the show.

For all the random comings-and-goings that occupy most of the roles and much of the business of the show, at the heart of *Street Scene* is a clear-cut story with a beginning, middle, and end. It is a story which concerns only four characters: Anna and Frank Maurrant, their daughter Rose, and her friend Sam Kaplan. From the evidence of the score it is

---

41. Among the many other essential differences between the Broadway and the epic approaches, one structural principle must not be overlooked: with *Street Scene* Weill talked about integrating the book and musical components in "a show that flows naturally from dialogue into music and back" (Philadelphia tryout notes, 12/21/46), whereas with *Die Dreigroschenoper* Weill asserted "music is no longer plot-advancing, but rather the actual entrance of music is synonymous with an interruption of plot" (Kowalke, p. 514).

42. Weill, "Score for a Play," p. 3.

43. Weill/Lenya Archive (Box 32: Folder 31/433).

STREET SCENE AND THE ENIGMA OF BROADWAY OPERA

these four characters whose music, unlike that of their neighbors, constitutes "the opera I wanted to write," as Weill stated. That opera, almost a self-contained piece, has virtually nothing to do with the Broadway-style view of "the streets of New York themselves." But what obscures its musical focus are the Broadway melting-pot episodes which interrupt the operatic momentum too often to provide the slice-of-life background that might otherwise have brought the *opera* into relief. If the two musical worlds thus demand equal attention, the problem is that they are made simply to coexist without one shedding much light on the other.

Unlike Weill's next show, *Love Life*—a kind of "epic" musical in which vaudeville numbers interrupt the continuity of the "show songs" in order to comment, amplify, or undercut their meaning—the confrontation of musical styles in *Street Scene* doesn't seem to have much point to it. Weill's appeal to the musical variety "from popular music to operatic ensembles" to which "the play lent itself" is an attempt to justify the conflict of styles as if there *were* some point to be made by it. But its appearance remains unmotivated. To compare *Street Scene* with *Porgy and Bess* in this regard demonstrates how much more the sound of Broadway can be at home in Charleston than in New York: it may be the wrong local color, but it is the right dramatic one. Every time "Broadway" intrudes into the opera on Catfish Row it is essential that it do so since a crucial turn of plot hinges on a major character's being drawn into its corrupting domain: Bess's rape ("What You Want Wid Bess?"), Crown's blasphemy ("A Red-Headed Woman"), Sportin' Life's seduction ("Dere's a Boat Dat's Leavin' Soon for New York"). But when "Broadway" invades *Street Scene,* it is not similarly motivated.[44] There is no structural investment (and so no emotional involvement) at stake when cameo roles appear in order to perform "throwaway" numbers in Broadway-style that don't affect the outcome of essential matters: Dick and Mae from the original play now simply sing, jitterbug, and vanish ("Moon-faced, Starry-eyed"); Jennie Hildebrand is invented for the show in order to sing a charm song ("Wrapped in a Ribbon . . ."); Henry Davis, a black janitor, is also imported only to sing a blues number ("I Got a Marble and a Star"). All these Broadwayisms could be cut from *Street Scene* without disturbing the heart of the work in the least. Clearly "Broadway" is not the street where *Street Scene* lives.

If Weill mistrusted "Broadway" enough not to let it intrude *functionally* into the music of his "opera," his aesthetic and economic positions nevertheless forced him to accept the Broadway theater as the medium

---

44. The sole exception is Harry Easter's singing "Wouldn't You Like To Be on Broadway?", which owes no small debt to Sportin' Life's corresponding seduction song in *Porgy and Bess.*

through which to transmit his operatic ideal.[45] He did so at the obvious
risk of artistic and commercial failure, for "Broadway" and "opera" have
traditionally been deemed incompatible, and profoundly so; he remained
keenly aware of the difficulty involved in bringing them together. With
Street Scene's opening in New York only two weeks off, he continued to
badger his collaborators: "We have not succeeded yet in blending the
elements of the show. In some places we try to be too legitimate, in other
places, too musical comedy."[46] Perhaps the dilemma was built into the
very structure of Weill's endeavor from the start, and so it might not have
been any different with another theatrical project; yet the ultimate enigma of "Broadway opera" remains with Weill's particular choice of play to
exemplify the genre itself. When he wrote to Lenya in 1944 that he was
within reach of "what you and I have been waiting for: my first Broadway
Opera,"[47] he wasn't referring to *Street Scene* at all, but to *The Firebrand of
Florence!* *Street Scene* seems only to have "lent itself" to the notion of
"Broadway opera"—and not the other way around. The result is a work
whose fascination lies more with its discovery of "new grounds" than with
any artistic riches they were to yield.

   45. With regard to *Street Scene*, Weill attempted to defend his aesthetic posture: "Certainly it would be much healthier for an American musical theater to make certain conces-
sions to Broadway showmanship than to a traditional opera form which is European in
concept and purpose." Kurt Weill, "Broadway and the Musical Theater," *The Composer's
News-Record* 2 (May 1947): 1.
   46. Kurt Weill, "Notes on *Street Scene*, Dec 21st [1946]," p. 1; Weill-Lenya Research
Center.
   47. Letter dated 12 July 1944 to Lenya; Weill-Lenya Research Center.

Examples

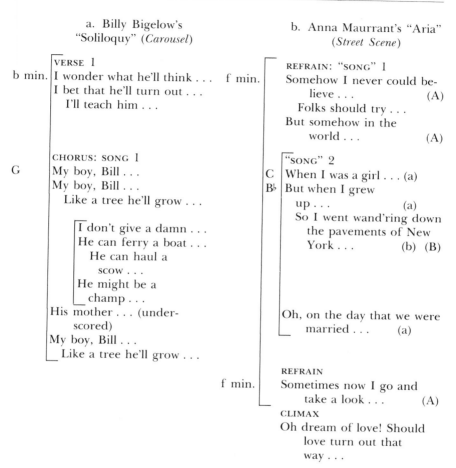

a. Billy Bigelow's
"Soliloquy" (*Carousel*)

b. Anna Maurrant's "Aria"
(*Street Scene*)

b min.   VERSE 1
I wonder what he'll think . . .
I bet that he'll turn out . . .
I'll teach him . . .

f min.   REFRAIN: "SONG" 1
Somehow I never could be-
lieve . . .   (A)
Folks should try . . .
But somehow in the
world . . .   (A)

G   CHORUS: SONG 1
My boy, Bill . . .
My boy, Bill . . .
Like a tree he'll grow . . .

C
Bb   "SONG" 2
When I was a girl . . . (a)
But when I grew
up . . .   (a)
So I went wand'ring down
the pavements of New
York . . .   (b) (B)

I don't give a damn . . .
He can ferry a boat . . .
He can haul a
scow . . .
He might be a
champ . . .
His mother . . . (under-
scored)
My boy, Bill . . .
Like a tree he'll grow . . .

Oh, on the day that we were
married . . .   (a)

f min.

REFRAIN
Sometimes now I go and
take a look . . .   (A)
CLIMAX
Oh dream of love! Should
love turn out that
way . . .

Example 1. A comparison of Rodgers's "Soliloquy" and Weill's "Aria."

a.   b.

RECITATIVE
a min. And I'm damned if he'll
                   marry . . .

INTERLUDE   INTERLUDE ("New York"
                                                                       transformed)
(F⁷)   I can see him when he's   C   But then the babies
                   seventeen . . .   came . . .

VERSE 1   RECITATIVE
a min. │What would I do . . .   f min. I don't know . . .
            │(underscored)
            │She mightn't be so bad . . .

VERSE 2*
F   │When I have a daughter . . .

CHORUS: SONG 2
            │My little girl, pink and
            │   white . . .
            │ Dozens of boys . .
            │She has a few pink and
            └   white . . .

CODA: CLIMAX   CLIMAX (developed)
B♭   I got to get ready . . . or die!   There's got to be a little
                                                                       happiness some-
                                                                       where . . .

                                                                   REFRAIN
                                                       f min. → F I never could believe . . . a
                                                                        brighter day.

Example 1 continued

*This verse is usually cut in performance, although John Raitt sings it on the original
cast album (Decca DL 7-9020).

Example 2. Street Scene: Anna Maurrant's "Aria."
a. Mm. 3–10.

Example 2 continued
b. End (mm. 123–31).

Example 3. Carousel: Billy Bigelow's "Soliloquy."
a. Mm. 12–20.
b. Mm. 196–204.

Example 4. Street Scene: Anna Maurrant's "Aria."
a. Mm. 47–51.
b. Mm. 83–90.

Example 5. Anna Maurrant's "Aria." mm. 111–20.

Kurt Weill, conductor (front left center) with cast from *Zehn Mädchen und kein Mann* (an 1862 operetta by Franz von Suppé), 12 May 1920, Lüdenscheid. The director of the theater, Kistenmacher, is kneeling (front right center). Cast members include: Frau Widder, Frau Dr. Bonkart, Fräulein Linden, Fräulein Schreiber, Fräulein Gerhardi, Sr., Fräulein Gross, Frau Jardon, Frau Emmy Bogler, Herr Heumann, Fräulein Gerhardi, Jr., (?) and Fräulein Funten. Courtesy of the Yale University Music Library.

Der Protagonist, November 1928, Städtische Oper Berlin. Final scene of a production directed by Brügmann and designed by Vargo. Cast members (left to right) are Pechner, Heermann, Burgwinckel, Zador, Bassth, Heyer, and Nitsch. Photo: Suse Byk. Courtesy of the Weill-Lenya Research Center.

Royal Palace, scenic design by Hein Heckroth (1925, Berlin) for the original production at the Berlin Staatsoper with Erich Kleiber conducting. Courtesy of the Yale University Music Library.

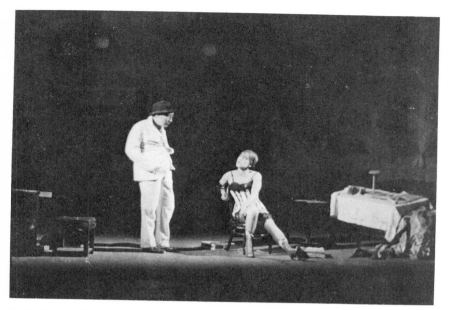

Happy End, original production at Theater am Schiffbauerdamm, Berlin, September 1929. Peter Lorre (Dr. Nakamura) and Helene Weigel (Die Dame in Grau). Courtesy of the Yale University Music Library.

Die Bürgschaft, act 1, no. 9 of the original production at the Berlin Städtische Oper, March 1932. Caspar Neher, designer. Carl Ebert, director. Photo: Joseph Schmidt. Courtesy of the Yale University Music Library.

Der Jasager, first U.S. production at the Henry School Settlement, New York, April 1933. R. A. Jones, designer. Sanford Meisner, director. Photo: Paul Parker. Courtesy of the Yale University Music Library.

Der Silbersee, act 1, scene 2 (the grocery store) of the original production at the Stadtstheater, Magdeburg, February 1933. Ernst Rufer, designer. Photo courtesy of Jürgen Schebera and the Weill-Lenya Research Center.

Kingdom for a Cow, scenic sketch by Hein Heckroth (1935, London) for the original production at the Savoy Theatre. Courtesy of the Yale University Music Library.

The Eternal Road, act 2, scene 1 of the original (and only) production, Manhattan Opera House, January 1937. Norman Bel Geddes, designer. Max Reinhardt, director. Photo: Lucas-Pritchard. Courtesy of the Museum of the City of New

Lady in the Dark. Gertrude Lawrence dancing in the Glamour Dream ("The Girl of the Moment"). Harry Horner, designer. Hassard Short, director. Photo: Richard Tucker. Courtesy of the Yale University Music Library.

The Firebrand of Florence, act 1, scene 1 of the original production which opened at the Alvin Theatre, March 1945. Jo Mielziner, designer. Photo: Lucas-Pritchard. Courtesy of the Weill-Lenya Research Center.

Love Life, Nanette Fabray (center), winner of the Antoinette Perry Award for her portrayal of Susan Cooper, sings the "Women's Club Blues" at the 46th Street Theatre, October 1948. Boris Aronson, designer. Elia Kazan, director. Courtesy of the Yale University Music Library.

Chronology of Weill's Life and Works

DAVID FARNETH

Compositions are entered in the chronology under the date of completion according to the following format: *Title* (author of the text), place of composition. Annotation (premiere performance: date, theater, city [omitted if obvious from entry], major performer). Titles of compositions untitled by Weill are taken from David Drew's forthcoming *Kurt Weill: A Handbook* and are indicated by brackets. The information for each entry draws heavily upon the major sources cited for the other essays in this publication (especially David Drew's Weill handbook) as well as scores, correspondence, and other primary documents in the collection of the Weill-Lenya Research Center.

1900 March 2	Born to Albert Weill (1867–1955) and Emma Ackermann Weill (1872–1957), Leipzigerstrasse 59, Dessau. The third of four children: Nathan (b. 8 January 1898), Hanns Jakob (b. 14 January 1899), Ruth (b. 6 October 1901).
1907	Weill family moves to quarters in the parish house ("Gemeindehaus") next to the new synagogue.
1909	Attended Herzogliche Friedrichs Oberrealschule. Music teacher: August Theile. German teacher: Dr. Max Preitz.
1913?	*Reiterlied* (H. Löns), Dessau. Modern premiere: 9 September 1975, Berliner Festwochen, Akademie der Künste, Barry McDaniel.
1913	Albert Bing engaged as a conductor at the Dessau Hoftheater.
1913–14?	*Mi Addir: Jüdischer Trauungsgesang,* Dessau.
1914	*Ich weiss wofür,* Dessau. Modern premiere: 13 September 1975, Akademie der Künste, Uwe Gronostay, conductor.
1914–16?	*Zriny,* opera after the play by Karl Theodor Körner, Dessau.

1915–17	Studies theory and composition with Albert Bing, Dessau.
1915?	*Schilflieder*, Dessau. *Volkslied* (A. Ritter), Dessau. *Im Volkston* (A. Holz), Dessau. Modern premiere: 9 September 1975, Berliner Festwochen, Akademie der Künste, Barry McDaniel.
1915 January	Earliest known public performance by Weill as pianist: "Für uns" (January 1915, Zentrale Restaurant, Dessauer Feldkorps).
December 18	Performs a Chopin Prelude and the Third Nocturne from Liszt's *Liebesträume* in a recital at the Ducal Court, Dessau.
1915–16?	*Gebet* (Emanuel Geibel), Dessau. Composed for sister Ruth's confirmation.
1916	*Ofrah's Lieder* (Jehuda Halevi), a cycle of five songs, Dessau. *Sehnsucht* (Eichendorff), Dessau.
c. 1917	*Das schöne Kind*, Dessau. Modern premiere: 9 September 1975, Berliner Festwochen, Akademie der Künste, Barry McDaniel.
1917	Employed as accompanist at the Dessau opera. *Maikaterlied* (Otto Julius Bierbaum), Dessau. 6 February 1918, Saal des Evang. Vereinhauses, Dessau, Clara Ohent and Gertrud Prinzler. *Abendlied* (Otto Julius Bierbaum), Dessau. 6 February 1918, Dessau, Clara Ohent and Gertrud Prinzler.
December	*Intermezzo*, piano, Dessau.
1918 March	*Andante aus der A♭ Sonate von C. M. von Weber*, orchestrated by Kurt Weill, Dessau.
April	Attends classes at the Hochschule für Musik, Berlin and the University of Berlin. His teachers include Cassirer and Dessoir.
September	Begins full-time studies at the Hochschule für Musik, Berlin. His teachers include Humperdinck, Koch, and Krasselt. *String Quartet in B Minor*, Berlin? Modern premiere: 9 September 1975, Berliner Festwochen, Academie der Künste, Berlin, Melos Quartet.
1919?	*Weberlied* (Gerhart Hauptmann), Berlin.
1919	*Orchestra Suite in E major*, Berlin.

March–July	*Die Weise von Liebe und Tod des Cornets Christoph Rilke,* symphonic poem, Berlin. Manuscript lost.
August	Vacations at the Convalescent Home Ebert, Beneckenstein in the Harz.
September?	Returns to Dessau to accept a post as Repetiteur at the Dessau Hofoper under Hans Knappertsbusch.
December	Begins a six-month tenure as Kapellmeister at the newly formed municipal theater in Lüdenscheid.
1919–20	*Sonate für Violoncello und Klavier,* Lüdenscheid and Berlin. Probably begun Spring 1919. Possible premiere: February 1921, Albert Bing, Hannover. Modern premiere: 9 September 1975, Berliner Festwochen, Akademie der Künste, Siegfried Palm, cello; Aloys Kontarsky, piano.
Ninon von Lenclos, opera after the play by Ernst Hardt, Lüdenscheid. Manuscript lost, probably unfinished.
1920	*Sulamith,* Lüdenscheid. Incomplete draft survives.
April	Conducts *Die Fledermaus, Cavalleria Rusticana, Der Zigeunerbaron,* and a premiere, all within one week in Lüdenscheid.
Invited to work in the summer theater in Norderney with Kistenmacher, director of the Lüdenscheid theater.
Die stille Stadt (Richard Dehmel), Berlin or Dessau. Probable first performance: 22 June 1920, Saal des "Casino," Halberstadt, Elisabeth Feuge, soprano.
May 15	Parents move to Leipzig where his father accepts directorship of the B'nai B'rith children's home.
September	Moves back to Berlin; Zehlendorf, then Lichterfelde.
December	Accepted to study in Ferruccio Busoni's masterclass, Akademie der Künste, Berlin. Other students include Luc Balmer, Robert Blum, Walter Geiser, and Vladimir Vogel.
1921 April–June	*Sinfonie in einem Satz* (No. 1), Berlin. Four-hand piano version performed in Busoni's masterclass, 1921. Modern premiere: 1957, Sinfonieorchester des Norddeutschen Rund-

funks Hamburg, Wilhelm Schüchter, conductor.

Die Bekehrte (Goethe), Berlin. Modern premiere: 2 November 1983, Yale University, New Haven, Connecticut, Robin Tabachnik.

Supplements composition studies with counterpoint lessons from Phillip Jarnach.

Rilkelieder, for piano and voice (Rainer Maria Rilke), Berlin.

1922

Psalm viii, Berlin. Incomplete. January 1972, BBC Chorus, Peter Gellhorn, conductor.

Divertimento für Flöte und Orchester, op. 52 von Ferruccio Busoni, arrangement for flute and piano, Berlin.

Divertimento für kleines Orchester mit Männerchor, Berlin. Last movement: 7 December 1922, Sing-Akademie, Berlin Philharmonic Orchestra, Heinz Unger, conductor. Entire work: 10 April 1923, Berlin Philharmonic Hall, Berlin Philharmonic Orchestra, Heinz Unger, conductor. Reconstruction by David Drew in 1971: 10 January 1972, Südwestfunk, Baden-Baden, Ernest Bour, conductor.

Sinfonia sacra: Fantasie, Passacaglia und Hymnus für Orchester, op. 6, Berlin. 12 March 1923, Berlin Philharmonic Orchestra, Alexander Selo, conductor.

Zaubernacht, ballet-pantomime with scenario by Vladimir Boritsch, Berlin. 18 November 1922, Theater am Kurfürstendamm, Berlin, Franz-Ludwig Hörth, director. This is the first of Weill's works to be performed in the United States: 1925, New York.

1923

From 1923 until probably 1926, Weill supplements his income by giving private theory and composition lessons. His early students include Claudio Arrau, Nikolas Skalkottas, and Maurice Abravanel.

March

String Quartet No. 1, Op. 8, Berlin. 24 June 1923, Frankfurt Kammermusikwoche, Hindemith-Amar Quartet.

April

Quodlibet, Op. 9 ("Orchestersuite aus der Pantomime *Zaubernacht*"), Berlin. 15 June 1923, Friedrich-Theater, Dessau, Albert Bing, conductor.

June–July	*Frauentanz, sieben Gedichte des Mittelalters, Op. 10,* Heide and Berlin. February 1924, Akademie der Künste, Berlin, Nora Pisling-Boas, soprano; Fritz Stiedry, conductor.
September	*Recordare, Op. 11* (Text: Lamentations V), Berlin. 2 July 1971, Holland Festival, Utrecht, NCRV Radio Vocal Ensemble; Marinis Voorberg, conductor.
December	Concludes studies at Akademie der Künste.
1924 February–March	Visits Nelly Frank, Villa Bergfried, Davos, Switzerland, and extensive tour of Italy.
February–July	*[Pantomime],* scenario by Georg Kaiser, Berlin. Unfinished.
April 22	Signs first publishing contract with Universal-Edition, Vienna.
April–May	*Konzert für Violine und Blasorchester, op. 12,* Berlin. 11 June 1925, Théâtre de l'Exposition des Arts Décoratifs, Paris; Marcel Darrieux, violin; Walter Straram, conductor.
May	Moves to a new apartment in Berlin: Winterfeldstrasse 21, bei Berger.
Summer	Meets Lotte Lenya at Georg Kaiser's home in Grünheide.
September	*Das Stundenbuch: Orchesterlieder nach Texten von Rilke* (Rainer Maria Rilke), Berlin. Begun in Winter 1923. 22 January 1925, Berlin Philharmonic Hall, Manfred Lewandowsky, baritone, Berlin Philharmonic Orchestra; Heinz Unger, conductor.
1925 January	Begins writing musical criticism for *Der deutsche Rundfunk.*
April	*Der Protagonist* (Georg Kaiser), Grünheide and Berlin. Begun September 1924. 27 March 1926, Dresden Staatsoper; Fritz Busch, conductor.
May	Moves to a new address in Berlin: Berlin-Charlottenburg, Luisenplatz 3, bei Hassfort.
July–September	*Der neue Orpheus* (Iwan Goll), Berlin. 2 March 1927, Berlin Staatsoper unter den Linden, Delia Reinhardt, soprano; Rudolf Deman, violinist; Erich Kleiber, conductor. *Klops-Lied* (Traditional), Berlin. 14 December 1927, Berlin.

1926 January	*Royal Palace* (Iwan Goll), Berlin. Begun October 1925. 2 March 1927, Berlin Staatsoper unter den Linden; Erich Kleiber, conductor.
January 26	Marries Lotte Lenya, née Karoline Wilhelmine Blamauer, in Charlottenburg.
March 27	The premiere of *Der Protagonist* marks Weill's first major success in the German theater.
June–July	Travels to Zürich with Lenya for negotiations and vacations in Milan, Genoa, Alassio, and Cannes.
July–August	*Herzog Theodor von Gothland*, incidental music, Berlin. 1 September 1926, Berliner Rundfunk, Bruno Seidler-Winkler, conductor.
1927 April	*Na Und?* (Felix Joachimson), two-act comic opera, Berlin. Unperformed. Sketches survive.
May	*Mahagonny Songspiel* (Bertolt Brecht), Berlin. 17 July 1927, Deutsches Kammermusikfest, Baden-Baden; Ernst Mehlich, conductor; Walter Brügmann, director.
August	Visits Lenya in Prerow on the Baltic Sea. *Der Zar lässt sich photographieren* (Georg Kaiser), Berlin. 18 February 1928, Leipzig Neues Theater, Gustav Brecher, conductor; Walter Brügmann, director.
September	*Vom Tod im Wald* (Bertolt Brecht), Berlin. 23 November 1927, Berlin Philharmonic Concert, Heinrich Hermanns, bass; Eugen Lang, conductor.
October	*Gustav III*, incidental music for the play by Strindberg, Berlin. 29 October 1927, Theater in der Königgrätzerstrasse, Berlin, Walter Goehr, conductor; Victor Barnowsky, director. A suite, *Bastille Music*, was devised by David Drew, 1970–75: 13 September 1975, Berliner Festwochen, Akademie der Künste, London Sinfonietta, David Atherton, conductor.
1928 February?	*Leben Eduards des Zweiten von England*, incidental music for the play by Bertolt Brecht and Lion Feuchtwanger, Leipzig-Berlin. Fragment survives.
March	*Konjunktur*, incidental music for the play by Leo Lania with song texts by Felix Gasbarra, Berlin. Partly missing. 8 April 1928, Lessing Theater, Berlin, Erwin Piscator, director; Edmund Meisel, conductor. A suite, *Öl-Musik*,

	was prepared by David Drew: 13 September 1975, Berliner Festwochen, Akademie der Künste, London Sinfonietta, David Atherton, conductor.
March–April	*Katalaunische Schlacht,* incidental music for the play by Arnolt Bronnen, Berlin. Manuscript lost. 25 April 1928, Staatliches Schauspielhaus, Berlin.
May	Travels to the south of France with Brecht, Weigel, and Lenya to begin work on *Die Dreigroschenoper.* On 3 May Weill is in Bandol, near Marseilles and on the 26th they are staying at Hostellerie de la Plage, Cyr sur Mer. Brecht rents a villa in Le Lavandou.
August	*Die Dreigroschenoper* (Bertolt Brecht), Berlin–Cyr sur Mer–Berlin. 31 August 1928, Theater am Schiffbauerdamm, Berlin, Theo Mackeben, conductor.
October	Moves to a new address: Berlin-Westend, Bayernalle 14.
	Berlin im Licht (Kurt Weill), Berlin. Military band version: 15 October 1928, Berlin im Licht Festival, Wittenberg Platz, Hermann Scherchen, conductor. Song version: 16 October 1928, Kroll Opera, Paul Graetz, voice.
November	*Petroleuminseln,* incidental music for the play by Lion Feuchtwanger, Berlin. 28 November 1928, Berlin Staatstheater.
November–December	*Das Berliner Requiem* (Bertolt Brecht), Berlin. 22 May 1929, Frankfurt Radio, Ludwig Rottenberg, conductor.
December	*Kleine Dreigroschenmusik für Blasorchester,* Berlin. 7 February 1929, Staatsoper am Platz der Republik (Kroll), Berlin, Preussische Staatskapelle, Otto Klemperer, conductor.
1929 March 6	Supervises the first production of *Die Dreigroschenoper* in Vienna.
April–May	*Der Lindberghflug,* original version with Paul Hindemith, text by Bertolt Brecht, Berlin. 27 July 1929, Kurhaus, Baden-Baden, Frankfurt Radio Orchestra; Hermann Scherchen, conductor.
May	Resigns as chief music critic of *Der deutsche Rundfunk* in a dispute over the radio's treatment of *Das Berliner Requiem.*

May–June	Vacations at Hostellerie de la Plage, Cyr sur Mer, France.
May–August	*Happy End* (lyrics by Bertolt Brecht; play by Elisabeth Hauptmann), Berlin. 2 September 1929, Theater am Schiffbauerdamm, Berlin, Theo Mackeben, conductor.
August	*Dantons Tod*, incidental music for the play by George Büchner, Berlin. 1 September 1929, Volksbühne, Berlin.
September	*Aufstieg und Fall der Stadt Mahagonny* (Bertolt Brecht), Berlin. Begun in 1927. 9 March 1930, Neues Theater, Leipzig, Gustav Brecher, conductor; Walter Brügmann, director.
September?	*Die Legende vom toten Soldaten* and *Zu Potsdam unter den Eichen* (Bertolt Brecht), Berlin. November 1929, Berliner Schubertchor, Karl Rankl, conductor.
September–November	*Der Lindberghflug*, second version with music entirely by Weill (Bertolt Brecht), Berlin. 5 December 1929, Staatsoper am Platz der Republik (Kroll), Otto Klemperer, conductor.
1930 January–May	*Der Jasager* (Bertolt Brecht), Berlin. 23 June 1930, Zentralinstitut für Erziehung und Unterricht, Berlin, Kurt Drabek, conductor.
July 21	Travels to London and stays at the Bushy Hall Hotel.
July 26	Travels to Unterschöndorf (Ammersee) to work with Brecht, possibly on the Pabst *Die Dreigroschenoper* film.
1931 January?	*Mann ist Mann*, incidental music for the 1931 Berlin production of Bertolt Brecht's play, Berlin. 6 February 1931, Berlin Staatstheater.
February	Premiere of *Die Dreigroschenoper* film directed by G. W. Pabst. The well-publicized court trial over the film's treatment of the material (Weill and Brecht vs. Nero Films) took place 19 October to 4 November 1930.
May	Vacations at the Provence Hotel, Le Lavandou, France.
June 8	Travels through Madrid on the way to Zazaux near San Sebastian and stays at the Grand Hotel in Zazaux while working with Caspar Neher on *Die Bürgschaft*.

June 20	Travels through Paris, staying at the Hotel Astor.
October	*Die Bürgschaft* (Caspar Neher), Berlin and Zazaux. Begun August 1930. 10 March 1932, Berlin Städtische Oper, Fritz Stiedry, conductor; Carl Ebert, director.
1932 March	Moves to a new address: Berlin-Zehlendorf, Wissmannstrasse 7.
December 11	Acclaimed performance at the Salle Gaveau in Paris of *Mahagonny Songspiel* (with four additional numbers from *Aufstieg*) and *Der Jasager* conducted by Maurice Abravanel with Lenya performing.
1933 January	*Der Silbersee* (Georg Kaiser), Klein-Machnow. Begun in August 1932. 18 February 1933, three concurrent productions in Leipzig, Erfurt, and Magdeburg.
March 4	The last public performance of any Weill work (*Der Silbersee*) in Germany until 1945.
March 21	Potsdam Day—Weill flees Berlin by car, arriving in Paris on 23 March.
April 1	Writes to Lenya from the Hotel Splendide in Paris, but soon stays at the home of Charles and Marie-Laure de Noailles, 11 Place des Etats-Unis, Paris.
April 13	American premiere of *Die Dreigroschenoper* in an English translation by Gifford Cochran and Jerold Krimsky, Empire Theater, New York. 12 performances.
April–May	*Die sieben Todsünden* (Bertolt Brecht), Paris. 7 June 1933, Théâtre des Champs Elysées, Paris, and 1–15 July 1933, Savoy Theatre, London, Maurice Abravanel, conductor. This was the first work by Weill to be produced in England. A concert of the "Paris version" of *Mahagonny* and *Kleine Dreigroschenmusik* was presented on 18 July.
June–July	Vacations in Italy (Alassio, Positano, Rome, Florence) while *Die sieben Todsünden* plays in London.
September	*Es regnet* (Jean Cocteau), Paris. *Der Abschiedsbrief* (Erich Kästner), Paris.
September 3	Writes to Lenya in Berlin from the Hotel Splendide, Paris.

September 18	Divorce from Lotte Lenya is finalized.
October	*La grande complainte de Fantômas* (Robert Desnos), Paris. 3 November 1933, Radio Paris, Alejo Carpenter, conductor.
	Weill is released from his Universal-Edition contract and on 31 October signs a new publishing agreement with Heugel, Paris.
November 9	Writes to Lenya from his new apartment: 9 bis Place Dreux, Louveciennes (outside of Paris).
December 9	Travels to Rome for a production of "Paris version" of *Mahagonny*.
1934 February	*Symphony no. 2*, Berlin-Paris. Begun January 1933. 11 October 1934, Concertgebouw Orchestra, Amsterdam, Bruno Walter, conductor.
May	Travels to Zürich, Basel, Venice, Novi (Yugoslavia) and Salzburg to work with Reinhardt and Werfel on *Der Weg der Verheissung*.
	Complainte de la Seine (M. Magre), Louveciennes. 1934, numerous cabaret performances by Lys Gauty.
	Je ne t'aime pas (M. Magre), Louveciennes. 1934, numerous cabaret performances by Lys Gauty.
September	*Marie galante* (Jacques Deval), Louveciennes. 22 December 1934, Théâtre de Paris, Edmond Mahieux, conductor.
December	*Der Kuhhandel* (Robert Vambery), Louveciennes. Unperformed in the original German version; adapted January–May 1935 for a production in England under the title *A Kingdom for a Cow*.
1935?	*Youkali* (Roger Fernay), Paris.
1935 January	Travels to London to work on *A Kingdom for a Cow*.
June	*A Kingdom for a Cow* (English lyrics by Desmond Carter; English book adapted from Vambery by Reginald Arkell), London. 28 June 1935, Savoy Theatre, London, Muir Matheson, conductor.
Summer?	Weill's parents move to Palestine.
August	*Der Weg der Verheissung* (Franz Werfel), Louveciennes, London, Salzburg. Never performed in the German version; revised for an American production between October 1935 and

	December 1936 under the provisional title *The Road of Promise*.
September 10	Arrives with Lenya at New York Harbor aboard the S.S. *Majestic*. They stay at the St. Moritz Hotel, Central Park South, New York.
1936 May	Travels to Chapel Hill, North Carolina to work with Paul Green.
June–August	Weill, Lenya, Paul Green, and Cheryl Crawford join the Group Theatre at Pine Brook, Trumbull, Connecticut, to work on *Johnny Johnson*.
June–November	*Johnny Johnson* (Paul Green). 19 November 1936, 44th Street Theatre, New York; 68 performances.
Summer	*The Fräulein and the Little Son of the Rich* (Robert Graham), New York. Unpublished and unperformed.
August	Weill and Lenya live at Cheryl Crawford's house in Bridgeport, Connecticut.
1937	*The Eternal Road* (Franz Werfel, with an English translation by Ludwig Lewisohn and additional lyrics by Charles Alan), Paris, Salzburg, and New York. 4 January 1937, Manhattan Opera House, New York, Max Reinhardt, director; Norman Bel Geddes, designer; Isaac van Grove and Leo Kopp, conductors; 153 performances.
January 19	Remarriage of Weill and Lenya in North Castle, Westchester County, New York, by Julius A. Raven, Justice of the Peace.
January–June	Travels to Hollywood to pursue opportunities. Stays at the Roosevelt Hotel, then moves to 6630 Whitley Terrace on 18 February. Lenya stays at Cheryl Crawford's apartment, 455 East 51st Street, New York.
March–April	*The River Is Blue*, film score, Hollywood. The film's title was first changed to *Castles in Spain* and then to *Blockade*. Only one song from Weill's score was ultimately used.
August	*Deux Chansons D'Yvette Guilbert* (Yvette Guilbert), New York. Written for the 1937 Paris production of *Die Dreigroschenoper;* 29 September 1937, Théâtre des Etoiles, Paris.
August 27	First application for American citizenship after a short trip to Canada and reentering on an immigrant visa.

September	Moves to duplex apartment at 231 East 62nd Street, New York.
November	*Albumblatt für Erika*, New York. Unpublished piano transcription for Erika Neher.
December 13	Returns to Hollywood with Lenya and rents a cottage at 940 Ocean Front Street in Santa Monica.
1938	*Two Folksongs of the New Palestine*, arranged for voice and piano, New York.
	The Common Glory (Paul Green), New York. Unfinished.
January–April	*Davy Crockett* (H. R. Hays and Kurt Weill), New York. Unfinished.
March–May 20	Travels to Hollywood to work on *You and Me*. Address: Villa Carlotta, 5959 Franklin Avenue, Hollywood.
Spring	*You and Me*, film score, lyrics by Sam Coslow and Johnny Burke, directed by Fritz Lang, Hollywood.
Summer	Rents a country house on the "Eastman Estate," Route 202, 3½ miles from Suffern, New York.
March–September	*Knickerbocker Holiday* (Maxwell Anderson), New York. 19 October 1938, Barrymore Theatre, New York; 168 performances.
1939 Spring	*Railroads on Parade* (Edward Hungerford), New York. 30 April 1939, New York World's Fair.
March–August	*Ulysses Africanus* (Maxwell Anderson), Malibu–New York. Unfinished.
June	Accepted as a member of ASCAP.
November	*Madam, Will You Walk?*, incidental music for the play by Sidney Howard, New York. 13 November 1939, Baltimore, with prerecorded music.
December	*Two on an Island*, incidental music to the play by Elmer Rice, New York. 20 January 1940, Broadhurst Theatre, New York.
	Nannas Lied (Bertolt Brecht), New York. First performance unknown.
	Stopping by Woods on a Snowy Evening (Robert Frost), New York. Manuscript missing.
1940 January	*Ballad of Magna Carta*, radio cantata (Maxwell Anderson), New York. 4 February 1940, Columbia Broadcasting System, New York.
February–November	*Lady in the Dark* (lyrics by Ira Gershwin, book

July 15

1941 May

May 21

Autumn

1942 January

February

March

March

Spring

by Moss Hart), New York. 21 January 1941, Alvin Theatre, New York; 467 performances.

Weill and Lenya welcome their close friends Darius and Madeleine Milhaud on their arrival in New York.

Film rights to *Lady in the Dark* are sold to Paramount for the highest price to date for a Broadway musical.

Purchases Brook House, New City, Rockland County, New York.

Fun to Be Free, pageant by Ben Hecht and Charles MacArthur, New York. 5 October 1941, Madison Square Garden, New York.

Walt Whitman Songs ("Oh Captain! Oh Captain!", "Beat! Beat! Drums!", and "Dirge for Two Veterans"), New York. A fourth song, "Come up from the Fields, Father" was composed in 1947; first performance unknown.

Your Navy, incidental music for a radio program by Maxwell Anderson, New York. 28 February 1942, NBC, New York.

Und was bekam des Soldaten Weib? (Bertolt Brecht), New York. 3 April 1943, Hunter College, New York, Lotte Lenya, voice; Kurt Weill, piano.

[Four Patriotic Melodramas], New York: "Battle Hymn of the Republic," "The Star Spangled Banner," "America," "Beat! Beat! Drums!" First recording: 30–31 March 1942, Helen Hayes, Roy Shields, conductor, Victor M 909.

Becomes chairman of production committee for "Lunch Time Follies," presented by the American Theatre Wing.

[Songs for the War Effort], New York: "Schickelgruber" (Howard Dietz); "One Morning in Spring" (St. Clair McKelway); "The Good Earth" and "Buddy on the Nightshift" (Oscar Hammerstein); "Song of the Inventory" (Lewis Allan); "We Don't Feel Like Surrendering Today" (Maxwell Anderson); "Oh Uncle Samuel!" (Maxwell Anderson, melody by Henry C. Work); "Toughen Up, Buckle Down, Carry On" (Dorothy Fields).

Song of the Free (Archibald MacLeish), New York. 4 June 1942, Roxy Theatre, New York, Bob Hannon, vocalist.

	Correspondence with Brecht and Adorno regarding an adaptation of *Die Dreigroschenoper* for an all-black cast in California.
August	*Russian War Relief* (J. P. McEvoy), New York. August 1942, Nyack, New York.
October 1	In California, Weill and Brecht meet for the first time since 1935.
1943 February	*We Will Never Die* (Ben Hecht), New York. 9 March 1943, Madison Square Garden, New York.
May	Brecht visits Weill at Brook House where they begin work on an operatic version of *The Good Soldier Schweyk* and *The Good Woman of Setzuan*, which is to be "half-opera."
June?	Works on film versions of *Lady in the Dark* and *Knickerbocker Holiday* in Hollywood.
June–September	*One Touch of Venus* (lyrics by Ogden Nash, book by S. J. Perelman and Ogden Nash), New York. 7 October 1943, Imperial Theatre, New York; 567 performances.
August 27	Awarded U.S. citizenship.
November	Works on *Where Do We Go from Here?* with Ira Gershwin in Hollywood.
1944 January	*Where Do We Go from Here?*, film score with lyrics by Ira Gershwin, screenplay by Morrie Ryskind, directed by Gregory Ratoff. Released by 20th Century Fox.
Spring	*Wie lange noch?* (Walter Mehring), New York. First recording: Spring 1944, New York, for the Office of War Information.
April–May	*Salute to France,* music for a propaganda film produced by the U.S. Office of War Information, New York.
July–December	*The Firebrand of Florence* (lyrics by Ira Gershwin, book by Edwin Justus Mayer), Hollywood–New York. 22 March 1945, Alvin Theatre, New York; 43 performances.
1945 April	Goes to Hollywood to work on the film score of *One Touch of Venus.*
August–November	*Down in the Valley,* version for radio (Arnold Sundgaard), New York. Never broadcast or published.
1946 January–November	*Street Scene* (lyrics by Langston Hughes, book by Elmer Rice), New York. 9 January 1947,

	Adelphi Theatre, New York; 148 performances.
March	*Kiddush,* for cantor, chorus, and organ, New York. 10 May 1946, Park Avenue Synagogue, New York.
Summer	Elected to full membership in the Playwrights' Company.
August	*A Flag Is Born,* music for a pageant by Ben Hecht, New York. 5 September 1946, Alvin Theatre, New York.
1947 May 6	Leaves New York on the S.S. *Mauretania* for a vacation in Palestine, England, France, Italy, and Switzerland. This is Weill's first trip to Europe since his departure from France in 1935 and the first meeting with his parents since 1933.
June	Receives a "special" Antoinette Perry (Tony) award for distinguished achievement in the theater. This was the inaugural year of the awards.
November	*Hatikvah,* arrangement for orchestra, New York. 25 November 1947, Waldorf-Astoria Hotel, New York.
1948 April	*Down in the Valley,* stage version (Arnold Sundgaard), New York. 15 July 1948, Indiana University, Bloomington.
August	*Love Life* (Alan Jay Lerner), New York. 7 October 1948, 46th Street Theatre, New York; 252 performances.
1949	*Lost in the Stars* (Maxwell Anderson), New York. 30 October 1949, Music Box Theatre, New York; 273 performances.
October 27	Performance of *Der Zar lässt sich photographieren,* Juilliard School of Music, New York.
1950 January–March	*Huckleberry Finn* (Maxwell Anderson), New York. Unfinished.
March 17	Suffers coronary at Brook House and on 19 March is taken by ambulance to Flower Hospital.
April 3	Dies, Flower Hospital, New York.
April 5	Buried, Mount Repose Cemetery, Rockland County, New York.

Contributors

Alan Chapman, associate professor at Occidental College, received his Ph.D. in music theory from Yale University, where he studied with Allen Forte and developed a general theory of atonal harmony and voice-leading.

•

Susan C. Cook received her Ph.D. degree from the University of Michigan with a dissertation entitled "Opera during the Weimar Republic: Weill, Hindemith, and the *Zeitoper.*" She is assistant professor of music at Middlebury College.

•

David Drew, director of publications for Boosey & Hawkes, is the editor of *Über Kurt Weill, Kurt Weill: Ausgewählte Schriften,* and numerous editions of Weill's music. His Kurt Weill handbook and critical biography are forthcoming from Faber & Faber.

•

David Farneth is archivist and director of programs of the Kurt Weill Foundation for Music, Inc. He serves as coordinator of the Archives Roundtable of the Music Library Association, and he contributed the article on La Monte Young for *The New Grove Dictionary of American Music.*

•

John Fuegi is director of the Comparative Literature Program at the University of Maryland. One of the foremost Brecht scholars, he is the author of *The Essential Brecht* and *Chaos, According to Plan,* as well as the editor of ten volumes of the *Brecht Jahrbuch.*

•

John Graziano, Ph.D. Yale University, is professor of music at the City College of New York. A composer and theorist, he is the author of many articles on American music and is currently writing an opera based on Stephen Crane's "The Blue Hotel."

•

Christopher Hailey has edited the correspondence of Franz Schreker-Paul Bekker, and Berg-Schoenberg. He is currently writing a biography of Schreker and translating the Weill-Universal Edition correspondence.

•

Stephen Hinton received his Ph.D. from the University of Birmingham and assisted Carl Dahlhaus at the Technische Universität in Berlin. He now teaches at the Freie Universität and is preparing a monograph on *The Threepenny Opera* for the Cambridge Opera Handbook series.

•

Douglas Jarman teaches at the Royal Northern College of Music in Manchester, England. A director of the International Alban Berg Society, he is the author of *The Music of Alban Berg* and *Kurt Weill: An Illustrated Biography.*

•

Ian Kemp is professor of music at the University of Manchester. He is the author of *Hindemith* and *Tippett: The Composer and His Music* and serves as an editor of the New Berlioz Edition. He has written several articles on Weill and conducted many performances of his works.

•

Kim H. Kowalke, associate professor at Occidental College, is president of the Kurt Weill Foundation for Music. He is the author of *Kurt Weill in Europe* and has published extensively on Weill's music. He is currently editing the Weill-Lenya correspondence with Lys Symonette.

•

Michael Morley is professor of drama at the Flinders University of South Australia. Author of *A Student's Guide to Brecht* and *Brecht: A Study,* he has also conducted and performed Weill's and Eisler's music.

•

Alexander L. Ringer, the senior musicologist at the University of Illinois, has published extensively in various areas of nineteenth- and twentieth-century music, most recently with special emphasis on Arnold Schoenberg and Kurt Weill.

•

John Rockwell, music critic for *The New York Times,* is the author of *All American Music: Composition in the Late Twentieth Century* and *Sinatra: An American Classic.* His doctoral dissertation at Berkeley was "The Prussian Ministry of Culture and the Berlin State Opera, 1918–1931."

•

Matthew Scott is working on a Ph.D. at the City University of London on the American works of Kurt Weill. Also active as a composer and musical director for television, film, and theater, he is currently a music director of the National Theatre of Great Britain.

•

Ronald K. Shull is business manager for the Lexington Children's Theatre. He is the coauthor, with Joachim Lucchesi, of *Musik bei Brecht,* a two-volume book scheduled for publication by Henschelverlag in 1987.

•

Larry Stempel is associate professor of music at Fordham University. He contributed the article on Weill for *The New Grove Dictionary of American Music* and is writing a book about the American musical theater to be published by W. W. Norton.

•

Guy Stern is the cofounder of the Lessing Society and the Society for Exile Studies and the founding editor of the Lessing Yearbook. A Distinguished Professor at Wayne State University, he coedited *Invitation to German Poetry* and is the author of books on Efraim Frisch and Alfred Neumann, as well as *War, Weimar, and Literature.*

Index